DIARY OF A PSYCHOSIS

How Public Health
Disgraced Itself
During COVID Mania

Thomas E. Woods Jr., PhD
Foreword by Jay Bhattacharya, MD, PhD

The
LIBERTARIAN
INSTITUTE

DIARY OF A PSYCHOSIS

How Public Health Disgraced Itself During COVID Mania

Thomas E. Woods Jr., PhD

Foreword by Jay Bhattacharya, MD, PhD

Diary of a Psychosis:
How Public Health Disgraced Itself During Covid Mania

Published in the United States of America by

The Libertarian Institute
612 W. 34th St.
Austin, TX 78705

LibertarianInstitute.org

ISBN 13: 979-8-9884031-6-6

To Jenna,
who made the dystopian years of Covid
the happiest of my life

Table of Contents

Foreword

by Jay Bhattacharya, MD, PhD

Memory is a funny thing. Our minds suppress our past traumas and difficulties because they are sometimes too difficult to bear unfiltered. But it's not that we simply forget them. Instead, we replace them with ersatz recollections that soften the edges of the hard times. Our minds infuse those times instead with a patina of destiny or purpose that gives meaning to them that was often not present at the time we were going through them.

It is for this reason that the pandemic diary that you hold in your hand is so important. The trauma of the pandemic years demands crystal clear recollection.

At the same time, these memories and the difficult pandemic times demand that we imbue them with purpose. All those kids whom the pandemic planners robbed of their futures by denying them school. All those people who lost their jobs because they did not think the vaccine was for them. That time when you couldn't celebrate the life of your father or mother and grieve with your family because it was too dangerous for you to hold a funeral.

The tyrannical public health response extended deep into the most intimate circumstances. Do you remember how invitations to Christmas dinner split families because public health propaganda convinced some that the unvaccinated were dangerous biohazards while the vaccinated were clean? Or advice from the top medical officer of Canada, Teresa Tam, that it was dangerous to kiss your paramour or partner without a mask? Or advice from Andy Slavitt, one of President Biden's top coronavirus advisors, to segregate your child returning from college in the garage during his Thanksgiving visit?

We know the end of the story: despite all the nonsense, the disease spread everywhere anyway. But did we sacrifice all that for nothing?

Though not a doctor or scientist himself, Tom was a voice of reason and science throughout the pandemic. I remember seeing a video of one of his speeches in which he put up two charts of the spread of Covid cases in two different regions over time. You will remember, I'm sure, how ubiquitous such graphs of cases were in the plague times. Perhaps you remember the sense of dread and déjà vu that I had that Covid and the lockdowns were here again every time you saw them.

Anyway, Tom put up these two graphs and informed the audience that one represented a region that had had a mask mandate throughout the period, while in the other, the public health authorities permitted free masking and bare faces at will. With these charts visible but without labels to say which was which, Tom challenged the audience to identify which region had the mandate and which did not. The catch was that the charts were nearly identical, with cases rising and falling over time with a predictable cadence in both regions.

The punchline was clear for anyone with eyes to see. Though political leaders and public health authorities, clothing themselves in the moral authority of The Science™ itself, might claim the credit for the waning of the virus, in fact, the mandates, lockdowns, and other anti-scientific interventions they promulgated and imposed had little or nothing to do with the spread of a highly infectious virus spread by breath.

In these pages, you will see how clearly Tom saw this essential fact — the inefficacy of much Covid policy in protecting the vulnerable — long before most scientists were willing to concede this obvious truth. And you will see his frustration with the scientists, public health officials, and government apparatchiks who propagandized and ultimately harmed the public — especially children, the poor, and the working class — with their destructive lockdown policies. And you will feel his frustration (and perhaps relive your own) as time marches on in the diary and the apparatchiks learn nothing.

Ultimately, the purpose of reminding ourselves about the hard times is to help ensure that they do not come back, and if they do, to make sure we do not repeat the same mistakes. The diary you hold in your hands will help make that happy future a reality, which makes it a good thing indeed.

Jay Bhattacharya, MD, PhD
Stanford, California

Introduction

(Don't skip, or the book won't make sense.)

.

In late 2019 news outlets around the world reported that a novel virus — SARS-CoV-2, they said — had appeared in China.

Further news items would go on to report its gradual spread around the world.

Nobody quite knew how the world's governments would react, but in early 2020 authorities like Dr. Anthony Fauci, director of the National Institute of Allergy and Infectious Diseases, were assuring us that we shouldn't go around wearing masks, and he said that younger people should feel free to continue to travel on cruise lines and carry on with their ordinary behavior.

As you know, dear reader, that didn't last long.

Before we knew it, everything was being shut down. Culture and the arts were shuttered. People (other than those deemed to have "essential" jobs) were ordered to stay in their homes, with some countries enforcing this requirement more harshly than others. Gyms, restaurants, schools, retail stores — everything closed down, though restaurants could serve food to go, and stores selling necessities remained open.

If you had to be in public you were ordered to observe "social distancing"; this amounted to keeping six feet of space between yourself and another person — although it was later admitted that the six-foot rule was in fact arbitrary.

By complying with these and a considerable array of other requirements, we were told we would "flatten the curve."

This oft-repeated phrase referred to spreading out the presumed burden on the health care system over time. Instead of everyone getting sick all at once and overwhelming hospitals, we would spread out the timing of the various infections, thereby easing the burden on the health care system.

"Fifteen days to slow the spread" was the public-health slogan in March 2020. But the official public-health emergency would not be discontinued for over three years.

During that time, people who questioned the wisdom of these policies, noting their dubious basis in science and horrendous and widespread collateral effects, found themselves demonized and their voices suppressed.

Like most people, I initially didn't know what to think. But I actively sought out dissident voices. Things looked grim in March and April. It seemed as if restrictions would go on indefinitely. So I wondered: is there anyone out there with a more optimistic perspective, and if so, what data were they using?

And I wasn't going to let the public health establishment ruin my life without even bothering to see whether it was doing any good.

That's when I began to discover that none of their interventions seemed to make any difference.

So I began reporting on this, the most significant event of my lifetime, to my newsletter audience. Every weekday I would find charts and data, or recount people's personal stories, or report on what the official sources were saying (and seeing if any of it made sense), and send what I found to my subscribers.

In so doing, I assembled, in effect, a diary of these three years.

There have been some great books on Covid and the government response, and I've been happy to promote them and feature their authors on the Tom Woods Show, the podcast that celebrates its tenth anniversary in 2023, the year of this book's release.

What makes this one different is that thanks to all that writing, I recorded a lot of crucial detail that's been left out of other versions of the story.

So much lunacy was passed off as public health wisdom over the past three years, and I'll bet even some of the closest observers have forgotten 75 percent of it.

I myself sure had, until I revisited what I had written.

By preserving this diary aspect, I am able to walk the reader through what those days, weeks, months — even years — were like.

And again and again — and again and again and again and again — the alleged experts would predict one thing, and the opposite would happen.

The sheer relentlessness of what you are about to read should make it impossible for any truly open-minded reader to conclude anything other than: people's lives were torn apart, and massive collateral damage (including huge numbers of avoidable, non-Covid deaths) occurred, for no good reason.

Some people will be unsatisfied with this book. For example, those who wish I would focus on the sinister forces directing world events will be disappointed (even though I agree there are plenty of nasty people out there)

I have the humble purpose of demonstrating that the so-called mitigation measures of 2020 onward were a dramatic failure. If people come to accept this, their minds will be opened to consider deeper questions. But this is the essential starting point.

Now, a few clarifying items.

From time to time you'll hear me speak of "my private group," because someone in there had a helpful insight. The group I'm referring to is what I call, tongue in cheek, the Tom Woods Show Elite, a no-censorship discussion group for people who support the Tom Woods Show. It's been a lifeline for people trying to navigate a world gone mad. (Entry is via my SupportingListeners.com website.)

I have not included every single entry I wrote during these years. The book would be unwieldy if I did. I included enough to tell the story, and to make what I consider an overwhelming case against what was done to us.

You'll find some repetition in this book. Some of that is a function of my having wanted each of these entries to be a standalone composition. I chose to retain some repetition because (1) some of these points bear repeating, and (2) I wanted to convey something of the exasperation we felt at trying to explain the obvious, and nobody in the public health establishment bothering to listen.

Although you'll find acknowledgments at the end of the book, I want to take a moment right here to thank Ian Miller, many of whose charts I make use of in these pages and whose work was of critical importance. I highly recommend his book *Illusion of Control: Covid-19 and the Collapse of Expertise*.

I'm very happy with and proud of this book, but I think it really gets going once enough time has passed in 2020 to begin deciding whether any of the recommended measures were actually generating results. Then the book becomes an outright bludgeon, mercilessly smashing the propagandists.

I want to give you a special gift for buying this book: my companion volume, *Collateral Damage: Victims of the Lockdown Regime Tell Their Stories*. The lockdowns caused enormous suffering and loss, but you were shamed into not sharing your story. If the true history of this period is to be recorded, we need to hear those stories.

So I strongly urge you to grab your free copy of *Collateral Damage* at DiaryOfCovid.com. *These stories need to be heard.*

Tom Woods
October 2023
St. Cloud, Florida

Part I: Spring 2020

March 23, 2020 | Backlash building against the shut-everything-downers

How is everyone so sure of what is going to happen? "We are Italy," people say. "It's just getting started."

Maybe. But there appears to be zero curiosity about strange anomalies. Like: why has the German number of deaths amounted to practically zero? Why has there been no real outbreak in Japan? Some things were closed but no society-wide lockdowns, and rush-hour trains are still full. Why has Vietnam seen zero deaths?

These questions genuinely stump the experts, though nobody you talk to on Twitter seems stumped. They have answers for everything.

Over the weekend I posted an outrageous headline from the *New York Post* on Twitter about a 20-year-old who died, and I noted that they waited until paragraph ten to tell us he had leukemia. Surely we can all agree this is irresponsible?

Nope. Someone from my high school class commented to remind us about the seriousness of Covid — irrelevant to the point about the misleading headline. She added that lots of young people were dying.

Lots of young people are not dying. The headlines about this are the most irresponsible of the whole episode. Without fail, stories about this handful of young people — a rounding error in the grand scheme of things — end with, "Oh, by the way, this one had this disease and that one had that." Hardly cases of robust young people struck down in the prime of life.

A doctor in Michigan made everyone go berserk when he said his hospital was full of twentysomethings on ventilators "fighting for their lives" against the virus.

He later admitted that this was not true:

> Beaumont's ICUs are not full of young people on ventilators. In reality, much of what I wrote in that text message is exaggerated and untrue. During this time of crisis, truth and accuracy are more important than ever. I sincerely apologize for sharing false information.

Then this same high school acquaintance went to somebody else's thread to report on me. Why, have you seen what our friend Tom Woods is saying?

Imagine that: Tom Woods holds an opinion other than the one we've all been instructed to hold. Go gawk at him!

Yes, I think it has the potential to be serious, and yes, I think people should take reasonable precautions. But thank goodness we have dissident voices, because sometimes the herd gets it wrong.

For instance, David Katz, the founding director of Yale University's Yale-Griffin Prevention Research Center, just wrote in the *New York Times*: "The path we are on may well lead to uncontained viral contagion and monumental collateral damage to our society and economy. A more surgical approach is what we need." Katz says the shutdown of virtually everything will have other consequences that will likely worsen the situation on all levels. "Let's shut everything down and see what happens" is supposed to be the sophisticated response of the so-called adults in the room, but it's actually extremely naive.

This is what other scientists have not been good at: cost-benefit analysis. They are not trained for it. And this is why we need the analytical abilities of other people, particularly economists, coupled with the medical knowledge of specialists, if we are going to devise a sensible approach to what we may be facing.

April 9, 2020 | In defense of the angry

A friend of mine who's a very credentialed physician wrote to scold me gently for the nastiness of a few of my Facebook friends after I'd written a post there.

I replied:

> *I appreciate your point of view. I'm sorry if some people are rude. In their defense, they have been told for a month now that if they express skepticism of the Fauci regime they must care only about the stock market or a 0.1% increase in GDP.*

> *Dr. Zeke Emanuel is not alone in calling for an 18-month lockdown. This is pure insanity. The collateral damage of a shutdown of that length is multifaceted and incalculable — and no, I don't mean only in stock values, it should be unnecessary to point out. Although since we're*

on the subject I shall impertinently note: all the wealth in the entire world today amounts to three years' worth of current production. We're talking a degree of impoverishment on that scale.

Eighteen (or even fewer) months of "lockdown" means the destruction of people's hopes, dreams, and aspirations. It means the loss of their life savings. It means the shuttering of their businesses. It means a kind of "living" that to me is a kind of death.

Meanwhile, we're being told with a straight face that the reason this preposterous model is being revised downward yet again is that we've all been doing such a super job. But the model already assumed school closures, business closures, and lockdown. I know you know this.

I think people have every right to be upset at people lording it over them, equipped with their clipboards and models, explaining why we're so sorry but your life has to be ruined and a non-trivial portion of it effectively erased.

That is just a no-go. That is not going to happen. Only a lunatic would tolerate such a situation. I think at this point everyone realizes that what we will need to acclimate ourselves to is a regime in which we take special care of certain vulnerable people while allowing the rest of mankind to resume their lives, of which they get only one, so that they may engage in the very production and wealth creation that makes the care of the vulnerable possible in the first place.

April 14, 2020 | The goalposts keep changing

Remember when the rallying cry was "flatten the curve" — i.e., to stretch the number of infections out in time so they wouldn't "overwhelm" our hospitals by happening all at once?

Yeah, that's gone.

Now it's: you just can't leave your house, flat curve or no flat curve, overwhelmed hospitals or no overwhelmed hospitals.

Someone in my private group just wrote:

I am getting the sense that the noose is tightening. I just saw that Pisgah National Forest, a 500,000-acre national forest in North Carolina, was closed yesterday for an indefinite period. To say that it was modestly used this spring would be a gross overstatement of the activity there.

There is zero chance of people getting sick with Covid because they were in a national forest. This is insanity.

Meanwhile, that model they keep "updating" told us on April 1 that we'd need 262,000 beds at the peak. The other day it told us we'd need 57,000 at the peak — and that the peak had been three days earlier.

We are living in a Kafka novel.

April 15, 2020 | How the laissez-faire country is faring in the pandemic

It would be nice if people could be honest and say: we really don't understand a lot of what's going on with Covid.

Whenever you point out anomalies, there's always a quick and cartoonish answer: why, this country adopted more lockdown measures than that one!

Oh? Then why have twice as many people per million died in locked-down Belgium than in the more relaxed Netherlands?

Why has Vietnam seen zero deaths? Zero! What extremes would it have had to implement for the "lockdowns explain everything" thesis to work there?

A week ago I pointed out a CNN article from March 23 lecturing Hong Kong about reopening too soon. Headline: "Hong Kong appeared to have the coronavirus under control, then it let its guard down."

We read at that time that the number of confirmed cases had doubled in the previous week.

When I noted on April 8 (sixteen days after the article was published) that the number of deaths in Hong Kong was still unchanged (just four), I got a little lecture: don't you know the average case-fatality day is 20?

Well, it's now day 23. You'll never guess: still just the four deaths, despite that "doubling of confirmed cases."

Sweden, too, has been lectured for not implementing "lockdown" (how I hate the regime's terminology, which is instantly adopted by the populace). They're supposed to be having terrible results. There was an outbreak in Stockholm nursing homes, it's true, but the rest of Sweden's experience is actually quite interesting.

In fact, a Swedish expat in the Tom Woods Show Elite has been giving us a daily update about conditions in Sweden. Here's today's (minus his charts):

I said yesterday that I feared that we would see a spike in newly reported cases, both in terms of just confirmed new cases, as well as deaths and ICU admissions, due to the long 4-day Easter weekend in Sweden. I'm happy to say that I was wrong, and that I'm now cautiously optimistic that the trend is turning downwards from now on. The data reported for today is obviously not complete, and so we'll see a correction of that tomorrow.

In any case I downloaded the data sets from the Public Health Department in Sweden, and made the charts below for people to see [they are posted in the group]. I still do not have access to the breakdown by nationality, unfortunately, but I'm writing to them and asking them for it.

Just a general observation is that we can now see how the curve is actually flattening, and the reported daily cases are going down. It should be added that as of yesterday there were 530 Covid patients in ICU. Today there are 525. So that is also an indicator that more people are leaving the ICU than being admitted to the ICU. The ICUs across the country as a whole are not operating at full capacity, and the field hospital in Stockholm is still empty.

On an additional note, the state epidemiologist, Anders Tegnell, has been subject to a very coordinated attack from the "experts" in academia. Twenty of them took to the media in an op-ed published by one of the biggest newspapers in the country, where they call his approach "extremely dangerous." They (the academics) are calling for a complete shutdown of Stockholm, and also for Anders Tegnell's resignation.

They are viscerally disturbed that this state epidemiologist is not listening to them, and is leading with an independent, different approach. Yesterday, he was grilled at the prime news hour, Aktuellt, by one of these so-called experts, who went after him on national television. Nevertheless, the Public Health Department is not changing strategy. And so far, from what I can tell, Tegnell will reign supreme when this is done with. But I'm not going to be too optimistic yet, because this can change, and I'm very aware of that.

April 16, 2020 | Warning: forbidden questions enclosed

I've had people tell me that Covid is a real threat to the young, even though there have been more deaths from it among people over age 100 than among people under age 30. "But my friend knows someone who died" is the actual response I hear from people who claim to be listening to The Science.

This is like saying, "Men are generally taller than women," and having someone reply, "What? My wife is 6'1"!"

People who claim to support The Science say the numbers are being revised downward because we've been doing such a super job "social distancing," even though the model they're talking about not only took social distancing into account, but also assumed it would be universally observed.

Supporters of The Science told me that when Hong Kong was reporting a doubling of "confirmed cases" last month, I should start expecting deaths within a couple of weeks. Three and a half weeks later, not one additional death.

Can we just admit what is obvious, namely that we're making sweeping statements about something elusive? Or would that puncture people's near-religious devotion to The Science and its priesthood?

Finally, here's what someone who belongs to the Tom Woods Show Elite wrote yesterday:

> *I relinquish any claim on the lives of the young. As an oldster who is presumed to be peculiarly susceptible to the ravages of Covid-19, I will not ask anyone to sacrifice days, weeks, or months of their time, love, life, and livelihood on my behalf. It is grotesque for the old to ask the young to sacrifice for them. Go. Live your lives. Enjoy the beautiful spring weather. I have no claim on you for my welfare.*
>
> *Who among my fellow oldsters will release any claims on the lives of young people?*

April 17, 2020 | Fauci the liar

Dr. Anthony Fauci, the virologist and immunologist who has advised half a dozen presidents, gets very high ratings from the American people.

Personally, I don't get it. I can barely stand the sight of the guy.

Leave aside his opinions on locking down the country. That's a topic for another day. Right now let's just look at the false impressions he has given about how soon he was warning of the need for drastic measures. My erstwhile co-author Chris Ferrara just examined all this in great detail in *The Remnant*, where I used to have a column years ago.

On January 21, Fauci said: "This is not a major threat to the people in the United States. And this is not something that the citizens of the United States right now should be worried about."

Before I get unjustified pushback: I am not criticizing him for having been wrong. I am simply establishing what his opinions were at what time.

On February 18:

> I don't think people should be frightened. The risk right now, today, currently, is really relatively low for the American public. But that could change....So right now, don't worry about it, be more concerned about influenza, which is going into a second peak for the season, than coronavirus....People wearing masks now is just not relevant. You don't need to be walking around with a mask right now.

On February 29:

> No, right now, at this moment, there is no need to change anything that you're doing on a day-by-day basis. Right now, the risk is still low, but this could change. I've said that many times....You gotta watch out, because although the risk is low now — you don't need to change anything you're doing — when you start to see community spread, this could change.

Now let's see how, in media interviews, Fauci has tried to paint the picture of these months. There are numerous examples; I'll draw excerpts just from his interview with Jake Tapper on Easter Sunday; Tapper and Fauci in bold:

> **TAPPER: The *New York Times* reported today that you and other top officials wanted to recommend social distancing and physical distancing guidelines to President Trump as far back as the third week of February, but the administration didn't announce such guidelines to the American public until March 16, almost a month later. Why?**

That's strange wording, isn't it? "Wanted to recommend"?

> **FAUCI: You know, Jake, as I have said many times, we look at it from a pure health standpoint. We make a recommendation. Often the recommendation is taken; sometimes it's not. But it is what it is. We are where we are right now.**

Reading that, would you not conclude that Fauci had been recommending "social distancing and physical distancing guidelines" during the third week of February? But as we've seen, on the very last day of February Fauci was saying publicly that no behavioral changes were required!

TAPPER: Do you think lives could have been saved if social distancing, physical distancing, stay-at-home measures, had started the third week of February instead of mid-March?

Of course, Fauci himself hadn't come close to recommending stay-at-home orders in the third week of February, but the viewer could be forgiven for thinking he had, based on this response:

FAUCI: Obviously you could logically say that if you had a process that was ongoing and you started mitigation earlier you could've saved lives, obviously. No one is going to deny that. But what goes into those kinds of decisions is complicated. But, you're right: obviously, if we had right from the beginning shut everything down, it may have been a little bit different. But there was a lot of pushback about shutting things down back then.

There was pushback to social distancing and shutting the country down in the third week of February? Who was even *suggesting* those things back then? And of course the implication is that Trump was doing the pushing back. But these things were not recommended, by Fauci or anyone, at the time. The shutdowns began in numerous states in the middle of March, after which time Trump indicated his desire to see the country reopened by Easter. It was in response to this, in mid-to-late March, that Birx and Fauci urged the President to keep things locked down longer.

Finally, on April 13, Fauci came clean:

> The first and only time that Dr. Birx and I went in and formally made a recommendation to the President to actually have a "shutdown" in the sense of — not really shutdown but to have really strong mitigation…the President listened to the recommendation and went to the mitigation.
>
> The next, second time, that I went with Dr. Birx in to the President and said, "Fifteen days are not enough; we need to

go thirty days." Obviously there are people who had a problem because of the potential secondary effects. Nonetheless, the President at that time went with the health recommendations and we extended it another thirty days.

So, I can only tell you what I know and what my recommendations were. But clearly as happens all the time, there were interpretations of that response to a hypothetical question [by Tapper] that I just thought it would be very nice for me to clarify because I didn't have the chance to clarify it.

When another reporter asked Fauci for the date when he first made these recommendations, all of a sudden Fauci couldn't remember: "You know, to be honest with you, I don't even remember what the date was. I can just tell you that the first and only time that I went in and said that we should do mitigation strongly the response was 'Yes, we'll do it.'"

Ferrara writes:

The problem for Fauci is that if he admitted it was not until at least mid-March that he advised Trump not to "open up the country" by Easter then it would be clear that everything he had implied during his previous media interviews about Trump's failure to act promptly in January and February was a lie and that, in truth, during those months Trump was merely following Fauci's own advice that no drastic measures were necessary. Hence Fauci's convenient memory lapse about a date he could not possibly have forgotten.

April 21, 2020 | Are all of these Covid deaths Covid deaths?

Here's something plenty of people have been wondering about: is the number of Covid-19 deaths artificially elevated because it's being promiscuously blamed for all kinds of deaths?

As with everything on this subject, the answer is murky.

Alex Berenson, the voice of reason on Twitter against Team Apocalypse, solicited answers to this question among medical professionals. A physician who's practiced in West Palm Beach for 31 years and signed hundreds of death certificates replied:

I believe that doctors are using death by Covid-19 as a convenient diagnosis when they don't really know what caused their death. Unless someone has tested positive for the virus and had symptoms and died there is no way to attribute their death to Covid-19.

Another physician, taking the opposite view, wrote:

> There is a significant amount of people who are starting to believe that Covid deaths are being falsified. This cannot be further from the truth.…There's also the myth that people are dying *with* Covid and not *of* Covid. A terminally ill cancer patient who dies of the flu is a flu death and that is how it has been coded for years. It's no different with Covid.

Still another physician says that doctors are

> definitely erring on the side of coding everything Covid that presents with those symptoms.…This is going to result in real problems doing research on the disease. We need accurate death counts and accurate co-morbidity and pre-existing condition studies to understand the disease.

The key questions we are trying to answer, he concludes, are "harder to answer if you have a bunch of false data included in the set."

With good guys on both sides of this issue it's hard to know what to think.

April 22, 2020 | "If it saves only one life," say the shysters

We heard it from Andrew Cuomo, governor of New York, and plenty of people since then: if we save even one life with these draconian measures, it will have been worthwhile.

Well, ol' Woods is here to throw cold water on that.

Here are two recent items:

(1) The U.K.'s *Sunday Express* — so not exactly an obscure dispatch — reports that increased cancer fatalities will result from the redeployment of health resources caused by Covid hysteria. In fact, says Richard Sullivan, a professor of cancer and global health at King's College London and director of its Institute of Cancer Policy, "The number of deaths due to the disruption of cancer services is likely to outweigh the number of deaths from the coronavirus itself." Sullivan continues:

The cessation and delay of cancer care will cause considerable avoidable suffering. Cancer screening services have stopped, which means we will miss our chance to catch many cancers when they are treatable and curable, such as cervical, bowel and breast....When we do restart normal service delivery after the lockdown is lifted, the backlog of cases will be a huge challenge to the healthcare system.

(2) As Reuters reported, this week a UN report warned that

economic hardship experienced by families as a result of the global economic downturn could result in hundreds of thousands of additional child deaths in 2020, reversing the last 2 to 3 years of progress in reducing infant mortality within a single year.

The report further warned that 42 million to 66 million children could fall into extreme poverty as a result of the crisis.

(In case it isn't obvious: I place no confidence in the UN. I cite them to show that these predictions aren't coming from right-wing ideologues and are therefore more difficult to dismiss.)

Well, how about that: the world isn't as cartoonish as Team Apocalypse thinks. Shutting down the world, coupled with demands that we accept living like vegetables as the "new normal," has consequences.

It isn't just that our side wants to go out and get haircuts, as these geniuses keep saying. It's that we're against destruction.

And that we realize there are often additional consequences, beyond the immediate, to the kinds of approaches states have been taking.

The latest gimmick from Team Apocalypse is to ask, "Would you take a handful of jelly beans from a bowl of 100 in which one was poisoned?" This is supposed to show me that cowering in my house is the only rational response to Covid.

The case is being framed like this: "Would you reach in and take something if there was a chance it was poison?" Well, it depends on what I would suffer *if I didn't reach in.*

The people using this analogy are misleadingly suggesting that my only possible concern is Covid. But I have other concerns, too — namely, not spending months and possibly years living like a vegetable. When I reach into the bowl, they are suggesting that this is the equivalent of returning to normal life, and taking a risk. But yes, I am prepared to take that risk because I want a life that's worth living.

If the jelly beans represent everything I've worked for my whole life, if they represent financial solvency, if they represent all my hopes, dreams, and aspirations, you'd better believe I would grab and eat that handful.

April 29, 2020 | Wait, do the lockdowns even work?

Somebody finally analyzed the data, in a *Wall Street Journal* column. Here are the results (emphasis mine):

> We ran a simple one-variable correlation of deaths per million and days to shutdown, which ranged from minus-10 days (some states shut down before any sign of Covid-19) to 35 days for South Dakota, one of seven states with limited or no shutdown. **The correlation coefficient was 5.5% — so low that the engineers I used to employ would have summarized it as "no correlation" and moved on to find the real cause of the problem.**

> With 10 million people, Sweden's death rate — without a shutdown and massive unemployment — is lower than that of the seven hardest-hit U.S. states — Massachusetts, Rhode Island, Louisiana, Connecticut, Michigan, New Jersey and New York — all of which, except Louisiana, shut down in three days or less.

> Despite stories about high death rates, Sweden's is in the middle of the pack in Europe, comparable to France; better than Italy, Spain and the U.K.; and worse than Finland, Denmark and Norway. **Older people in care homes accounted for half of Sweden's deaths.**

> **We should cheer for Sweden to succeed, not ghoulishly bash them. They may prove that many aspects of the U.S. shutdown were mistakes — ineffective but economically devastating — and point the way to correcting them.**

A Swedish expat in my private group gives us regular updates on Sweden. Here's an excerpt from his latest (again, emphasis mine):

> I have seen a bunch of articles shared here, and even a claim that Sweden isn't much different in terms of restrictions compared to some states in the U.S. I don't think that's true at

all. I think it's very different. **Where in the U.S. are the schools, gyms, cafes, restaurants, bars, swimming pools, playgrounds, parks, and regular "non-essential" shops open?** You tell me, because I would be very interested in hearing about those places....

Some people had requested that I do a comparison chart with other European countries, so that's what I did. I downloaded data sets for Italy, Spain, France, U.K., Belgium, Norway, and Denmark, and I plotted those countries against Sweden. The numbers are normalized in terms of deaths per 100,000 people in order to account for the population sizes of these different countries....[He posted these charts and the specifics of what they show inside the group.]

I think these charts are helpful to use against the lockdowners, because I see zero correlation between locking down everything and a lower rate of deaths.

On the other hand, looking at the comparison between Denmark, Norway, and Sweden, Sweden is worse off. They are ahead in the curve, but something dramatic must happen for Norway and Denmark to catch up. But as I've said before, Stockholm, which has half of all recorded cases in Sweden, already has achieved a degree of herd immunity. Between 1/4 and 1/3 of the population in Stockholm have been infected, estimates say based on a few serology tests. Do Norway and Denmark have the same partial immunity or are they just prolonging the agony? I don't know, obviously, but I can speculate.

April 30, 2020 | Just ate in two restaurants. Here's what I saw

I'm spending a few days in Georgia, where the governor has allowed some restaurants and various other establishments to reopen. The hysteria is beyond even what we've come to expect from Team Apocalypse. One media outlet even called it an experiment in "human sacrifice." The usual left-wing sobriety, in other words.

In Atlanta in particular most restaurants' dining rooms are still closed. Among the reasons: the health department's requirements for restaurants — which operate on razor-thin margins as it is — make it challenging for restaurants to function at a profit. Also, there's a fear of consumer backlash: Atlanta is heavily left-liberal, and restaurants prefer not to be accused of trying to murder their customers and employees.

Another thing: the mayor of Atlanta and the city's left-liberal inhabitants want to stick it to the governor, who says they can open, by not opening.

Wondering what it was like?

Both restaurants were what you might call fine dining, so not the kinds of places that would generally be packed on a Wednesday night — especially when most people don't even realize they're open.

In both cases our server wore a mask, and in both cases we were spread out from other diners. In one case the restaurant was operating from a limited menu — not because it expected fewer patrons, but because, as we were expressly told, "there are some items we just can't get right now."

But you're darn right it felt good to be a normal person again. We can't yet do this in Florida, even though the health officials advising the governor say at his own press conferences that conditions seem fine to begin reopening.

I might note in passing that the CovidActNow.org model predicted 465,000 hospitalizations in Florida by last week. Back on planet Earth, it's been about 2,200.

Even in New York we're starting to hear voices advocating a return to normal life.

(And isn't that what we hear whenever we try to insert some sanity into the discussion? "Tell that to New York!" As if we haven't heard of New York. These allegedly "pro-science" people are exasperatingly juvenile.)

Dr. Daniel Murphy chairs the department of emergency medicine at St. Barnabas Hospital in the Bronx. He says it's time to open back up. He notes that he can pinpoint the moment the wave crested: April 7 at 1:00pm. From that moment on, things slowed down noticeably.

He adds:

> This was striking, because the community I serve is poor. Some are homeless. Most work in "essential," low-paying jobs, where distancing isn't easy. Nevertheless, the wave passed over us, peaked and subsided. The way this transpired tells me the ebb and flow had more to do with the natural course of the outbreak than it did with the lockdown.

Why is it slowing? Not for the reason most people think, he says:

> As of today, over 43 percent of those tested are positive in the Bronx. We are developing a significant degree of natural herd immunity. Distancing works, but I am skeptical that it is playing as predominant a role as many think.

Another reason to open back up is that the Covid hysteria has people who need to go to the hospital staying home instead: "We usually average 240 patients a day. For the last week, we averaged fewer than 100. That means our patients in this diverse, low-income community are afraid to come to the ER for non-Covid care."

There will be more people like Dr. Murphy.

In the meantime, many people *need* Covid to be the end of the world. They need it to be a catastrophe. It's a deranged cult. I've never seen anything like it.

May 4, 2020 | What we saw in a semi-free state last week

Well, we spent several days in Georgia last week, eager for some semblance of normal life.

If you're curious, here's my report.

I already mentioned in a previous email our experiences at a couple of fine dining restaurants. Those experiences turned out to be similar to those we would have at other restaurants: tables were spread out (tables that were out of commission were taped off and/or had a large X taped on them), servers wore masks, and special care was given to keeping surfaces clean.

One restaurant actually took our temperature (using one of those forehead thermometers that doesn't actually touch your body) before we entered.

We also made a 3:00am visit to Waffle House, one of the few locations whose dining room was open. We had to stand in line at the register (they didn't take our order from a table), then wait outside for the food to be prepared, and then be called back inside to be seated when it was ready. This is Georgia, so at least the weather was mild at night.

(We wondered what kind of things a Waffle House server who works the graveyard shift must have to deal with when we heard ours say to someone, "Sir, you're bleeding.")

In Roswell, we were in what must have been the downtown area Saturday night and plenty of people were out and about and in good spirits. They appeared to have decided: the world has become very marginally more dangerous, but rather than live like vegetables we think it's better to proceed with our lives.

I got a haircut from a guy who'd been featured in local media stories about establishments opening back up again. He had little patience for the "it's too dangerous to open" folks. Under the circumstances, he said, they get paid more not to work, so of course they don't want to open. But instead of being honest, they cloak this venality in a veneer of moral superiority.

The pool was closed at our hotel and they weren't offering their usual breakfast buffet, but there was a brown-bag grab-and-go breakfast in its place. And no housekeeping for the entire stay.

My personal opinion: With every week that goes by, even the blue state moral preeners get more stir-crazy.

Some of them say they'll sit and wait for a vaccine.

Maybe.

I think instead they'll try to claim victory, using whatever metrics necessary, and start opening back up.

I also think people will seriously consider moving out of such states. When fall comes along and their kids still can't do things that bring them joy and fulfillment, while in other states everything is proceeding just fine, those decisions will be made.

May 5, 2020 | Whoa: Main Covid modeler abruptly resigns

Perhaps you know the name Neil Ferguson.

He has spent his life making wild predictions of doom. He said 200 million could die from bird flu; the grand total was 282 people. He said 65,000 people in the U.K. would die from swine flu; the actual number was 457. And so on.

More to our current point, Ferguson is the man behind the Covid-19 models on the basis of which most of the world has shut down. According to his model the U.K., where he lives, would have seen 500,000 deaths without radical interventions. Stay at home, he demanded. "Social distancing!"

Well.

It turns out that ol' Neil, rather than abide by the rules he would impose on others, believes he ought to be able to assess the risk level for himself. We peons aren't allowed to make these determinations, of course. No, we have to stay home alone (even though in some states as well as in Europe around 50 percent of the deaths from Covid-19 are occurring in nursing homes).

But ol' Neil? He can have visitors. Evidently he had a visitor quite recently. His married lover stopped by. Twice. Once after she had told friends that her husband may have been showing symptoms.

Oops.

Ferguson has stepped down from his government advisory position.

You really can't make this up. These are the people running the world right now. These are the people who have your neighbors scared out of their wits, to the point that they cannot have a rational conversation with you.

May 6, 2020 | The bastards won't let us live

Life is riskier in the age of Covid-19. But for the vast majority of people, it's not that much riskier.

Thankfully, we know precisely the kinds of people who require special consideration and attention. We had no right to expect this from Covid. This should help us as we try to cope with it.

Or so you would think.

Instead, Doomers genuinely want to discontinue those life-giving pleasures that give meaning and fulfillment to otherwise drab existences. Oh, well, they say, there's nothing we can do.

There *is* something you can do! You can live!

You have an infinitesimally small chance of being someone who contracts and dies from Covid-19. Was your risk level precisely where you needed it to be, down to three significant digits, before Covid came along? Because that would be an extraordinary coincidence: you were at the exact risk profile you could tolerate, and then a very slight increase in risk meant you had to shut your life down.

The people most likely to suffer serious consequences from Covid are free to isolate themselves, but I'm certainly not going to render judgment on a grandmother who decides she'd rather take her chances embracing her family members than spending her time isolated in a nursing home, wasting away physically, mentally, and emotionally.

If we don't agree to focus our efforts on safeguarding the elderly in particular (remember, more people older than 100 have died from Covid than have people under 30), then life becomes a miserable series of deprivations.

Consider this social-media testimony from a choir singer. Imagine living like this:

> I'll sum up for those who couldn't attend the ACDA/NATS/ ChorusAmerica/BarberShop/national Pandemic webinar:
>
> There is no safe way for choirs to rehearse together until there is a vaccine or 95% effective treatment in place, most likely one to two years. Perhaps occasionally outside in small groups, but only when the wind is not at your back. Masks and spacing do not protect your singers from contagion, and singers are super spreaders.
>
> Though there may be some mitigation using a combination of UV lights and fan/atmosphere scrubbing inside, it is not 100% effective and the UV in particular may be both expensive and dangerous.
>
> No concerts or public performances this fall, and frankly, maybe not for 1 to 2 years, though we actually don't know.
>
> Once rapid testing becomes available, possibility to rehearse with immediate testing before every rehearsal with ironclad agreements from choir members.
>
> AUDIENCE: liability insurance for your arts organization. Temperature checks at the door and required masks. U.S. government phase THREE recommendations for actual safe return to public performances.

So instead of isolating the sick and vulnerable, every activity that brings people joy is to be made miserable or discontinued.

When will someone say: *we refuse to live like this?*

We already have some immunocompromised people, including friends of mine, saying: *We don't want you to live like this! We're not even asking for this!* Go enjoy the one life you get, and we will do our best until conditions change!

At least that way we can focus our resources on people who really need it, instead of fruitlessly trying to ship millions of "tests" all over the place.

In the U.K., Lord Sumption just wrote:

> What sort of life do we think we are protecting? There is more to life than the avoidance of death. Life is a drink with friends. Life is a crowded football match or a live concert. Life is a family celebration with children and grandchildren. Life is companionship, an arm around one's back, laughter or tears shared at less than two metres. These things are not just optional extras. They are life itself. They are fundamental to our humanity, to our existence as social beings. Of course death is permanent, whereas joy may be temporarily suspended. But the force of that point depends on how temporary it really is.

Right on.

I for one intend to live. If that means underground events and gatherings, then so be it. Agorism has never been needed more than now.

May 7, 2020 | Look who else says we need to open up

Dr. Steven Shapiro, chief medical and scientific officer of the University of Pittsburgh Medical Center, just made a statement from which I have drawn the following excerpts (emphasis in original):

> We indeed saw a steady stream of patients but never "surged." At peak in mid-April, Covid-19 patients occupied 2% of our 5,500 hospital beds and 48 of our 750 ventilators. Subsequently, admissions have been decreasing with very few patients now coming from the community, almost all now being from nursing homes. Of note, in the 36 UPMC-owned senior facilities we have had zero positive cases.

Our outcomes are similar to the state of Pennsylvania, where the median age of death from Covid-19 is 84 years old. The few younger patients who died all had significant preexisting conditions. Very few children were infected and none died. Minorities in our communities fared equally as well as others, but we know that this is not the case nationally. In sum, this is a disease of the elderly, sick and poor.

We are now actively bringing back our patients for essential care following CMS guidelines. To assure a safe environment, we use adequate PPE and test all, even asymptomatic, preoperative patients for active viral infection with PCR. To date, 0 out of 1,000 tested positive in western Pennsylvania, New York and Maryland. 3 of 500 are positive in central Pennsylvania. Our community prevalence is low, which we will soon confirm with antibody testing.

And now, for some rare humility:

Despite rapid progress, there are critical gaps in our knowledge as well as selective use of what we know. For example, we don't know why many who are infected never develop symptoms while other, seemingly similar patients, get very sick. Crowded indoor conditions can be devastating in nursing homes, while on the U.S.S. *Theodore Roosevelt* 1,102 sailors were infected, but only seven required hospitalization, with one death. This contrast has significant implications that we have not embraced. Epidemiologic prediction models have performed poorly, often neglecting critical variables. Seasonality is rarely considered, yet we know that coronaviruses are seasonal. Hope is not a plan, but it is quite possible that the virus is not very healthy in the U.S. right now.

The question before us is **what will happen as we re-open society and how should we manage it?** For New York and a handful of other cities with high case rates as a result of density, travel and socioeconomic issues, they must open up in a measured step-wise manner with extensive testing, tracing and treatment.

But for the rest of the country, as people come out of their homes cautiously and safely, if we protect our vulnerable seniors, particularly those in nursing homes, we should be able to keep case rates low, buying time for a potential resurgence as we bolster our supply chain and find effective intervention.

Covid-19 is a disease that ravages those with preexisting conditions — whether it be immunosenescence of aging or the social determinants of health. We can manage society in the presence of this pathogen if we focus on these preexisting conditions.

And here it comes: there are health consequences of lockdown:

What we cannot do, is extended social isolation. Humans are social beings, and we are already seeing the adverse mental health consequences of loneliness, and that is before the much greater effects of economic devastation take hold on the human condition....

In this particular case, the problem we're not going to be able to fix in the short term is the complete eradication of the virus. The problem we can fix is to serve and protect our seniors, especially those in nursing homes. If we do that, we can reopen society, and though infectious cases may rise as in the *Theodore Roosevelt*, the death rate will not, providing time for the development of treatments and vaccines.

That's coming from locked-down Pennsylvania. We've never needed federalism more than now.

May 8, 2020 | The 75,000 deaths the lockdowners forgot

How about that: locking down a whole society has negative consequences.

Benjamin Miller of the Well Being Trust in Oakland, California, is co-author of a study that seeks to determine how many "deaths of despair" (from drug or alcohol abuse or suicide) will occur as a result of all this.

Their estimate: about 75,000.

To be sure, some of this has to do with anxiety about Covid itself, but according to the study it's also related (obviously) to the unprecedented shutdown, extremely high unemployment, and months-long social isolation with (in many places) no clear endpoint.

Miller says it's crucial that people be allowed to get back to work. "People have to be working and we have to get people connected to other people," he said.

Dr. Elie Aoun, vice chairman of the American Psychiatric Association's Council on Addiction Psychiatry, said that this result, while shocking, wasn't surprising: "I've been seeing this in practices and my colleagues have been talking about it, too."

Aoun said social isolation has more consequences for the many vulnerable patients who suffer from depression, anxiety and addiction. "Addiction patients are relapsing, and a lot of patients who don't have drug use or alcohol problems are drinking more now, sometimes every day from 4 or 5pm, and they don't stop until they sleep," he said.

You don't need me to tell you that this is very bad news.

The good news: more and more people are hearing about these effects of the lockdown. Even CBS News ran a story about this study.

May 13, 2020 | How are the ghouls taking good news?

Axios is reporting, "Some of the states that skeptics were most worried about, including Florida and Georgia, haven't seen the rise in total cases that some experts feared. Florida's new cases have actually declined by 14% compared to the previous week, and Georgia's fell by 12%."

"Some experts" have been predicting piles of corpses in Florida for weeks. Our governor didn't lock down soon enough, they said.

These experts also predicted piles of corpses in Japan. Just wait two weeks, they said, and Japan will get what's coming to it. You'll see!

Then…nothing.

Then it was, "Oh, the Japanese wear masks and wash their hands," etc. Nice try, Bozo. You already knew they did these things before you made the ghoulish predictions.

What's so hard about admitting: we're not entirely sure what's going on here?

And although the news about declining cases in Georgia and Florida is good, "cases" are not primarily what should concern us. The more we test, the more "cases" we find. The point is, most "cases" wind up amounting to precisely nothing. There were over 800 "cases" at that South Dakota meat packing plant, and so far over 800 recoveries. In March we got lurid reports of a doubling of "cases" in Hong Kong. We'd better wait two weeks! Piles of corpses! Eight weeks later, zero additional deaths.

Now I'll be honest with you: I am afraid to see how these good numbers are being received by Doomers. Some of them seemed to be practically licking their chops when describing the wave of deaths they were sure awaited jurisdictions that hadn't adopted their panoply of closures and restrictions. It was downright ghoulish.

So I just posted this on Twitter:

Tom Woods
@ThomasEWoods

I'm sure everyone is delighted at the good news that the numbers are looking great in Georgia and Florida, which are reopening. We are all celebrating this, right? Nobody would be ghoulish enough to be secretly unhappy, right?

11:25 AM · May 13, 2020 · Twitter for Android

⊣l View Tweet activity

273 Retweets **1.2K** Likes

May 14, 2020 | Hate the lockdowns? You're racist

Why are people protesting the lockdowns?

I'll bet you can think of a dozen perfectly good reasons off the top of your head.

And since we are dealing with what is substantially a nursing-home epidemic, you'd think we could figure out a way to be more targeted and therefore more effective (and less disruptive to the healthy) in our approach.

Now let's turn to Twitter for an answer! Why are people protesting the lockdowns according to Twitter?

One user's answer: "Because people who have never truly been oppressed are being inconvenienced for the first time in their lives and don't understand what it means to sacrifice in the name of the greater good. Individualist culture, institutionalized racism, commodity fetishism, and selfishness."

You're selfish and a racist and a "commodity fetishist" if your state has 10 deaths and everything is shut down, your livelihood is destroyed, and your children's hopes and dreams are indefinitely postponed.

These are the people who think you and I care only about "the economy," and to them "the economy" is the stock market, which they do not understand but which they think is useless and serves no social function.

People are closing businesses they have devoted their lives to because of this, and people like the person above can't even be human enough to say: hey, I get that the sacrifices being demanded here are severe.

May 15, 2020 | Grandmas against lockdown

The lockdowners — or civilization wreckers, as I prefer to call them — sure are satisfied with themselves, aren't they? They're willing to sacrifice everything you've worked your whole life for. And if you disagree with shutting down society, why, you must want to kill people's grandmothers. A pleasant bunch.

Sure, you might actually think we'd do a better job protecting grandmothers if we focused our energies on old folks specifically instead of fruitlessly shipping millions of "tests" all over the place, or if (unlike certain governors) we hadn't forced Covid patients back into nursing homes; but the lockdowners can't hear you.

I've been thinking: what the world needs now is an organization called Grandmas Against Lockdown.

Plenty of older folks are appalled at what's going on, and are terrified to contemplate their grandchildren's future if this goes on much longer.

They don't like their grandkids wasting away in front of computer screens on "virtual playdates." They don't want every activity that once enriched their grandkids and gave them joy canceled indefinitely (and that's no straw man: plenty of so-called respectable people are calling for precisely that). They want their grandkids to be kids — the same way they themselves once had the chance to be.

And for that matter, they don't want to spend their final days locked in a sterile room watching their families over Zoom. That may seem normal and desirable to the lizard people who rule us, but not to actual human beings.

I just spoke to David Stockman, who was director of the Office of Management and Budget under Ronald Reagan. He's 73 and staying home. But he agrees with everything I'm saying here: younger people should resume their lives immediately, and he will take care of himself in the meantime until things improve.

The current strategy is: you can't have anything back that gave your life meaning.

If you perform in front of an audience, forget it. Sorry, dancers, musicians, comedians, magicians, singers, actors, athletes, and many others. Other people were allowed to follow what gave them joy, but you cannot.

Maybe someday — in 18 months, after you've had to give up on that dream anyway. Or maybe never.

Not to mention, of course, the destroyed businesses, the ruined lives, the domestic violence, the depression, the suicide, and the confusion of mere biological life with truly human living.

When will someone prominent have the courage to say: *we refuse to live like this*?

I spoke to a musician at dinner the other night, and he told me that the small venues he'd normally book for his band's tour are saying they will never reopen. The lockdowns have destroyed them for good. Are we sure this is the world we want?

The wild predictions did not come to pass. People have criticized Sweden, but if the lockdowners were correct Sweden should be a giant cemetery. There should be mountains of corpses everywhere. Their outcome should not be comparable to plenty of other European countries.

We are destroying every good thing, and tearing apart friendships and families in the process.

Let's just stop.

May 19, 2020 | More good news the ghouls will hate

Remember when Dana Milbank wrote a piece for the *Washington Post* called "Georgia Leads the Race to Become America's No. 1 Death Destination"?

All the robots shared it. Georgia's reopening is going to kill everyone!

Well, here's what we just found out today.

The number of Covid-positive patients hospitalized in Georgia is down 34 percent since May 1.

Normal people are happy about this. The ghouls won't even acknowledge it. In fact, the *Post* ran an op-ed today called, "Will Republican Governors Pay a Price for Their Recklessness?" It's like they're living in a different universe from the rest of us.

If Republican governors deserve to "pay a price," it's for falling for the hysteria in the first place.

May 24, 2020 | The country that recovered without lockdown (not Sweden)

For weeks and weeks and weeks the ghouls have insisted that a massive wave of death was bound to pour over Japan. Tokyo is pretty dense, and the whole country has plenty of interaction with China. Japan doesn't even have a Centers for Disease Control. Not to mention: they didn't "test" enough, which is supposed to be the cardinal sin.

And then…nothing.

In fact, Japan could lift the state of emergency in Tokyo as soon as tomorrow.

How did it do this?

Mikihito Tanaka, a professor at Waseda University who belonged to a public advisory group of experts on SARS-CoV-2, was blunt: "Even experts don't know the reason."

It's almost as if the ebb and flow of illness occurs according to its own dynamic.

One of the best parts of the Japanese experience has been that humility: "Even the experts don't know the reason."

Man, that's refreshing.

The ghoulish certainty with which we've been told to "wait two weeks" until refractory locales get what's coming to them has been one of the most grotesque parts of these weeks and months.

Japan is so eager to get back to normal that there is a serious proposal, beginning as early as July, to subsidize half of foreign visitors' travel expenses.

Amidst all the panic and fearmongering, it's nice to report on some good news.

May 25, 2020 | Take a guess at the dangerous, irresponsible thing I'm doing

This week I'll be spending time at various Florida beaches, beginning with a nice visit to author and friend Tom DiLorenzo.

That's right: I'll be sitting on the beach. Possibly even swimming!

You can imagine what the fact-free hysterics think about that. You'll kill people if you go to the beach! Even though research (remember "The Science"?) suggests there's about a zero percent chance of outdoor transmission.

Well, one Doomer takes the cake: Daniel Uhlfelder, @DWUhlfelderLaw on Twitter. He's been going around Florida beaches dressed as the Grim Reaper. This weekend, for Memorial Day, he says he's been handing out body bags to beachgoers. Of course, precisely zero deaths will occur as a result of people going to the beach.

Ask yourself this: if your chances of being struck by lightning increased by three times, would you stay home because your overall risk profile had changed, or would you venture out anyway, because life is worth living?

Oh, we're worried about infecting others, comes the answer, and that's another matter for another day.

But I've encountered some people — as has my 15-year-old daughter, whose peers are at zero risk — who are genuinely frightened even now.

That's no way to live.

And even the older and more vulnerable folks are starting to say: I can't live my final days not embracing my grandchildren, and talking to my family only through Zoom. This is not living.

May 26, 2020 | Are the lockdowners starting to crack?

As Homer Simpson would say: wellity, wellity, wellity.

Michael J. Stern, a member of *USA Today*'s Board of Contributors, just published an op-ed called "Coronavirus: I was in the stay-home-until-it's-safe camp. But I just can't take it anymore."

Much of the article is nonsense: he says, for example, that Texas, which recently reopened, had its highest day of new "cases" on May 16, after the reopening.

The truth: I visited Dallas two weeks ago and can assure you that the city was barely "opened." More to the point: the rise in "cases" comes from a massive increase in testing.

Meanwhile, the number of Covid *deaths* in Texas over the past weekend was the lowest for any two-day period since March 31–April 1. So in other words, the usual obfuscation.

But some common sense manages to creep in:

> Reopening the country due to economic considerations is not the same as saying money is more important than human life. We face economic realities every day, independent of the coronavirus. Gun violence, drunken drivers, transmissible diseases and a panoply of other dangers could all be brought to a screeching halt if we locked down indefinitely. But a life of home confinement is not a world in which most of us would want to live.

Remember that picture of Dr. Fauci holding a document with the headline "15 Days to Slow the Spread"? That was 71 days ago. And as time drags on, this bizarre situation does more and more damage.

Thus Stern:

> Moving into the third month of home isolation, the toll on each of us is different. Some face financial hardship. Some have seen their education thrown into limbo. For me, the longer I'm home alone, the more my obsessive-compulsive disorder flares. I didn't realize this until a phone call in which a friend asked whether I was staying safe.

> I explained that I had found a way to test myself for coronavirus: Loss of taste is one of the first signs of infection, so I bought a 5-pound tub of jelly beans with 49 flavors. I eat several handfuls daily, one bean at a time. If I recognize each of the different flavors, I figure that I'm safe.

> The dead silence on the line convinced me it was time to book a Zoom therapy session.

It's borderline criminal what the hysterics have reduced this person to. But even he sees that we have to emerge from our homes.

May 27, 2020 | Social distancing did nothing

I find it hard to believe myself.

But I've now seen what the data looks like graphically, and, well, it's not what they're telling us on TV.

We have Google mobility data now, so we can see if people's mobility levels have any connection to Covid deaths per million. So why not plot these numbers for all 50 states and look at them?

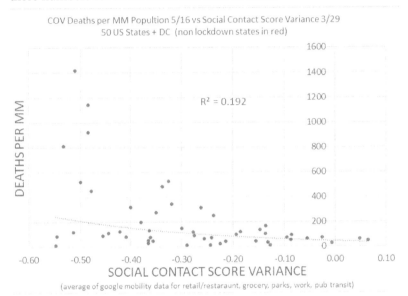

COV Deaths per MM Popultion 5/16 vs Social Contact Score Variance 3/29
50 US States + DC (non lockdown states in red)

$R^2 = 0.192$

DEATHS PER MM

SOCIAL CONTACT SCORE VARIANCE
(average of google mobility data for retail/restaraunt, grocery, parks, work, pub transit)

Do you see a relationship between mobility (social contact score) and deaths per million in that chart? Are the dots not rather all over the place?

Let's look now at the shelter-in-place policy. Does increased time at home correlate with fewer deaths per million?

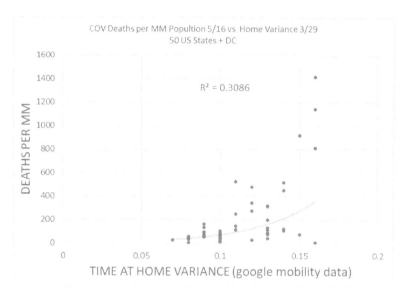

If anything, this chart shows the opposite.

We all know that correlation doesn't prove causation. But is it plausible to have causation without correlation?

Now could it be a case of harder-hit places having more extreme social-distancing responses? The person who plotted the numbers (@boriquagato on Twitter) considered this: "Many have posited that this inverse relationship is driven by worse outbreaks driving stronger distancing reactions. I suspected this, too. So I tested it. I ran U.S. state case counts to see if higher counts drove stricter policy. Nope."

"This result," he adds, "holds all over the world and in every component data series there as well."

If we had to choose a date, social distancing can be said to have begun in earnest on March 15, when the "social interaction score" went negative for the first time.

Two weeks later, March 29, was when peak distancing response was reached, and it continued fairly consistently at that level for about four weeks.

Average the social-distancing response on March 29 for the states that got worse and the states that got better, and…the result is exactly the same. You have to go down to four decimal places to detect any difference at all.

The CDC itself admitted earlier that "the effectiveness of pandemic mitigation strategies will erode rapidly as the cumulative illness rate prior to implementation climbs above 1 percent of the population in an affected area." Since we were surely past that level of disease prevalence in major American cities by then, could this all have been a huge exercise in political theater, accomplishing nothing?

If we had real reporters asking real questions, maybe we'd be getting somewhere.

May 28, 2020 | Lockdown was unnecessary, this country now admits

Over in the U.K., the *Spectator* just made note of a report coming out of Norway that will surprise folks who haven't been following the lockdowns and the course of the virus closely.

The rest of us are just happy someone is admitting it.

What are they admitting? That the lockdowns were unnecessary. It turns out that the virus was already on the decline when the lockdowns were ordered, and it was not spreading nearly as fast as the most extreme numbers — on the basis of which the lockdowns were implemented — suggested it was:

> It looks as if the effective reproduction rate had already dropped to around 1.1 [and not 2 or 3, as a frightened public was being told] when the most comprehensive measures were implemented on 12 March, and that there would not be much to push it down below 1....We have seen in retrospect that the infection was on its way down.

And according to the director of Norway's public health agency:

> Our assessment now, and I find that there is a broad consensus in relation to the reopening, was that one could probably achieve the same effect — and avoid part of the unfortunate repercussions — by not closing. But, instead, staying open with precautions to stop the spread.

She added that "the academic foundation was not good enough" to justify lockdown.

Now, I wonder: will the people who touted Norway as an example of a country that locked down early continue to promote that country as an example, now that its officials are admitting they made a mistake? Or were we supposed to respect Norway only when it lived up to our preconceived ideas?

It's exhausting trying to keep up with what we're supposed to believe from one day to the next.

Part II: Summer 2020

July 9, 2020 | Are we ready to be reasonable?

A few more people — in this case, health experts — are starting to fight back against the lockdown regimes.

Yes, society does need to balance all considerations, and Covid is not the only (or even the most important) of these.

A group of physicians in Canada just released an important statement, whose first portion I reproduce for you here:

> Covid-19 is a serious public health threat and will remain so until we have a universally available safe and effective vaccine or similar medical treatment. There have been many deaths due to Covid-19 and every single one represents a tragic outcome. However, in overall population health terms Covid-19's direct impact on premature mortality is small. While those under the age of 60 account for 65% of cases, they represent just 3% of deaths. With ready access to health services, severe outcomes can be averted in those who do not have pre-existing risk factors.

> In March 2020, unprecedented public health measures were implemented in Canada in response to the rapid rate of growth of cases and the potential threat to health systems. Because of the potential for exponential growth in cases and the situation in other parts of the world our governments took these actions that applied to the entire population in order to protect our health care system. These interventions were meant to buy the time necessary to develop a longer-term response. They should not be used as a means of eradicating the disease.

> While some countries have been successful in suppressing the disease, most continue to see sporadic cases and outbreaks. Only a few countries, primarily island nations, appear to have eliminated the disease, but it is uncertain how long those countries can completely isolate themselves from the rest of the world.

> The public health measures did protect our health care system, to the point that Canada had excess capacity. Our leaders and public health authorities had to use strong language to support universal acceptance of these measures.

As a result, many Canadians have become fearful of Covid-19 and are worried about the impact of working, seeking routine and preventative medical care, participating in religious and cultural events, interacting with their family and friends, using public transportation, shopping and other normal activities.

Covid-19 control is an important public health priority but it is not the only nor the most important challenge to the health of people in Canada. We need to examine the broad social determinants of health and their impact on citizens, particularly with an equity lens, as the consequences of the public health measures have not been shared equally in society. Those in lower income groups, black and other racialized groups, recent immigrants and Indigenous people are bearing a disproportionate burden. The public health efforts must take account of the impacts of both the disease and the consequences of the control measures on all segments of the population.

The fundamental determinants of health — education, employment, social connection and medical and dental care — must take priority. Measures for Covid-19 control need to accommodate these health determinants. Children need to go to interact with their peers, in child care, schools, sports and social activities, and summer camps. Adults need to go to work. Family and friends need to meet.

The societal costs of maintaining these public health measures, even with some gradual relaxation, are too high. Canadians are missing scheduled medical appointments and surgeries, which will lead to increased deaths. There are significant challenges for our young with impact on early childhood development, one of the strongest predictors of lifelong health and social outcomes. Education is compromised. There are increases in domestic violence, alcohol and drug intake, and food insecurity. The economic consequences are huge. This leads to increased unemployment, which is related to increased deaths. And the toll on mental health is just beginning to be felt. Personal concerns about the disease, cases and deaths in friends and family, loneliness and isolation, worries about jobs and finances, parents having to juggle childcare and general insecurity, are leading to increased levels of anxiety, depression and stress.

We need to shift from a mindset of attempting to eradicate this disease, which is not feasible and will lead to continued devastation of our society, to a new goal.

Our new goal: minimize the impact of Covid-19 using methods that are practical, effective and compatible with our values and sense of social justice.

July 17, 2020 | Reality vs. "expert" predictions, example #44,772

You know those people who feel qualified to tell you how many lives would have been saved if we'd done X, Y, and Z earlier — most of which they themselves weren't recommending at the time?

You'd think these people would have a little humility by now.

Here's what a peer-reviewed model for Minnesota, at a $1.5 million price tag, concluded about what was supposed to happen in that state (the higher line in each graph). The essentially flat bottom line, by contrast, is what's *actually* happening.

Ready?

Here it is:

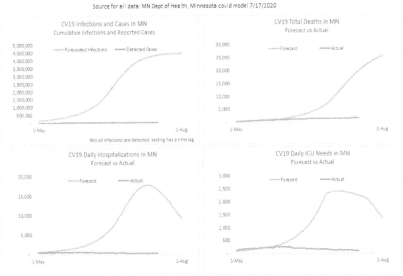

About what we've come to expect, in other words.

Meanwhile, in education: Sweden kept the kids in school and Finland didn't, and the health outcomes have been the same. In Germany, Saxony sent kids back to school and no hotspot has emerged. After the summer break they plan to drop the mask requirement as well.

In the U.S., the plans for school range from semi-reasonable to downright dystopian. Either way, it's an opportune moment to consider homeschooling. And since I myself helped create the self-taught, K-12 Ron Paul Curriculum, I'm rather partial to that: RonPaulHomeschool.com.

July 20, 2020 | Wait, you mean there won't be 100 New Yorks?

Ten days ago ProPublica released an article with this headline:

"All the Hospitals Are Full': In Houston, Overwhelmed ICUs Leave Covid-19 Patients Waiting in ERs"

Now were the hospitals all full? Not even close.

The author, Charles Ornstein, is an adjunct professor at Columbia Journalism School. When called on this, he responded that somebody in the article had *said* they were all full, so the quotation in the headline was accurate in that sense.

Just five days ago, the same journalist insisted: "Houston's coronavirus situation is dire," and linked readers to an MSNBC interview.

Now today, Ornstein has taken us from "dire" to "good news" (which means the situation could not have been dire to begin with — as you, dear reader, surely knew): "Data from the Texas Medical Center in Houston shows that it is past the peak and is looking at gradual decreases in hospitalized Covid-19 patients."

Here in Florida, incidentally, we're doing much better than the crazies predicted. Because of all the backdating, you have to make a special effort in order to get the number of deaths that actually occurred on each particular day, as opposed to being retroactively classified as Covid later on.

The highest number of deaths on a particular day so far in July was 99, all the way back on July 8. By a week ago we were already supposed to have been hitting 600 deaths per day, according to Bloomberg.

We are not looking at multiple New Yorks all over the country.

You'd think people would be delighted at this good news, but I've never seen people more resistant to good news in my life.

July 30, 2020 | Doomers wrong again, episode #4277

Let's check in with Arizona. That's another state that a month ago we were told would be a catastrophe. "Wait two weeks," remember?

As of yesterday, how's it going?

Covid admits have been falling as fast as they rose. Hospitalization, as well as ICU and ventilator usage, have been consistently declining as well.

As the sensible people predicted, the rise in "cases" vastly outpaced the rise in hospitalizations.

Total hospital usage was pretty much unchanged.

Meanwhile, teachers' unions are insisting they won't return to school — *and* that they don't like online instruction.

One such teacher, a very young woman, sobbed on local news about how terrified she was to return to school.

These are the people teaching your children. That woman has a better chance of being killed in a car accident on the way to school while being simultaneously attacked by werewolves than she does of dying of Covid.

These are the same people who say, "Listen to the science."

August 3, 2020 | Masks: the non-miracle workers

Thought things were crazy in the U.S.?

Here's the situation in Melbourne, Australia. After a meaningless rise in "cases" following their brutal and hysterical lockdown, they're locking down even harder. Here's a sample:

So another pointless, soul-crushing lockdown.

Google mobility data already show no difference in outcomes between societies with a lot of mobility and societies with little. Germany and the U.S. have had very different health outcomes despite having virtually identical mobility numbers.

And no, it isn't masks. Spikes keep happening in places with mask mandates and/or widespread mask wearing. By contrast, practically the only Scandinavians wearing masks are Asian immigrants, and Scandinavia is down to practically zero deaths.

Japan, we were told, escaped serious harm because they wore masks (this Tweet is from late May):

Eric Topol ✓
@EricTopol

And why did Japan do so well without a lockdown and so little testing?
Masks.
They gave masks out to 50 million households. An expert panel believes this was the main reason for their success.

japantimes.co.jp/news/2020/05/2...

by @IsabelRTokyo

Let's see how Japan is looking right now:

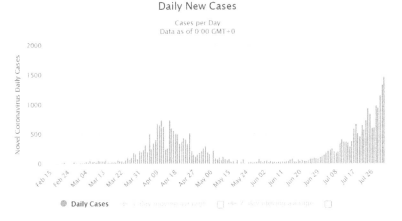

So much for that theory.

Japan will be fine, because very few of these cases are serious. But the idea that "masks" account for their low case numbers doesn't seem sustainable anymore.

(Especially because the masks the Japanese government supplied to everyone were much too small, and became a national joke. Our experts here, like Eric Topol, are completely unaware of this, naturally.)

Meanwhile, there's the usual good news we get every day that most people for some reason don't want to hear — and thanks to the media, most of them never do hear.

Like: the spike in the Sun Belt is over. ICU and hospitalization rates are plummeting in Arizona. In Florida, despite 300,000 new "cases" reported over the past month, hospital capacity is essentially unchanged.

August 4, 2020 | Lockdowns do nothing

What if people get Covid despite our nonpharmaceutical interventions? That's what the data sure seem to be telling us. Lockdown or no, masks or no, Covid has its way with people and societies.

Mobility data yields no obvious relationship between stay-at-home orders and health outcomes.

We are supposed to hate Brazil for not locking down. Here's its chart:

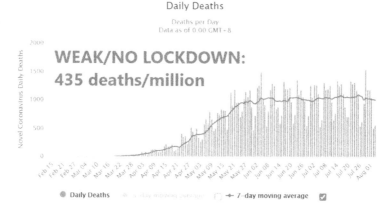

Now here's Peru, a country which by contrast we are not supposed to hate because it locked down:

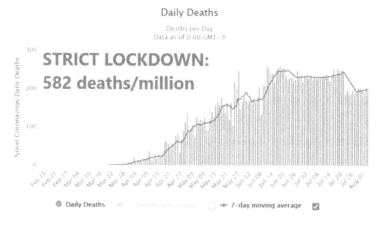

Of course, this is perfect for governments everywhere. They can panic the public, and then take credit for declines that were going to occur anyway. Governments always do this.

The Occupational Safety and Health Administration (OSHA), created in 1970, boasts of having reduced workplace accidents and fatalities. What they don't point out is that *these things had been declining at an even faster rate for the previous 25 years*, in the absence of OSHA!

The National Highway Traffic Safety Administration (NHTSA) takes credit for a 3.5 percent annual decline in traffic fatalities per mile traveled.

Care to guess what the annual decline was *before* we had a NHTSA? 3.5 percent.

So again, governments love taking the credit for developments that are already happening on their own.

Incidentally, here's people's mobility in Massachusetts plotted on the same graph with Covid hospitalizations:

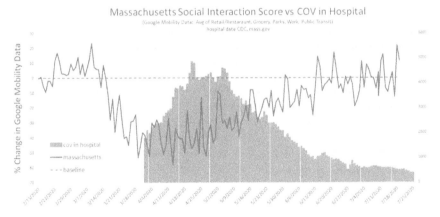

As you can see, there is no connection at all.

August 5, 2020 | The country (not Sweden) Doomers ignore

Doomers really are determined to pretend Japan doesn't exist.

When they thought Japan would suffer badly after refusing to lock down, they couldn't talk about Japan enough. When Japan did fine, they temporarily lost interest.

That is, until they thought they could use the example of Japan on behalf of mask wearing. "Japan did well because they wore masks" became the conventional wisdom. Well, here's the problem there: right now Japan is having a bigger outbreak of cases than at any time during the pandemic, despite the mask wearing.

So the Doomers have gone back to pretending Japan doesn't exist. Here's a typical interventionist on Twitter with nearly half a million followers:

Amy Siskind 🏳️ ✅
@Amy_Siskind

Look at every other country who has succeeded on Covid-19. What does it entail? The same thing - national lockdown, mass testing and contact tracing.

See what I mean?

Japan had neither a national lockdown nor mass testing. Its results have been fine (and will continue to be fine despite the current surge in "cases"). Therefore, it no longer exists in the Doomer consciousness.

Meanwhile, the Philippines had one of the toughest lockdowns of any country in the world, and were threatened with on-the-spot execution for violations. A recent survey, moreover, found them to be the most consistent mask wearers in the world.

Result:

Another spike.

Government response:

Another lockdown of a poor country.

The vast majority of people there, as anywhere, are at trivial to zero risk from Covid. Therefore, let's lock down and impoverish absolutely everyone.

So apparently the plan is simply to keep locking countries down. For all our vaunted "science," this wreckage of whole societies is the best these geniuses can come up with.

Meanwhile, if you take the data from the Oxford Covid-19 Government Response Tracker index and plot it against health outcomes — in other words, if you look to see if there's any apparent connection between severity of lockdowns and health outcomes — you find no connection at all. The distribution is entirely random.

As future ages look back on the 21st century, our "public health" establishment will be a laughingstock: dressed in white coats and holding clipboards, but prescribing leeches and rain dances and human sacrifice and calling it "science."

August 7, 2020 | How to panic people with b.s. numbers

Daphne Zohar is founder and CEO of her own biotech firm. Here she is trying to claim a few days ago that Massachusetts — where the virus has obviously receded — is in "bad shape":

Daphne Zohar
@daphnezohar

With testing delays this is a look back to a week or more ago, meaning that Massachusetts is in bad shape. Mass.reports 438 new confirmed coronavirus cases. @MassGovernor @MassLtGov

Mass. reports 438 new confirmed coronavirus cases, 9 new deaths - The Bos...
The uptick in COVID-19 cases in Massachusetts continued its march forward, as the state reported a 438 rise in confirmed cases on Tuesday — the first tim...
🔗 bostonglobe.com

Now for one thing, she's focused on a "day of report" number, a bunch of tests that were reported on the same day. People make this mistake with deaths all the time, which is why my state of Florida looked a lot worse than it was: if there are 150 deaths "reported" today, but only 35 deaths today and the others are retroactive classifications from as long as six weeks ago, well, that's relevant to how we understand the overall trajectory.

But then there's the fact that there's been a massive rise in testing there — by 90 percent since late June. And yet the number of confirmed "cases" has risen by much less than 90 percent, which means prevalence is falling. Good news, for the dwindling number of people who appear to welcome good news these days.

And a lot of these "cases" are not cases at all, because of the sensitivity of the PCR tests everyone is taking. [TW note: this will be discussed in a later entry.] Many weeks after recovery people can still test positive, but they are not sick and not contagious.

How about hospitalizations? Here's the situation in Massachusetts, which is obviously not in "bad shape":

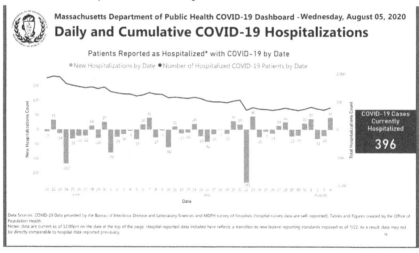

And as I've previously noted, there is no connection at all between health and the Massachusetts reopening (Daphne Zohar said in another Tweet that Massachusetts had reopened "too fast"):

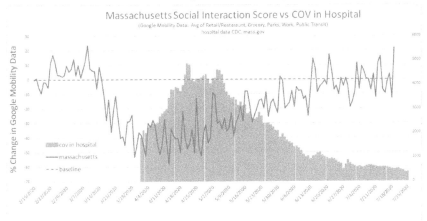

To be worried about Massachusetts right now, in light of these numbers, is bizarre.

The one thing Massachusetts should be worried about is that no matter how low their numbers get, they're going to be effectively imprisoned in their homes anyway and deprived of some of life's great pleasures for an indefinite period of time, thanks to ignorant people panicking everyone.

Do we even know what the goal is at this point? Zero cases? That's not what the public was told in March — *five months ago now*.

Incidentally, I responded to ol' Daphne Zohar. Many people had tried to explain to her that she was misinterpreting the numbers. Yet her Tweet stayed up. I would have thought embarrassment alone would have caused her to take it down. So I asked, "Why has this Tweet not been taken down after it was explained to you that you're misinterpreting the data?"

She responded by blocking me.

August 10, 2020 | Great news: unexpected resistance to the lockdowners

Surely somebody, somewhere, amidst the fact-free frenzy that has consumed America, was going to resist, right? Some organized group *had* to step up.

The idea that we should ruin everyone's lives in order to protect the vulnerable, instead of just protecting the vulnerable, makes no sense.

If I graph the progress of the virus in numerous states — some with bars open, others with them closed, some with restaurants open at 25 or 50 percent capacity (good luck staying in business like that) and some with restaurants fully open — you will not be able to tell me which is which. It's all theater, egged on by politicians who have a unique opportunity to exercise power righteously, and to portray themselves as having saved lives even though the virus appears to peak and taper off according to the same pattern everywhere, regardless of our non-pharmaceutical interventions.

Meanwhile, people have been shamed into not saying a single word when their lives and businesses are ruined and things that give their lives meaning are taken away indefinitely.

So surely someone is going to say: this is stupid and evil.

And it turns out:

It's college football players, and the #WeWantToPlay movement.

Big Ten presidents apparently thought they could collude with the hysterics in sports media to get the fall season canceled, and that would be that. They didn't count on a massive outcry from players themselves. That wasn't supposed to happen. The players, like the rest of us, are supposed to shut up like good peons and let their betters tell them that something they love is being taken from them regardless of what they think.

And for heaven's sake, if ever there were a group of people at no risk from Covid-19, it's college athletes.

The SOBs may still cancel the season, but how refreshing to see so many people willing to say *enough is enough* to the fact-free, anti-science lockdowners.

And the facts and figures suggesting that the lockdowns have been both devastating and pointless keep piling up.

August 11, 2020 | The normal person the lockdowners hate

I don't make a habit of cheering for politicians, as you surely know. But holy cow: Kristi Noem, governor of South Dakota, has been outstanding.

She refused to lock down her state. The crazies went berserk. Even some of her own people demanded to be locked down. An outbreak at a meatpacking plant made the crazies feel vindicated, even though prisons, nursing homes, and meatpacking plants are rather unrepresentative of society at large when it comes to Covid.

Back in April Rachel Maddow lectured Governor Noem: "You are aware that it's *infectious*, right? That it's a communicable disease?" That was the entirety of Maddow's analysis.

That there might be various forms of collateral damage of shutting society down was not considered. That we might be better off letting people live their lives — since, really, isn't that the default position? — and isolating the truly vulnerable, was not mentioned, either.

Meanwhile, even the *New York Times* reported last week that as a result of the lockdowns there will be 1.4 million excess TB deaths, 500,000 from HIV, and another 385,000 from malaria.

Thanks, geniuses.

Anyway: Governor Noem ignored them all.

South Dakota has had a death rate of 17 per 100,000 (compared to 127 per 100,000 for Massachusetts, for example).

(I might add, by the way: in neighboring Wyoming, the governor was urged to shut down by the head of the Wyoming Medical Society: "If we don't act now, it's certain we'll use up available supplies in weeks....Now's the time before it's too late." Wyoming has had a death rate of 5 per 100,000.)

On Twitter she's been publishing common sense:

Governor Kristi Noem ✔ @govkristinoem · Aug 10

There is a risk associated with everything that we do in life; more South Dakotans have died from accidental injuries than from #COVID19 in the past 5 months. We mitigate risks by taking proper precautions. (1/2)

💬 1K 🔁 10.9K ♡ 34.8K ⬆️

Governor Kristi Noem ✔ @govkristinoem · Aug 10

We take precautions when we get in our cars, when we operate farm equipment, and when we make choices about what we eat and how much we exercise. The same should be true about life as we continue getting back to normal. (2/2)

💬 331 🔁 2.8K ♡ 12.3K ⬆️

Then she's noted that life has gone on fairly normally in her state:

 Governor Kristi Noem ✔ @govkristinoem · Aug 7
#Sturgis2020 kicks off today. Welcome to South Dakota!

Our state had the Mount Rushmore Fireworks Celebration. We had the first national indoor sporting event with fans thanks to @PBR.

We've been "Back to Normal" for over 3 months, and South Dakota is in a good spot.

♡ 1.5K   ⟲ 9.4K   ♡ 31.1K   ⬆

And then, showing some genuine political savvy, she made a video urging people to move to South Dakota — because there you can have your business and your life:

⚲ Pinned Tweet

 Governor Kristi Noem ✔ @govkristinoem · Jul 16
There's no place in America like South Dakota. We'd love to have you join us. Come grow your company; live your life; achieve your dreams.

We can make it happen for you right now, because South Dakota Means Business.

▶ 737.6K views   0:00 / 1:00 ◁)) ↗

♡ 2.2K   ⟲ 10.6K   ♡ 36K   ⬆

Schools will be open in South Dakota, too.

August 17, 2020 | The lockdowners' unforgivable crime against the young

By now we've all gotten the message: you're selfish if you'd like to do the kinds of things that once gave your life meaning, and life is about nothing but the avoidance of death. Virtually everything you've looked forward to has been canceled, and nobody will tell you when you can have those things back. "When we have a vaccine," comes the raving lunatic's answer.

Nobody was giving you that answer when they were pushing "15 days to flatten the curve." They didn't dare.

Instead, they kept us in our homes for those 15 days, and then 15 days after that, and 15 days after that. Each time they pushed the date back we grew more demoralized, more resigned to a barren life without "large gatherings" — i.e., everything that makes life fun — and with "virtual" events over Zoom.

Oh, and no hugs, no weddings, 10 people at your father's funeral, and a long list of other grotesque demands.

What metrics were they using to decide when we'd be allowed back out again, when our businesses could open (and when they could operate at a level that made profit even a remote possibility), and when those life-giving pleasures that bring us meaning and fulfillment could be resumed? Who knows? All we heard was: everything is canceled. Maybe you can have it in 2021. Maybe you can have it when there's a vaccine — as if there's a guarantee of that.

Well, a terrifying statistic came out last week showing the grim — if entirely predictable — effects all this inhuman regimentation has been having on the young, particularly those between 18 and 25. Here are some figures from the federal government's Substance Abuse and Mental Health Services Administration. They are percentages of people who have considered suicide within the previous 12 months, organized by age. Note that the 18–25 group fluctuates between 6.8 percent and 11 percent:

Figure 58 Table. Suicidal Thoughts in the Past Year among Adults Aged 18 or Older: 2008-2018

Age	2008	2009	2010	2011	2012	2013	2014	2015	2016	2017	2018
18 or Older	3.7⁻	3.7⁻	3.8⁺	3.7⁺	3.9⁺	3.9⁺	3.9⁺	4.0	4.0	4.3	4.3
18 to 25	6.8⁺	6.1⁻	6.7⁺	6.8⁺	7.2⁺	7.4⁺	7.5⁺	8.3⁻	8.8⁻	10.5	11.0
26 to 49	4.0⁻	4.3	4.1⁺	3.7⁺	4.2	4.0⁺	4.0⁺	4.1⁻	4.2	4.3	4.7
50 or Older	2.3	2.3	2.6	2.6	2.4	2.7⁺	2.7⁺	2.6	2.4	2.5	2.1

Now, from the Centers for Disease Control, we find that percentage (for the 18–25 group) has leaped to 25.5 percent — and this survey asks not about the previous 12 months, but whether they've considered suicide *just in the past 30 days*:

TABLE 1. Respondent characteristics and prevalence of adverse mental health outcomes, increased substance use to cope with stress or emotions related to COVID-19 pandemic, and suicidal ideation — United States, June 24–30, 2020

		Conditions						
Characteristic	All respondents who completed surveys during June 24–30, 2020 weighted* no. (%)	Anxiety disorder[†]	Depressive disorder[†]	Anxiety or depressive disorder[†]	COVID-19-related TSRD[§]	Started or increased substance use to cope with pandemic-related stress or emotions[¶]	Seriously considered suicide in past 30 days	≥1 adverse mental or behavioral health symptom
All respondents	5,470 (100)	25.5	24.3	30.9	26.3	13.3	10.7	40.9
Gender								
Female	2,784 (50.9)	26.3	23.9	31.5	24.7	12.2	8.9	41.4
Male	2,676 (48.9)	24.7	24.8	30.4	27.9	14.4	12.6	40.5
Other	10 (0.2)	20.0	30.0	30.0	30.0	10.0	0.0	30.0
Age group (yrs)								
18–24	731 (13.4)	49.1	52.3	62.9	46.0	24.7	25.5	74.9
25–44	1,911 (34.9)	35.3	32.5	40.4	36.0	19.5	16.0	51.9
45–64	1,895 (34.6)	16.1	14.4	20.3	17.2	7.7	5.8	29.5
≥65	933 (17.1)	6.2	5.8	8.1	9.2	3.0	2.0	15.1

(Note also the huge jump in the numbers for people in their mid-20s through their 40s.)

We've taken away everything they love, deprived them of the opportunity to socialize and to experience those irreplaceable moments of youth, and demanded they accept this dystopia as the "new normal." Now *that's* selfish.

Part of the natural order is that parents make sacrifices for their children, not the other way around. If vulnerable people wish to isolate themselves, then *they should isolate themselves*, not demand that young people sacrifice everything dear to them and live atomized existences for a period of time that our overlords refuse to specify.

As I pass through middle age, the thought would never occur to me to make these demands of younger people. Am I prepared to tell them that while I enjoyed these pleasures when I was young, for the sake of my comfort they cannot have them? What kind of selfish bastard thinks like that?

Some of us — yes, even many of us in middle age and beyond — are prepared to say: this is no way for anyone, young or old, to live. We want a life that includes weddings, family celebrations, hugs, live concerts, drinks with friends, thriving businesses, the arts, school dances, theater, and friendship from less than six feet away — and we're willing to accept whatever risk accompanies these things, because no other kind of life is worthy of a human being.

As I've noted before, it's not just the deprivation of basic, non-negotiable joys that the lockdowns cause. Even the *New York Times* admitted that lockdowns will lead to 1.4 million excess TB deaths, 500,000 excess HIV deaths, and 385,000 excess malaria deaths. That's on top of the 1.2 million children UNICEF expects to die as a result of the lockdowns.

Not to mention how many people have been prevented — by deadly regulations driven by irrational fear, or by irrational fear itself, drummed into them by a grossly irresponsible news media — from receiving major medical care they need. In the U.K. they've been predicting more avoidable cancer deaths than Covid deaths because of this problem.

Meanwhile, Doomers have been peddling a comic-book version of events. When Wisconsin courts said bars could reopen, this was supposed to lead to a massive spike in deaths there. All the social-media scolds said so. No such thing happened. Did this cause them to rethink their comic-book approach? You can guess the answer.

They practically cheered when spikes hit Arizona, Texas, and Florida, and they blamed those states' reopenings — even though those states had been open for eight weeks before the spikes occurred.

Those spikes are over now, and they were brought down without lockdowns. Yes, some bars were closed, but what really happened, as Alex Berenson put it, is that they simply pretended they were restaurants so they could stay open.

August 19, 2020 | U.S. congressman has had it with Fauci/Birx

I'm spending the week in the free state of South Dakota, which never shut down despite the hysterical cries of the fact-free Doomer industry.

There's more mask-wearing here than you might expect, though most people at least don't wear them outdoors — which is, unfortunately, more than I can say for the superstitious masses in plenty of other states.

We had lunch today at a chain called HuHot, where you assemble your raw ingredients at a buffet-style bar, and the chef prepares them for you. I wondered if this would still be allowed. Evidently yes. They had taken some precautions to reassure people, but the experience was essentially as I remember it in the past.

The folks I've met have been friendly, and in general have appreciated that life has remained more or less normal in their state.

Back in Florida, where I live, the excellent news nobody told you is that Covid hospitalizations there are down by about half since the peak. The Sun Belt spike is truly over, and without the "hundreds of thousands of deaths" that the ghouls on social media predicted.

Anyway, my newsletter is a bit data-light this week as I try to enjoy semi-normal life during this fleeting visit, but I did want to bring one thing to your attention in case you missed it.

Last week on the Tom Woods Show I had a chance to talk to Rep. Thomas Massie, one of a handful of sane voices in the U.S. Congress. He is an extremely impressive guy all around, as you may know already, but you'll be even more impressed after you hear his answers in this discussion.

He's not any more of a fan of the Fauci/Birx axis than you and I are, and he had plenty to say about them and about the various "stimulus" packages that the Borg has been tossing around. Enjoy:

TomWoods.com/1711

August 21, 2020 | Lockdowns kill, exhibit Z

The side effects of the lockdowns keep getting harder to ignore.

Dr. Brian Stauffer is head of cardiology at Denver Health. He and his colleagues wanted to figure out why the number of people arriving at the hospital suffering from cardiac arrest had plummeted in recent months.

Surely, dear reader, you know where this is going.

According to the *Colorado Sun*:

> Looking at data on ambulance calls in Denver, they found
> that, while overall calls for service went down during the stay-

at-home period, the number of people dying from cardiac arrests at home shot up.

Stauffer's team found that cardiac arrests at home in Denver more than doubled in the two weeks after the statewide stay-at-home order was issued compared with historical averages. Even compared with more recent data, the weekly average of out-of-hospital cardiac arrests jumped to 46 during those two weeks, versus 26 or 27 in the three months prior.

Stauffer and his colleagues found that the number of people in Denver who died of cardiac arrests at home in the two weeks following the statewide stay-at-home order was greater than the total number of people who died of Covid-19 in the city during that time.

Oh, but "listen to the science," everybody!

According to the "listen to the science" crowd, "science" demands lockdowns. Apart from the zero connection between lockdowns and health outcomes, the bigger issue is this: "science" doesn't tell you how you should decide between pouring all resources into Covid-19 while leaving horrific wreckage — including massive loss of life — everywhere else.

It is superstition to think "the science" could possibly — or is even intended to — answer a question like this. Science can inform our decision-making, naturally, but it obviously can't tell us what we should value or how we should prioritize our various goals.

Not to mention: these days "the science" seems to be all about pretending there are no trade-offs, no competing goals. The wreckage keeps piling up, and our leaders obviously have no idea what the endgame is.

August 24, 2020 | Lockdown architect admits: "A monumental mistake"

We'll see if any American so-called experts admit their mistake — there's certainly no media pressure forcing them to, that's for sure — but here's what just happened in the U.K.

Mark Woolhouse is a professor of infectious disease epidemiology and a member of the Scientific Pandemic Influenza Group on Behaviors that advises the government. And he's now saying the lockdowns were a terrible mistake.

"At the time I agreed with lockdown as a short-term emergency response because we couldn't think of anything better to do," he confesses. It was a "panic measure." He now calls it a "monumental mistake":

> I believe history will say trying to control Covid-19 through lockdown was a monumental mistake on a global scale. The cure was worse than the disease....I suspect right now more people are being harmed by the collateral effects of lockdown than by Covid-19.

This is why we can't listen exclusively to "public health officials," none of whom evaluate tradeoffs. They are convinced that whatever happens to be their primary or exclusive concern at the time should also be everyone else's primary or exclusive concern, and they set policy as if this is simply uncontroversial.

(It's not clear whether the policies they advocate even help in the first place, but for the sake of argument we'll leave that aside.)

But there are significant side effects to the massive social engineering that the white coats and clipboards have imposed on society, whether those white coats deign to acknowledge them or not. Woolhouse says:

> This is why we need a broader range of people on the government advisory board SAGE [Scientific Advisory Group for Emergencies] with equal input from economists to assess the damage to incomes, jobs and livelihoods, educationalists to assess the damage to children and mental health specialists to assess levels of depression and anxiety especially among younger adults, as well as psychologists to assess the effects of not being able to go to the theatre or a football match.

And here's what he thinks about the strategy of some American governors: "I would not dignify waiting for a vaccine with the term 'strategy.'"

And then, finally:

> I never want to see national lockdown again. It was always a temporary measure that simply delayed the stage of the epidemic we see now. It was never going to change anything fundamentally, however low we drove down the number of

cases, and now we know more about the virus and how to track it we should not be in this position again.

We absolutely should never return to a position where children cannot play or go to school. I believe the harm lockdown is doing to our education, health care access, and broader aspects of our economy and society will turn out to be at least as great as the harm done by Covid-19.

Now that's an admission.

He adds that there was never any good reason to close the schools. I agree with that from a public health standpoint, but from an ideological standpoint it's in the schools where the naive confidence in the Establishment and its crazy demands and policies is born in the first place.

August 25, 2020 | Dr. Fauci: Worse than you thought

It's true: I'm a PhD, and not a medical doctor. But you obviously don't need to be a medical doctor to smell a rat.

Longtime readers will recall that years ago I had a public exchange with commentator Mark Levin on the subject of presidential war powers. He was defending Barack Obama's right to intervene in Libya on his own authority, and I was disputing that right. That exchange got nastier than it needed to.

But forget all that.

Levin's recent interview with Harvey Risch is to my mind the most valuable and important thing he's ever done. Risch is a professor of epidemiology at the Yale School of Public Health and Yale School of Medicine. He is associate editor of the *Journal of the National Cancer Institute*, editor of the *International Journal of Cancer*, and a member of the board of editors of the *American Journal of Epidemiology*. Risch has been outspoken in defense of hydroxychloroquine, administered correctly, as a treatment for Covid-19.

Now I know what you're thinking: "all the experts" say it doesn't work, etc.

Well, not really.

Before we get to the Levin interview, here's an excerpt from an article Dr. Risch wrote last month (emphasis mine throughout):

As professor of epidemiology at Yale School of Public Health, I have authored over 300 peer-reviewed publications and currently hold senior positions on the editorial boards of several leading journals. **I am usually accustomed to advocating for positions within the mainstream of medicine, so have been flummoxed to find that, in the midst of a crisis, I am fighting for a treatment that the data fully support but which, for reasons having nothing to do with a correct understanding of the science, has been pushed to the sidelines. As a result, tens of thousands of patients with Covid-19 are dying unnecessarily.** Fortunately, the situation can be reversed easily and quickly.

I am referring, of course, to the medication hydroxychloroquine. When this inexpensive oral medication is given very early in the course of illness, before the virus has had time to multiply beyond control, it has shown to be highly effective, especially when given in combination with the antibiotics azithromycin or doxycycline and the nutritional supplement zinc.

On May 27, I published an article in the *American Journal of Epidemiology* (*AJE*) entitled, "Early Outpatient Treatment of Symptomatic, High-Risk Covid-19 Patients that Should be Ramped-Up Immediately as Key to the Pandemic Crisis." That article, published in the world's leading epidemiology journal, analyzed five studies, demonstrating clear-cut and significant benefits to treated patients, plus other very large studies that showed the medication safety.

Physicians who have been using these medications in the face of widespread skepticism have been truly heroic. They have done what the science shows is best for their patients, often at great personal risk. I myself know of two doctors who have saved the lives of hundreds of patients with these medications, but are now fighting state medical boards to save their licenses and reputations. The cases against them are completely without scientific merit.

In his interview with Levin, Risch went even further:

In fact, the science is so one-sided in supporting this result that it's stronger than anything else I've ever studied in my entire career. The evidence in favor of hydroxychloroquine benefit in high-risk patients treated early as outpatients is stronger than anything else I've ever studied.

Risch goes on to recall that Dr. Anthony Fauci, who has resolutely denied any benefit from hydroxychloroquine, was similarly obstructionist (the similarity is almost eerie) in 1987, in the face of the AIDS epidemic. At that time, there was a drug (Bactrim) that worked better than AZT and was very inexpensive, and which had an excellent record of treating the particular kind of pneumonia that was then the leading killer of people with AIDS. But the testimonies of countless frontline AIDS physicians meant nothing to Fauci, who — in defiance of the scientific consensus — discouraged its use. As many as 17,000 people died unnecessarily. You need to hear Dr. Risch, a mild-mannered academic, tell the story.

Incidentally, if the organized LGBT movement weren't in the tank for the Democrats, they'd be screaming with outrage right now, alerting Americans that Fauci is today doing to Covid patients what he had done to AIDS patients in 1987. But they'd rather stick it to Trump than stand up for themselves or for other suffering Americans. Their cowardice and lack of self-respect are truly grotesque.

(Interestingly, even *HuffPost* criticized Fauci for this back in 2014: "Dr. Anthony Fauci is rewriting history. He is doing so to disguise his shameful role in delaying promotion of an AIDS treatment that would have prevented tens of thousands of deaths in the first years of the epidemic." Of course, this was back when Fauci hadn't yet become sainted and untouchable; *HuffPost* would never have the courage to publish such a thing today.)

August 31, 2020 | The panickers just had a big oopsie

Well, sometimes the truth has a way of trickling out, in the unlikeliest of places. The *New York Times* just ran this headline: "Your Coronavirus Test Is Positive. Maybe It Shouldn't Be."

We learn there that as many as 90 percent of positive Covid results are for people who are not contagious, and are therefore being ordered to quarantine and isolate for no reason.

It has to do with the PCR test and something called the "cycle threshold," which in the United States is set in most labs at a cutoff of around 40 or 37 instead of a more reasonable 30.

Do an Internet search for that headline and you'll have all the details at your fingertips.

Someone drew this analogy: "Imagine a neighborhood on fire. Here, the firefighters have defined even dying embers as a 'fire' and are so busy putting those out that they are missing entire homes that are burning down and setting others ablaze."

So these gigantic "case" numbers, which meant little enough to begin with, mean even less now.

Incidentally, the general problem of numbers without context has panicked people around the world into thinking the virus is worse than it is. We know this is true of the United States thanks to some recent polling data. It's also true of the U.K., according to *The Telegraph*, where the average person thinks the death rate from the virus is 100 times greater than it actually is.

One British journalist from the *Daily Mail* visiting Sweden, where life continues as normal, noted the "generally relaxed atmosphere" at the supermarket: "Nobody recoiled in horror when our trolley came within five meters of them. Nor did people shrink in terror when another shopper appeared in the aisle, as is the norm in British supermarkets these days."

Oh, and let me add one more recent headline (also from the *Daily Mail*): "The country with the world's strictest lockdown is now the worst for excess deaths." They're talking about Peru, a poor country that has been decimated by the lockdowns. The poor are much poorer, and the tourism industry is destroyed.

This is evil. And if you say anything, you're condemned.

How did so many people get caught up in this wave of irrational destruction — especially when the true numbers, and an identifiable demographic of victims, became clear?

Just when you thought you couldn't hold the press and the American political class in any more contempt, this happens.

September 1, 2020 | One insane governor's impossible reopening standards

I know some good people who live in California, and this is just awful.

These are the governor's guidelines for what it will take to get some of the restrictions lifted. Note that there is no stage that involves getting your life back, period:

WIDESPREAD	**More than 7**	**More than 8%**
Most non-essential indoor business operations are closed.	Daily new cases (per 100k)	Positive tests
SUBSTANTIAL	**4-7**	**5-8%**
Some non-essential indoor business operations are closed.	Daily new cases (per 100k)	Positive tests
MODERATE	**1-3.9**	**2-4.9%**
Some business operations are open with modifications.	Daily new cases (per 100k)	Positive tests
MINIMAL	**Less than 1**	**Less than 2%**
Most business operations are open with modifications.	Daily new cases (per 100k)	Positive tests

This means no return to normal, ever — if they remain true to these guidelines.

Given the problem of false positives alone, how can these numbers ever be reached?

A member of the Tom Woods Show Elite pointed out some pertinent facts here. Since 42 of the 58 California counties have fewer than 500,000 people, a mere five cases per day will keep restrictions in place. Some 23 counties will be forced to keep some restrictions in place with just one case per day.

These guidelines are being released at the very moment that hospitalizations are plummeting — but hospital capacity no longer guides state policy, even though that was the original pretext behind the initial "flattening the curve" propaganda.

Some 41 percent of the 12,000 deaths in California — population ~40 million — were in people age 80 or above.

Meanwhile, some 44 percent of adults report experiencing anxiety and/or depression. In June that figure was 11 percent.

At some point people are simply going to have to abandon the worst, most irrational parts of the country and move elsewhere, regardless of the sentimental attachment they may have to wherever they currently live. The shrinking of their tax base would be exactly what these governors deserve.

Some people fear that the people fleeing will bring the bad politics of their home state with them to their new state. That's possible. But I tend to think that the kind of people who are prepared to leave are the kind with the ability to think for themselves, and who haven't bought into the self-flagellation cult of Covid-19, according to which the more they deprive themselves of human happiness, the more morally upright they are.

I've said from the start that most Republicans have been very unimpressive during the crisis, mostly me-too'ing the various restrictions. At the same time, if the Democrats win in November, states like California will get bailed out — so in effect rewarded for their totalitarian lockdowns, and buffered against the consequences of whatever future inhuman restrictions they may want to impose.

September 2, 2020 | The Covid panickers sure hate this guy

Yesterday we discussed a nutball governor. Today we have someone better to cover: Ron DeSantis, governor of Florida.

DeSantis took a lot of abuse early on for not being totalitarian enough with his lockdowns. My own view was something like the opposite: I thought he was too timid about reopening, and was too much in thrall to a highly dubious "public health" (that's a laugh) establishment that would never be satisfied no matter how encouraging the numbers were.

I still think he's too timid. But he's been pushing back, hard, against the irrational Covid cult and its society-destroying pseudoscience. Instead of following in the footsteps of other governors, who run away from good news and introduce new metrics to justify lockdown when the old ones are looking much too good to sustain it anymore, he highlights the excellent news in our state:

Ron DeSantis ✓
@GovRonDeSantis

Florida COVID-19 update (1/8): The number of COVID-positive patients currently hospitalized is down nearly 60% since the July peak

9:47 AM · Aug 31, 2020 · Twitter Web App

3.2K Retweets **230** Quote Tweets **10.9K** Likes

Ron DeSantis ✓ @GovRonDeSantis · Aug 31
Replying to @GovRonDeSantis
(2/8): The number of COVID-positive patients in the ICU is down 52% since the July peak

◯ 35   ↻ 309   ♡ 1.5K   ⬆

Ron DeSantis ✓ @GovRonDeSantis · Aug 31
(3/8): The number of COVID-positive patients in Florida hospitals represents 6% of all licensed hospital beds

◯ 34   ↻ 302   ♡ 1.4K   ⬆

Ron DeSantis ✓ @GovRonDeSantis · Aug 31
(4/8): The number of hospital admissions for COVID on 8/30 was the lowest since June 15th

◯ 21   ↻ 238   ♡ 1.2K   ⬆

And now watch as he handles what by now, to a rational person, is the unhelpful and misleading number of "cases":

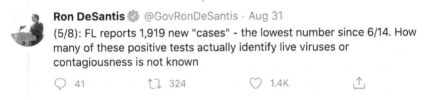

Ron DeSantis ✓ @GovRonDeSantis · Aug 31
(5/8): FL reports 1,919 new "cases" - the lowest number since 6/14. How many of these positive tests actually identify live viruses or contagiousness is not known

◯ 41   ↻ 324   ♡ 1.4K   ⬆

I love that he puts "cases" in quotation marks, just as I do.

More:

Ron DeSantis ✔ @GovRonDeSantis · Aug 31
(6/8): Antibody testing at Florida's drive-thru sites has continued to register at between 20-25% and the diagnostic positive % has fallen to the 5-6% range

💬 26   🔁 251   ♡ 1.2K   ⬆

Ron DeSantis ✔ @GovRonDeSantis · Aug 31
(7/8): 27% of hospital beds are empty; 24% of ICU beds are likewise empty

💬 54   🔁 292   ♡ 1.5K   ⬆

Ron DeSantis ✔ @GovRonDeSantis · Aug 31
(8/8): ED visits for COVID-like illness have returned to the levels seen during the first half of June.

💬 161   🔁 252   ♡ 1.4K   ⬆

On Monday DeSantis held a joint press conference with Dr. Scott Atlas, the Stanford academic the media hates because he doesn't stoke fear. The heroic writer Jennifer Cabrera reported on it:

Jennifer Cabrera @jhaskinscabrera · Aug 31
DeSantis: "We will never do any of these lockdowns again, and I hear people say they'll shut down the country, and honestly, I cringe, because we know places that have done that"

Jennifer Cabrera @jhaskinscabrera · Aug 31
DeSantis: "The most draconian lockdown in the world has been Peru, military enforced since March. They have the highest per capita mortality in the world from COVID. And at best, what a lockdown will do is delay. It does not reduce the ultimate mortality"

Jennifer Cabrera @jhaskinscabrera · Aug 31
DeSantis: "If there are 3 cases in a school somewhere, how many of those people developed any type of symptom? How many of them were ill? Like the University of Alabama had all these, quote, cases. I don't think a single one of them required hospitalization."

Jennifer Cabrera @jhaskinscabrera · Aug 31
Atlas: "There's a considerable cost to shutting down medical care, whether it's cancer, chemotherapy, live organ donor transplants, cancer screenings, biopsies, immunizations, all kinds of things went by the wayside in the prolongation of the lockdown..."

Jennifer Cabrera @jhaskinscabrera · Aug 31

Atlas: "Half of them didn't come in for their chemotherapy. You had thousands of tumors that weren't biopsied; 2/3 of cancer screenings that were not done; we had more than half of childhood immunizations not done; 85% of living organ transplant surgeries were not done."

Jennifer Cabrera @jhaskinscabrera · Aug 31

Atlas: "The purpose of testing is to stop people from dying, stop people from getting a serious illness from this disease, and allowing other people, who are very low-risk, to function."

Jennifer Cabrera @jhaskinscabrera · Aug 31

Atlas: "And that's what the new CDC guideline came out this week on testing, and I'm very much for that, as was every single doctor on the Task Force, despite what you may read, is that we do testing in a very smart way."

Jennifer Cabrera @jhaskinscabrera · Aug 31

Replying to @jhaskinscabrera

Atlas: "We know what's going on; this is not March or April; we've had a massive decrease in the case fatality rate since then; we know a lot more; length of stays in hospital are one-third of what they were at the peak; 50% less mortality, if you are hospitalized."

Meanwhile, isn't it interesting: the very people who lecture us about their devotion to education have been by far the most credulous, the most prone to panic, and the most willing to adopt groupthink when it comes to Covid. They think "the experts" should tell us how to live, as if "the experts" take a class in college that teaches them how to balance a so-called public health goal against its innumerable side effects. No "expert" has been trained to make such decisions, period.

September 3, 2020 | The numbers don't lie: lockdowns did nothing

No matter how you slice it, the numbers refuse to tell the story that lockdowns did any good.

Donald Luskin, in a *Wall Street Journal* article called "The Failed Experiment of Covid Lockdowns" (also adapted for the *New York Post*), tells us this:

> TrendMacro, my analytics firm, tallied the cumulative number of reported Covid-19 cases in each state and the District of Columbia as a percentage of population, based on data from

state and local health departments aggregated by the Covid Tracking Project. We then compared that with the timing and intensity of the lockdown in each jurisdiction. That is measured not by the mandates put in place by government officials, but rather by observing what people in each jurisdiction actually did, along with their baseline behavior before the lockdowns. This is captured in highly detailed anonymized cellphone tracking data provided by Google and others and tabulated by the University of Maryland's Transportation Institute into a "Social Distancing Index."

Measuring from the start of the year to each state's point of maximum lockdown, which range from April 5 to April 18, it turns out that lockdowns correlated with a greater spread of the virus. States with longer, stricter lockdowns also had larger outbreaks. The five places with the harshest lockdowns — D.C., New York, Michigan, New Jersey and Massachusetts — had the heaviest caseloads.

It could be that strict lockdowns were imposed as a response to already severe outbreaks. But the surprising negative correlation, while statistically weak, persists even when excluding states with the heaviest caseloads. And it makes no difference if the analysis includes other potential explanatory factors, such as population density, age, ethnicity, prevalence of nursing homes, general health or temperature. The only factor that seems to make a demonstrable difference is the intensity of mass-transit use.

They then repeated the study, this time to investigate the reopenings. They started from each state's peak of lockdown and ended on July 31. They found that the states that opened up had the lightest caseloads, though the relationship was "fairly weak." They also noted that the states that had the Sun Belt spike, which is over now, were not even the most opened up.

The Lancet, the prestigious medical journal, found similar results when comparing across countries: "A longer time prior to implementation of any lockdown was associated with a lower number of detected cases."

The TrendMacro study is better, though, because instead of relying on stated government policy, they use mobility data to examine what people actually did (so Doomers can't use the "people disobeyed the lockdowns" excuse).

September 4, 2020 | Grandma's dystopian life thanks to Covid-mania

Up to now, a lot of us in the reality-based community have focused on the crimes perpetrated against the young, who have had everything that makes life fulfilling yanked away from them, and a socially distanced dystopia put in its place.

But older — and indeed the very oldest — folks are suffering, too.

We're all certain that the most humane course of action is to require people who — if the average lifespan after being admitted to a nursing home is any indication — are in the final months of life to interact with their families only over Zoom, and be devoid of human contact?

Yes, they are biologically alive. I get it. I could spend my whole life biologically alive in a windowless room with no art or music and with cans of navy beans slipped through a slot in the door. But I would not be a human being according to any definition I would recognize.

Earlier this week someone in my private group shared (with the names removed) a couple of quite typical comments from a support group for people whose loved ones have been locked in nursing homes for the past six months. One such person wrote:

> *I think I've hit rock bottom today. I passed the nail salon and technician that did my loved one's nails. I stopped and told her I haven't touched my lady in six months and the tears just start pouring....How much longer can I do this? It's grieving every single day.*

Then another:

> *Tonight's window visit. She asks if church is filling up again. I tell her it is. She asked if she can get a pass to go out for church. I look at her. I cannot lie to her. I tell her, "If you go out, when you come back you have to stay in your room by yourself all day and all night for 14 days." She looks at me waiting, wondering. I tell her, "Just in case you might have caught the virus." There are no words for the look of disgust on her face. She cannot believe what is being forced on her. No one, absolutely no one, not even those caring for her, are subject to such isolation or lockdown. This is criminal. It's elder abuse. It's been six months since she stepped outside. I wonder if she even remembers how to get in the car.*

And then the woman writing this said to Texas Governor Greg Abbott and the Texas Health and Human Services Commission: "OPEN THESE

FACILITIES. YOU ARE STEALING PEOPLE'S LIVES. THE LAST BIT OF THEIR LIFE!"

Now:

I can share all kinds of charts with you.

I can chart Peru (with a harsh lockdown) against Brazil (with no lockdown), and you will not be able to tell which is which (except I'll give you a hint that Peru is the one with worse results).

I'll show you American states, and you try to figure out, based on the results, which ones locked down and which didn't, which locked down the hardest, which ones opened and when they opened, and you won't be able to make any consistent sense out of any of it.

I can show you over and over again that the lockdown regime is based on pseudoscience.

I can point out the collateral deaths caused by the lockdowns [as I will do in the "Death by Lockdown" chapter].

But at this point screw all that. This response is inhumane, period. Let people make their own decisions about their own lives.

September 5, 2020 | A lockdown victim they don't want you reading about

Yesterday's item about the fate of the old in the age of Covid evidently struck a chord. I got bombarded by responses.

As I wrote yesterday, most people (myself included) have protested what's being done to the young, with their every pleasure stolen from them indefinitely. But as I also wrote yesterday, we can't forget about the inhumane approach to the old.

One person wrote:

> *I know this is one example, but my grandma is 86 years old. Her best friend in the world was hospitalized with Covid, and on top of it all she lives in uptown Kenosha…not three blocks from where the worst of the* ~~*protests*~~ *arson took place. Yet when I called her on the phone this past weekend she was still of the attitude that she needs to get out and live her life, because as you say, there is more to life than merely surviving. If she can go about her life, anyone should be able to.*

Now take a look at a second reader's testimony:

Thank you so much for your newsletters. This particular one struck a chord, because my husband's grandfather killed himself early in July because of lockdown and social distancing. He and his wife were 91, but perfectly fit and healthy, of sound mind and living independently with their only form of assistance being grocery shopping.

According to my husband's Nan, he was suffering from anxiety, couldn't understand what was going on and kept muttering, "I've had enough now, I just want to go." He threw himself to his death at 4am, was taken by Life Flight to a hospital but died of head injuries. Suspiciously, they did not put suicide on the death certificate. He died of a "head injury sustained during a fall." As they massaged the numbers toward Covid, I have no doubt they are massaging the numbers away from suicide.

My mother-in-law has gone full Bedwetting Mentalist. I really quite respected the woman before all this hit, but she's gone crazy observing the guidance, and wouldn't even hug her own bereaved mother. After we set off for the funeral (we live 12 hours away in north Scotland), everyone panicked as the "guidance" on letting relatives stay in your home changed while we were en route, and they had to scramble to get us a hotel room.

(On a side note, hotel rooms are in short supply, because the U.K. government is housing an extraordinary number of illegal immigrants arriving in the hundreds on rafts every day.…It's all very bizarre, and I say this to you as a left-wing person who has been an immigrant several times in my life. I generally have compassion for these people and their situation, but something is very wrong here.)

At the funeral, I was the only person willing to hug the 91-year-old widow who just lost her husband of 71 years. It was a tiny funeral. Five people attended besides the minister and the gravediggers. I was told I couldn't sit by her, but I did anyway, and she was glad for it. She's not bothered in the slightest by this virus.

What the hell is wrong with people?

I just wanted to share that story with you. We told our MP that we don't know a single person who has had Covid, but we have a suicide in the family due to lockdown and social distancing, and empty condolences were all we got. We don't need condolences. We need this to STOP.

Meanwhile, Dr. Fauci has gone full-on berserk.

He's now saying that the Covid crisis will require us to reexamine and rebuild our relationship with nature. This 79-year-old bureaucrat thinks he should be able to implement the total transformation of society:

> Living in greater harmony with nature will require changes in human behavior as well as other radical changes that may take decades to achieve: rebuilding the infrastructures of human existence, from cities to homes to workplaces…to recreational and gatherings venues.

Um, how about not?

But there are people who superstitiously believe that Fauci, by virtue of his medical degree, is somehow qualified to reorder all of society — and would want him to do it.

September 7, 2020 | Masks had nothing to do with it

The great Jennifer Cabrera has been doing an excellent job smashing the government line on Covid. For example, the Sun Belt spike was supposed to have devastated Florida, according to hysterics on social media. It didn't. Why didn't it? Want to guess what the media wants you to think did the trick? Go ahead, guess.

You got it: "masks."

They need it to be masks, because that way they can claim that government mandates saved us. The trouble is, the numbers do not bear this explanation out at all. Not even a little.

On August 25, Dr. Michael Lauzardo, Chief and Assistant Professor of the Division of Infectious Diseases and Global Medicine at the University of Florida, nevertheless made this very argument: when people heard about the rising case count, he said, they wore masks more reliably and left their homes less frequently.

I've already given away the punchline: there is no evidence for this theory.

Florida saw a very minor decrease in mobility in July and August, but there is no statistically significant relationship between cases and mobility in Florida or in the United States in general.

The Phase 2 reopening has been blamed for the growth in cases, but the data show that the Phase 2 reopening did not affect mobility at all. Miami introduced a mask mandate as early as April 9, and required masks even outdoors as of July 2. Despite no changes to their lockdown policies, Miami saw a massive increase in cases in July, and then saw a decline in August — again, with no changes in policy.

There is no evidence that Floridians increased their mask usage during the spike, so it's not clear why Dr. Lauzardo would have said such a thing — unless he is assuming a priori that masks work and must be the explanation for a decline in cases and deaths, so therefore mask usage *must* have increased.

If you can see a connection between mask usage and health outcomes in the below, I owe you a Coke:

Deaths per 100K Population & Average Mask Use (Always+Frequently) - FL

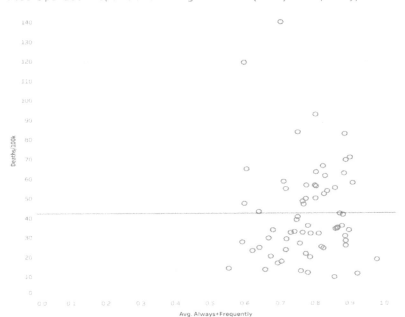

Once again, none of these interventions appear to accomplish a thing.

I am convinced that half the reason behind the mask mandates is that government officials can then try to take the credit ("it's because we forced you stupid rubes to wear masks!") when the numbers follow their inevitable path downward.

September 8, 2020 | Fauci keeps pretending the "case" count isn't a joke

By this point anyone who's informed about the situation knows that the count of "cases" — which doesn't actually mean people showing symptoms — is an absurd metric on which to base policy, for numerous reasons I've covered in the past.

Spikes in "cases" in various parts of the world have led the global midwit population to make all kinds of predictions about deaths that have consistently failed to materialize.

But we discovered — from the *New York Times*, of all places! — within the past week or two that the "case" metric is even more absurd than we could have imagined.

As I noted in this space eight days ago, the *New York Times* ran the headline: "Your Coronavirus Test Is Positive. Maybe It Shouldn't Be."

We learned there that as many as 90 percent of positive Covid results were for people who were not contagious, and were therefore being ordered to quarantine and isolate for no reason. It has to do with the PCR test and something called the "cycle threshold."

Anyway, Phil Kerpen of American Commitment was curious about the situation in the District of Columbia, so he contacted the health authorities there to ask what cycle threshold they're using for their tests (so we can get a sense of the extent to which their tabulation of "cases," already a notoriously unhelpful metric, is truly ludicrous).

After contacting them, Kerpen noted: "If it is 37 to 40 like Nevada, New York, and Massachusetts, then up to 90% of reported positives are from noninfectious, months-old viral debris."

Well, D.C. Health got back to him.

"D.C. Health does not have information about cycle thresholds."

What kind of a joke is this?

As one commenter put it, "What's worse? If they're lying or if they really don't have any?"

Meanwhile, our supposedly nonpolitical expert, Dr. Fauci (who revealed last week that he hopes the Covid crisis will lead to the adoption of something akin to the Green New Deal), to my knowledge has not acknowledged any of this. The other day he said the case count was unacceptably high heading into flu season, without acknowledging this report and the fact that we now know the "case count" is wildly inflated.

We are truly living in a giant insane asylum.

September 9, 2020 | When will people be normal again?

You've probably heard about the new paper purporting to show that the Sturgis Motorcycle Rally in South Dakota is responsible for 266,000 new Covid "cases."

Oh, and the health cost will be $12.2 billion.

Now if this all seems ridiculous and over the top to you, and conforms just a little too neatly to the narrative — dumb Trumpers who refuse to listen to "the science" are going and getting people killed — that's probably because it is.

I'll dig into that paper with you within the next few days. But the general thrust is this: no joy in your lives, citizens! For there is a virus!

So Los Angeles, for example, has just banned trick-or-treating this Halloween. You know, because they're super sciency in Los Angeles.

Trick-or-treating will go on in most places, and nothing will come of it.

On Twitter today someone asked: "What is the endpoint for people who still won't resume their pre-Covid lives? Are they waiting for Fauci or a wise governor to signal the 'all-clear'? What will it take?"

That's the question I've been stumbling toward but haven't quite asked so bluntly.

Doomers get upset when you mention the flu, but it's relevant: we learned to live with it. We didn't discontinue life-giving pleasures for young people (and indeed for all people). That's because we realize that truly human lives involve the very things that the world's Faucis are now demonizing, and warning us we may never get back.

If we get to a point where Covid claims 100 people per month, will this be sufficient? But if the "if it saves even one life" logic (such as it is) is correct, how can it be? Will these people still be cowering in their homes even then? Even if continuing restrictions are obviously causing other deaths, deaths that would have been avoidable otherwise?

How do these people ever climb out of this?

I don't mean how governments step back. I mean: how does someone who's convinced himself that he cannot leave his house go back to being a normal person? I honestly don't know.

We may have two parallel societies for some time. Unfortunately, the folks in the other society, the panic society, want to exercise power over you and how you make your living — in the name of "science."

September 11, 2020 | Now they're imposing a six-person limit on gatherings

You may not be aware of what the bastards are doing in the U.K. Here's the current situation:

Daily New Deaths in the United Kingdom

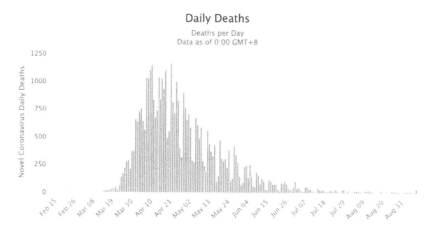

They're imposing more restrictions, despite the above. With a few exceptions, no social gatherings of more than six people. That applies to indoors and outdoors. It applies to your house. If you have six or more people in your household you are allowed to gather in public or private (how generous!) but not with anyone else.

These rules are expected to last through the spring. And all because of a modest rise in "cases," a stupid figure that should be savagely mocked.

Forget about the original concerns regarding overwhelming the hospital system. Everybody knows the hospitals will be fine. Now it's just a ban on death itself — as if the lockdowns themselves don't cause collateral deaths. (Not to mention: who can think this bizarre dystopia is a healthy place for children to grow up and develop in?)

Incidentally, Israel locked down hard, and required masks and curfews, and engaged in sophisticated methods for mapping contacts, and...now they're considering another lockdown because of a rise in "cases." If all that couldn't do the trick, what on Earth are we doing? (I shouldn't say *we*. You and I have nothing to do with this.)

Here, by the way, is a graphical reminder of the uselessness of lockdowns. The U.K., Lockdown Central, is represented in the line that goes higher. That other, lower line is Sweden, the country we're all supposed to hate:

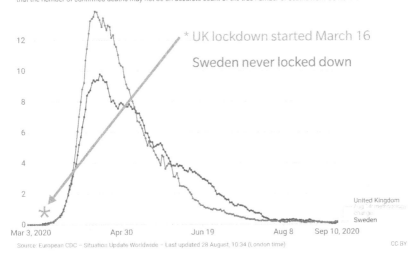

Daily new confirmed COVID-19 deaths per million people

Shown is the rolling 7-day average. Limited testing and challenges in the attribution of the cause of death means that the number of confirmed deaths may not be an accurate count of the true number of deaths from COVID-19.

* UK lockdown started March 16

Sweden never locked down

United Kingdom

Sweden

Source: European CDC – Situation Update Worldwide - Last updated 28 August, 10:34 (London time)   CC BY

I've said in numerous episodes of the Tom Woods Show that there are two parallel societies emerging, each living almost in its own reality. One lives in terror of Covid and almost refuses to acknowledge favorable trends. The other realizes that this is in fact manageable after all, and that we cannot continue to destroy people's lives — lives of both young and old, I might add — indefinitely, or even "until there's a vaccine."

September 13, 2020 | Why the Florida Covid spike vanished from the media

Two items for you this morning. First, a few social media remarks from a physician and academic (Dr. Victoria Fox):

> I'm sorry — it's time for public health officials to implement evidence-based pandemic mitigation solutions that are logistically feasible, sustainable and target the problem while

allowing society to function. Give people viable solutions they can implement day to day to protect their loved ones during outbreaks. You can't tell the world to stay home and "socially distance" — whatever that even means — and then act shocked, pissed and punish society because your vague, untested voodoo didn't work. Because the truth is there is no good solution to this — only tradeoffs. Public health doesn't want to be responsible for the adverse outcomes of the tradeoffs so they have developed a strategy that [claims] the pandemic [is] preventable and places blame on society for not complying.

So perfectly said.

Instead of being mature adults who understand that widespread shutdowns leave massive wreckage in their wake — and I've chronicled these numerous times in this space; they're so devastating that I cannot believe any compassionate human being could support lockdowns — we are instead to ignore the wreckage, make the whole thing into a simple morality play, and then lecture people for not complying if the numbers go the wrong way.

Again, I can show you charts of states and countries that locked down, with the names removed. You will not be able to tell me which ones locked down, how hard they locked down, how intense their so-called mitigation strategies were, or when or how widely they reopened. That is just a fact. Nitpick me all you want, but this is something I guarantee you cannot do.

Yet, just like Keynesian stimulus, when the approach doesn't work our overlords respond with an even heavier dose of the original poison. So when the Obama stimulus yielded terrible results, the response from its evidence-impervious architects was not that the whole approach might be juvenile and destructive to begin with, but (of course) that they hadn't done enough of it.

Same with the lockdowns — and in general it's the same people advocating them. As another observer recently pointed out, had Florida locked down to cope with the Sun Belt spike and gotten the results below, with numbers declining, this chart would have been "presented as scientific proof lockdowns prevented overwhelmed hospitals. Instead they didn't, so we just stop talking about Florida."

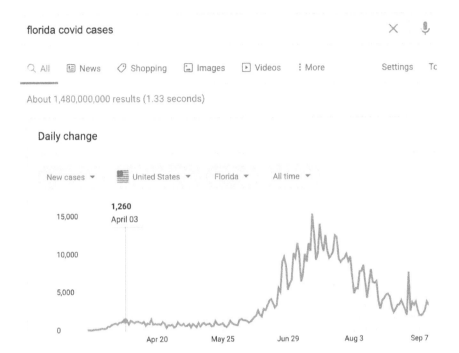

florida covid cases   ✕   🎤

🔍 All   📰 News   🏷 Shopping   🖼 Images   ▶ Videos   ⋮ More   Settings   Tc

About 1,480,000,000 results (1.33 seconds)

Daily change

New cases ▾   🇺🇸 United States ▾   Florida ▾   All time ▾

1,260
April 03

15,000 · 10,000 · 5,000 · 0 — Apr 20 · May 25 · Jun 29 · Aug 3 · Sep 7

Each day shows new cases reported since the previous day · Updated less than 3 hours ago · Source: Wikipedia · About this data

Second item:

You will no doubt recall — because it was everywhere on social media for days — a paper published by an "Institute for Labor Economics" claiming that the Sturgis Motorcycle Rally in South Dakota was responsible for over 266,000 new Covid "cases." The authors' contempt for the people they treat in that paper is evident throughout, starting from the very beginning: the paper opens with a quotation from the singer of Smash Mouth, a band that performed there, saying that enough is enough and it's good to see people living like human beings again.

There have been plenty of responses to that paper that have cut it off at the knees, but now even *Slate* — which isn't exactly eager to exonerate mostly pro-Trump motorcycle dudes — ran an article you can find in the search engines called "The Sturgis Biker Rally Did Not Cause 266,796 Cases of Covid-19." It concludes: "Exaggerated headlines and cherry-picking of results for 'I told you so' media moments can dangerously undermine the long-term integrity of the science — something we can little afford right now."

September 14, 2020 | Top doc drops 10-megaton bomb on lockdowners

Well, the skeptics are finding their voices at last.

In Ireland, Dr. Martin Feeley — clinical director of the Midland Fields Hospital Group and a senior executive of the Health Service Executive, Ireland's government-funded health care system — just made his dissenting views known to the *Irish Times*.

He said the lockdowns that we were told were essential can no longer be justified in light of what we now know about Covid-19. The lockdowns, he added, disproportionately harm the youth — and "you can't postpone youth." He said:

> The financial cost can be seen in any walk or drive through cities, towns and villages. Mortgage repayments and other financial setbacks are virtually all suffered by the young worker or business person and not by the over-65, who are guaranteed their pension, as indeed are the salaries of the individuals who decide to inflict these draconian measures.

Dr. Feeley condemned the obsession with "cases," a contextless number that only panics people, when we should instead be focusing on hospital strain:

> The number of deaths among recent cases is less than one in a thousand. This data reflects a disease much less severe than the average annual flu. The media reaction to these cases, i.e., with the gravity appropriate to reporting deaths from a major catastrophe, borders on hysteria. Opening a newscast with the number of people testing positive for a condition less dangerous than the flu, which many don't even know they have, is scaremongering.

The *Irish Times* also reports on Dr. Alan Farrell, who has made his unhappiness with the government's extreme measures known to the Minister for Health. He says:

> From a medical perspective I am not seeing an impact from Covid on the ground. What I am seeing is delayed diagnoses for other conditions — breast cancer, skin cancer in young people, an onslaught of anxiety and depression, an increase in loneliness in the elderly, recently a fractured humerus in an

elderly lady that has been like that for months as she was afraid to go outside.

Now here's a question no mainstream reporter will ask an epidemiologist, even though it's an obvious one: are you modeling the non-Covid human costs of lockdowns and restrictions and if so, what have you concluded?

Of course no epidemiologist will answer you, because none of them are doing this. They believe that the subject of their monomania must be as all-consuming for everyone else as it is for them. The very notion of tradeoffs simply does not enter the picture.

September 15, 2020 | No more lockdowns: how to beat back the society destroyers

Remember that Sun Belt spike?

The numbers now are excellent. Hospitalizations in those states (we're talking Florida, Georgia and Texas in the South, and then California and Arizona) are down 65.7 percent since their peak.

Out of the 108 million people living in those states, a grand total of 10,828 are currently hospitalized with Covid. The chart looks like this (thanks to Ian Miller):

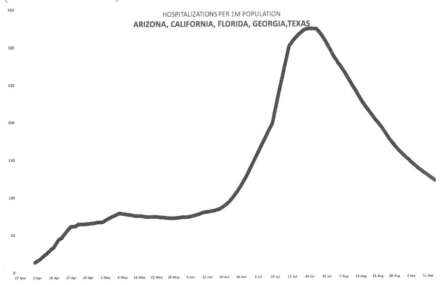

Florida reported 34 deaths yesterday. But even that exaggerates the situation, since yesterday was merely the day these deaths were reported, not the day they actually occurred. Here's when those 34 deaths occurred (with thanks to Jennifer Cabrera, who covers these numbers for Florida, for the data):

9/13: 1	8/30: 1	7/31: 1
9/11: 1	8/20: 1	7/30: 1
9/9: 1	8/19: 1	7/24: 1
9/8: 3	8/17: 1	7/8: 1
9/7: 5	8/16: 1	6/20: 1
9/6: 2	8/11: 1	
9/4: 5	8/6: 1	
9/2: 1	8/3: 1	
9/1: 1	8/2: 1	

This result was reached without hard lockdowns.

Yes, California locked down, but in light of the results in these other states, that was obviously pointless.

Meanwhile, which two countries in the world have suffered the least economically? Russia and China. It would be funny if it weren't so destructive: the very people who see Russian threats to America around every corner just got played in the most devastating and embarrassing way.

The hospital system — anywhere in America — is nowhere near being overrun. Fears that it would be were behind why we were urged to "flatten the curve." The curve has been flattened, hospitals are fine, and yet the lockdown/reopening voodoo pseudoscience continues.

At this point the White House has got to coordinate rational, fact-based messaging about Covid.

There are plenty of highly intelligent people who have been doing excellent work out there, and who can easily parry — and mock — the panic narrative being peddled in virtually every outlet you can think of.

It could even be packaged expressly as an antidote to fake news.

For example: when the media try to panic you about "cases," here's what you should know. And so on.

Doctors with unimpeachable credentials should be placed front and center. We have to hope that they'd be willing to take the slings and arrows for the sake of fighting for what's right, since the best doctors understand the wreckage all the restrictions are causing.

Show a bunch of charts, with the state/country names withheld, depicting places with different timings and degrees of lockdowns and reopenings, and challenge reporters to figure out which charts represent hard lockdowns and which don't. For the sake of humanity itself, hammer away at this.

Take every opportunity to line up aggrieved Americans against the people doing this to them. Like those kids at that massive rally in Connecticut protesting the state's decision to cancel high school football season. "Let us play!" the kids chanted. Tell those kids: never forget who did this to you.

September 16, 2020 | *New York Times* accidentally tells the truth

Every once in a while a bit of truth leaks out from the *New York Times*.

Don't worry, though: the next day the *Times* will just pretend they never said it, and continue with the official nonsense.

So on one day they'll say: lockdowns are going to lead to 1.4 million excess TB deaths, 500,000 excess HIV deaths, and 385,000 excess malaria deaths over the next five years.

Then the next day they'll say: lockdowns sure are super.

Or one day they'll say: up to 90 percent of all so-called "cases" of Covid turn out to be of people who are not infectious, because in America the tests have been calibrated to be absurdly sensitive.

Then the next day they'll say: look at all the cases in the Midwest! Panic!

Yesterday there were 38,000 new "cases" in the United States. That means as many as 34,200 people who are not infectious were forced to quarantine — with all the dislocation and wealth destruction that involves — for no reason.

Tomorrow it will have been six months since "15 days to slow the spread."

Meanwhile, Adar Poonawalla, chief executive of the Serum Institute of India, the world's largest manufacturer of vaccines, just said that "it's going to take four to five years until everyone gets the vaccine on this planet."

So the deranged "wait for a vaccine" people just got more deranged. Life-giving pleasures must now be canceled for years?

And they propose measures that clearly lead to the loss of other lives, and which take away (especially from young people, who cannot get their youth back once it's gone) so many of the joys that make life worth living, and are therefore themselves a kind of death.

All this over a problem that clearly does not overwhelm our hospital capacity, and certainly appears to be manageable (to say the least). The so-called experts genuinely have no idea what they're doing, but their white coats, advanced degrees, and clipboards have superstitious Americans convinced that this particular priesthood will save them.

Punish every politico who encouraged this, and (much as I hate to say "reward" and "politico" in the same sentence) reward the handful who kept their wits about them.

I hope South Dakota booms as a result of all this.

Surely there are still some people out there who want to live. I cannot be alone in this.

September 17, 2020 | City government caught concealing good news

Why anyone trusts state governments on anything related to Covid anymore is beyond me, but now it's just getting ridiculous.

A local FOX affiliate just made public a series of emails between the Nashville mayor's senior adviser and the health department. I'll let them summarize these emails:

> The coronavirus cases on lower Broadway may have been so low that the mayor's office and the metro health department decided to keep it secret. The discussion involves the low number of coronavirus cases emerging from bars and restaurants and how to handle that — and most disturbingly, how to keep it from the public.

Yes, that's correct. *The numbers are too low to scare the public with*, so they'll remain for internal consumption only.

Meanwhile, countless livelihoods have been destroyed on the presumption that the numbers are far worse than they actually are. For example, in mid-summer a newspaper reporter asked the health department about a rumor that bars and restaurants had been responsible for a mere 80 cases — not deaths, but "cases," which of course means essentially nothing. The reporter asked:

> The figure you gave of "more than 80" does lead to a natural question: If there have been over 20,000 positive cases of Covid-19 in Davidson and only 80 or so are traced to restaurants and bars, doesn't that mean restaurants and bars aren't a very big problem?

In the emails we see the health department's Brian Todd asking five department officials: "Please advise how you recommend I respond." One health official responds:

> My two cents. We have certainly refused to give counts per bar because those numbers are low per site. We could still release the total, though, and then a response to the over 80 could be "because that number is increasing all the time and we don't want to say a specific number."

A pretty stupid and evil response, obviously.

A month earlier, when exactly 22 "cases" had been traced to bars and restaurants, this exchange ensued:

> Leslie Waller, health department: "This isn't going to be publicly released, right? Just info for Mayor's Office?"
>
> Senior advisor Benjamin Eagles: "Correct, not for public consumption."

Now had there been 10,000 "cases" from bars and restaurants, you'd better believe the public would have been hearing about it.

City councilman Steve Glover says he has heard from a barrage of restaurant owners as well as bartenders and servers, and demands to know why the city government would not release the data: "We raised taxes 34 percent and put…thousands of people out of work that are now worried about losing their homes, their apartments, etc., and we did it on bogus data," he says.

Meanwhile, the CDC is telling us that we should be able to get back to normal life by, oh, the second or third quarter of 2021 — not exactly what they dared tell us back in March.

If you haven't yet started ignoring these people, it's time to start.

September 18, 2020 | Shock: Harvard prof talks sense about lockdowns

By now I'm sure you know Stanford's Dr. Scott Atlas, who is Public Enemy #1 to the Covid cultists because he takes a reality-based approach to the virus. He's also now an adviser to the President.

Well, a bunch of his colleagues, not exactly risking anything in this political climate, recently released a letter attacking him. (The vast majority of these colleagues have donated to Democratic candidates or other left-wing causes, we now know.) Why, how dare he say children are at essentially no risk! (Um, because children obviously are essentially at no risk?) How dare he suggest that we protect the vulnerable and let everyone else live? All should be punished equally!

Now comes Martin Kulldorff, a professor at Harvard Medical School, in defense of Atlas:

> While anyone can get infected, there is a thousand-fold difference in mortality risk between the old and young, and the risk to children is less than from annual influenza. Using an age-targeted strategy, Atlas wants to better protect high-risk individuals, while letting children and young adults live more normal lives. This contrasts with general age-wide lockdowns that protect low-risk students and young professionals working from home, while older higher-risk working-class people generate the inevitable herd immunity.

Unlike the signatories to the letter, Kulldorff continues, Atlas doesn't ignore the "collateral damage caused by lockdowns." He continues: "Among experts on infectious disease outbreaks, many of us have long advocated for an age-targeted strategy, and I would be delighted to debate this with any of the 98 signatories."

And then, knowing just the language to hit them with, he concludes: "Supporters include professor Sunetra Gupta at Oxford University, the world's preeminent infectious disease epidemiologist. *Assuming no bias against women scientists of color*, I urge Stanford faculty and students to read her thoughts" (emphasis mine).

Part III: Fall 2020

September 21, 2020 | We anti-lockdowners just got a new hero

Well, we have a rather unexpected and unlikely hero right now.

I've thought for a while that eventually performers would become realists about Covid, conclude that we obviously can't hide in our houses forever, that it's clearly manageable, that a life without the arts is itself a kind of death, and that in any case locking down causes lots of other kinds of deaths.

So far I've been disappointed. As with most things these days, performers have the same, predictable opinions about everything — and by what I'm sure is just a coincidence, these opinions just happen to be precisely the ones the establishment urges upon us.

Real mavericks, these people.

Ian Anderson (Tom Woods Show guest, episode #3, remember?) of Jethro Tull at least went to the trouble to draw up a fairly detailed plan regarding how musical performances could safely begin again. I mentioned it in my recent episode with metal vocalist Phil Labonte of All That Remains.

Well, our unlikely hero is going even farther than that.

It's…Van Morrison.

You may have heard in the news that Van Morrison, who's been complaining about "pseudoscience" and gig restrictions for months, is set to release three anti-lockdown protest songs — the first of which will come out just two days from now.

He is urging other performers to join him in demanding the return of live performance with no restrictions. "I call on my fellow singers, musicians, writers, producers, promoters and others in the industry to fight with me on this. Come forward, stand up, fight the pseudoscience and speak up."

Interestingly, just today the health editor at BBC News ran an article: "Is It Time We Learnt to Live with the Virus?"

Well, yes. The consequences of any other approach are horrific.

September 22, 2020 | Just caught a Covid liar red-handed

OK, folks, it's time for a quiz.

Here's the background:

I recently wrote to you about the Nashville mayor's office, which misled people about the contribution of bars and restaurants to the Covid "case" count, and then on the basis of these misleading remarks ordered bars shut down and restaurants crippled. Internal emails showed officials wanting to keep the low case numbers associated with bars and restaurants a secret.

Since then, the mayor's office has denied all this, but thanks to the Internet we have a video clip of Mayor John Cooper saying in July that bars were behind "*sharp recent case increases and clustering of cases.* Our public health investigators have found *a record number of clusters originating from bars* within the past week" (emphasis mine).

Then, just last week, under pressure, the mayor admitted: "Back when we were modifying phase two, *the bar case count was not at that time super high.* Of course we're happy to share all information, but we want the right interpretation behind all of this. Thank you" (emphasis mine). And he walked off.

Now in that context, here's your quiz. Feel free to share it with those friends of yours who still think the correct approach is to cancel everything that brings people joy and to hide in our homes indefinitely.

These are charts of case counts in four Tennessee counties. (I realize "case" counts are a dubious measure, but if the Doomers want to play that game, let's play.) Unless you live in Tennessee, you probably won't know which county Nashville is in.

One of these four counties shut down bars and limited restaurant capacity to 25 percent. Can you figure out which one?

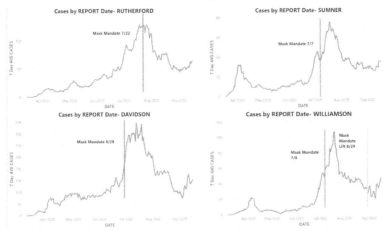

CASE TRENDS (7 Day AVG) by COUNTY

Does it not look instead as if it makes no difference what policies are implemented?

By the way, want to know which one is the correct county? It's Davidson, in the lower-left corner of the graphic. You couldn't tell, could you?

And that, my friends, is the story of the whole sorry episode: looking at charts of states and of whole countries, you can't tell which places shut down, or how hard they shut down, or how long they shut down, or whether they had mask mandates, or when the mask mandates were implemented, or when the mask mandates were lifted.

It's all been an episode in voodoo pseudoscience, perpetrated by tyrants who themselves do not fear Covid (else we wouldn't see them secretly going about their lives in defiance of the restrictions placed on the rest of us).

Opinion is slowly turning in favor of normality, though I have to admit I thought more people would have developed a rational outlook on the whole thing by now.

September 25, 2020 | Big-state governor just fully reopened

A major move in favor of rationality and decency occurred today.

In Florida, where I live, Governor Ron DeSantis announced Phase 3 of the state's reopening, in which essentially all restrictions are lifted, and private institutions of all kinds may operate at full capacity.

As Alex Berenson says, this makes him by far the best big-state governor.

Just yesterday, DeSantis held a virtual roundtable featuring Harvard Medical School's Martin Kulldorff, and Michael Levitt and Jay Bhattacharya of Stanford. Every minute of it is worth watching. No hysteria, no panic, and plenty of common sense.

DeSantis himself is impressive in the video. He has a real command of the state of the literature on Covid-19, and he also knows the weaknesses in the case for lockdowns.

When I saw this roundtable, I knew what it meant: DeSantis was getting ready for Phase 3 (which in Florida means complete reopening), and he wanted to cover himself by having unimpeachable experts go on the record with him in opposition to lockdowns. I had no idea that the Phase 3 announcement would occur the very next day.

DeSantis asks all three scientists: would you say at this point that lockdowns are off the table?

All said yes, of course. Bhattacharya described the cost of lockdowns as "catastrophic."

This is truly fantastic news.

Meanwhile, the roundtable is definitely worth watching. As reporter Jennifer Cabrera said about it, if you've been wondering where the adults have been in all this, well, here they are.

Enjoy: TomWoods.com/major-dose-of-covid-19-truth

September 28, 2020 | The lockdowners' voodoo is unraveling

Well, well, well: it's now looking as if Sweden, which was savaged by respectable opinion for not locking down, will end the year with zero or negative excess mortality.

It's funny, by the way: Doomers are so wedded to their voodoo pseudoscience that they have to keep dancing around Sweden rather than admit that their rain dances aren't actually what bring the rain.

When you used to bring up Sweden, the response was: they have a high death rate! What a disaster! Now, when Sweden is being vindicated every day, the response is: oh, they voluntarily complied with various mitigation practices, and that's why it worked out so well! (To a small degree yes, but I recommend looking through pictures from Stockholm during these months and drawing your own conclusion.)

Notice what they cannot say: "Hmm, maybe there was another way to go about this after all."

No way.

They are too invested in the voodoo to turn their backs on it.

And after the wreckage they've left everywhere, with deaths piling up in the Third World, depression and suicide spiking like crazy, millions of deaths now baked into the future because of missed screenings and other non-Covid procedures, and people's life savings wiped out and businesses destroyed, I doubt we can expect them to admit anything.

At this point, they wouldn't dare.

As for Sweden's death rate, by the way: they had about 5,000 deaths, in a country of 10 million. At least two thirds of those were in long-term care facilities, where they admit they did a poor job. *But the quality of long-term care facilities in Stockholm is obviously unrelated to the effectiveness of the pandemic mitigation strategy pursued by society as a whole.*

By June they had had 4,000 deaths. Neil Ferguson's model predicted that without lockdowns they were going to have 96,000 by June.

So again, instead of saying, "Wow, we must really not understand this as well as we think we do if Sweden beat our projections by a factor of twenty-four" — you know, the kind of thing an honest person who's genuinely trying to learn and has no axe to grind might say — they just change their story as I indicated above or, more commonly, they never mention Sweden again.

September 29, 2020 | How many millions do the lockdowners plan to kill?

The crazies who think "public health" should mean "a monomaniacal fixation on one issue" should have to answer more for the non-Covid wreckage they're leaving everywhere.

For instance, last week I wrote in my newsletter about Gret Glyer, the creator of the amazing DonorSee philanthropy app. Donors help individual people and small projects. And they mean the world to recipients. True to the name, donors really can see the results: hence DonorSee.

For example, you donate to help a blind person see, and then on your phone you receive a video of the person seeing for the first time. My listeners raised money to build a house for a widow in Malawi — and then we got a video tour of the house, and a message of thanks from her and her family.

It's a miracle, truly.

Well, I just had Gret on the Tom Woods Show again, and he talked to us about how the lockdown regimes are decimating the developing world. He himself lived in Malawi for three years, so he is intimately acquainted with their particular vulnerabilities.

These people are living hand to mouth, he tells us in the episode. That means that each day they earn enough money to eat for that day, and that's it. Now imagine ordering them to stay at home for weeks or even months at a time. Oh, the government will help them? These societies have no welfare state worth speaking of. This is pure devastation.

Even *The Atlantic* had to admit, "When you ask them to stay home, in many cases you're asking them to starve." And in the U.K., *The Telegraph* says, "The absurd demand that developing countries adopt economically disastrous lockdowns is driving untold misery."

Why are the perpetrators of this fiasco never required to answer for this?

October 1, 2020 | Scott Atlas just hit back at Fauci

Well, this Dr. Scott Atlas is a fighter.

The lockdowners can't stand him. So they point out that he isn't an epidemiologist. No, but (1) he's simply relaying what the epidemiologists are saying, and any intelligent person can do that; and (2) he is trying to encourage Americans to think about the long-term effects on everyone of the fanaticism over Covid. Is there any indication that Fauci recognizes collateral damage from shutdowns at all?

Atlas mentions names — drawn from Harvard, Stanford, and Oxford — that have never been uttered under the Fauci regime and would never have been heard by the American public if it hadn't been for him.

And just the other day, with Laura Ingraham, he hit back at Robert Redfield (of the CDC) and Fauci, pointing out that they've been all over the place. In particular, he made fun of Fauci for suggesting that we really ought to be wearing goggles (remember that?).

He insists that it's "destructive" to lock down healthy people, that we know who the vulnerable people are, and that "public health officials" have neglected the public-health effects of lockdowns themselves: these problems have "not been given the appropriate consideration by the public health officials who somehow think they have unique expertise," he says.

It's about time we had a non-hysteric in public life.

I was happy to see Atlas retweet the below (Kulldorff is from Harvard Medical School), after Dr. Fauci said it was "extraordinarily inappropriate" for Atlas to have contradicted Dr. Redfield at a press conference:

↻ Scott W. Atlas Retweeted

Martin Kulldorff @MartinKulldorff · Sep 26
This is weird! @SWAtlasHoover stated the simple fact that immunity is higher than those with antibodies, whereupon Dr. Fauci criticizes him without contradicting what was actually said. Stating a simple scientific fact is not "extraordinarily inappropriate". What is going on?

One thing we can be sure of: under Joe Biden it'll be all Fauci, all the time, with no dissident voices, and the handful of non-sociopaths we have as governors will have to summon plenty of courage to hold the line.

October 5, 2020 | Charts the Covid hysterics prefer to keep from you

In the midst of all the misinformation and panic, there's some good work being done on Covid, including at the state level. I've mentioned Jennifer Cabrera, who does excellent work on Florida. Today let's talk Minnesota, courtesy of the Twitter account @covid_clarity.

Remember when we were told to "flatten the curve" in order to relieve potential pressure on the hospital system? That was the stated purpose behind the so-called mitigation measures. And except very briefly here and there, hospitals wound up never in fact being overwhelmed. To the contrary, hospitals were emptier than usual. In April alone, 1.4 million jobs were lost in health care across the country.

Minnesota residents were told, during the "flatten the curve" stage, that every single hospital bed in the state of Minnesota would be occupied by a Covid patient. Hence the urgency of doing something.

That never came close to being true, as you can see below, where total beds available, beds used at the peak, and beds in use just under two weeks ago are depicted:

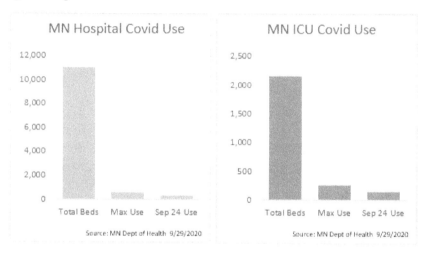

So the hospital problem is no problem at all. Hooray, right? We flattened the curve! Mission accomplished!

Nope. Now they just want to ruin your life for the hell of it.

So now it's just an obsession with — you guessed it — "cases." As you can see, "cases" generally track tests:

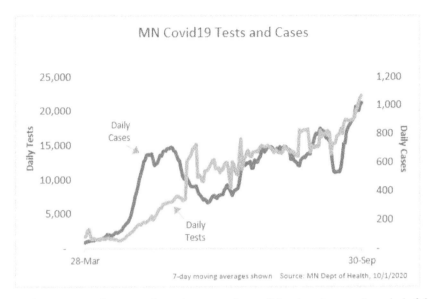

As you can also see, obsessing over "cases" in the abstract is unhelpful (note the divergence between "cases" and deaths beginning around the middle of the graph below):

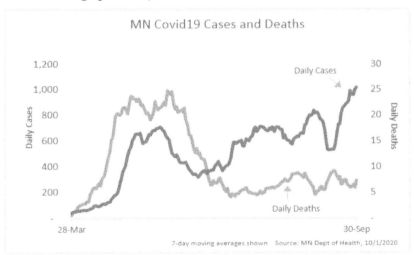

And then finally, note that the impact on the general population is pretty much unchanged (and extremely mild) throughout, regardless of the policy pursued:

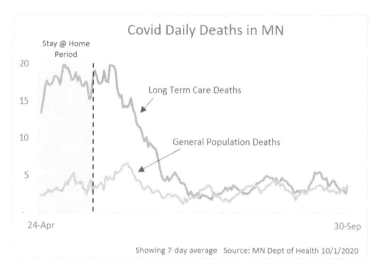

The Minnesota Department of Health observed a "somber milestone" on Twitter on October 1: Minnesota had passed 100,000 "cases." Of course, "cases" mean nothing, most people barely even notice they have the virus, and the survival rate in Minnesota outside long-term care is 99.92 percent. You'd think a department of health would note and celebrate that, but then you forgot you're living in an insane asylum.

October 6, 2020 | The non-hysterics just hit back hard

"Listen to the science!" has become the rallying cry of the most irrational, anecdote-driven, fact-free believers in voodoo I have encountered in my lifetime.

And now they're getting hit hard.

Just two days ago, three renowned experts — Martin Kulldorff of Harvard, Sunetra Gupta of Oxford, and Jay Bhattacharya of Stanford — released the Great Barrington Declaration, alongside a great many illustrious co-signers, deploring the public health consequences of lockdowns and advocating an approach that would allow more or less normal life to resume.

Excerpts:

> As infectious disease epidemiologists and public health scientists we have grave concerns about the damaging physical and mental health impacts of the prevailing Covid-19 policies, and recommend an approach we call Focused Protection.

Coming from both the left and right, and around the world, we have devoted our careers to protecting people. Current lockdown policies are producing devastating effects on short and long-term public health. The results (to name a few) include lower childhood vaccination rates, worsening cardiovascular disease outcomes, fewer cancer screenings and deteriorating mental health — leading to greater excess mortality in years to come, with the working class and younger members of society carrying the heaviest burden. Keeping students out of school is a grave injustice....

Those who are not vulnerable should immediately be allowed to resume life as normal. Simple hygiene measures, such as hand washing and staying home when sick should be practiced by everyone to reduce the herd immunity threshold. Schools and universities should be open for in-person teaching. Extracurricular activities, such as sports, should be resumed. Young low-risk adults should work normally, rather than from home. Restaurants and other businesses should open. Arts, music, sport and other cultural activities should resume. People who are more at risk may participate if they wish, while society as a whole enjoys the protection conferred upon the vulnerable by those who have built up herd immunity.

They are urging both health-care professionals as well as members of the general public to affix their signatures as well. I have already done so.

October 8, 2020 | "Whoops, we starved 130 million people. Our bad!"

The editors of the *New England Journal of Medicine* just published an editorial essentially urging people to vote for Joe Biden. "When it comes to the response to the largest public health crisis of our time," they write, "our current political leaders have demonstrated that they are dangerously incompetent."

They didn't engage in enough lockdown voodoo for the *NEJM*, apparently.

"The federal government has largely abandoned disease control to the states," they continue. "Governors have varied in their responses, not so much by party as by competence. But whatever their competence, governors do not have the tools that Washington controls."

Translation: "science" demands that federalism and the Constitution be abandoned and a Fauci dictatorship be installed.

Note that when discussing the "governors" who "varied in their responses," there is not a word of condemnation of the governors who sent Covid patients into nursing homes.

The rest is the usual nonsense. Not enough "tests," they say:

> While the absolute numbers of tests have increased substantially, the more useful metric is the number of tests performed per infected person, a rate that puts us far down the international list, below such places as Kazakhstan, Zimbabwe and Ethiopia, countries that cannot boast the biomedical infrastructure or the manufacturing capacity that we have.

Japan and Taiwan rejected the mass testing craze, and they're fine. In fact, when I spoke to Harvard Medical School's Martin Kulldorff, an infectious disease epidemiologist, he was pretty clear that far too much testing was being done, and that it's essentially a lot of white noise. Especially college students, who he says should not be tested at all unless they're showing symptoms.

Of course, the states that followed the crazy lockdown voodoo most closely did considerably worse than states that didn't, but that won't shake the religious fervor of these super-important scientists.

Now:

Did they criticize "public health" experts for not having factored into their Covid mitigation strategies the problem of collateral deaths in other areas of health? Some *130 million people* are at risk of starvation as a direct result of this approach! Not a word, of course. "Public health" for these people means the monomaniacal fixation on one issue to the exclusion of everything else.

(Whatever enormities someone may wish to lay at the feet of Donald Trump, not one is in the same galaxy as a catastrophe like that.)

Did they criticize "public health" experts for constantly changing the goalposts for reopening, and for their complete lack of transparency regarding the metrics they're using and what achievable goals would have to be reached in order to bring about reopening?

Did they criticize politicians for bizarre, anti-science edicts — like the county commissioner in Gainesville, Florida, who approved a one-person-per-1,000-feet rule for private businesses "because it's easy math for everybody to do"? The question answers itself.

October 12, 2020 | Lockdown victim: "This isn't human"

An acquaintance of mine knows someone in Melbourne, Australia, where the lockdown has been especially severe. I read this person's testimony and decided to share it with you as today's installment. We're told that these crazy measures are designed to "save lives" — but what is human life to these people? Read on (I have left the punctuation and usage unchanged):

Three months since i saw another human face besides [my partner's]

7 months since [my partner] and I had a little break together in the form of going and having a coffee down the street

Over a year since i last sat out in nature

Sitting staring at the wall for 2 hours, again…unable to move

Despair

Horrible negative emotions virtually all day

Awake entire nights, distress

I cant think of anything to look forward to because i dont know when we will be allowed to do anything

Just go for a drive, go to the forest

Just go somewhere together, far from all of this

We are not allowed

The police could enter our homes at any point and arrest us if we say the 'wrong' thing online

This doesnt feel human

I don't smile

I dont laugh

I worked out the other day and felt nothing, no pain

Nothing would register as pain

I couldn't feel anything

I feel far away from myself

Sometimes i forget how long the day has been going for

Does it matter?

You're not allowed to leave? Even if family members are terminally ill? They could die before we are let out of Melbourne, got told it isnt a good enough reason to be let out of the state

Literally not allowed to move house

I think WA is letting Victorians in now but we cant get to the airport to fly out of here because the airport is more than 5ks from our house

You arent allowed more than 5ks from your house

You arent allowed to buy a takeaway coffee and sit under a tree or on the ground anywhere that isnt your house

Inhuman

This isnt human

This isnt human

This isnt human

This isnt human

There is no empathy here

No price is too high

Suicide is not too great a price to pay

Self harm is not too great a price to pay

Structural brain changes in large portions of the population is not too high a price to pay

Do you know what prolonged social isolation does to the brain?

We are made to feel it does not matter

Because all we are, are numbers

We are not people we are the masses without a say

Without a time period to look forward to when we can hug again

I am sharing my experience because you should know the truth

Sincerely

A faceless number in melbourne

That about sums it up, doesn't it?

The architects of this dystopia refuse to acknowledge collateral damage, including mental health, from the lockdowns, even though at this point it positively swamps the number of deaths from Covid itself. Now the CDC is saying you really shouldn't go trick-or-treating, and you should have a "virtual Thanksgiving." When can we stop doing these inhuman things? Who knows? They change the goalposts so much it's impossible to say.

October 13, 2020 | Death by Lockdown

I almost don't blame people who are unaware of the following information, because you have to go to the U.K., usually, or the international press in general, to find it. But here is some of the collateral damage caused by lockdowns.

(1) In the U.K., cancer authorities have been warning that the lockdowns will wind up leading to as many or more avoidable cancer deaths than Covid deaths there — as many as 60,000, according to one estimate.

The U.K.'s *Sunday Express* — not exactly some obscure dispatch — reports that increased cancer fatalities will result from the redeployment of health resources caused by Covid hysteria. The BBC says the same. In fact, says Richard Sullivan, a professor of cancer and global health at King's College London and director of its Institute of Cancer Policy:

> The number of deaths due to the disruption of cancer services is likely to outweigh the number of deaths from the coronavirus itself. The cessation and delay of cancer care will cause considerable avoidable suffering. Cancer screening services have stopped, which means we will miss our chance to catch many cancers when they are treatable and curable, such as cervical, bowel and breast. When we do restart normal service delivery after the lockdown is lifted, the backlog of cases will be a huge challenge to the healthcare system.

According to the *Daily Mail* on October 6:

> Vital operations were canceled and patients missed out on potentially life-saving therapy in the spring because tackling Covid-19 became the sole focus of the health service, instead of cancer and other cruel diseases.
>
> Almost 2.5 million people missed out on cancer screening, referrals or treatment at the height of lockdown, even though the NHS was never overwhelmed — despite fears it would be crippled by the pandemic.
>
> Experts now fear the number of people dying as a result of delays triggered by the treatment of coronavirus patients could even end up being responsible for as many deaths as the pandemic itself.

(2) A United Nations report in April warned that economic hardship generated by the radical interruptions of commerce could result in hundreds of thousands of additional child deaths in 2020. The report further warned that 42 million to 66 million children could fall into extreme poverty as a result of the crisis.

(3) The Well Being Trust in Oakland, California, released a study that seeks to determine how many "deaths of despair" (from drug or alcohol abuse or suicide) will occur as a result of the pandemic, including the lockdowns. Their estimate, according to CBS News: about 75,000.

(4) UNICEF warned of 1.2 million child deaths — "visits to health care centers are declining due to lockdowns, curfews and transport disruptions, and as communities remain fearful of infection."

(5) Oxford University's Sunetra Gupta has pointed to warnings by global authorities that as many as 130 million people are at risk of starvation thanks to the possibility of famine in several dozen places around the world, brought on by lockdown-induced disruptions of supply chains.

(6) Suicidal ideation is massively on the rise in the United States. The federal government's Substance Abuse and Mental Health Services Administration reports on percentages of people who have considered suicide within the previous 12 months, organized by age. People between the ages of 18 and 25 fluctuate between 6.8 percent and 11 percent. Now, from the Centers for Disease Control, we find that percentage (for the 18–

25 group) has leaped to 25.5 percent — and this survey asks not about the previous 12 months, like the earlier one, but whether they've considered suicide *just in the past 30 days.*

(7) The CDC estimates 93,814 non-Covid "excess deaths" this year, including 42,427 from cardiovascular conditions, 10,686 from diabetes, and 3,646 from cancer, and many of these were caused by the cancellation of "nonessential" care in the midst of the Covid panic.

Meanwhile, almost no American hospitals were actually "overwhelmed" during 2020, despite what your Facebook friends told you. In April alone, 1.4 million health care workers were furloughed because the hospitals were empty. In May NPR reported on those field hospitals that were assembled to take care of the surge of people who were supposed to appear: "U.S. Field Hospitals Stand Down, Most without Treating Any Covid-19 Patients."

(8) According to *The Lancet*, "During lockdown people with dementia or severe mental illness had a higher risk of excess death." Dementia patients had a 53 percent greater chance of death because of lockdowns, and elderly patients with severe mental illness had a 123 percent greater chance of death.

(9) As a direct result of the lockdowns, the *New York Times* reports that there will be 1.4 million excess tuberculosis deaths, 500,000 excess HIV deaths, and 385,000 malaria deaths.

See why "public health" shouldn't be confused with the monomaniacal fixation on one problem?

Meanwhile, if you look at the charts for country after country and state after state, you will not be able to tell which ones locked down, how hard they locked down, when they lifted their lockdown, whether they had a mask mandate, when they imposed such a mandate, and when and if they lifted that mandate. The charts show zero correlation.

Non-pharmaceutical interventions — voodoo, we might well call it now — appear to have accomplished nothing, apart from creating all this avoidable misery around the world.

October 13, 2020 | How "public health" became voodoo

I just received an email that I thought you'd want to see. I have to keep the author anonymous. It confirms what many of us had already begun to suspect:

> *I've been following your podcast since it started and I was in high school! Now I'm a third-year student in medical school.*
>
> *I've been following your commentary on the Covid pandemic with great interest. I don't have anything original to tell you about the virus, and I personally don't have the time to vet everything that's said by the medical experts or you because I have to keep up with my studies.*
>
> *But the reason it is interesting to me is because this event is bringing the medical community to the public's attention. When I entered medical school I was extremely unaware to what degree the left had taken over the medical field. For the first two years it was extremely concerning to me and and I wondered if the public would ever realize this. And I think this pandemic is doing just that.*
>
> *In my opinion the medical intelligentsia is in complete lockstep with far-left politics. It is so fully ingrained that I personally don't think it's possible for it to change from the inside. I think outside forces need to become aware of it. Without going into too much detail, the public health field is generally made up of people who define medicine to be such a broad term that almost no area of our lives would not be subject to control by it. For example, gun control leads to trauma, so health experts should make policy on it. Poor housing leads to worse health outcomes, so health experts should make policy on housing subsidies/projects, etc.*
>
> *It is the orthodox opinion that the medical community should advocate and push for policies (that always line up with left-wing politics). A large part of my first two-year curriculum consisted of sessions where we learned how to advocate for policy changes, and how we could convince congressmen to our cause. A notable example is where we had a gun control session and the made-up scenario consisted of us trying to convince a rural population and a conservative congressman to pass gun control legislation.*
>
> *Anyway, I think this is actually a very important issue specifically considering the times about how politicized the medical profession has become, at least at the academic and national organization level.*

This is all the more crazy and dangerous because Americans have so convinced themselves that "the experts" know everything on every subject that they'll actually think "the science" demands rent control and other destructive ideas.

And of course, the state will decide for us who the "experts" are. Any other credentialed person who has a different opinion is to be shunned.

October 16, 2020 | Did Scott Atlas just say Fauci must be held accountable?

Every now and then, something I see on Twitter makes me want to stand up and cheer, as opposed to committing an atrocity.

An example from yesterday: someone shared a clip of Dr. Scott Atlas, adviser to the White House on Covid-19, on Laura Ingraham's show.

Oh, was it good.

It began with Ingraham asking if Atlas thought Biden would lock America down again if "cases" began to rise in January. Atlas replied:

> Anyone who's talking about doing another lockdown has really not been paying attention for the last seven months and is simply out of touch with average Americans....The prolonged lockdowns are a complete disaster. They're a complete disaster for missed health care; they're a complete disaster for average working families and particularly for people who are working class and lower-income people.

> People have been killed by people who want to have prolonged lockdowns. And when I say "killed," I look at the data. And that means, for instance: this week it was shown that forty-six percent of the most common types of cancers were not diagnosed during the lockdown. Those cancers didn't disappear. They're there. People will present with much later, more widespread disease.

Some 650,000 Americans missed important cancer treatment, Atlas added, thanks to "the fear instilled by our so-called public health experts. You could go on and on: 40 percent of people with acute strokes."

After mentioning the statistic that I've shared with you, that an astonishing 25.5 percent of people between 18 and 25 contemplated suicide in the month of June alone, Atlas concluded:

It's just completely off the rails....And it's much worse — not for the elites who are sipping lattes working for a tech company where I live, in Silicon Valley — for people who are average, working-class Americans, they are destroyed by prolonged lockdowns.

And then, in direct response to a question about Dr. Fauci:

History will record the faces of the public health expertise as some of the most sinful, egregious, epic failures in the history of public policy. They have killed people with their lack of understanding and their lack of caring about not just the impact of cases of Covid-19, a virus that the overwhelming majority of people do well in. They never cared to consider the impact of the policy itself, and the policy itself has been a complete epic failure, and honestly some people say a crime against humanity — these people should be held accountable for what they did.

October 19, 2020 | Are college kids terrified of Covid?

A student at an Ivy League university just wrote to me:

I'm a senior college student at [X] and back in March when we shut down, I was genuinely concerned about Covid.

However, I study hospitality and as I read about layoffs at restaurants and hotels, my heart broke for the staff there. By May, I was fully skeptical. At first, I thought we'd be done with this by now. Back home in New York, my high school friends are terrified and the one time we saw each other, we sat in my backyard 6+ feet apart from each other. As a business student, I hope that I understand how the markets work and how every single week of lockdown affects our society in every shape and form.

Where I live, we are a wealthy town and most parents are businessmen/lawyers and can afford to stay home. However, having worked in the hospitality industry, I understand how so many people are being affected while families in my community are ordering for $100+ delivery and $200+ Instacart orders. They're so phony — they think that the federal government could snap their fingers for small businesses and its employees and they'll be saved. Whether it's Trump or Biden, these people are not being helped.

One interesting anecdote: my friend's sister has really, really bad eyesight. Both of her parents are doctors and she's still scared to go get her eyes checked. When I was with her, I had to read her the menu from her phone when we were ordering in. She's 22 years old. 22!

Trust me, I know I'm privileged but was disgusted by the lack of empathy. I worked in restaurants and hotels and I know that these workers are suffering. Meanwhile, my high school friends think that the federal government will help them. They don't understand how it works. They keep thinking that we're going to have a vaccine or treatments by next year. I tried to explain that the U.S. population is over 300 million across the country and that you can't vaccinate everyone overnight. Somehow all my friends go to Ivy League schools and they don't understand that logic. And trust me, my major at [X] is known to be the "dumb" major and compared to the engineers, they have no clue.

Now, for some good news. I'm now back at [X University]. Some challenges are having to wear masks everywhere and having twice weekly tests. Aside from that, it's almost like being back in college. I've hosted parties with my best friends hosting pong, getting drunk, and being a college student. The first few days back, my friends and I were a bit scared to hug and all. Since then, we've had so many great social events. We even played spin the bottle and had such great experiences. While when I meet another friend that I haven't seen for a while, we don't hug or do anything....Soon after, after a drink or two, we've all hugged. I talked to my friends about Covid and we're all under the impression that by March 2021, somehow life has to go on.

Lastly, I do not understand this conversation about waiting until a vaccine or treatment. How long can we go on? Luckily, I'm a senior and will have had most of my college years. But how will education be affected? When I was in high school, I worked with students on the spectrum and with autism; I can't imagine what they are living.

Now much of this is quite discouraging: the 22-year-old woman who's terrified to get her eyes checked, even though she quite literally has a greater chance of dying in a car accident on the way to the eye exam than she does of Covid, is beyond ridiculous.

At the same time, I'm glad to hear that when push comes to shove, college students are being college students, regardless of the hysteria, and that they seem to have decided on a date in their minds beyond which the insanity simply cannot go on.

October 20, 2020 | Is everyone dead in Florida after reopening?

As you know, Florida governor Ron DeSantis announced three and a half weeks ago that the state was entering Phase 3 reopening. That essentially means that all businesses may operate at full capacity.

The day before the announcement, DeSantis held a virtual roundtable featuring professors from Harvard and Stanford, in which everyone denounced lockdowns as a grotesque mistake with terrible health outcomes.

Naturally, the hysterics went into overdrive. Wait two weeks, they demanded.

(Hard to believe anyone is still saying "wait two weeks" after all the times they've been embarrassed, but I suppose if these people were capable of embarrassment the world would look very different right now.)

Dr. Fauci called it "very concerning."

Well, I've been a real sport: I waited *three* weeks.

The great Jennifer Cabrera, whom I interviewed on episode #1750 of the Tom Woods Show, tracked down the data. Hospitalizations:

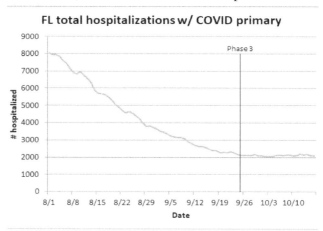

Percentage of people visiting the ER for a "coronavirus-like illness" (the second line from the top; you can see it heading ever lower):

Percentage of ED visits by syndrome in Florida: COVID-19-Like Illness, Shortness of Breath, Pneumonia, and Influenza-Like Illness

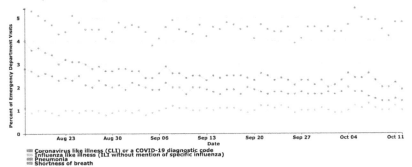

"Cases" are a pointless metric and we should be paying attention instead to hospitalizations and deaths, Harvard Medical School's Martin Kulldorff told me, but here are the charts anyway:

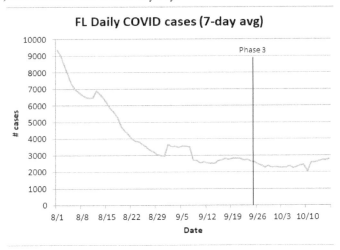

Here's what "cases" look like on the Worldometers site:

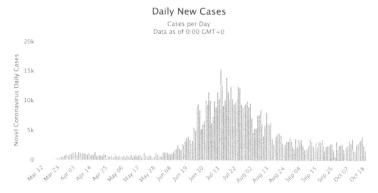

I wouldn't describe any of this as exactly catastrophic.

And yet I feel sure you know — or are perhaps even surrounded by — people who seem to be living in another universe from you. No matter what data you present, they're stuck in panic mode, months and months after they should have figured things out.

October 21, 2020 | Back to lockdown in Europe; is that our fate, too?

I keep following Scott Atlas, and I keep being impressed.

He's the anti-Fauci in the White House. He doesn't quite put it that way, but we all know that's who he is.

I just watched another interview with him, where he answered a lot of the same questions he's covered in the past — with regard to the damage done by lockdowns, the importance of reopening society, and the strategy of taking special care to keep the elderly safe.

But he said a couple of things I hadn't heard him say before, which I thought were worth sharing with you. First, in terms of what life is all about (spoiler: it's more than just the avoidance of death):

> I have a 93-year-old mother-in-law, and she said to me two months ago, "I'm not interested in being confined in my home. I am not interested in living if that's the life….I'm old enough to take a risk; I understand social distancing. I'm going to function; otherwise there's no reason to live." This sort of bizarre, maybe well-intentioned but misguided idea that we are going to eliminate all risk from life, we are going

106

to stop people from taking any risk that they are well aware of, we're going to close down businesses, we're going to stop schools — these are inappropriate and destructive policies.

There are between 30,000 and 90,000 people a year that die — that are high-risk elderly — in the United States every flu season. We don't shut down schools in response to that.

Then, in answer to: is he angry?

I am angry at the people who were wrong and who insist on prolonging these policies that are killing people, particularly people who are not in their socioeconomic class. It's no problem for a person who has a high-level job in government, or an academic job, to sit there and pontificate when the average guy is being destroyed. That I am angry about. And I think history will record these people very harshly — it is an epic failure of massive proportions that they have abandoned regular people here with their own hubris and political agenda. In that sense, yeah, I'm angry.

And then:

All of these harms are massive for the working class and the lower socioeconomic groups. The people who are upper class, who can work from home, the people who can sip their latte and complain that their children are underfoot or that they have to come up with extra money to hire a tutor privately — these are people who are not impacted by the lockdowns.

I'm telling you, we need this guy.

We need him so we won't be — for example — Ireland, which has just returned to a severe lockdown because of a rise in "cases," even though, as the BBC explains, "Hospitalizations have been rising, but they're not at the level seen earlier in the year and again while deaths are slowly rising, they're nowhere near what they were at the peak."

And yet despite that, for at least the next six weeks the following restrictions are being imposed:

• People are allowed to venture only 5km from their houses.

• People may meet, outdoors, with one other household.

• No social or family gatherings are allowed in homes.

• Many "non-essential" businesses will have to close.

• Bars and restaurants have to close their dining rooms.

• Only 25 guests can attend weddings (this rule holds until the end of the year).

• Funerals may have only 10 mourners.

In the U.S., the lockdowners are pretending they're not for full lockdowns anymore. But repeat lockdowns are happening in Europe — in the Czech Republic, people are limited to groups of two — and even in some parts of the U.S.

Lockdowns accomplished nothing at all apart from killing people from other causes, sucking the joy from life, and simply delaying when people get Covid, so of course our overlords intend to push them even harder.

This is why I'm a fan of Scott Atlas. He represents a middle finger to all of this anti-life b.s.

October 23, 2020 | We have two choices

Remember when Dr. Fauci was telling us that we were too stupid to do lockdowns right, and that Italy did it the correct way?

He said in July:

> When we shut down as a nation, in reality only about 50% of the nation shut down....In many of the European countries, 90, 95% of all activities were shut down. So that is one of the reasons why [in Italy] the cases came down…and then stayed.

Now Italy is having its biggest case numbers of the whole episode. Oops!

The Daily Beast just wrote: "What's particularly troubling about the return of Covid in Italy is that the country has done everything experts like Dr. Anthony Fauci have been advising."

Gee, what a surprise! Who could have predicted that — except, I guess, everyone who's been paying attention for the past seven months.

In the presidential debate last night, Joe Biden made clear he'd listen to Dr. Fauci, which he equates with "listening to the science."

Also, Biden warned about teachers dying, even though nowhere in the world have teachers been found to have higher Covid-19 mortality than people in any other profession. That was just a fact-free sop to the unions.

He also ridiculed the suggestion that ultimately we'd have to learn to live with Covid, as if this was some kind of bizarre, misanthropic proposal as opposed to a brute fact of reality that was clear to a lot of us from the beginning.

As a matter of fact, a search for "learn to live with the virus" yielded the following radical right-wing results (I apologize for having to point out that that term is meant to be satirical):

"Covid: Is it time we learned to live with the virus?"
    – BBC News

"We're going to have to learn to live with the virus, says EU health boss"
    – euronews

"Covid-19: Virologist Urges 'Learn to Live with the Virus'"
    – Bloomberg

"Europe Is Learning to Live With the Coronavirus"
    – *New York Times*

October 27, 2020 | *New York Times* reports: lockdowns are deadly

The *New York Times* just reported on "excess deaths" caused not by Covid but which would not have occurred in its absence. You and I have known about and indeed predicted this from the start, but it's nice to see our wise overlords acknowledge it once in a while.

In an article called "The pandemic's real toll? 300,000, and it's not just from the coronavirus," the *Times* writes:

> In many cases, patients may have delayed seeking medical attention or going to the emergency room, either out of fear of contracting the virus or because medical care was not available. Substance abuse disorders and psychological stress may also be playing a role in excess deaths.

The *Times* quotes a doctor as saying:

> It's important for people who have these conditions to not delay or forgo medical care because of their fears of the virus. In many cases, the danger of not getting care is much greater than the risk of exposure to the virus.

Indeed.

Meanwhile, despite the repeated failures — and indeed the outright deadliness — of lockdowns, they're being urged all over the world once again.

That means limiting people to groups of two, confining them to a few miles from their houses, preventing them from visiting practically anyone, and canceling everything they love — and repeating this periodically, as if a society can be run like this.

Look at the curves for deaths, for lockdown and non-lockdown countries, and you'll see that the curve follows the same pattern everywhere. So I call it voodoo.

When "cases" fall, the people in charge congratulate themselves that their voodoo did the trick. When "cases" rise, the people in charge scold us peasants for noncompliance with the voodoo, whether it's mask mandates (as the charts show, mask mandates correlate with nothing) or staying locked in our houses.

Now consider this, sent to me by a reader:

> *Attached is a local story of recent "outbreak" at a hospital. This is the premier hospital in the Northwest. It is the Level 1 trauma center and burn center for a four-state area. The outbreak occurred in surgical unit and 40 staffers and four patients have tested positive. Sadly, one of the patients died.*
>
> *You'll notice this line from the article: "This virus spreads among patients and staff because of gaps in adherence to the precautions we know are very effective."*
>
> *Seattle is the most masked city I've been in (I drove up from AZ in August through UT, ID, MT, and WA), and the surgery unit is the most adherent to masking in the hospital even before Covid. And not just masks, but clean scrubs, shoe covers, hair covers, eye protection, etc. And it's well ventilated. It's the cleanest place in the hospital.*
>
> *So if a staff trained in how to keep their environment clean or even sterile, with all of the PPE that Fauci could dream of, in the most masked unit in a hospital in the most masked city can't prevent the spread of the virus, what hope is there for the rest of society?*

A good question.

I don't see how it will be possible, in the long run, not to fall back on this: people will need to take whatever precautions they think appropriate, and we'll ultimately have to make our own decisions.

October 28, 2020 | Another prediction of Covid doom falls apart

Myanmar is a country of nearly 54 million people. It has had 1,000 Covid-19 deaths. It has been subject to a severe lockdown.

"People are eating rats and snakes," one resident said. "Without an income, they need to eat like that to feed their children."

Meanwhile, the panic that feeds into anti-life decisions like lockdowns in Myanmar continues apace. Nothing seems to be able to puncture it. No matter how many failed predictions of doom, or how obvious it is that we're going to have to live with Covid at some level (and we are quite capable of doing so), there's no changing some minds.

On September 25, the *Los Angeles Times* reported that California was expected to see an 89 percent increase in Covid hospitalizations over the next month. Now even if that had happened, it wouldn't have been a problem, since California's hospitals have more than enough capacity to handle that.

But I'm sure you already know what I'm about to tell you: there was no 89 percent increase in hospitalizations. Instead, hospitalizations *decreased* by nearly 14 percent.

Florida governor Ron DeSantis held a rally with the President 16 days ago. It was a "superspreader" event, said the midwits.

Here's what the deaths chart for Florida looks like for the past month (and this includes Florida's crazy backdating of deaths months later):

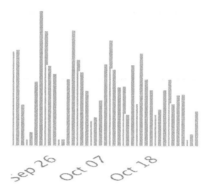

October 29, 2020 | Hysterics smashed in 3 charts (thanks, Scott Atlas)

The crazies who thrive on bad news and panic just got smashed good and hard.

Opponents of Ron DeSantis, governor of Florida, have called him "DeathSantis" because he decided against locking everyone in their homes.

They kept up their stupidity in response to the Trump rally in Sanford two and a half weeks ago that DeSantis attended. As I noted yesterday, this alleged "superspreader" event was followed, two and a half weeks later, by a continuing decline in deaths.

On September 26 DeSantis moved Florida to Phase 3 of reopening, which essentially means normal life. Oh, the crazies went nuts over that. Some of them are trying to stoke panic even now. Including CNN, evidently.

But the numbers don't lie.

The heroic Dr. Scott Atlas just posted the charts below on Twitter.

First, here are Covid-19 hospitalization rates by age and month. The first section is for ages 0–44, the second for 45–64, and the third for 65+. The percentages for each group come down pretty consistently, as you can see:

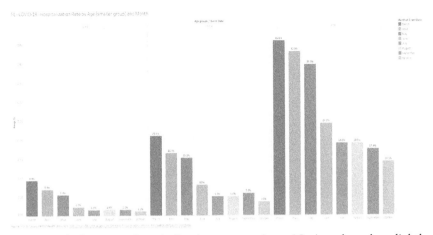

Second, here are hospitalizations over time. Notice that the slightly darker section at the top, which represents Covid hospitalizations, is smaller or stable as you move into the future:

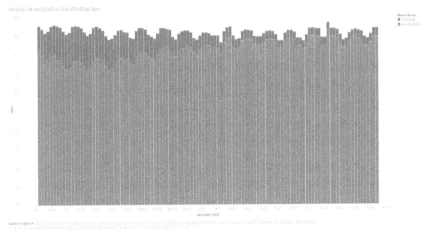

And finally, here's Florida deaths by date of death:

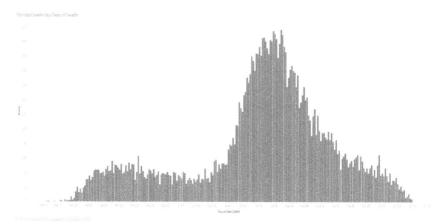

Maybe this thing doesn't behave the way I thought it did, or *maybe lockdowns aren't so necessary after all,* or *maybe the issue is less simple than I supposed* seem to be thoughts that some people are constitutionally incapable of entertaining.

October 30, 2020 | Guess what Biden's virus adviser wants to do

Remember Dr. Zeke Emanuel? I'll refresh your memory:

> We cannot return to normal until there's a vaccine. Conferences, concerts, sporting events, religious services, dinner in a restaurant, none of that will resume until we find a vaccine, a treatment, or a cure....
>
> We need to prepare ourselves for this to last 18 months or so and for the toll that it will take. We need to develop a long-term solution based on those facts. It has to account for what we are losing while this fight goes on, things like schooling and income and contact with our friends and extended family.

He wanted you to go for 18 months without "schooling and income and contact with [your] friends and extended family."

Dr. Emanuel is advising Joe Biden on Covid.

If you're curious about what he would advise Joe to do, here's what he said back when he thought Italy had "crushed the curve":

> One of the important things...to look at is Italy. Italy did a nationwide lockdown....We've never gotten as low as Italy is today....We needed that kind of process nationwide, and we did not have that. So that's one thing: a nationwide lockdown

that lasts eight weeks until we have a number of new cases in the 2 to 3 per 100,000 level.

He said this in September.

Italy just reported 217 deaths from Covid yesterday, which is the equivalent of 1,200 deaths in the U.S.

Gee, Dr. Emanuel, it looks like locking people in their houses only delays the inevitable — as everyone at the time tried to tell you.

Meanwhile, let's check in with Sweden, which never locked down and where almost nobody wears masks. Here's Sweden versus Illinois, which is going into another lockdown:

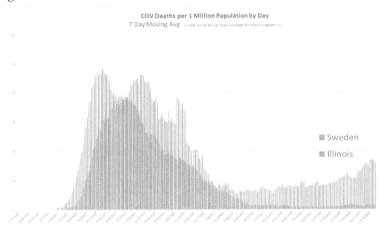

Here's Sweden against several other European countries:

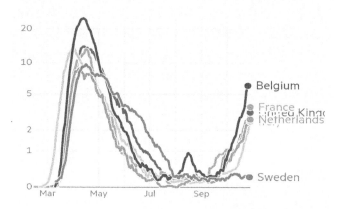

New deaths attributed to Covid-19 in United Kingdom, France, Italy, Netherlands, Belgium and Sweden

Seven-day rolling average of new deaths (per million)

And here's Sweden against still other countries:

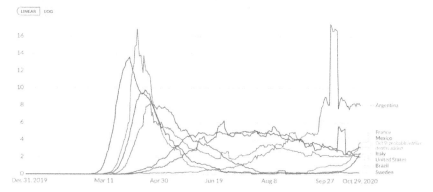

Daily new confirmed COVID-19 deaths per million people

Shown is the rolling 7-day average. Limited testing and challenges in the attribution of the cause of death means that the number of confirmed deaths may not be an accurate count of the true number of deaths from COVID-19

Well, how about that! Lockdowns don't even work — except to suck the joy out of life; decimate people's savings; ruin their livelihoods; delay necessary health procedures; disrupt supply chains, thereby threatening famine; cause 2 million excess deaths from TB, HIV, and malaria; and lead to depression and despair.

116

This should be obvious by now, and yet we have a shocking number of people who think this is what needs to be done. More of what failed the first time!

October 31, 2020 | The "listen to the science" cult

With Massachusetts seeing a rise in "cases," I saw someone on Twitter lamenting that he and his fellow Massachusetts residents had "dropped the ball."

Notice that this person cannot admit that the voodoo doesn't work. It's always because the peasants didn't comply enough. If you stupid people would just obey us, this thing would go away!

I understand why progressives might be attracted to this way of thinking:

(1) They hold a superstitious belief in the powers of the state — so if the state says it can wipe out Covid, who's to say it can't?

(2) It involves "experts" dictating to the stupid rubes, which is their preferred model of governance.

(3) It allows them to ridicule the working-class people they despise — why, if only these backward hicks would "follow the science," we'd be out of this thing already!

But let's face facts: lockdowns only delay the inevitable, and they leave wreckage in their wake.

(And forget about masks: as I've shown before, mask mandates have no discernible effect. If they were as effective as people say — e.g., if we'd just wear masks for six weeks, we'd be out of this! — there should be *some* obvious effect on the charts, but there just isn't. Believe me, I wish masks could solve the problem so I could get the rest of my life back.)

Peru, Belgium, and the U.K. (to name three of many examples) had hard lockdowns, and high death rates. Belgium and the U.K. are locking back down, as is much of Europe.

The crazies, when faced with this data, try to claim that such-and-such country didn't lock down early enough. It can't be that lockdowns don't work, remember. (It's super-scientific to assume a priori that the approach works!) No, it's always that those stupid people didn't "listen to the science," even though there is precisely zero "science" behind lockdowns.

There's no guidebook, no nothing. Lockdowns weren't even a thing until 2020.

But you certainly can't say that Spain didn't lock down early and hard. Or Italy, for that matter.

Now the same European countries whose insufferable intellectuals have been lecturing the U.S. for its handling of the crisis are seeing spikes in deaths again.

In Italy, and in the U.K., and here and there in other places, at least some people are fighting back. The last lockdown took everything they had. One video, which has gone viral, shows an Italian woman crying that she has lost everything and has nothing to feed her child.

I guess she'd better "listen to the science," right?

What a sick, deranged cult this is.

And what is the point of indefinitely depriving ourselves of what makes life worth living, so we can live in an antisocial dystopia? What are we staying alive for, then? So we can sit at home and stare at the wall?

There are other concerns in the world apart from Covid-19. Incredible that this should have to be said. Even some of the elderly are starting to say: I'm at the end of my life, and you want me to spend my final months and years like a vegetable? What's the point?

Meanwhile, vastly more deaths are being caused elsewhere by the policy. Oxford's Sunetra Gupta just published a column in the *Daily Mail* arguing that the response to Covid has been worse than Covid itself.

Even the *New York Times* noted that excess deaths from TB, HIV, and malaria caused as a direct result of the lockdowns will exceed two million.

I could go on and on about the collateral deaths, but I'm probably sounding like a broken record by now.

As Professor Gupta puts it, "Lockdown is a luxury of the affluent; something that can be afforded only in wealthy countries — and even then, only by the better-off households in those countries."

By the way, Prof. Gupta describes her politics as "left-wing," and is aghast that people think that because she opposes barbaric lockdowns she's part of a right-wing conspiracy.

November 8, 2020 | My day with Ron Paul and other normal people

Yesterday I spoke at an event alongside Ron Paul in Angleton, Texas, and it was glorious.

The room was filled to capacity, and we had the kind of normal fellowship and interaction that makes human life worth living. I spoke about the media's laughable and absurd portrayal of Covid, and how it's made people cheer villains and boo heroes.

There were no masks at the event, either.

I haven't focused much on masks, incidentally, because I think lockdowns and restrictions are much worse and that that's where our focus should be. But these days even the masks are making me crazy. As I showed in my talk, mask mandates have had zero effect anywhere. The charts don't lie, and once you see them you can never unsee them.

The claim that "if we'd only worn masks for six weeks, we'd be out of this" is thoroughly refuted by them.

There is little to no mask wearing in Scandinavia, and that doesn't seem to have made any difference.

I get that the left enjoys the egalitarian aesthetic of universal masking, but masks to me are dehumanizing and hideous. Seeing people's facial expressions is a non-optional necessity when it comes to proper communication and the avoidance of misunderstandings. Smiling at people ought to be a non-negotiable part of life.

In my private Tom Woods Show Elite group, a member of my SupportingListeners.com recently shared a highly revealing mask experience she just had:

> *I work in a supermarket, where wearing a mask is required by my employer. I'm also a grandmother, so smiling at babies and small children is second nature to me.*
>
> *I recently began noticing that babies and very young children rarely smile back these days when I'm wearing the mask, but I get huge smiles — smiles that seem to come from sheer joy — when I'm outside and sans mask. (Although [my area's] mask ordinance applies to outdoor areas as well as indoors, as soon as I exit the store, whether walking to my car or to a break area, I pull the mask below my chin and so far no one has said anything to me.)*

Yesterday, as I was walking to my car, a baby around 8–10 months old not only smiled but held out her arms like she wanted me, a complete stranger, to pick her up. I was stunned, as were her parents, who were loading groceries into their car. Her mother said, "It looks like she likes you," and I replied, "Yes, it does," and as I walked by I waved at the baby, smiled, and said "bye-bye" (the way grandmothers do), and she reached for me again. We all smiled and shrugged, and I continued to my car.

But driving home I got to wondering how all this mask wearing might be affecting the development of babies and toddlers, considering the role that facial expressions play in developing communication and social skills. Given this particular baby's apparent age, she was probably born around the time the pandemic began, so up to this point in her life it may be that the only people she has seen without a face mask are her family and their close friends. I know some babies are just naturally outgoing and friendly, but this seemed unusual.

Considering all that's going on these days, I realize this is hardly a major issue, but I just can't help but wonder about possible unforeseen consequences if this masking of human faces goes on much longer.

The wreckage all over the world caused as our so-called experts have claimed to be protecting our health is easy for anyone to see, but there are also subtle damages being done, like the one I think this supporter is correct to point out.

November 9, 2020 | How the Covid dystopia affects babies and kids

Yesterday my newsletter had to do with masks, a topic I haven't discussed much except to note that the charts of health outcomes around the world don't appear to back up the claim that they are particularly effective.

In response, I received this from a reader, and it really struck me:

I look forward to your emails every day to help me keep a sane perspective on this world. Your latest email below, however, struck such a chord with me that I just had to reply.

I am the mother of three children. Our youngest is five months old. Masks have been a very sore subject with me from the beginning for many reasons. Our oldest is four years old. His preschool teachers are required to wear them and our son is extremely troubled by them. He's never seen his teachers' faces! It's a daily struggle to help him deal with this abnormal and disturbing world he all of a sudden lives in.

While this is endlessly upsetting for me, what has me even angrier is the world our baby has been born into. In her five months on this earth, aside from our family, she has never seen another human face! When we go out in public, she doesn't know that there are human faces and perhaps a smile behind those ridiculous masks. She just sees figures wrapped up like mummies. What must she think of the world? What is she learning about her surroundings? To her, this dystopia is going to be "normal."

Our baby is extremely alert and engaged, smiles in response to every smile she's given, and studies our faces intently when we talk and sing to her. I know that as a father, you know that this is how babies learn to talk and learn to communicate with facial expressions. Every parent knows this. Doesn't it concern anyone else that millions of babies are being deprived in a significant way of this opportunity to learn and develop the way God intended? To flourish in the presence of normal human interaction? No one seems to think or care about the psychological and developmental damage these masks are doing to our children and babies. It makes me sick.

We pray constantly for a better future for our children.

Meanwhile, we're hearing that masks will have to be semi-permanent even with a vaccine.

Nope.

That's inhuman.

Even if the only argument against them were that it screws up infants trying to read people and learn about the world if they all look like they're from *The Twilight Zone*, that would be plenty.

November 11, 2020 | Lockdowns vindicated by the vaccine, say the crazies

Since the dual announcement of the Pfizer vaccine and the monoclonal antibody treatment, I've heard some people say: it's time for the lockdown skeptics to stand down. We'll have things getting back to normal within two to four months, they say, so just shut up until then. (These are the same people who, eight months ago, spoke of 15 days to flatten the curve.)

Now, for the sake of argument, suppose these folks are right. Does that mean it's time to give up pointing out facts?

The standard Covid-19 mitigation narrative cannot be smashed hard enough, because we need people to understand what a catastrophe it was the next time they try to impose it on us, who knows how many years down the road.

I saw someone saying that lockdowns have been vindicated by the arrival of the vaccine. What that person really means is: millions of deaths in the developing world from non-Covid illnesses as a direct result of lockdowns *do not matter*.

Now, another issue:

You know how when there are spikes in red states, we get a lot of stern moralizing about the reckless behavior of the peasants?

What happens when there are spikes in blue states, which are replete with restrictions? For example, Minnesota, Colorado, and New Mexico:

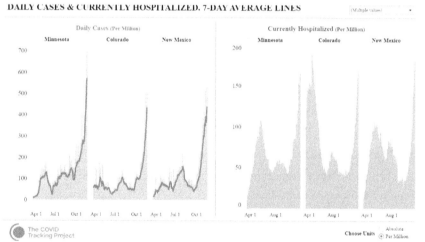

Are those governors going to be lectured to and denounced? The question answers itself, dear reader.

The state desperately needs to take the credit here, so they'll claim that mask mandates, lockdowns, and ruined lives — carried out by people who believe in The Science — were the keys to success.

We were told that Europe had "done it right" and "crushed the curve" by ruining people's lives. Now Covid is back in those places.

We've been told that wearing masks will do the trick, but some of the biggest spikes in the world right now are taking place in countries that have been heavily masked for months.

When sane scientists drafted the Great Barrington Declaration, denouncing society-wide lockdowns as both inhumane and unhelpful and recommending "focused protection" instead, we were told that it would not be possible to shelter vulnerable people. That's way too difficult!

No big deal, on the other hand, was decimating people's life savings, ruining their businesses, roping off playgrounds and depriving children of socialization, disrupting supply chains and risking famine, shutting down everything that brings people joy and meaning — no problem! Not difficult at all!

This has been the worst public-health fiasco in world history, but the media has somehow managed to get half the country cheering for villains and booing heroes — and, even more bizarre, cheering the destruction of their own lives.

You know these people — they're your neighbors, your co-workers, even your family members. They think you're evil, even though the policies they've supported have led to catastrophic outcomes far surpassing the damage from Covid itself.

November 12, 2020 | The "listen to the science" cult wants to ruin your life again

So now they all want lockdowns again.

Poor Tyler Cowen: he just got done telling everyone that hard lockdowns were a "straw man" and a thing of the past, and that the authors of and signatories to the Great Barrington Declaration decrying them were wasting their time.

Remind me not to consult Cowen for predictions.

France is reporting 500+ deaths per day at this point, which would be like 2,500 deaths per day in the U.S. — higher than we ever had.

France is also home to intellectuals who sniffed at the U.S. for its allegedly unscientific response. The same goes for the U.K., Italy, Spain, and elsewhere.

So here's the chart, which includes the country the lizard people hate to mention:

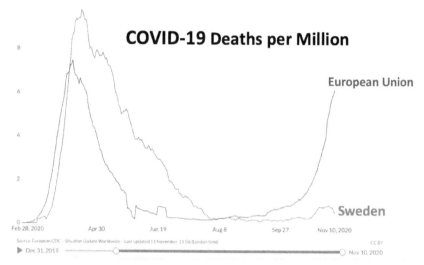

COVID-19 Deaths per Million

European Union

Sweden

Feb 28, 2020   Apr 30   Jun 19   Aug 8   Sep 27   Nov 10, 2020

Source: European CDC - Situation Update Worldwide - Last updated 11 November, 11:06 (London time)   CC BY

▶ Dec 31, 2019 ─────────────────────────────────────○ Nov 10, 2020

There's Sweden at the bottom, the country that never closed businesses or schools and never had a mask mandate.

By the way, see that tiny blip at the end of Sweden's line, where it goes up a little bit and then comes back down? A couple of weeks ago people were pointing at that tiny thing and screaming that Sweden was finally going to get what was coming to it.

Mmkay.

They can't just be happy for Sweden and curious to learn more about why it's been doing so well month after month — in fact, September 2020 was the least lethal month in the entire recorded history of Sweden.

It's as if they want to make us suffer, they want to take away what brings us joy, they want us to feel pain — and Sweden spoils that party.

Woods, you may say, how can you attribute that kind of motive to them?

At this point, what other explanation is there? They keep proceeding according to the same failed practices of the past, and they keep ignoring the one major country that took a different path. Does that sound like what someone with a truly dispassionate, scientific frame of mind would do?

The rule seems to be: we don't know what we're doing, but if something brings pleasure we should probably limit it, and if something involves great inconvenience and sacrifice, we should impose it.

"Science," everyone!

Meanwhile, the Republican Party, with a few notable exceptions, has been borderline useless through the crisis.

Just one example: Ohio's Mike DeWine. More restrictions coming from Mike, and more masking — because masks have done just a bang-up job around the world!

November 16, 2020 | It's almost as if none of the "virus mitigation" measures work

Steve Sisolak, governor of Nevada, recently scolded citizens of his state. Why, only irresponsible behavior can account for a rise in "cases" there! So he's telling Nevadans that they have two weeks to get things under control.

He warned, "I'm not going to come back in two weeks and say I'm going to give you another chance."

And then, three days later, Governor Sisolak himself tested positive for Covid-19.

Should we treat him like he's 7 and scold him for his irresponsible behavior, the way he just did to his citizens?

The governor was forced to admit: "You can take all the precautions that are possible and you can still contract the virus. I don't know how I got it."

An anonymous professor who posts on Twitter about the virus just presented this graph for our consideration. It's a plot of Covid deaths in North Carolina and Oklahoma. Those states have adopted very different approaches. And yet, somehow, they more or less track each other anyway:

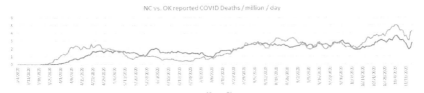

125

Yesterday former Secretary of Education Arne Duncan posted the following:

I so appreciate everyone's good wishers!
How did we catch it?
I don't know

We wore masks
We socially distanced
We avoided crowds
We haven't had people in our house

And, I'm sure whoever gave it to us felt they did the same
COVID is in the air now- in almost every room you enter

1:59 PM · Nov 15, 2020 · Twitter for iPhone

"How did we catch it? I don't know. We wore masks. We socially distanced. We avoided crowds. We haven't had people in our house."

We can either accept some humility about what we can accomplish, and take steps to protect those among us who are most at risk while others resume the one life they are given, or we can destroy our social fabric.

Meanwhile, we have families and friendships being torn apart over all this. You're a bad person if you reject the propaganda. Why, you don't care about saving lives! You're "selfish"! Never mind the countless lives lost by lockdown itself, a point I've made again and again. Those lives don't count.

November 18, 2020 | Rising "cases" are your fault, you awful person

There's no pleasing everyone.

Some of you started following me because of my recent video "The Covid Cult," which between YouTube and Facebook has had well over 1,000,000 views since it was released last week.

Well, not everyone liked it. On Twitter, I just received this stimulating intellectual response:

@ThomasEWoods I just listened to your YOUTUBE on the Covid Cult....my husband and i are in healthcare and have a busy medical office practice. You sir, should be ashamed of your self

2:32 PM · Nov 18, 2020 · Twitter Web App

Was anything I said in the talk disputed? Of course not. So I replied:

Tom Woods @ThomasEWoods · 33m
Replying to ███████
Which one of the nine devastating consequences of lockdowns that I listed is untrue?

She disputed none of them. I was then told that what "got us into this horrid situation" was "carelessness and not caring about one another."

This conventional line of argument makes me crazy.

So I came back with, "I just showed you that 130 *million* people are at risk of starvation because of your preferred policies, and you're telling me about not caring about people! Unbelievable! Physician, heal thyself!"

I then pointed out that much as it might satisfy our urge to be able to blame someone, it just doesn't work: places with major shutdowns are having spikes, while we in Florida saw our spike recede without any lockdowns. Moralizing is completely misplaced here.

Not to mention, of course, that some of the most mask-compliant places on Earth have had some of the roughest outcomes.

She then asked what I favored: just letting the virus ran rampant?

My answer: "I am saying that people at risk should take the precautions they think necessary, but that most of the present one-size-fits-all strategy deprives extremely low-risk people of the things that make life worth living *with no benefits to show for it.*"

This Friday night in Melbourne, Florida, I have a chance to speak to 100 state legislators from around the country, and I'll be speaking on this topic. I'll say something like this:

People who are living in irrational fear already have their representatives: the entire entertainment world, the media, and virtually all of the political class.

The rest of us have almost no one.

People whose family members died because their procedures were indefinitely postponed, or who lost a loved one to suicide, or who have had everything they've poured their hearts into crushed and destroyed — they have no one.

Elderly people dying of social isolation, and who are told they can see their grandkids through a window or over Zoom, but who think they themselves can best judge what kind of life they want to live, likewise have no one to speak for them.

The physical and mental health toll of the restrictions and shutdowns is staggering — and nobody is allowed to mention it for fear of being told they want grandmothers to die.

No one will speak for them.

Except you.

People will hate you for this. Automatons who can do nothing but repeat CBS News talking points will think you're terrible.

The rest of us will consider you a hero.

You must be the voice of the voiceless. Because if it isn't you, it will be no one.

November 19, 2020 | Superstition-based policy keeps failing

Here's the first thing I saw on Twitter this morning. I promise this is real and not a parody:

Andrea @intouchfornow · Nov 18   ooo

Hey @SAPoliceNews for the sake of my stupid husband, who's doing a #KarenFromBrighton moan, can you please broadcast very specific information about walking the dog.
#lockdown

  💬 327   🔁 211   ♡ 266

South Australia Police ✓
@SAPoliceNews

Replying to @intouchfornow

Hi Andrea, You cannot leave the house to walk the dog or to exercise.

1:21 AM · Nov 18, 2020 · TweetDeck

1.8K Retweets   **4.9K** Quote Tweets   **1.4K** Likes

Andrea @intouchfornow · Nov 18
Replying to @SAPoliceNews
Thanks for replying
It's what I've been trying to tell him ...
Good work, stay safe too.

💬 591   🔁 97   ♡ 95   ↑

So she's delighted to learn that indeed they cannot leave the house to walk the dog or to exercise.

This is for everyone's health, of course. Because a society can be run successfully when it's allowed to operate, then suddenly shut down, then started again, and then shut down again. No problems there!

Second, I wanted to share a few charts with you. The heroic Ian Miller has more of them.

The CDC credited masks with bringing down Arizona's curve. Are they planning a follow-up statement now? (I'm just playing with you with that question; we already know the answer.) And here's New Mexico as well, for good measure:

Here's New Jersey. The governor there said masks played a significant role in bringing their curve down. And it's true that this is one of the rare charts in which that story at least has a surface plausibility. The problem is that there's a right-hand side to that chart now:

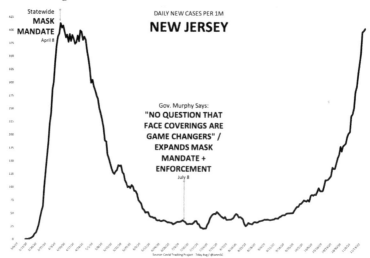

Then there's Minnesota, which has had all kinds of crazy restrictions, and Florida, which was mostly open for a while before becoming completely open on September 25. Isn't it odd that their case counts are the opposite of what the hysteria would lead you to expect?

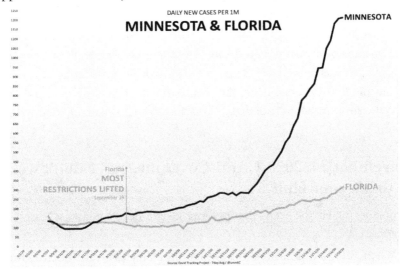

And finally, here are three states that "believe in science"! That's funny: I guess by an interesting coincidence they all abandoned their sciency strategies at exactly the same time (because remember: rising case counts are always somebody's *fault*!):

In short, the world looks *nothing at all* like it should if the cartoon version of events and the government responses were correct. And yet people continue to believe it. And not only do they believe it: but they shame and condemn you if you don't believe it.

Why, you're "selfish"!

I'll never forget, earlier this year, when people protested lockdowns because their livelihoods were being destroyed, everything they'd devoted their lives to was being taken away, and their kids were suffering very badly — and the lockdowners, being the compassionate lovers of mankind they always claim to be, responded, "You just want a haircut, you selfish person."

November 24, 2020 | Anti-Covid measures don't work, so that's your fault

Remember when the CDC credited masks for bringing down "cases" in Arizona?

When they say ridiculous things like this, they give the green light to people who want to blame their neighbors for rises in cases. "Why, since we know masks work, the rise in cases must be because of you stupid anti-science people who refuse to wear them!"

Even though mask compliance is as high as ever, these "pro-science" people just *know* it can't be, because they just *know* masks at the very least go a long way toward solving the problem.

Well, anyway, how about we check out Arizona's curve now?

How about that.

Could it be that masks didn't bring the curve down after all? That these curves seem to do more or less the same thing no matter what?

Right now one blue state after another that supposedly "followed the science" is seeing a rise in "cases." And all their people can do is blame their neighbors. Because, don't you know, the "science" works! So if the "science" isn't working, that means someone somewhere must not be sciencing.

Let's check in with "pro-science" Rhode Island. Are masks keeping "cases" down there?

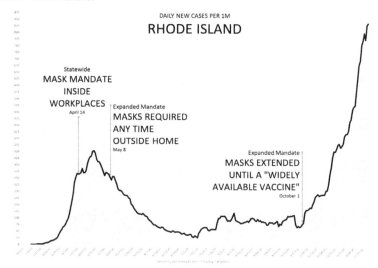

That's quite a coincidence: people in Arizona and Rhode Island chose the same moment to stop sciencing.

Red-state Utah is in a similar situation. People are screaming at their neighbors to wear masks. And as you can see, that has had a clear and unmistakable effect:

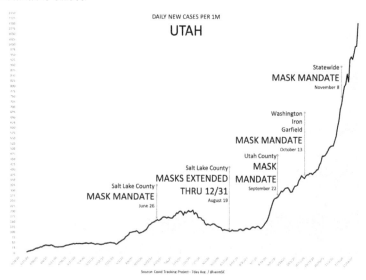

(Yes, I was being sarcastic.)

November 25, 2020 | "Must love lockdowns" now part of YouTube's Terms of Service

Well, I have an update for you: YouTube has taken down "The Covid Cult," my remarks that between Facebook and YouTube had had nearly 1.5 million views.

This is the first time this has ever happened to me.

Oh, and why did they do it? It violated YouTube's "Terms of Service" — which apparently include the provision that you may not question lockdowns, which are a brilliant idea and have no side effects.

You can still watch it here: TomWoods.com/the-covid-cult

Not one stitch of anything in that video was false, as you can see at the link if you haven't watched it already.

There are now other platforms you can use to post videos where you can be confident they'll stay up. That's a good thing, but it's also symbolic of the current divide. You don't need me to tell you that the country had already been divided well before Covid came along, but once all this passes there will be a profound and lasting division that is probably beyond healing.

On the one side, you have people who think half the country selfishly ignored sound public health advice and put people at risk because they wanted to get haircuts. They're not going to want to make nice anytime soon.

Then you have our side.

We're the ones who tried to empathize with people who had lost everything they'd worked their whole lives for; people suffering from depression, for whom "social distancing" was a death sentence; people whose medical treatments were indefinitely postponed; people around the world at risk of starvation from supply-chain disruptions; elderly people dying of "failure to thrive" because the deprivation of human contact had made them lose the will to live — you know as well as I do that it's a long and very grim list.

Now look: I disapprove of making all of life about politics, or having litmus tests for friendships. For that matter, I shouldn't have to investigate where my ketchup company donates its profits.

But I'll be honest: I don't particularly want to associate with people responsible for this fiasco.

They're surrounded by collateral damage and the destruction of societies and the things that make life worth living, and all they can do is tell us Covid is bad? They can't think about more than one thing at a time?

Meanwhile, they didn't bother to notice that the charts of places with radically different policies were often exactly the same. That realization would have disrupted their ordinary course of action: namely, *blaming people for Covid*.

If people get sick no matter what government policies are instituted, it becomes more difficult to portray oneself as morally superior and super concerned with saving human lives.

And frankly, imagine the kind of person to whom the expression "stay home, save lives" appeals. You can finally matter, and all you need to do is...absolutely nothing.

December 3, 2020 | The Covid catastrophe that never occurred

The mask obsession won't go away.

The ridiculous Facebook "fact-check" of one of my videos claimed that I "cherry picked" my examples of heavily masked countries. Why, Japan wears masks and did fine, they said.

I'm glad they brought up Japan, which is a fascinating case. Japan has had about 17 Covid deaths per million, despite a lackluster "lockdown" and a large elderly population. This compares to 1,472 in Belgium, 1,106 in Peru, 972 in Spain, 946 in Italy, 891 in the U.K., and 830 in the U.S.

Starting in April, we were told for weeks that Japan would be an absolute catastrophe. We have an Internet that keeps a record of botched predictions. Japan did relatively little of the sacred "testing," maybe five percent of what South Korea did. They didn't bother obsessively testing asymptomatics. They had only a halfhearted lockdown.

Now if we followed that relatively laissez-faire plan in the U.S. but wore masks, the mask obsessives would say (and indeed have said), "We never said masks could solve the problem on their own! They need to be coupled with other measures!"

Well, Japan didn't take the "other measures" recommended by the hysterics. So all the hysterics have is masks. And wouldn't you know: your social media friends now claim masks solved the problem in Japan.

"Masks aren't enough," they say when I show charts of the Czech Republic, Belgium, the U.K., France, Italy, Germany, Austria, etc. But when it comes to Japan, The Science now says: masks are enough!

Just for fun, let's recall the warnings of doom from April, with a sampling of mainstream headlines:

> *Science*: **Did Japan miss its chance to keep the coronavirus in check?**

My comment: Nope! I guess it didn't!

> *Washington Post*: **Japan's coronavirus response is too little, too late**

My comment: Get a load of the arrogance of these people. Not even a question mark, as in, "Too little, too late?" No, in April they know enough about Covid already to state with certainty that Japan's response was inadequate.

> Also *Washington Post*: **How hostess bars and cherry blossoms helped undermine Japan's coronavirus response**

My comment: I have no idea what this means, but plenty of countries only wish their response could have been so "undermined" that they'd have a mere 17 deaths per million!

> *New Statesman*: **How Japan's refusal to impose a coronavirus lockdown is dividing the country**

My comment: Yes, dividing it between people who were right, and people who were prepared to ruin others' lives for no reason.

> **ABC (Australian Broadcasting Corporation): How Shinzo Abe has fumbled Japan's coronavirus response**

Again, plenty of countries only wish they could have "fumbled" their response the way Japan did!

You don't get to spend weeks screaming about the inadequate Japanese response, during all of which Japan was wearing masks, and then, when everything turns out extremely well, turn around and say: I knew all along they'd be fine, because they wore masks!

We've heard people try to claim that this or that Asian country did really well because it implemented strict contact tracing, widespread testing, hard lockdowns, etc. Of those, Japan did only contact tracing, and even that it did differently from how Western "public health experts" recommend. As the *Japan Times* put it, "Encouraging people with mild or no symptoms to take PCR tests would have revealed nothing but resulted in isolating false-positive cases."

It does not seem implausible to suggest that the staggering differential between Japan's death rate and those of Western Europe and the Americas indicates that pre-existing immunity may be heterogeneously distributed around the world. This is far more plausible than to believe that government interventions, widely differing throughout Asia and yet yielding roughly similar results — results that are orders of magnitude better than what's been seen on other continents — account for the difference.

December 7, 2020 | The creepiest rule about Covid lockdowns

Once in a while I like to share something I receive in my inbox.

The lockdown insanity has crushed who knows how many people — tens, hundreds of millions? billions? — some of whom write to me.

Publicly, none of these people are allowed to say anything about it. That's what I consider the creepiest rule about Covid lockdowns. If you break this rule you'll be called cold and callous — for daring to care about your own life and everything you've poured your heart into.

Because the only thing that matters in the world is Covid. Not your kids, whom the lockdowners have gleefully sacrificed. Not your life savings — why, who can think about money when we're all obsessing monomaniacally about one thing?

Oh, and not your business (obviously!), not your physical health (sorry we canceled all those procedures!), not your family, not your friendships, not your mental health, not normal human connection, not relationships, nothing.

Only Covid.

Because, don't you know, it spreads "exponentially" — as every midwit screamed at us in March. (Except it doesn't, obviously.)

At any rate, here's what I received from a Californian today:

> *While I'm sure this is repetitive, I can't imagine it's never not good to hear that your emails are a godsend. Throughout quarantine my husband and I have been stuck in California, or as I like to call it, Newsom's sadistic playground.*
>
> *We had plans to move to Tennessee to help family in failing health and pick up more responsibilities in the family business, but all of that was dashed with the lockdowns. Work has dried up, our savings are now gone, and with everyone literally fleeing the state, Tennessee real estate has skyrocketed well beyond what we had been looking at in February. To say we are disheartened is probably one of the top ten understatements of this year.*
>
> *Our friends and family are fairly like-minded, but even my brother — who has a BS in economics — couldn't understand why stimulus checks hurt more than they helped. Even my cousin — who is an ER nurse — drank the lockdown Kool-Aid and warned against my skepticism of tests in the beginning, though I'm happy to say she's slowly coming around....I have felt so alone in my outrage for months.*
>
> *Relationships have been strained, and a handful actually severed over the quarantine. I can't even talk about it in my own home now, because it's too upsetting and unfruitful to complain about the current state of things. Needless to say, reading each morning about how you crush the Covid cult is one of my few sources of sanity these days.*
>
> *I will be honest, my family technically broke the state-mandated rules for Thanksgiving. We had a multi-household camping trip at the beach, in the sunshine and fresh air, and about twenty of us crammed onto a couple of picnic tables under the stars for our turkey dinner. We didn't wear masks between bites, and we definitely consumed alcohol and sang songs together.*
>
> *You know what the darnedest thing is, though? Not one of us got sick.*
>
> *Newsom has now dropped us and all neighboring counties a tier (his arbitrary system for how strict a lockdown he will impose) and now we can't even eat outside at restaurants anymore. We have a local favorite that we've frequented throughout the quarantine in hopes that we can keep it afloat, but being closed until Christmas might be what does it in. What does all of our local businesses in. I've never known this amount*

of despair and impotent rage before. Clearly, California's definition of life is different from mine....

Thank you for your voice in the midst of this chaos. Thank you for letting people like myself know that we aren't alone in this insanity. And if you could somehow bring the fight to California, you'd save more lives than Newsom claims his tactics have saved.

Gratefully, A Reluctant Californian

I am receiving boatloads of emails like this every day. Nothing I've ever written about has resonated with more people. *You are keeping me sane,* people tell me.

I have never heard that before.

I've covered lots of topics before, but this one is truly unique. It's as if you and I are living in different realities from some of the people around us. Major cities are at 95+ percent mask compliance, and some people really think a lack of masks is the problem. They think staying home is the key to making progress, when heavily locked down California has more hospitalizations per million than completely open Florida. (Not to mention, Florida has the country's fifth-oldest population, while California is all the way down at number 44.)

December 9, 2020 | Did Thanksgiving lead to a spike in hospitalizations?

By now, reality stubbornly refuses to conform to the public health establishment's narrative. If it did, Florida should be catastrophic: very old population, lots of travel in and out, completely open and with no state-imposed occupancy restrictions. And yet right now it's doing better in terms of hospitalizations per million than California, whose lockdown is downright inhuman.

Georgia was supposed to be catastrophic. Not even close. Sweden should certainly be in the top five, or top ten, or at least the top 20 worst places, yet it isn't.

People's mobility, which you'd think would correspond to more deaths, or "cases," or whatever, corresponds to nothing.

There are theories as to why these outcomes occur, but the standard public-health narrative proceeds as if these mysteries did not exist.

So:

Don't you dare visit people for Thanksgiving, they said.

Thanksgiving was November 26, thirteen days ago. Travel for Thanksgiving occurred 14 to 17 days ago.

Here are the numbers for weekly changes in national Covid hospitalizations, courtesy of Alex Berenson. There was already a spike before Thanksgiving, and it has slowed since:

Nov. 10–17: +24%
Nov. 17–24: +14%
Nov. 24–Dec. 1: +12%
Dec. 1–8: +6%

As you can see, the most recent week's figure is one-fourth as high as that for the week of November 10. If the numbers had been reversed, we'd have been lectured nonstop: see what you stupid rubes did by traveling? Since the numbers once again do not correspond to what the cartoon version of things would lead us to expect, Team Apocalypse has simply moved on to something else, not chastened in the slightest.

Meanwhile, check out this graph, showing the massive divergence in deaths by continent.

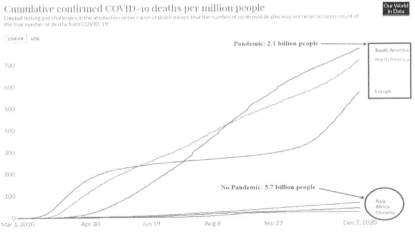

Differences of that scale can hardly be attributed to policy differences between continents, much as the "listen to the science" crowd wants us to believe that wise government policy can navigate us through a spreading virus.

141

Not to mention: there has been wide variation in response among East Asian countries, and yet the same kind of results have been achieved in each. As Jay Bhattacharya of Stanford said on the Tom Woods Show yesterday, "There seems to be some policy invariance in East Asia: no matter what policy you pick, you get a good result....I think the only explanation must be something like pre-existing immunity."

December 10, 2020 | Enclosed: a 10-megaton bomb against the panickers

One place after another is using "cases" as the metric to decide whether people are allowed to experience joy or not.

So let's meet them on that ground.

Yinon Weiss (@yinonw) has been heroic through this fiasco, and he just released a series of charts, along with commentary, that I can't improve upon. So for today's issue I'm sharing them with you:

> Santa Clara County (CA) was the first in the U.S. to lock down. They "followed the science" with perhaps the longest lockdown in the world. Gyms never opened. Indoor dining *never* opened. How did that work out?

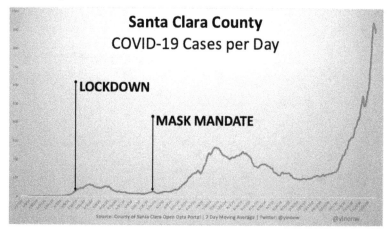

> Connecticut is the home of Yale and many intellectuals, so surely they followed the science. Except now they have the highest per-capita case count in the country. What about all those masks, lockdowns, and the almighty #science?

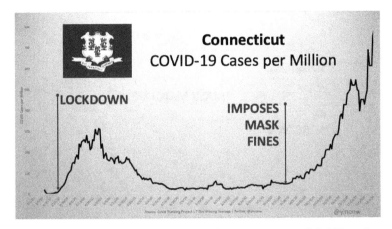

Surely progressive Massachusetts, home to Harvard, MIT, and so many esteemed scientists, would follow the science. They used #science to require people to wear masks even if miles away from others in November. No schools, closed businesses, and a curfew. Surely that would work?

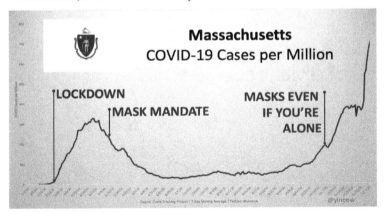

Let's visit the West Coast, where highly scientific California loves following the science! Remember all those beach closures? Curfews, no schools, and destroyed businesses are a high price to pay, but surely it's worth it at the altar of #science. How is that working out?

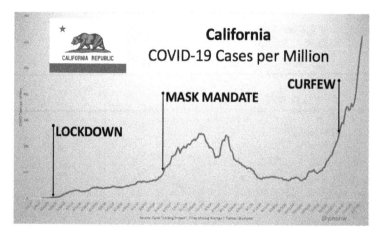

But wait, maybe science was right and it's the people's fault! Even when separated by 2,500 miles, the evil residents of CT, MA, and CA all decided to get lazy at the exact same time. So let's not blame false idol scientists and clueless politicians. Let's blame the people!

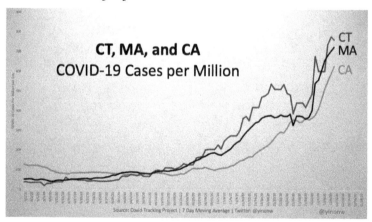

Okay, okay, but it would be so much worse if they didn't follow the #science, right? Let's look at Florida, which effectively ended Covid restrictions on Sept 25th. Those crazies with their open schools, open business, and people who get to live their lives. Barbarians!

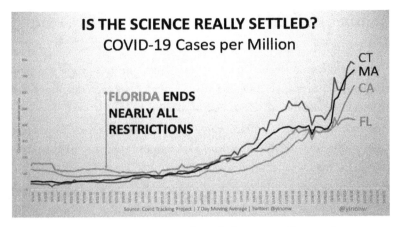

Not to be left out, New York and Governor Cuomo love to brag about all the science they follow. It's all about the #science! Only problem is that NY/NJ have the highest per capita death rate in entire world. If that's what it means to be a scientist in 2020, I'd rather be a pagan.

COVID Deaths Per Million

NEW JERSEY	1989
NEW YORK	1811
MASSACHUSETTS	1620
BELGIUM	1508
CONNECTICUT	1482
ITALY	1022
SPAIN	1005
ARIZONA	973
UK	919
FLORIDA	906
USA	894
FRANCE	867
TEXAS	822
SWEDEN	720
SWITZERLAND	658
NETHERLAND	574

Source: worldometers.info | Data as of 12/9/2020 | Twitter: @yinonw

What further comment is necessary? The ruined lives, the global wreckage — was it all for nothing? We are not permitted to raise the question.

As always, those are the very questions we need to ask.

December 11, 2020 | The country with zero Covid deaths

One place we haven't heard much about amid the hysteria is Cambodia. Cambodia is reporting zero deaths from Covid. Not zero deaths yesterday, or last week, or last month. Zero deaths, period.

Now you know the standard view: places that "listen to The Science" manage to minimize deaths, and wise government policy is what makes the difference between one country and another.

How anyone can still believe this in December 2020 is beyond me. The phrase "policy invariance" is now one of my favorites. It doesn't seem to matter what we do. The mayor of Los Angeles even admitted that the behavior of the people there hadn't changed at all and they were seeing a major spike anyway. He's so close to an important truth, but you know what they say: none so blind…

Cambodia was ranked 89th in the world for its preparedness for an infectious disease outbreak. Eighty-ninth! Are we supposed to believe that the reason Cambodia is at zero is the huge supply of public-health PhDs they have there?

Could there be explanations *other than government policy*? Practically every chart in existence screams out this conclusion at us.

Dr. Fauci has been doing his level best to give the impression that Covid is an equal-opportunity killer. He will emphasize extreme outliers to give the impression that the average 35-year-old is at genuine risk, when the average 35-year-old has a vastly higher chance of dying in a bicycle accident.

Not only is Covid *not* an equal-opportunity killer for individuals, but it is evidently also not an equal-opportunity killer for countries and regions, either.

Africa has barely been touched by it — and again, not because public-health PhDs have been having their way.

In East Asia we've seen "policy invariance," according to Stanford's Jay Bhattacharya. Hard lockdown in China, lackluster response in Japan, and evidently good results in both cases.

The Covid crazies in the West want to blame us: why, if only we'd been like East Asia, etc. But it's obvious, given the policy invariance, that something other than government policy is at work.

That could be: overall health, Vitamin D levels, age, or low obesity levels — or T-cell immunity (Bhattacharya's supposition).

In Japan, in fact, a September seroprevalence study yielded an astonishing result of 47 percent, which suggests masks and social distancing aren't the explanation for the low death count. Lots and lots of Japanese had it (so they failed to "stop the spread"), but they didn't get sick or die — almost certainly because of preexisting immunity. Not because of the public-health PhDs.

If government policy were the explanation, there should be piles of corpses in Florida at the moment, where even theater and live music have made a comeback. And yet such blue-state, "follow the science," ruin-people's-lives states like New York, California, Illinois, Michigan, Wisconsin, New Mexico, and New Jersey, among others, have worse hospitalization numbers per million right now.

All of this should be excruciatingly obvious. And yet chances are, you're surrounded by people trying to blame you and your neighbors for their bad behavior — for bad behavior is what makes "cases" rise!

December 15, 2020 | Forbidden comparisons

Mayors and governors have been ordering soul-crushing shutdowns yet again.

When I try to explain that these measures don't seem to accomplish anything, since places that don't do them get similar results, I get reader feedback saying: *don't bother making this argument. The political class has a secret agenda it's pushing, and it's not about health.*

Well, the political class always has an ulterior motive for what it does, but that doesn't mean there's no value in explaining to ordinary people that what they're doing hurts rather than helps. And what shocks me is how many ordinary people continue to go along, and continue to shame dissidents, without having bothered to look into whether any of it has done any good.

So I like to draw comparisons.

As I noted in a recent talk, much more open Oklahoma has if anything done better in terms of deaths per million (524 vs. 558) than relatively closed North Carolina, for example.

We could generate similar comparisons all day.

Whenever you draw comparisons, though, the lockdowners try to pretend that the places you're comparing are just too different from each other for the comparison to be valid.

So if Oklahoma and North Carolina had exactly the same death chart, well, that's just a coincidence caused by the precise balancing of drastic differences between those places and populations.

Sure it is.

(These are the very same people, by the way, who don't hesitate to compare isolated New Zealand to the United States.)

I found it interesting to look at three places that are right next to each other, in order to minimize differentiating factors like weather, demographics, etc. And yet despite different policies implemented at different times, Maryland, D.C., and Virginia follow exactly the same pattern. Isn't that *at least odd?*

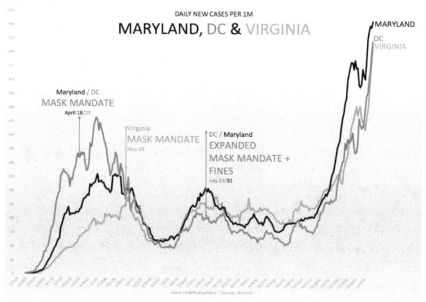

Or how about Arizona, Nevada, and California. Different policies, same result:

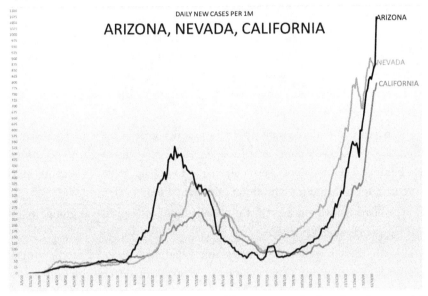

I realize this isn't as much fun as blaming people for the virus, and I realize that's what so many people want to do. *This is your fault!*

Eli Klein, who runs an art gallery in New York City, just pointed out that New York has 25 percent more Covid hospitalizations per capita than Florida, and is worse in every other cumulative and current metric. Florida is completely open, while New York is irrationally closed. "Nobody I talk to in NYC knows that data," he says. "Nobody."

If we had an honest media, everyone would know this, *especially* New Yorkers.

December 16, 2020 | You can knock off all the sanitizing

You know all that mad disinfecting everyone has been doing?

You'll never guess: it's pointless.

Even the *Washington Post*, in an article last week called "We Are Over-Cleaning in Response to Covid-19," wrote: "We don't have a single documented case of Covid-19 transmission from surfaces. Not one. So why, then, are we spending a small fortune to deep-clean our offices, schools, subways, and buses?"

Meanwhile, though, lots of restaurants are still using disposable menus. Now that's what you call not following the science.

And now here's the problem.

We know surfaces aren't the issue, and that we're wasting enormous time and resources pointlessly deep-cleaning. The reason we're still doing it is that the general public is still in panic mode, even after all we now know. And because the public, convinced it's "listening to the science," is in fact not following the science at all.

So when you endure some pointless practice here and there, whose only effect is to cause you pain or at least serious inconvenience, it's very often not because a private entity seriously wants to engage in it. It's because they have to cater to hysterics who don't know anything.

This isn't just a matter of the government. It's public opinion that's making the craziness possible.

I knew there were a lot of Americans I had nothing in common with. I had no idea how many Americans had a completely different definition of life from mine.

If I'm elderly and in a nursing home and cannot see or embrace anyone in my family, and I cannot socialize or do anything, please don't congratulate yourself for keeping me alive. You've already killed me.

We're being told that masks and social distancing will be necessary even after the vaccine. Are these people prepared to go along even with that? Surely some will decide enough is enough. But who knows how many.

Some people are fighting back, like the coffee shop owner I interviewed on episode #1796 of the Tom Woods Show yesterday. I'm doing what I can by spreading as much helpful and revealing information as possible. Still, a lot of people are demoralized: how can this still be going on? How can anyone still think these alleged mitigation measures do anything but crush people's spirits?

Believe me, I get that.

Where I live (Florida), everything is open. But if I lived anywhere else, I'd be going out of my way to support businesses that refuse to comply. And although their number is smaller than we might hope, it's growing.

December 17, 2020 | Is the hospital system "overwhelmed"?

Remember how awful Thanksgiving was supposed to be? Well, here's what happened in the Midwest:

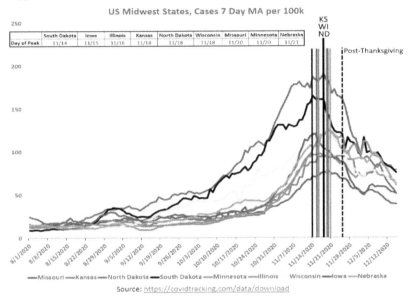

Source: https://covidtracking.com/data/download

Was everyone in every single one of those states behaving recklessly, and then suddenly, right at Thanksgiving, thought better of it? Or might all these interventions be useless?

Meanwhile, what about hospitalizations? These, too, are supposed to be our fault, as insufferable "health care professionals" lecture us with made-up stories about people whose dying words were supposed to have been, "I thought it was a hoax."

Absolute guarantee nobody ever went to his grave saying those words. If you're going to invent a b.s. story, at least make it plausible.

Yinon Weiss (@yinonw) has dug up the relevant information on current hospitalization trends. Let's start with what the big picture looks like:

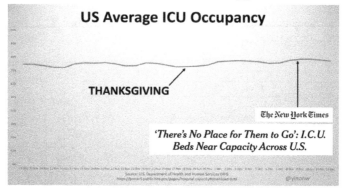

I'll bet most people don't think the chart looks like that.

Now given that the U.S. has 6,000+ hospitals, some number of them will experience high occupancy from time to time, as has happened numerous times in the past. The chart above shows the aggregate numbers, which do not appear to be abnormal.

With Covid hospitalizations increasing, though, how can this be? Weiss explains:

1. Wide Covid spread means people coming in for non-Covid issues but still count as Covid patients.

2. Covid patients replacing flu patients.

And hence this:

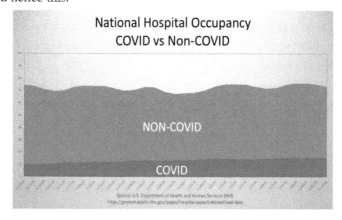

Finally, what's happening in Los Angeles? This:

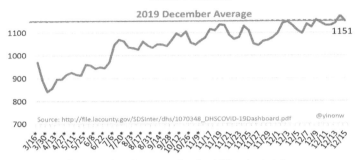

Los Angeles Department of Health Services Hospitals Total Patients

Important to know what last year looked like, isn't it?

This is why decontexualized numbers don't help us. We need to know what's typical. Saying an ICU is 85 percent occupied sounds scary to people who don't know anything. But they generally have to be at least that occupied for a hospital to stay afloat.

Part IV: Winter 2020–2021

December 21, 2020 | Charts your panicking friends can't explain

You may have noticed something about your social media contacts: they think cases go up when people disregard state-imposed restrictions, and go down when they comply.

These are people who haven't seen any charts.

Some of the ones that follow were generated by Ian Miller (@ianmSC), and some by me using the Worldometers site.

Let's start with two Orange Counties, one in California and one in Florida. The one in California has been shut down for eight months. It is the home of the only Disney property in the world that is still closed. California has a young population: it's the 44th oldest of the 50 states. The one in Florida is completely open, including theme parks and entertainment venues, with no state-imposed occupancy restrictions. Florida is the fifth-oldest of the 50 states.

Isn't it funny how closely the two track each other — until the end, of course, when California's goes through the roof?

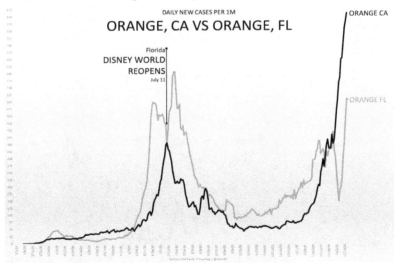

I guess California and Florida obey and then disobey at exactly the same time. What a coincidence!

Let's check in on California at large. All those restrictions must really be helping! Here's the chart:

Ahem.

Let's check on Mississippi and Alabama. They're right next to each other, with very similar populations, but they've imposed mask mandates at different times and had different timetables and policies for the reopening of various kinds of businesses. Their charts must be wildly different, right?

And yet:

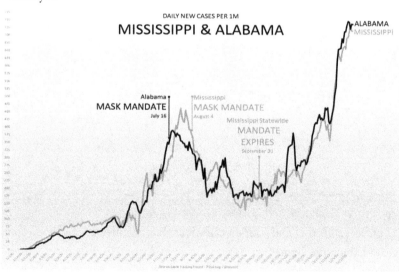

Poland had a mask mandate as of April 17. Apparently they must have started ignoring guidelines and begun traveling for some kind of Polish Thanksgiving in early October:

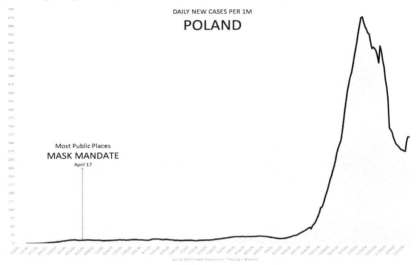

Here's what deaths in Poland look like:

Daily New Deaths in Poland

Back in May, we got stories about Slovakia like this one in *The Atlantic*: "Lessons From Slovakia – Where Leaders Wear Masks. The country's politicians led by example, helping it flatten its curve."

Here's Slovakia right now:

Daily New Deaths in Slovakia

I guess there's some Slovakian tradition in October where they burn their masks.

Or how about Hungary:

Daily New Deaths in Hungary

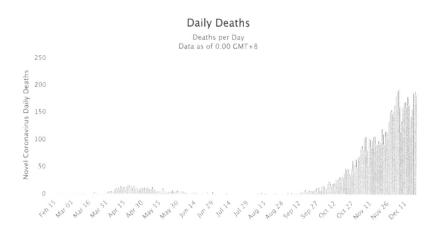

And here's Germany, the land of $5,000 fines for not wearing masks:

Daily New Deaths in Germany

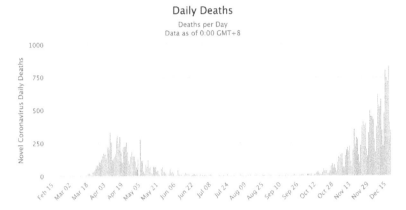

Isn't this weird? It's like all the peoples of central Europe conspired to ignore public health recommendations at exactly the same time!

Let's make a quick trip to Asia. Check out the similarity of the curves in Japan and South Korea. How weird that their peoples followed, then disregarded, then followed, and then again disregarded public health recommendations at precisely the same time in both places!

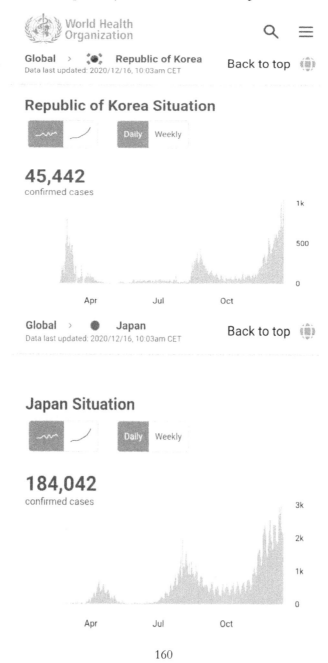

Remember being told how bad we all were for visiting people during Thanksgiving? What we see above is that there were major spikes in many countries of the world even without a Thanksgiving there, but our betters aren't letting that stop them from blaming us for a rise in hospitalizations. (The rate of growth in hospitalizations in the U.S. actually slowed after Thanksgiving, incidentally.)

Oh, and here are North and South Dakota. North Dakota imposed a bunch of occupancy restrictions to "stop the spread." South Dakota didn't.

Gee, isn't that funny — their numbers look exactly the same:

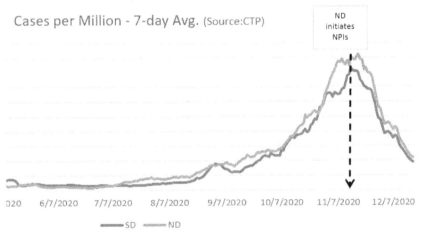

December 28, 2020 | Doctor accidentally tells truth about Covid, then pretends it never happened

Two items for you today.

First, I couldn't resist this Politico headline from last week: "Locked-down California runs out of reasons for surprising surge." After all, they've been among the most brutal, if not the most brutal, of the hard lockdown states. And yet they're claiming that their hospital system is on the verge of collapse.

And for those trying to pretend that it's noncompliant Republicans driving the surge, why did the numbers shoot up in heavily leftist San Francisco as well?

California Restaurant Association President and CEO Jot Condie said in a statement:

> Nationally, there has been a kaleidoscopic application of every imaginable type of lockdown order, with California being the most restrictive and inflicting the most devastation on small businesses and the most economically vulnerable service workers. And still, we are none the better as far as Covid is concerned....In fact in L.A., where indoor and outdoor dining are completely shut down, with indoor dining [closed] since July, the virus rages on.

Excellent point, which means California will ignore it.

Second item:

Most people reading this will be familiar with the Great Barrington Declaration, written by professors at Oxford, Harvard, and Stanford, urging a rejection of lockdowns in favor of keeping the elderly and immunocompromised safe. "Focused protection," they call it.

According to Harvard Medical School's Martin Kulldorff, this is actually the majority opinion among infectious disease epidemiologists, even though it's portrayed in the media as dangerous extremism.

And before everyone decided to throw previously existing science out the window in 2020, it seemed obvious even to those who now favor ruining people's lives.

Take, for example, Jeremy Samuel Faust, emergency medicine physician at Brigham and Women's Hospital in Boston and an instructor at Harvard Medical School. In early March, Dr. Faust wrote the following in *Slate*, if you can believe it, in an article called "Covid-19's Mortality Rate Isn't as High as We Think":

> This all suggests that Covid-19 is a relatively benign disease for most young people, and a potentially devastating one for the old and chronically ill, albeit not nearly as risky as reported. Given the low mortality rate among younger patients with coronavirus — zero in children 10 or younger among hundreds of cases in China, and 0.2–0.4 percent in most healthy nongeriatric adults (and this is still before accounting for what is likely to be a high number of undetected asymptomatic cases) — we need to divert our focus away from worrying about preventing systemic spread among healthy people — which is likely either inevitable, or

out of our control — and commit most if not all of our resources toward protecting those truly at risk of developing critical illness and even death: everyone over 70, and people who are already at higher risk from this kind of virus....

In particular, we need to focus on the right people and the right places. Nursing homes, not schools. Hospitals, not planes....

Healthy people who are hoarding food, masks, and hand sanitizer may feel like they are doing the right thing. But, all good intentions aside, these actions probably represent misdirected anxieties. When such efforts are not directly in service of protecting the right people, not only do they miss the point of everything we have learned so far, they may actually unwittingly be squandering what have suddenly become precious and limited resources.

Focused protection, in other words.

Since early March, the trend has been entirely downward in terms of the fatality rate of the virus. It is far less lethal than initially feared. And yet the panic and the willingness to abandon this initial common-sense approach has skyrocketed. You'd think it would be the opposite, but you'd be wrong.

The Central Florida Metal Fest was scheduled to take place in my area in March. At first, people on the Facebook event page scoffed at the virus. We're metal people, they said. We're not afraid of any virus!

But months later, when we learned that the virus was far *less* lethal than we first thought, *the very same people were urging everyone to stay home*, even if it meant destroying the very venues that play the niche music those people enjoy.

The less reason there is for alarm, the greater the panic. Bizarre.

January 4, 2021 | Australia succeeded thanks to lockdown? Not so fast

For those of us who have closely followed the policy response to the virus around the world, it's been obvious that something other than policy has to account for the widely varying health outcomes.

Seriously: Cambodia, which was ranked 89th in pandemic preparedness, managed to escape with zero Covid deaths? And we're supposed to believe that this is because of the amazing health and science infrastructure in…Cambodia? Come on.

On episode #1792 of the Tom Woods Show, Stanford University's Jay Bhattacharya used the helpful term "policy invariance" (which I've used a number of times so far) in connection with the situation in East Asia. Whatever policy you adopt, he said, you seem to wind up with a good result. China imposed vicious lockdowns, whereas Japan was so lax that for weeks Western headlines were screaming about an apocalypse that they just knew was going to strike — these people are not known for their humility — and of course never did.

Australia's relative success has of course been attributed to — what else? — lockdowns and the public's willingness to adhere to "public health" guidelines. In the standard narrative all results must be explainable by policy, because the story these people want to tell, as usual, is one of wise, dispassionate public servants nobly attempting to protect the people's health on the one hand, and foolish, backward American hicks who (for reasons never fully explained) mysteriously despise science on the other.

Well, here's the problem with that little morality tale: we can actually measure the mobility of the public, and therefore know how strictly people observed stay-at-home orders and instructions. And it turns out that the mobility patterns between the two countries track each other almost exactly, with the exception that Australia lagged behind the U.S. by about a week.

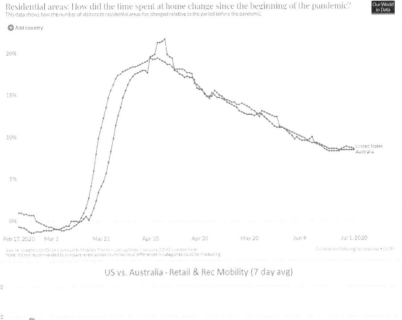

Residential areas: How did the time spent at home change since the beginning of the pandemic?
This data shows how the number of visitors to residential areas has changed relative to the period before the pandemic.

US vs. Australia - Retail & Rec Mobility (7 day avg)

[Note: in 2022, following the mass vaccination campaign, Australia suffered the greatest surge in excess deaths since World War II — but nobody who pointed to Australia's alleged success would bother to point that out.]

Back in the United States, the graphs below were generated by Johns Hopkins. First, we have South Dakota, where the numbers are coming down dramatically even though they didn't do anything:

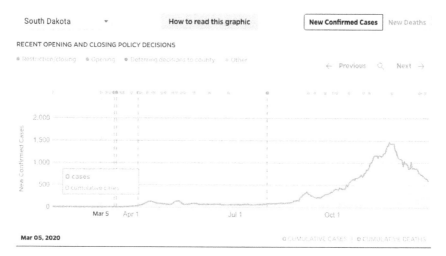

South Dakota ▾ How to read this graphic **New Confirmed Cases** New Deaths

RECENT OPENING AND CLOSING POLICY DECISIONS

Mar 05, 2020

Governor Noem and the South Dakota Department of Health commissioned an agency task force for coordination and planning with partners and other state agencies, developed an action plan for information management, incident management, and monitoring for persons at risk of infection, among other actions.

Then we have New York, where numbers remain high despite the usual government lunacy:

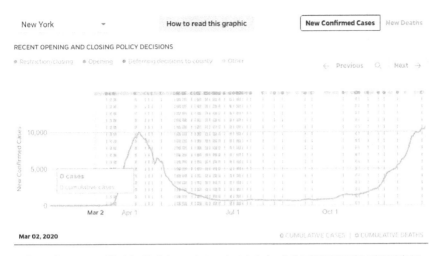

New York ▾   How to read this graphic   **New Confirmed Cases**   New Deaths

RECENT OPENING AND CLOSING POLICY DECISIONS

● Restriction/closing   ● Opening   ● Deferring decisions to county   ● Other   ← Previous   Q   Next →

Mar 02, 2020   0 CUMULATIVE CASES | 0 CUMULATIVE DEATHS

- Governor Cuomo announced the state will institute a new cleaning protocol at schools and in the public transportation system to help stop any potential spread of the virus.

- The Governor will also propose legislation to clarify authority for governor to take certain statewide actions and measures in response to the novel coronavirus outbreak as needed.

- The public health laboratory housed within the State Department of Health (DOH) is partnering with hospitals to expand surge testing capacity to 1,000 tests per day statewide for the novel coronavirus. The Wadsworth Center will provide these hospitals with instructions on how to replicate the States test, as well as help them purchase some of the equipment necessary to develop and validate the test.

- DOH is convening local health departments and hospitals statewide to review protocols, best practices and procedures to help ensure they are prepared to combat the spread of the novel coronavirus.

- Under a directive by the Governor, the State Department of Financial Services will require health insurers to waive cost sharing associated with testing for coronavirus.

Nobody in a position to ask questions of our overlords seems to think this is the least bit curious or is something they ought to inquire about.

January 8, 2021 | Researchers: people irrationally reject anti-lockdown findings

You've probably noticed a refusal on the part of some of your friends and family to acknowledge drawbacks to the lockdown strategy advocated by "public health" officials. They doubt the scientific validity of such claims, and they think you're a bad person even for offering criticisms. Irrational and bizarre, right?

Well, I don't know if this makes it better or worse, but researchers have found this to be a general phenomenon, and not confined to your crazy friends. A study conducted at New Zealand's University of Otago and published in the *Journal of Experimental Social Psychology* looked at people's readiness to overlook negative consequences of lockdown.

It's called "Moralization of Covid-19 Health Response: Asymmetry in Tolerance for Human Costs." The "asymmetry" in the title refers to people's extreme unwillingness to tolerate Covid-related suffering on the one hand, and their much-reduced concern for lockdown-related suffering on the other.

Participants were presented with two research proposal descriptions. Both proposals involved the same research and gave the same information about the methods used. Yet people described the anti-lockdown research as having less rigorous methods and relying on less accurate information, and they trusted the research team less.

Pure irrationality, in other words, from the very people who urge us to "follow the science."

The New Zealand Doctor website had this to say about the study:

> Both failing to properly contain Covid-19 and implementing restrictions to contain Covid-19 carry collateral costs. Collateral human costs that may result from failing to combat Covid-19 include increased cases, overwhelmed healthcare systems, health complications, and deaths. Prioritizing control or elimination of Covid-19 also carries collateral human costs, such as unemployment, extreme financial stress, social isolation, substance abuse, and delayed cancer diagnoses. Left unaddressed, these forces may generate "deaths of despair," whereby individuals perish from behaviors or worsened illnesses as a result of perceived bleak prospects. Other costs include public shaming of those who violate or question health-based policies, abuse of law-enforcement and government power, and deterioration of human rights.

> Lead author Dr. Maja Graso, a Senior Lecturer in Business Ethics at the University of Otago's Department of Management, says results supported the hypothesis, suggesting Covid-19 elimination efforts became moralized to an almost sacred level.

> Although moralization may be a natural response to such an imposing health threat, this process may also blind people to potential human costs resulting from a Covid-19 elimination strategy (e.g., extreme financial strain, undiagnosed illnesses). Importantly, moralization of Covid-19 may also mean that merely questioning elimination strategies is not acceptable. Indeed, this is exactly what their findings revealed.

"As a research team, we don't take a stance on whether moralizing elimination is good or bad, nor on how Covid-19 should be handled. Instead, we examine how people assess human costs, and we invite people to consider the possibility that the moralization of Covid-19 elimination may lead us to overlook other, less visible forms of suffering, such as loss of livelihoods or deaths of despair. It may also lead us to discount peer-reviewed scientific evidence that documents human costs resulting from elimination-based strategies," Dr. Graso says.

At the very time when we could most use a bit of nuance and common sense, we've instead been overwhelmed by hysterical monomania.

January 16, 2021 | The attorney who smashes Covid restrictions

In the midst of all the Covid nuttiness, something quite nice happened the other day.

In 2002, attorney Chris Ferrara and I wrote *The Great Façade*, a book about the Second Vatican Council and the craziness in the Catholic Church that followed in its wake.

Several years later, Chris and I had rather an unfortunate public falling out, and we probably went at least a dozen years without speaking to each other.

Then came 2020.

The world became so insane that we decided we had to make peace. At a time like this, people of good will need to work together. So I invited Chris onto my show this week, and the result was Tom Woods Show episode #1813.

What you hear in this episode is the first conversation Chris and I have had in over a dozen years. And I happen to think it's really darn good.

Chris has racked up several victories in the courts (in New York, New Jersey, and California) from a religious liberty angle, successfully challenging the arbitrary restrictions on houses of worship.

But as you'll hear in the discussion, Chris's opposition to the Covid regime goes well beyond that. He smashes it all to smithereens, and he's entertaining while he's doing it.

We have some laughs together, and it's like old times. Enjoy: TomWoods.com/1813

January 18, 2021 | Pretend this Covid chart doesn't exist, or get canceled

Back in May, *Vanity Fair* ran this headline: "If 80% of Americans Wore Masks, Covid-19 Infections Would Plummet, New Study Says."

Now that that didn't work out (despite mask compliance being at about 88 percent overall), the mask religionists are falling back on what they call their "Swiss cheese" model of virus mitigation. I would explain that to you, but come on. (It starts with, "We never said masks alone would do the trick!")

When you challenge the grandiose claims made for masks by pointing out the endless charts showing no discernible effect anywhere, or comparing places with masks to places without, the excuse factory shifts into high gear.

There are too many other factors at work between two given places, we're told, so it's not fair to compare their outcomes with and without masks. (Incidentally, if the situation were reversed and the charts showed deaths going down after the introduction of mask mandates, do you think we'd be getting these lectures about careful distinctions and nuance, or do you think the mask religionists would be shoving the charts in our faces?)

All right, then. Let's look at just *one* place, Arizona, and compare it *with itself*.

Given the importance attached to masks, there must surely be a clear difference, evident in the data, between Arizona counties that mandated masks and Arizona counties that didn't.

Are you ready to see that radical difference for yourself? Here it is:

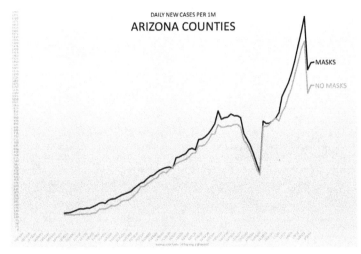

DAILY NEW CASES PER 1M
ARIZONA COUNTIES

Now nonbelievers in the mask religion, like me (and I hope you, too, dear reader) may look at this chart and say: there is no difference. But we know what happens to mask religion heretics — they're deplatformed and destroyed. So: why, yes, Mr. Science Man, sir, I sure do see the big difference masks made in Arizona!

Now I have another chart for you, this one illustrating media distortion. Iowa and New Mexico had very similar curves, separated only by time. In both places the curve went up sharply, and then came down steadily.

As the curve was going *up* in Iowa, *The Atlantic* ran the headline on the left. As the curve was coming *down* in New Mexico, *Scientific American* ran the headline on the right:

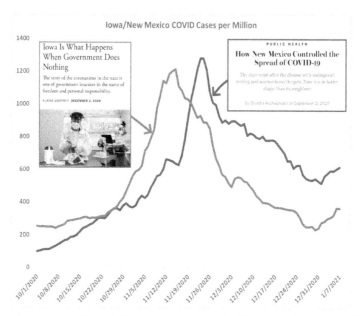

Iowa/New Mexico COVID Cases per Million

Do these seem like reliable sources to you? (The question is intended to answer itself.)

January 19, 2021 | The lockdowners tore my family apart

I just received the following from a subscriber. I told her it was worthy of sharing with my other subscribers, but that it was so personal that I wouldn't dream of doing it.

She replied: go ahead and do it. If it makes other people in my situation feel less alone, it will have done some good.

> *Dear Tom,*
>
> *I hope you do not mind me addressing you as Tom, as I feel like I have made a new friend. I discovered you when I happened upon your video "The Covid Cult." I was immediately hooked. I looked you up, signed up for your newsletter, and I listen to your podcasts. Soon after I found you, I learned that your video was taken down and I followed all of that. I, along with countless others I would imagine, agree that you keep me sane. I am my own island in my home and it can be a lonely existence.*
>
> *Like you, I live in the beautiful free state of Florida. I am a middle school teacher. My husband of almost 29 years has been completely brainwashed. When this all started back in March, I had to relearn how*

to teach remotely. My husband already did work from home, so his world hardly changed. In addition, he put restrictions on me as he was so fearful if I went out, I might bring home the virus.

Then I went back to work and life got even more crazy. He didn't want me sleeping in the same bed, wanted me to go to a hotel if I so much as started to feel a wee bit out of sorts, and it was just ridiculous.

But I digress. I have since learned not to engage in any Covid talk with him because it is useless. I have to accept his faulty perception of me. I even tried to rattle off statistics from your newsletter comparing California to Florida. It was of no use. My 24-year-old son just texted us in a group thread about Cuomo's tweet regarding the opening of New York. After he copied the tweet, he sarcastically added, "Never would have thought," with the appropriate emoji. I think it was an eyeroll.

I then responded with your exact words: "…pretty much what every sensible person has been saying…" Well, the husband didn't like that one bit. Here's his response: "Florida is averaging over 10% daily positive rate. Mease Dunedin, Mease Countryside, and Morton Plant have 2, 3, and 4 ICU beds available currently. Restaurants and bars should not be open. Completely healthy men my age [he is 58] are dying from this thing daily."

Yes, I see the bodies lying in the streets.

I should add that my husband is overweight but does nothing to rectify that. Oh, and he then asked to be removed from our family thread as he no longer wants to be a part of these texts concerning Covid anymore.

Thank goodness for my smart son. Unfortunately, my 20-year-old daughter has fallen to the other side as well. She is a student at UF, but came home to finish the year remotely because she was so afraid of catching Covid up in Gainesville. Guess what? She caught it here (did a sleepover with a friend who was infected and didn't know at the time) and spent the entire Christmas break quarantined.

She was terrified of Covid and had literally thought that she would be hospitalized. Well, she recovered and is doing just fine. Lost some smell and taste, but it is returning. Again, I cannot take the hysteria. Nor can I take her stance on Covid. It is heartbreaking. She now has formed an alliance with my husband.

I have learned over these past months to take care of myself and to live the best life I can in spite of everything. I do see friends, and I have figured out ways to do things, and go to restaurants so that my husband won't know. It's not easy but I do not feel guilty. I refuse to live a fear-based life. I am 56 and life is too short.

At the end of the day, I think it's about finding nuggets of happiness wherever and however we can. Because we have no idea of the future right now. Everything is just so weird, for lack of a better word. As a teacher, I am very concerned for our youth — my children as well as my students. I tell my students all the time that school is just about the only thing they have any control over. I say to them, "Stay in your lane! Don't throw in the towel! You can do this! Make happy happen!"

I remind them that I know how hard it is to come to school in a mask. I don't even know what my kids look like! It's horrible. Very oppressive. But I do what I can to lift their spirits. I am about that. I don't care about data or scores right now. I just care about them as humans. Because this is just a difficult time.

Your own children are so lucky that they have you to navigate as normal of a world for them right now as you can. My husband's best friend, who also keeps me sane, shares with me that his world has hardly changed. He plays golf, hangs out with his brother and their kids, and has traveled to Colombia to visit family there. He has not seen my husband since Covid because my husband refuses to see anyone, even outside from a distance. I tell him that the "science says you can," but he's still fearful. I have no words. He's had too many Cocoa Puffs.

I completely agree with you. Cultivate your own garden. Work in concentric circles. Find your happiness.

Thank you for letting me vent. I love your podcasts, I love how you write (I am an English teacher) and I love that I found you. I wish you and your family all the best.

When the phonies say, while sipping lattes from their home offices, that "we're all in this together," they aren't referring to this good woman. Nobody is "in this together" with her. She is on her own.

What the crazies have taken from us can scarcely be quantified. Stories like this woman's will not appear in official histories of these years, but if we're going to get the full picture of what happened, they need to be.

[Remember: I am giving away my book *Collateral Damage: Victims of the Lockdown Regime Tell Their Stories* for free at DiaryOfCovid.com. Please read it, because these people deserve to be heard.]

January 21, 2021 | Lockdownistan is embarrassing the lockdowners

Last week I had a couple of people angrily write to me: you're saying Florida's outcomes are better than California's! But California's deaths per capita are lower! Don't be irresponsible!

What I actually said was: *right now*, California is doing worse in terms of hospitalizations per million than Florida. And that's true. Here's what's also true: California just overtook Florida in cumulative cases per million:

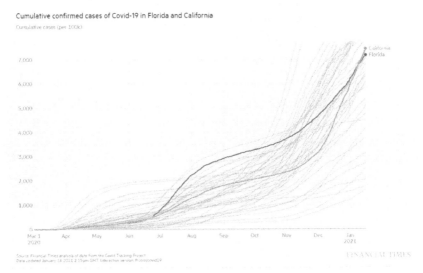

Cumulative confirmed cases of Covid-19 in Florida and California

Cumulative cases (per 100k)

Source: Financial Times analysis of data from the Covid Tracking Project
Data updated January 18 2021 2.15pm GMT. Interactive version: ft.com/covid19

FINANCIAL TIMES

Now look, I agree: "cases" are a dumb metric. But it's the metric the hysterics themselves love to use.

As a friend puts it:

> If Covidians were doing science, this would be a big deal. It would mean that their core hypothesis — that the key to good outcomes is the stringency of control measures — has yet again made a prediction that has failed. But since the glory of lockdown is a dogma known to be true a priori, not an empirical hypothesis to be tested a posteriori — we simply correct the data in light of the dogma, not the other way around.

[As you'll see at the end of this book, the difference in age-adjusted Covid mortality between California and Florida wound up being trivial, and

California actually wound up doing worse than Florida in all-cause mortality.]

So how do the hysterics deal with this? Does it make them wonder whether all this devastation has accomplished much of anything after all? Of course not. They know a priori that ruining people's lives just has to work. So generally they ignore it.

If that doesn't work, they adopt one of two strategies to avoid having to admit anything:

(1) "Florida is lying about its statistics." This is pretty rich coming from people who regularly denounce "conspiracy theorists." In fact, the Covid Tracking Project at *The Atlantic* gives Florida an A+ for its "current data completeness grade," and California only a B.

(2) "People haven't been complying." Well, I think we can take a drive through the devastated businesses of California and see whether people are complying or not. This is an idiotic line of argument: obviously there's at least *some* compliance in California, while in Florida, with no state-imposed restrictions, *there is nothing to comply with in the first place.*

Not to mention: I'd be willing to bet that a heck of a lot more tourists have been coming in and out of Florida than California over the past ten months — another advantage for California that should be showing up in their numbers. (By the way, if Californians really weren't complying, presumably there'd still be a lot of travel there — but I'm going to wager that the hospitality industry in California is completely devastated precisely because [1] nobody is visiting California right now because [2] there's nothing to do in California right now because [3] people are indeed complying.)

Notice that they absolutely cannot say: maybe these measures are just creating misery for no good reason.

January 26, 2021 | The latest peril: hugging your kids

Last week, U.K. readers found this headline in the *Evening Standard*: "Vaccinated Brits told not to hug kids amid fears millions will ignore Covid rules once they have jab."

So after the vaccine you still can't hug your children?

That's weird enough, but weirder still is:

Have people actually not been hugging their own children all this time? Was that really one of the "Covid rules"?

I could sit here and cite paper after paper that emphasizes the importance of hugging to children's mental health — honestly, I could — but is there anyone who actually needs a paper on that?

Meanwhile, Prime Minister Boris Johnson has just asked for a six-month extension of government powers to impose lockdowns and related "mitigation" measures.

Esther McVey, co-founder of the Blue Collar Conservatives caucus and a former cabinet minister, is among the resistance (an actual resistance, not the phony-baloney leftist "resistance" of the past four years in the United States), and she says the kinds of things we wish more public figures in the United States would say.

McVey insists:

> It is absolutely essential that once the most vulnerable groups have been vaccinated the government start easing the lockdowns....

> These restrictions are doing huge damage to people's livelihoods and mental health in particular, and the government must start to stand up to those siren voices who want lockdowns and restriction to become a near-permanent feature of our lives.

If the government doesn't "start making rapid headway in doing that," she warns, "it will be the duty of Parliament to remove these swingeing [severe] powers from them."

She has also accused the government of stoking fear by using exaggerated numbers.

Thus the government insisted on a mass early release of prisoners because an estimated 2,700 would die of the virus. In the event, 47 died.

McVey said:

> I appreciate that these estimates aren't an exact science, but the difference between a prediction of 2,700 to the reality of 47 is embarrassing to say the least, and shows why the government must not hand over total policy control to the scientists who are clearly not infallible with their predictions.

Conservative MP Sir Desmond Swayne demands that there be public discussion of the ending of the lockdowns and when it will occur:

> It seems to me that Boris has been completely taken over. He's completely given over to these people and as a consequence there's a complete lack of any sense of urgency on the need to lift restrictions....

> Remember, the issue was to protect the NHS, stop the NHS being overwhelmed by hospital admissions. Clearly, as we vaccinate that proportion of the population most likely to be hospitalized were they to be infected, that risk of the NHS being overwhelmed diminishes.

> They should be planning now at what stage they will lift the restrictions. At what proportion of the most vulnerable being vaccinated will the risk be acceptable?

> That's the sort of thing they ought to be taking us into their confidence [about] and debating in public now. But what we're getting is this mission creep.

January 27, 2021 | Lockdownistan just reopened — I wonder why

I guess you saw that Governor Gavin Newsom of California lifted the stay-at-home orders across the state and reopened the state.

Was that because the numbers started looking great? After all, Newsom had had all kinds of crazy tiers with metrics it seemed impossible to meet in order to allow this or that degree of opening. Yes, California seems to have passed the peak of its recent surge of deaths, but it's still far higher than it's been at any time since the whole thing began.

Naturally I favor reopening, so I'm not criticizing the governor for that part. I'm just wondering how he justifies locking the state down when the numbers were so much better, and opening it now when they're so much worse (there are 50 percent fewer ICU beds available than when the order went into effect). If the state can reopen now, then why couldn't it have done so in June, or any other time?

Of course, there is no answer.

They can't answer, remember, because you and I are too dumb to understand their advanced thinking. Just the other day the Bay Area's

KTVU tweeted: "State health officials said they rely on a very complex set of measurements that would confuse and potentially mislead the public if they were made public."

So what could have motivated this move?

I can't know for sure, but I'm rather partial to the explanatory power of this graphic:

Word is that Joe Biden is "furious" at Newsom for lifting the stay-at-home order, believing that he's doing it out of concerns about his re-election; but some wonder if this is all a bit of theater, that maybe Biden is playing along to make Newsom appear bolder for having defied the President. Who knows.

January 28, 2021 | How do the hysterics explain these Covid charts?

First, the ol' California vs. Florida issue again.

The best the excuse factory has been able to do is to pretend that Californians aren't complying with the regulations or they're not staying home. Why, they're still going to restaurants! This is supposed to be why California is doing worse than Florida at the present moment.

In fact, the evidence is the other way around. Here's a plot of restaurant visits in Florida (top line) alongside restaurant visits in California (bottom line):

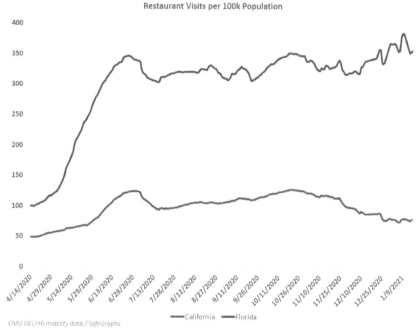

Arizona, meanwhile, has been substantially more open than California. At the very least, they've had different policies implemented at different times. Their population is older than California's, too. And yet, here are hospitalizations per million in each place:

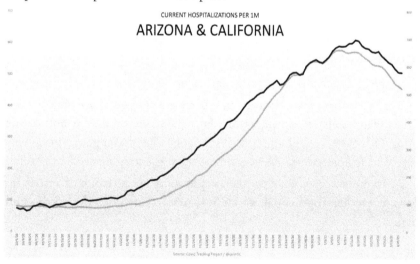

When Alabama fans gathered in huge numbers outdoors to celebrate after the college football national championship game, the hysterics were out in force: it's a "superspreader"! Look at those maskless fans! Look at those crowds in the streets!

CBS News ran an article compiling all kinds of warnings: let's check back on Alabama in a week! They were licking their chops. These stupid hicks will get what's coming to them for not listening to Dr. Fauci!

Here's what case numbers have looked like since, both in Alabama (remember when looking at the chart that the game took place January 11) and in Miami-Dade County, where the game itself took place:

Daily New Cases in Alabama

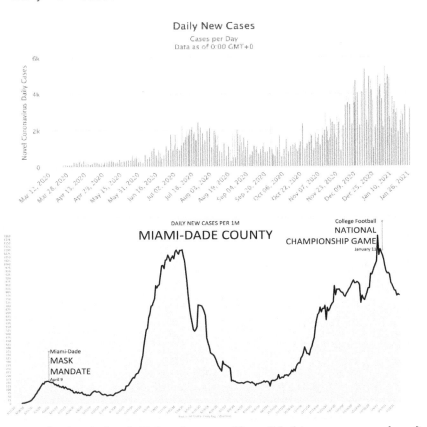

Finally, here's South Dakota's curve. How did this curve come down? These numbers are supposed to decline via human intervention. Mobility data shows people didn't voluntarily adopt stay-at-home measures, so the excuse factory can't pretend that's what did it. The curve just came down, regardless. Why? Do the hysterics even have an explanation?

New confirmed cases of Covid-19 in South Dakota

Seven-day rolling average of new cases (per 100k)

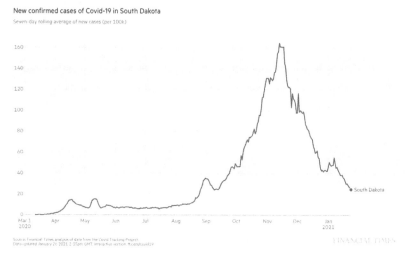

Source: Financial Times analysis of data from the Covid Tracking Project.
Data updated January 20 2021 2.05pm GMT. Interactive version: ft.com/covid19

FINANCIAL TIMES

Can we at least agree that this whole thing is a little more complicated than the propaganda would lead us to expect?

February 1, 2021 | Make the lockdowners squirm

As you know, lots of people want to make a morality play for simpletons out of the lockdowns and restrictions. Backward hicks in baseball caps refuse to "follow the science," the story goes, and if only they would, we'd be out of this.

I keep sending out examples that undermine this story.

Just today, I came across a fellow on Twitter who, unable to explain Florida's result, described it as "very average," adding: "I think we have to assume some noise and/or non-policy factors (e.g., FL being warmer and better suited to outdoor dining)."

My response to him:

> California, with one of the country's youngest populations, is also "warm," and its numbers on hospitalizations, deaths, etc., are worse right now than at any time in Florida, and the overall death rate is only trivially different, with the age of their populations explaining that differential entirely.

Then, in another Tweet, I added:

Even if the results were "very average," isn't it astonishing that the state with the fifth-oldest population would have achieved even average results? Our results should be absolutely catastrophic, not "very average." People are going to theaters, concerts, etc., here. How?

In fact, when Florida reopened, the hysterics screamed about what they were sure was about to happen. I assure you, they weren't warning us: "If you reopen, your results will be *very average!*"

Now for some graphics.

The first one involves the comparison no lockdowner wants to deal with, as the pathetic response of the critic above makes clear. (He's reduced to saying that Florida — which has no state-imposed restrictions — has had only average results, when you know darn well people like him were predicting outright catastrophe, not average results.)

So here it is: Los Angeles, where life has been canceled for close to a year, compared to Florida, where I have tickets to three concerts over the next two months:

One more.

Your next-door neighbor thinks it's lack of compliance that explains differences in Covid results. When you compare one state with another, your neighbor either changes the subject or tries to pretend that there are too many factors at stake to compare one state with another.

All right, then how about we just stick to one state?

California counties have implemented different policies at different times, yet their ICU usage numbers seem exactly the same — almost as if Covid doesn't care what we do. How odd!

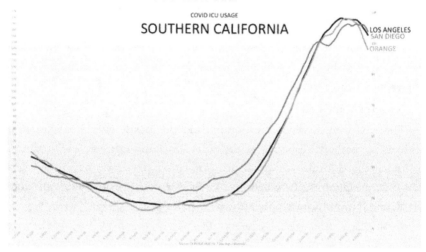

February 2, 2021 | How many masks, Dr. Fauci?

My old friend Tom Elliott, who produced the *Peter Schiff Show* back when it was on terrestrial radio, recently summarized Dr. Fauci's instructions on masks:

— Don't wear them

— JK, definitely wear them

— Actually wear two

— NM, wear one

— On 2nd thought, two

I got a haircut yesterday and the subject of two masks came up. Both people working there couldn't believe how ridiculous that sounded. "You'd barely be able to breathe!" one of them said.

It encourages me when I run into random people with sensible thoughts.

Meanwhile, Dr. Michael Osterholm, who's on the Biden Covid team, warns that two masks could be harmful. As he said on *Meet the Press*:

> If you add on another mask, you may actually make it tougher
> for the air to move through the two-cloth area, and then at

that point it causes more air to actually leak around the sides, which actually enhances your ability to get infected.

Now, for another chart. Remember the Christmas surge we were warned about, because of stupidheads who refused to "listen to the science"? This is a chart of 15 states, with different policies, and amounting to some 80 million people.

What do we note about them? Despite these different policies, they all peaked and declined at the same time, and despite the Fauci warning of a Christmas surge, they all peaked weeks before Christmas in each case:

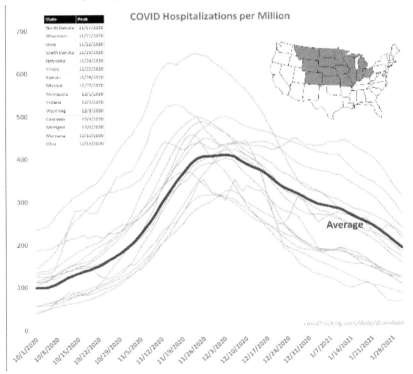

All year long I've been showing charts like this, demanding answers from the hysterics. If you've been sucked into supporting lockdowns, and you think living like a vegetable has been the right thing to do, you've been had. I don't know what else to tell you.

February 4, 2021 | The evil store with no masks, shamed by Shep Smith

Yesterday Shepard Smith shared a "shocking" (his word) video of a store in Naples, Florida, where people weren't wearing masks. As a Florida resident, I can attest to how unusual that store is — contrary to the implication in the story, masks are in fact everywhere here.

But of course the hysteria about this store has been off the charts.

So Ian Miller decided to plot the county where that Florida store was located against a California county that had one of the country's first mask mandates. You'll never guess what he found:

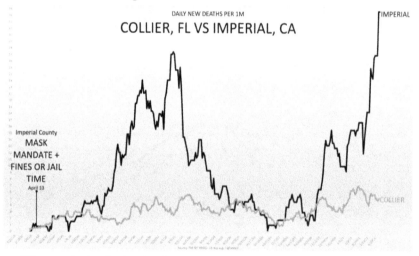

I'd say *that's* what's shocking, and *that's* what Shep should be talking about.

You may say this next chart isn't fair — after all, the two places are different:

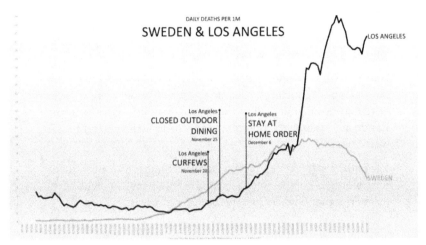

DAILY DEATHS PER 1M
SWEDEN & LOS ANGELES

LOS ANGELES

Los Angeles
CLOSED OUTDOOR DINING
November 25

Los Angeles
STAY AT HOME ORDER
December 6

Los Angeles
CURFEWS
November 20

SWEDEN

But if these alleged mitigation measures are really so crucial, and if the results would be genuinely catastrophic without them, *shouldn't there be a clear and unmistakable difference* between Los Angeles and Sweden, in favor of the former?

February 5, 2021 | I caught a glimpse of the Old Normal

I share a lot of data and charts with you, but data and charts can convey only so much about the inhuman regime of the past year — and the zombies who think living this way is not only acceptable, but even morally superior.

So I want to share a portion of a Tweet thread I just came across from a woman named Emily Burns, who just visited Florida from Massachusetts:

> Last weekend I escaped to Florida from Massachusetts, the fascist hellhole I am cursed to call home. Everything you have heard is true. They have real people there, not the zombies that people the blue wastelands. People smile, they laugh, they acknowledge you. Join me.
>
> I was in Miami, where there is a mask mandate which is mercifully unenforceable. On the boardwalk, 75% of people were unmasked. In town 50% of people on the sidewalks were unmasked. Miami has lower activity than much of the state, at 60% of normal.
>
> It was enough for a humanity-starved soul like me.

187

The restaurants were packed, no plexiglass in sight, and only those catering to the most affluent (and hence "liberal") appeared to have any reduced capacity at all.

But the bars. Inside, outside, it didn't matter. People were alive. Covid-"courtesy" was forgotten. People forgot your potential contagion and pushed past you to order a drink. Random strangers butted into your conversations. It was…normal.

I found myself excited by the smallest things: water fountains that worked, people who stopped to help me up without a moment's pause when I tripped on my 5" heels.

One of the things that struck me more than anything was resident Miamians' ability to do something as normal as being catty. I was so bemused talking to a woman who was complaining about how fake people there were.…

It made me realize the social riches we used to enjoy, and that they still enjoy. The ability not just to be around people, but to be exposed to such a surfeit of humanity that you might have the luxury of choosing with whom you wanted to associate, or not.

She talked about how nice it was to be around someone "normal." I told her I felt the same way…and didn't mention that now I was just happy to be around anyone at all.

It's probably worth noting that the world is truly a bizarre place when you go to Miami in search of "normal," or take comfort in being called "normal" by someone from Miami. But this is where we are, a world where Florida is a shining ray of hope for humanity.

I know that sounds snarky, but it's not meant to. What most people don't know was that one of the chief goals of the Enlightenment was to move people away from the bloody "higher" pursuits of glory (war) and "improvement of humanity" (evangelism, usually coupled with war).

And towards the more pedestrian (and much less bloody) focus of their selves, and simply tending to their own garden (re: Candide), their own happiness and family — their own "petty" concerns. Those Enlightenment peeps, they were on to something. And Florida is a perfect example.

All right, enough with Voltaire et al.; back to the topic. Our new friends, she from Romania, he from Argentina, invited us to an Asado the next time we came down. Naturally, our flights are already booked, and I am looking forward to the chimichurri.

Some people will now be spluttering, "That's why things are so bad in Florida!!" The data tell a different story. With our universal outdoor mask mandate (in Massachusetts) enforced by the social distance Stasi and mask mafia, we perform WORSE on every single metric.

And then she moves into the data, of a kind I review here on a daily basis.

Yes, the data is important. But mainly because it shows us, as she notes in her thread, that we have given up precious and nonnegotiable things…for nothing.

Now to be sure, writing to you every day is the right thing to do. But when I held a supporters' event at my house last year, that was worth all the newsletter issues in the world to the people who attended. The sign that greeted people on my name tag table read, "Welcome to the Old Normal."

February 8, 2021 | Another Covid surge that wasn't: watch a journalist cover her tracks

You know how it works by now:

According to our opinion molders, any movements in the Covid numbers are a reflection of the compliance, or otherwise, of the public with the state's so-called mitigation measures.

Now if we had any actual journalists, some of them would observe the absurdity of all this. After all, societies with little in common and remote from each other have seen exactly the same curves; we're supposed to believe that this is because their peoples all complied, and then didn't comply, and then complied again, on exactly the same timetable?

Can people be this thick?

Thus Elaine Godfrey at *The Atlantic* just wrote, "In November I wrote a story about how Covid-19 was overwhelming Iowa's hospitals. Back then, public-health experts predicted another big surge after the holidays, but it never came. I went back to those experts to find out why."

She went back to *those* "experts" to find out why.

She'd better follow up with these people who were totally wrong, ask them why they were totally wrong, and then uncritically repeat their answers to her audience!

Now of course, she could have consulted people who have been right, and who have been critical of the public-health apparatus, to see if maybe these folks have some insight into why the always-wrong people were wrong yet again, but that would be journalism, and that is not Elaine Godfrey's field.

Instead she wrote a follow-up article called, "Iowans Were Scared into Taking the Virus Seriously."

Yes, this is the best she can do: public-health officials did such a good job panicking everyone about a "surge" that they persuaded people to change their behavior!

Know what the trouble with this is?

Iowan public-health officials must have been so effective at scaring people that the scariness spread into North Dakota, South Dakota, Nebraska, Minnesota, Missouri, Illinois, Montana, Wyoming, Colorado, and Kansas, too, *which had identical curves and declines in their numbers with no change in public-health messaging and no change in the public's behavior.*

Oops!

They also try to claim that Iowa's November mask mandate brought the numbers down, but again: why the simultaneous declines in so many other places?

Not to mention: you've seen the charts I've shared. In country after country and state after state we got "masks flattened the curve!" in the first half of 2020, and then in the fall, with mask compliance higher than ever and the numbers worse than before…total silence.

They can't possibly admit that none of it worked, that our feeble interventions seem to do nothing to prevent people from becoming ill. They can't admit that they depleted people's savings, caused millions of avoidable deaths, and ruined people's lives, for nothing.

So it always has to be: the numbers came down because of our wise policies.

When the numbers skyrocket with those same policies still in effect or even increased in severity, that's supposed to be the fault of the vanishingly small percentage of noncompliant folks.

Meanwhile, California's death numbers (118 per 100,000) are approaching Florida's (129 per 100,000), even though California has one of the country's youngest populations and Florida one of the oldest (and therefore Florida's numbers should be *vastly* worse, not trivially worse). Not to mention: Florida has been open with no state-imposed capacity restrictions since September, and was mostly open before that.

How is this possible, if the cartoon version of events is correct?

Human happiness is not an optional extra. Our lives should not be at the mercy of governments operating from bogus science, to be turned on and off at whim.

February 10, 2021 | The teensy-weensy thing they left out of their study

In March of last year I didn't know what to think about Covid, but like many people I was concerned.

I had tickets to a concert on March 17. Should I go? (The band made that decision for me by postponing.)

I read what I could, and waited to see what would happen. The key thing that changed my mind? The doggone graphs. From what I can see, we are depriving ourselves of what it means to be human — not to mention impoverishing people and decimating the developing world — for nothing.

I understand why people would think that the various mitigation measures imposed on us make sense and must do some good. But for whatever reason, they don't. I've been sending you example after example that are impossible to explain if these measures did much good.

I just read yesterday about Los Angeles officials in October and November blaming Lakers and Dodgers fans for the spike there. Here's the problem: San Diego's numbers have followed the same trajectory. We can be quite certain that San Diego wasn't celebrating for Los Angeles teams — San Diego folks aren't exactly known for being Dodgers fans, to put it gently.

But another thing that's kept me a skeptic is the poor quality of the research that is supposed to refute me.

Here's the latest: a mask study by the CDC. It is supposed to show that masks have a significant effect. Except: the study stopped in October. Notice the tiny, almost imperceptible trend (yes, that's sarcasm) that occurred after October:

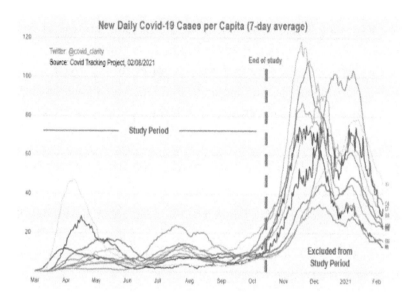

When you're told to listen to the research, remember the image above. That is "the research."

February 11, 2021 | What the path to normality will involve

Sometimes I like to share with you some of the correspondence I receive (names withheld if the authors prefer, of course).

This time I'm sharing a story from someone who's completely ordinary — in the sense that the lockdowns haven't destroyed this person's business or impoverished him or caused him to miss urgent surgery.

The point of sharing this is: there's plenty of suffering out there even for those not enduring outright catastrophe.

My correspondent writes:

Thanks for all you've been doing this past year to combat the narrative of fear surrounding Covid. Count me among those who have found your podcast, emails and videos to be helpful in maintaining my sanity.

I have a wife and four young children and we live in Ohio. If you compare our experience this past year to those of people suffering under more brutal lockdown regimes, we probably got off fairly easy. We already home-schooled, my job was considered "essential" so I never missed work and Ohio's actual lockdown was relatively brief. Unfortunately there's more to the madness than just the hardcore lockdowns.

My wife is one of the people who have an actual medical condition that makes it very difficult for her to wear a mask. So every trip to the grocery, every outing that requires going indoors, garners looks of derision and sometimes minor conflict with a mask "Karen." It has added such stress that she has been battling depression most of the year.

Additionally, we've seen things our kids love get closed and canceled. The dance studio they were part of last spring had to permanently close due to the lockdown. By chance, all of our kids have March birthdays, so we had a big birthday party planned for last March, but the week of the party Governor DeWine kicked off the lockdown. It was heartbreaking to them to have that taken away.

There have been many other issues that have popped up throughout the year: family conflicts over the virus, increased property taxes and school taxes (particularly infuriating since we home-school, and the #$%^ schools were closed at the time!), we even lost our church since they closed down and have been very strict on mask enforcement after reopening.

Those things, plus the low-level, constant shame/humiliation I feel wearing a mask at work every day have led us to consider moving to Florida. While exchanging one political jurisdiction with another obviously isn't a panacea, I am at the point where I have to do something. To that end, we have a trip planned to the Panhandle in early March to vacation and explore, with the intent of getting a feel for whether we want to make a permanent move. But now, it sounds like the Biden administration is threatening to cut off domestic travel to Florida to score a petty political point. It will devastate my kids if we are not able to make our trip next month.

So, I guess my point with all of this is to say that these mandates hurt people, even those who may seem to have it "easy." But more importantly to say "thank you," and to add my voice to those whom you've helped make it through the last year. Keep fighting the good fight!

Whatever the path forward is, it seems that it has to involve rational people identifying each other, interacting with each other, helping each other, and building normality again together.

February 16, 2021 | Can you be friends with a Covid Doomer?

Some people want to live in a completely politicized world, in which the very brand of ketchup you use makes a political statement.

This holds zero appeal for me, or any normal person.

Politics pits people against each other in a zero-sum game. The less it intrudes in our lives, the better.

But we all know people who, if you hold opinions that haven't been approved by the *New York Times*, will certainly shun you.

This seems sick and deranged to me.

And yet:

After nearly a year of Covid hysteria that has involved obviously voodoo science and sacrificing so much of what it means to be human (and as Florida would seem to demonstrate, there was no need to do this), I seriously wonder: can I really be friends with people who cheered this on?

James Delingpole, the British writer who was my guest for Tom Woods Show episode #1834, says he certainly can't. And frankly, I think he's right.

If you had a friend who destroyed your business, canceled a year of your children's lives, and deprived you of things that brought you joy, would you keep that person as a friend?

You may say: this is different. They thought they were helping.

But for heaven's sake, the evidence is everywhere, if anyone has the least curiosity to investigate, that none of this wound up doing a bit of good. We can modify the example: you have a friend who would do these things to you while thinking he's helping people, but without bothering to look beyond a few headlines he saw in the *Washington Post*.

Still bad.

Yes, I'll be polite to the old high school friends who still show up in my social media timelines. But stay the hell away from me.

I'm genuinely sorry that it's come to this. On some things we can be friends with people who disagree with us. But at this stage of my life I for one am making a deliberate effort to seek out the company of people who opposed stealing a nontrivial chunk of my life from me.

February 17, 2021 | So, you want to live despite Covid?

Yesterday's newsletter generated more feedback than anything I've written in a long time.

As you'll recall, in that issue I wondered, with the U.K.'s James Delingpole, whether it was possible to be friends with people who promote the Covid hysteria, and everything that comes with that: stealing a year of your kids' lives, destroying your business, and robbing you of things that bring you joy.

If you had a friend who did those things to you, would you remain friends?

I am so angry at the destruction wrought by this one-dimensional thinking, and the absolute indifference to the avalanche of contrary data, that I'm going out of my way these days to associate with people whose first instinct wasn't destruction and blind trust of authority.

And as I noted, I was wondering aloud about this even though I can't stand people who insist on politicizing all of life. They have to use this deodorant and that brand of mustard because of the political stances of the companies involved. And they can't be friends with people who disagree with them. I don't want to be like that.

I got some pushback, to be sure, and that's fine. I'm not infallible, and I'm very open to other perspectives on this. And in some ways it's more difficult than I made it sound: I myself have a college friend in medicine with otherwise excellent judgment who went for all this, though at least she recognized tradeoffs from the start and thought we should do everything possible to mitigate any collateral damage.

Still, I got a massive response from people with whom my misgivings resonated. Here's a sample:

> *This note hits home as I'm in the same boat. It's not just the Covid craziness or Trump hatred or contempt for the Trumpsters that has me on the ropes. It's the lack of grace, the righteousness, the indifference to the fact that we're all human and all struggling. I'm looking for a type of connection that's not present in my friendships, and that's very sad. The hypocrisy and virtue signaling are just symptoms. And since I come*

from the same part of the briar patch, ultra-Progressiveville, it's left me wondering: why have I changed and they haven't?

Meanwhile, as we endure the Biden Administration's looniness, the U.K. has it far worse: they've announced that lockdown will continue until cases fall to under 1,000 per day.

What that actually means:

Lockdown will not be lifted until the positivity rate falls to one-quarter of the *false positive rate* seen in the summer of 2020.

This is inhuman.

As I noted in my episode with James, in the beginning we got some acknowledgment, at least, that we were making a significant sacrifice. For 15 days we need you to drop everything and stay home. We realize we've never asked something like this of you before, but it will make a big difference.

Now it's: yeah, your life is shut down for at least five more months; we'll get back to you.

On social media yesterday I wrote: "We need a clearinghouse where normal people who defy the Covid stupidity and who seek goods and services that normal people enjoy can find other normal people who provide them, so we can help each other survive and thrive."

Yes, that could mean that the crazies won't buy from you (though it may not; they may never even find out), but the crazies are staying home anyway, and at this point you may as well go all-out to appeal to the folks who want to live — your natural market in 2021.

February 18, 2021 | Doomer chokes on national TV

Well, a member of the mainstream media — on MSNBC, no less — finally, after months and months, asked The Question. Her guest: Doomer and White House Covid adviser Andy Slavitt.

She asked him: "Contrast states like Florida and California, California basically in lockdown and their numbers aren't that different from Florida."

Slavitt proceeded to do everything but answer the question.

Before I get to his answer, let me say this: I'll bet there are some people on our side who wonder if the experts may after all have a good explanation for things like the California/Florida comparison, or why

Covid curves come sharply down in some places despite no changes in behavior, etc. As this clip with Slavitt demonstrates, they are indeed clueless. But since nobody ever asks them a tough question, the full extent of that cluelessness is seldom on full display.

Now on to Slavitt. He begins with this: "Look, there's so much of this virus that we think we understand, that we think we can predict, that's just a little bit beyond our explanation."

This is all I've been asking them to say for the past year. Admit that they don't fully understand it, and that it doesn't behave the way their mitigation guidance seems to suggest it does. Finally someone admits it.

And then, on to the evasion of the question:

> What we do know is that the more careful people are, the more they mask and social distance, and the quicker we vaccinate, the quicker it goes away and the less it spreads, but we have got to get better visibility into variants, we don't know what role they play, large events, etc. As we all have learned by this time, this is a virus that continues to surprise us. It's very hard to predict. And all around the country, we've got to continue to do a better job, and I think we are, but we're not done yet.

That's it. That's all he has to say.

Sorry we decimated your savings, took away your sources of joy, destroyed your business, and stole a year of your children's lives. We're just learning, you see.

And we "know," says Slavitt, that the more people "mask and social distance," the "quicker it goes away and the less it spreads." In fact, we "know" no such thing. Graph the results any way you like: lockdown stringency, people's mobility patterns, mask mandate dates, whatever. The results are completely random. They absolutely do not show a clear pattern whereby ruining your life solves the problem. Not to mention: the very California/Florida comparison the anchor is asking him about clearly contradicts this claim, but Slavitt just repeats it robotically anyway.

Slavitt also mentions "large events," of which there have been precious few in California over the past year. But there have been a ton in Florida, where I live. Shouldn't our state be marked by piles of corpses at the side of the road, and California be a paradise — especially since our state has a much higher elderly population?

Andy, you realize there's a camera on you and we're all seeing your responses, right?

Slavitt doesn't know what the explanation is for California and Florida, but he urges you to keep staying poor and socially isolated anyway.

February 22, 2021 | That awful superspreading Super Bowl

It's been the magical "two weeks" (of "wait two weeks" fame) since the Super Bowl.

This was supposed to be a "superspreader" event, or a series of mini-superspreaders (as Dr. Fauci put it) in the country as a whole, because of people's Super Bowl parties.

Here is the chart, taken from Worldometers. Decide for yourself whether the numbers appear to be going up or down over the past two weeks.

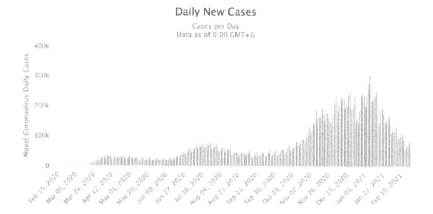

Daily Deaths

Deaths per Day
Data as of 0:00 GMT+8

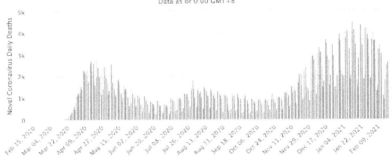

Why were the so-called experts wrong yet again?

Remember the admission — which I will never tire of quoting — from White House Covid adviser Andy Slavitt, who, when faced with a comparison between locked-down California (with its young population) and open Florida (with its older, much more vulnerable population), was reduced to saying, "There's so much of this virus that we think we understand, that we think we can predict, that's just a little bit beyond our explanation."

You don't say.

Now, let me draw again from the ol' mailbag. Folks are still responding to my note about the difficulties of staying on good terms with people who have bought into the panic and have thought nothing of ruining your life to allay their own misplaced fears.

Here's one of the many responses I received:

I find myself generally able to be friends with people who hold a variety of beliefs and options (as long as they are kind people). I have always enjoyed discussions and debates and learning from others.

But what I have noticed with "friends" who are on Team Hysteria is I don't want to be close friends with most of them anymore. I wish them well but I feel like the clinging to lockdowns and safety, the inability to look at data and discuss, the wishing of harm to people who "aren't being safe" or "aren't doing it right" (i.e., Florida) is insane and hateful to me. The shaming and the blaming. The divisiveness. All of it is just not something I want in my circle.

I was talking with a friend who lives about an hour from me. (We live in downtown Chicago and she lives in the burbs.) My husband and I were going to dinner and a movie. And she was going to a friend's home where four ladies were going to sit in the garage, in the four corners, with a space heater in the middle and bring their own food and drink...to be "safe" (mind you, it is also single-digit temps outside). She thought I was crazy. I thought she was crazy. I don't know if she is "my people" anymore. Maybe I am not "her people"?

I just don't know how some people are going to survive psychologically from all of this.

February 25, 2021 | Brutal smackdown

Journalist Brett Kelman just walked into a buzzsaw.

Promoting his latest article on Twitter, he began: "As Covid-19 swept the American South over the past 12 months, our uninformed and selfish choices worsened the pandemic in every way. We paid the price in lives."

In other words, the usual line: you stupid rubes wouldn't listen to your "public health" experts, so the deaths are all your fault.

Well, Ian Miller, who compiles so many of the charts I share with you, happened to see this.

The result was a brutal, bloody beatdown.

Ian began: "Hey Brett, wondering if you can explain this to me…if behavior and rules are so important, why do all of these curves look the same?"

Ol' Brett came back with: "Short answer? Because the behavior was largely the same. My story covers 4 of these states, and in those states residents generally followed the same gathering patterns, resulting in similar infection curves."

Ian wasn't about to let him get away with that.

"You think people in South Carolina and Louisiana behaved the same way? Despite totally different rules and mandates? That's the explanation?

"How about Kansas and Illinois and West Virginia, same behavior there, too?"

Ian keeps going.

"Nevada opened the largest casinos and hotels in the world last spring while California's been one of the most closed states in the country since March. So we know the behavior's been different there. What happened?"

Ian won't stop.

"Southern California counties have all had different rules at different times with wildly varying levels of compliance. Didn't matter here either. Ever thought that maybe behavior is an excuse used by politicians to explain why their policies aren't working?"

Kelman responded:

"Have I thought about it? Yes. I would like to look more at these charts you are posting, but not as Twitter screenshots. Mind sharing your source for these images?"

Ian proceeds to do so (they're listed at the bottom of each chart), with most of the data coming from the CovidTracking.com site.

Kelman thanks him, and the exchange ends.

It is virtually certain that Kelman had never seen any of this. He had bought the "it's your fault" argument hook, line, and sinker.

The example of Arizona, Nevada, and California is especially important, because the *Los Angeles Times* and the government of California are trying to take the credit for the decline in cases. But Arizona and Nevada didn't have such extreme lockdowns, and their curves are about the same.

If we had actual journalists, our "public health officials" (I cannot use that phrase except inside mocking quotation marks) would be mercilessly interrogated about all this on a daily basis.

What we have instead are curious, honest citizens like Ian Miller who report the truths we should be reading in the news.

February 27, 2021 | Student writes: my world has become a Covid prison

I received this email from a young person the other day, and all I can say is: I cannot understand how we've allowed the deranged lunatics who are doing this to him to claim the moral high ground.

This isn't pleasant to read, but as you'll discover, it needs to be read:

> *I am a college student at a major U.S. university pursuing a degree in STEM. A few years ago I was diagnosed with a very mild form of schizophrenia. I am considered extremely high functioning. I have friends, do well in school, and I am able to hold a part-time job where I get along with everyone.*

> *Ever since the lockdowns began, our school has treated us in a manner that can only be described as abusive. Our online education has essentially meant that we have to teach ourselves, because our instructors won't. The workload for every single class for everyone I know doubled as soon as we got sent home, since every instructor believes we have all the time in the world now. Homework and exams have been made more difficult in an absurd attempt to prevent "cheating." (This is their own explanation.) They have given us no resources to work with, and instructors treat us in an almost combative manner.*

> *I am a hard worker, but I can't do this anymore. Last semester, I was working for about 16 hours every day, seven days a week, with no outside assistance outside of our halfhearted lecture videos. Near the end,*

I had five weeks in a row where I worked for 48 hours straight with no sleep to try and make deadlines I couldn't even hit. A friend of mine was falsely accused of an academic integrity violation, given virtually no chance to appeal, and is now on probation for the remainder of his time here.

Our families are paying a fortune for us to teach ourselves through YouTube.

Walking onto campus feels like going to a wake. There is a morose atmosphere in the air, and everywhere is as quiet as a library. There is absolutely no social interaction except amongst friends who already know each other. There are volunteer students who act as the school's Stasi to enforce Covid guidelines.

I myself am reduced to a broken mess. I feel like I have nothing. All my friends are depressed from stress and work. My family cares for me but doesn't know how to console me. The doctors just want to experiment with a cocktail of medications that have every side effect imaginable, and they aren't even confident it would help me. I have nobody anymore.

I have always appreciated the work you and others have done to help advance the cause of liberty. I know you were aware of how much of a racket higher education was before all this madness began, but now it feels like a hostage situation. I can't think of ever starting a family now if my child would have to go through this just to do decently well in life. I needed to write this so I could know that someone out there understands what they are doing to us.

I can't stress how bad it is, sir. There are freshmen killing themselves here. My mental health can't take this. I feel like my youth has been stolen from me, and turned against me. Life doesn't feel worth living anymore.

Please never stop fighting against this. This is a horrific institution run by genuinely evil people. The people at these universities are more soulless than anyone in office. People like you are all we have left.

March 1, 2021 | What the lockdowners really think about you

Well, the mask slipped (so to speak) a bit over the weekend.

The World Economic Forum (WEF) published — then clumsily retracted — a Tweet claiming that lockdowns were "quietly improving cities around the world." It included a one-minute video.

What did we learn in this video? You'll never guess: lockdowns made cities a lot quieter. Gee, you don't say!

That silence is music to the ears of the mankind-hating lizard people who evidently run the WEF.

So we learned about how much less ambient noise there was during the lockdowns. This was great, we were told, because it allowed scientists to detect earthquakes somewhat more accurately.

These are not normal people.

Also, pollution came down a little bit.

But now things are returning to normal. And we'd better watch ourselves because…climate change.

The video ended by asking, "How quiet was your local area?"

The lizard people were evidently expecting us to say, "You know, doggone it, things sure were quiet around here! It was wonderful not hearing children playing, or live music coming from clubs and restaurants, or the hustle and bustle of a living city! How refreshing it was to experience a city with all the life and heart sucked out of it!"

Since that's not the way normal people look at the situation, what the WEF got instead was a reaction so hostile that they had to withdraw the Tweet.

But very reluctantly. They loathe us rubes.

"We're deleting this tweet," they wrote. "Lockdowns aren't 'quietly improving cities' around the world. But they are an important part of the public health response to Covid-19."

But even this retreat is all wrong.

A.J. Kay (@AJKayWriter), who's been excellent on the virus, responded like this:

> If by "important" you mean:
>
> *authoritarian*
> *grossly disproportionate*
> *deadly*
> *anti-public health*
> *power abusive*
> *lucrative*
> *poverty-inducing…*

then you nailed it.

March 2, 2021 | How will the excuse-makers defend this?

Someone introduced himself to my private group, the Tom Woods Show Elite, this week with the following:

> *Last year my daughter Abigail was born a few days before the lockdowns started in Massachusetts. She was diagnosed with an incredibly rare genetic disorder called CHARGE Syndrome (a little less than 1 in 100,000), which has a 40% survival rate. Once the lockdowns kicked in it was literally illegal for me and my wife to see or be by our preemie daughter, who was convulsing in painful, uncontrollable spasms for months, and on the brink of death.*
>
> *Eventually the lockdowns "relaxed" so one of us could visit our daughter once daily for a generous two hours. I cannot put into words how traumatic it is to have a daily conversation with your wife about who gets to spend the potentially last day ever with your baby girl. Thankfully she survived after multiple surgeries, but is blind (compared to death that is a blessing). However, developmental services for special needs children in Massachusetts have been deemed a "nonessential service."*
>
> *We have been lucky to have secured some in-person OT visits with our daughter, but it has been criminally illegal in our state to have critical in-person visits with developmental specialists to help our daughter overcome challenges associated with her disabilities. She is months behind and will face permanent developmental delays because of the lockdowns set forth by our lovely Republican governor.*
>
> *I joined this legendary group to share my personal Covid tragedy, which is unfortunately one of millions, to a sympathetic group of like-minded individuals. I'm finishing up my public health PhD at [X University], and am a political science professor at a state school up in Massachusetts, so I'm sure you can imagine how I'm surrounded by Covid Doomers 24/7. Tom Woods literally gave me the strength to look death straight in the eye last year and overcome it, so I will be forever grateful.*

This is indeed a tragedy, albeit one that could have been even worse.

The Covid monomania has had the effect of erasing these tragedies from the public's attention. All that matters is Covid.

And there are lesser tragedies, too. Kids prevented from socializing. Widespread impoverishment. Neighbors pitted against neighbors.

Businesses that people poured their lives into, destroyed. Depression, alcoholism and drug abuse, and suicide, all up. And make no mistake: everyone knows it.

And if you say *my life has been devastated by all this*, you will be shamed. You must want people to die because you're capable of thinking about tradeoffs and aren't consumed by monomania.

The whole social shaming thing is taking place at a fifth-grade level. It should embarrass the people doing it, but they seem incapable of embarrassment.

And to think these people have the nerve to tell us we're in this together.

I'll tell you who's in it together: the rational people who have been shamed by superstitious and terrified fools, and who have had their lives turned upside down, and even ruined, for no good reason.

[Remember: I am giving away my book *Collateral Damage: Victims of the Lockdown Regime Tell Their Stories* for free at DiaryOfCovid.com. Please read it, because these people deserve to be heard.]

March 3, 2021 | I defied the restrictions in Lockdownistan

Last night I did something human.

I spoke at a speakeasy event in Southern California. No pointless and dehumanizing masks, no inhuman "six feet apart" signs, no cowering in our homes.

We weren't allowed to hold an event like this. We held it anyway.

Hundreds of people thanked me as I'd never been thanked before. Finally, they said, we can feel human again.

Here's a recording of what I said there: TomWoods.com/1849

Meanwhile, our friend Ian Miller (@ianmSC) just released these charts about Montana, with this commentary:

> It's remarkable to me that people can look at a chart like this and think "yes, masks are an effective intervention." Cases went up 1,446% after Montana's mask mandate on 7/15....Now it's been 2.5 weeks since they lifted the mandate and cases are down -35.2%. I just don't get it.

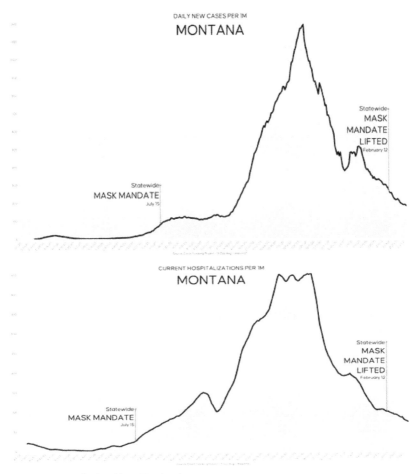

(Source: Covid Tracking Project)

Honestly: if you hadn't been propagandized into believing that masks play an important role in all this, would you seriously look at those charts and say, "Thank goodness for masks"? Nobody would. And yet everyone repeats the obligatory paeans to masks.

Here's a chart from Colorado. As one commentator put it, the people claiming that "it would have been worse without masks" are moving the goalposts. They used to cheer masks for preventing spikes like the one in the chart. Then we get a spike anyway, and instead of admitting they were wrong, they suddenly retreat to the unfalsifiable "it would have been worse" b.s.

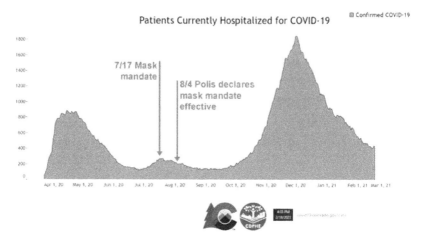

(Source: Covid19.Colorado.gov/data)

And now, daily deaths. The quotation in the chart below is from Eric Feigl-Ding, the nutritionist who has managed to pass himself off as an infectious disease expert and who has done nothing but spread fear and panic from the very beginning. He took an indirect swipe at the U.S. early on by claiming that the Czechs had "basically conquered Covid" after two months of mask wearing. Did he ever retract this? Need I even ask the question?

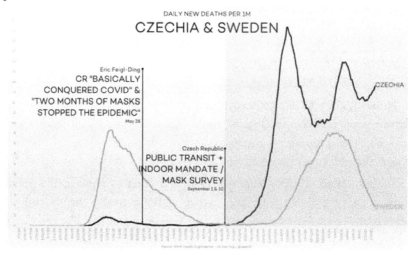

(Source: World Health Organization)

March 4, 2021 | The lockdowns are crumbling, and the hysterics are melting down

I presume you've heard the news: Texas and Mississippi are opening up fully.

Before that, the University of Alabama announced it would resume its normal academic practice and schedule in the fall, and return to full stadiums.

People who can't read charts are screaming about this. *Vanity Fair* says, "Texas and Mississippi are apparently duking it out to see who can kill more people with Covid-19."

Remember when the *Washington Post* said in April 2020 that Georgia was angling to become "America's number-one death destination"? It never came close. Did that make the hysterics curious, or cause them to stop saying idiotic things like this? You know the answer.

On February 7, Iowa dropped its mask mandate and its restrictions on businesses and gatherings. Three days later, the *Post* ran an article: "Welcome to Iowa, a State That Doesn't Care If You Live or Die."

I want you to try to pick out from this chart which one of these Midwestern states' lines — all of which show falling, not rising, numbers since then — is Iowa:

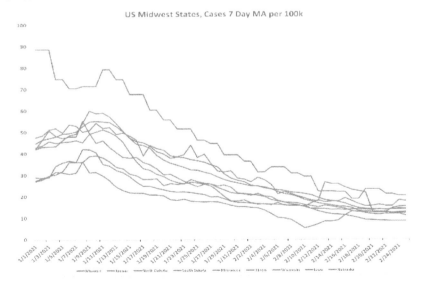

US Midwest States, Cases 7 Day MA per 100k

Give up? It's the bolded one:

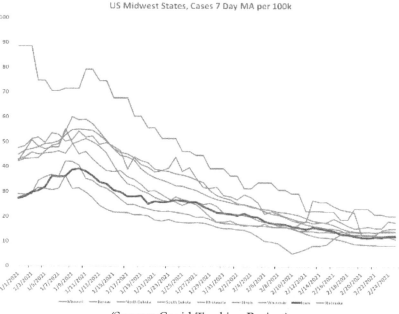

(Source: Covid Tracking Project)

And now, just as I'm writing this, this news just in from WNBC-TV in Connecticut:

"Effective March 19…Connecticut is lifting ALL capacity limits on restaurants, retail, libraries, personal services, indoor recreation, gyms, museums, offices and houses of worship."

That's Connecticut, folks. We have reached the beginning of the end.

March 10, 2021 | Covid Doomer caught red-handed

Today's is a potpourri issue, with three items.

(1) I still can't get over how tone-deaf it was for Andrew Cuomo to publish a self-congratulatory book (*American Crisis*) in the midst of the Covid-19 problem. Well, things are getting downright embarrassing on that front.

In a recent email to the *New York Times*, Crown Publishing Group's Gillian Blake noted "the ongoing investigation into N.Y.S. reporting of Covid-related fatalities in nursing homes" and added, "Pending the ongoing investigation, we have paused active support of *American Crisis* and have no plans to reprint or reissue in paperback."

From late January through late February, the book had sold only 400 copies.

Ouch.

(2) If you're on Twitter, you surely know Eric Feigl-Ding, the incorrigible Covid Doomer.

Feigl-Ding has portrayed himself as an epidemiologist, but he is actually a nutritionist. In mid-March, Marc Lipsitch, a professor of epidemiology at Harvard (who has been critical of the Great Barrington Declaration and is certainly not on our side), described Feigl-Ding as a "charlatan exploiting a tenuous connection [to Harvard] for self-promotion."

According to the *Times Higher Education*, Feigl-Ding's "expertise is in nutrition, not infectious disease, meaning that he makes 'no original contributions to analysis of this epidemic and is laser-focused on self-promotion,' pointed out Professor Lipsitch on Twitter."

Feigl-Ding also appeared in a Joe Biden commercial wearing a white physician coat, giving the impression that he's a doctor who sees patients. Nope again.

Journalist Jordan Schachtel, who's been a guest on the Tom Woods Show, has followed the peculiar story of Dr. Feigl-Ding:

> At the beginning of 2020, Feigl-Ding was an unpaid, visiting scientist in Harvard's nutrition department. His academic research centered entirely around nutrition, diet, and exercise. If Eric Feigl-Ding was interested in pandemics and the study of viruses, his research and academic credentials did not reflect that.
>
> When the coronavirus pandemic began to make waves in the media, everything changed. Feigl-Ding, an aspiring politician, appeared to see an opening to influence the masses and build up his brand.
>
> Feigl-Ding's rise to coronavirus stardom began with a since-deleted tweet falsely describing the coronavirus as "the most virulent virus epidemic the world has ever seen."

Well, now there's a new development.

Schachtel reports that Feigl-Ding, while giving the impression that he is still in the United States, quietly moved his family to Austria (where his wife is from) last year so his child could attend in-person school. In publicly available messages (not being shared to respect his family), it was emphasized that his child was experiencing emotional trauma from social isolation in the United States.

So Feigl-Ding understands the effects of social isolation on children but still favors school closures in the U.S. and the U.K., and never acknowledges the struggles of isolated kids — even though he is aware of those struggles first-hand.

Yet another ghoul on Team Apocalypse.

(3) Let's check in on North Dakota and Iowa, which ended their mask mandates over 50 and 30 days ago, respectively. Must be absolute devastation, right?

You'll never guess: Covid hospitalizations have dropped 75 percent and 47 percent, respectively:

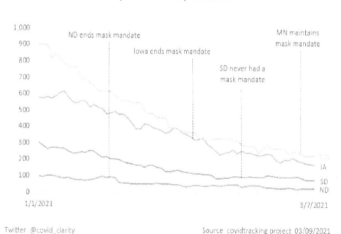

March 12, 2023 | How to make "public health" shysters squirm

Someone just did the very thing I would give my right arm to do.

The heroic Kathryn Huwig, who runs the important Understanding Ohio Covid Data Twitter account (@ohio_data), testified at the State House several days ago. What she did was brilliant. She held up this chart:

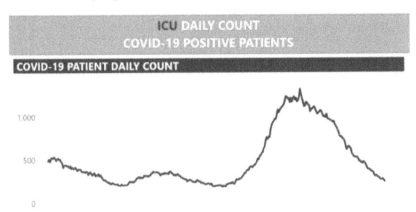

Notice that the X-axis, indicating time, has been omitted. This is on purpose.

She noted that Ohio's alleged "public health" authorities had picked out certain events and certain state policies as being significant with respect to Covid, either in terms of spread or mitigation.

All right, she said. If these things — like Thanksgiving and Christmas (which should have led to an explosion in Covid numbers, according to the "public health" establishment), or the implementation of the mask mandate and the curfew (which should have led to lower numbers) — really had such a significant effect that severe interventions into people's lives were justified, we should surely be able to identify them on the graph even without the help of the dates.

So go ahead, she said. Show me where the following things belong on the graph:

- Mask mandate implemented
- Businesses open in spring
- Liquor sales curfew initiated
- Stay at home order rescinded
- George Floyd protests
- 10 pm curfew goes into effect
- Thanksgiving
- Christmas
- New Year's Eve
- 10 pm curfew lifted

Of course it's impossible to identify any of these things.

213

If they're going to call us murderers and all the usual low-IQ b.s., let's shoot back: show me that what you're demanding of me has actually done any good. If it has, I'm sure you can tell me where on this graph the various mandates went into effect, right? The effects are surely significant enough for it to be obvious, right?

March 15, 2021 | Covid heretic strikes back

From the standpoint of what we laughingly call our "public health" establishment, the most dangerous heretic of 2020 was Scott Atlas.

Atlas, who served in the White House during 2020 as a public health adviser on matters related to Covid-19, recently spoke to a group of students at Stanford University about his experience.

Atlas was treated absurdly by his fellow academics and (of course) by the media, who accused him of all kinds of wickedness because he dissented from the lockdown consensus.

He reviewed all the key points from the past year.

First, in order to explain away the clear failures of lockdowns and other alleged mitigation measures, the lockdowners have tried to pretend that Americans weren't really all that locked down after all, and that in any case Americans didn't really change their behavior terribly much.

Atlas threw cold water on both of those claims:

> Here's the unacknowledged reality: almost all states and major cities, with a handful of exceptions, have implemented severe restrictions for many months, including closures of businesses and in-person school, mobility restrictions and curfews, quarantines, limits on group gatherings, and mask mandates dating back to at least the summer.

> And let's clear up the myths about the behavior of Americans — social mobility tracking of Americans and data from Gallup, YouGov, the Covid-19 Consortium, and the CDC have shown significant reductions of movement as well as a consistently high percentage of mask wearing since the late summer, similar to Western European countries and approaching those in Asia.

He then proceeded to lay out some of the costs of lockdown, of which I offer a sample here:

A recent study confirms that up to 78% of cancers were never detected due to missed screening over three months. If one extrapolates to the entire country, up to a million new cases or more over nine months will have gone undetected. That health disaster adds to missed critical surgeries, chemotherapy, organ transplants, presentations of pediatric illnesses, heart attack and stroke patients too afraid to call emergency services, and others, all well documented.

Beyond hospital care, CDC reported four-fold increases in depression, three-fold increases in anxiety symptoms, and a doubling of suicidal ideation, particularly among young adults — college age — after the first few months of lockdowns, echoing the AMA reports of drug overdoses and suicides. An explosion of insurance claims for these psychological harms in children just verified this, doubling nationally since last year; and in the strictly locked down Northeast, there was a more than 300% increase of teenagers visiting doctors for self-harm.

Domestic abuse and child abuse have been skyrocketing due to the isolation and specifically to the loss of jobs, particularly in the strictest lockdowns.

Was anybody even bothering to consider these effects? You know the answer. And that, said Atlas, was why someone like him needed to be part of the discussion:

To manage such a crisis, shouldn't policymakers objectively consider both the virus harms and the totality of impact of policies? That's the importance of health policy experts — my field — with a broader scope of expertise than that of epidemiologists and basic scientists. And that's exactly why I was called to the White House — there were zero health policy scholars on the Task Force; no one with a medical background who also considered the impacts of the policies was advising the White House.

He also spoke about the policy of universal masking:

Regarding universal masks: 38 states have implemented general-population mask mandates, most since at least the summer, with almost all the rest having mandates in their major cities. Widespread, general-population mask usage has shown little empirical utility for stopping cases, even though that evidence has been censored by Twitter and Amazon. Widespread mask usage showed only minimal impact in Denmark's randomized controlled study. Those are facts. And facts matter.

I posted a list where mask mandates empirically failed to stop cases, along with direct quotes, without any edit, from WHO, CDC, and Oxford University. That was censored by Twitter. And I stated numerous times that it would be irrational to wear a mask "when alone riding a bicycle outside, when driving your own car alone, or when walking in the desert alone." I stand by those words.

Those who charge that it is unethical, even dangerous, to question broad population mask mandates must not realize that several of the world's top infectious disease scientists and major public health organizations explicitly question the efficacy of general population masks. The public needs to know the truth.

For instance, Jefferson and Heneghan of University of Oxford's Centre for Evidence-Based Medicine wrote: "It would appear that despite two decades of pandemic preparedness, there is considerable uncertainty as to the value of wearing masks." Oxford's renowned epidemiologist Sunetra Gupta said there is no need for masks unless one is elderly or high risk. Stanford's Jay Bhattacharya stated, "Mask mandates are not supported by the scientific data. There is no scientific evidence that mask mandates work to slow the spread of the disease."

Throughout this pandemic until December, the WHO's "Advice on the use of masks in the context of Covid-19" stated: "At present, there is no direct evidence (from studies on Covid-19 and in healthy people in the community) on the effectiveness of universal masking of healthy people in the community to prevent infection with respiratory viruses, including Covid-19." In December, the WHO changed their wording to today's "At present there is only limited and inconsistent scientific evidence to support the effectiveness of masking of healthy people in the community to prevent infection with respiratory viruses, including SARS-CoV-2."

The CDC, in a review of influenza pandemics, "did not find evidence that surgical-type face masks are effective in reducing laboratory-confirmed influenza transmission, either when worn by infected persons (source control) or by persons in the general community to reduce their susceptibility." And until the WHO removed it on October 21, 2020 (almost immediately after Twitter censored my tweet highlighting the WHO quote), the WHO had written, "At the present time, the widespread use of masks by healthy people in the community setting is not yet supported by high quality or direct scientific evidence and there are potential benefits and harms to consider."

Atlas went on to slam the academic community, particularly at Stanford (his home institution), which conducted itself appallingly in his case.

March 16, 2021 | This state should have piles of corpses; let's check in

Today let's check in on Iowa — remember Iowa, a state "that doesn't care if you live or die," according to the *Washington Post*?

Iowa dropped its restrictions five weeks ago (so the initial deaths in that part of the graph are lagging from before the restrictions were dropped). Notice that the trend not only isn't moving into the stratosphere, but is actually downward:

Oh, and "cases" are at their lowest level since August 2020.

While we're at it, here's Tennessee:

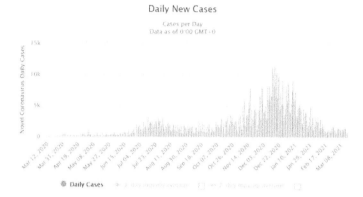

Scott Morefield wonders, "Would any of the so-called 'experts' care to explain how on earth Tennessee got to summer-level Covid-19 cases *without* a statewide mask mandate *and* with masked vs. unmasked counties at the same infection level?"

And finally, a Fauci update. The *Boston Globe* just ran this headline: "Fauci says Covid-19 restrictions could be lifted before U.S. reaches herd immunity." Martin Kulldorff of Harvard Medical School responded: "The futility of past/present lockdowns and their enormous collateral public health damage are obvious to more and more people. Politicians understand public opinion and are gradually shifting, and Anthony Fauci is superb at reading the political winds."

When you're pulling the so-called "science" out of your you-know-where, it's easy to shift on a dime.

March 19, 2021 | What I saw in Alabama

I'm writing to you from an in-person conference. No capacity limit, no dehumanizing masks, because it's on a property not open to the general public: the Mises Institute.

I'm here for their Austrian Economics Research Conference, where the brightest scholars gather to share their work in pushing our intellectual tradition forward.

But although this conference, which is 100% Old Normal, is great, there's still lunacy in Alabama. I had to run to the dry cleaners, where I saw a sign informing me that because of Covid-19, they would no longer be recycling coat hangers. No doubt eleventy bajillion lives will be saved.

At the hotel, meanwhile, there are no housekeeping services being offered. States where hotels do typically offer housekeeping services have no worse outcomes than states that don't, so this strikes me as simply an excuse not to offer a standard service.

When checking in, I was asked to hold up my ID rather than handing it to the hotel clerk. (Again, think of the millions of lives saved by avoiding contaminated drivers' licenses.) They also had me make my own magnetic key by picking one up from a pile and then placing it on the machine.

How have we allowed these people to claim the mantle of science?

Now, a couple of miscellaneous items you'll enjoy:

(1) The *Washington Post* just wrote, "Some studies indicate that mask mandates and limitations on group activities such as indoor dining can help slow the spread of the coronavirus, but less clear is why states with greater government-imposed restrictions have not always fared better than those without them." Well, well, well.

(2) The *New York Times* just wrote, "The origin of the six-foot distancing recommendation is something of a mystery. 'It's almost like it was pulled out of thin air,' said Linsey Marr, an expert on viral transmission at Virginia Tech University." You don't say!

Part V: Spring 2021

March 23, 2021 | One poll reveals the MSM's failure on Covid

It's been over six weeks since Iowa dropped all state-level Covid restrictions.

Well, how about this: hospitalized patients are down 54 percent.

I promise you that when the governor lifted restrictions, the hysterics were not saying: "If you drop restrictions, hospitalized patients will plummet 54 percent." They had rather more grim predictions. And yet here we are — once again.

To the retort that cases have leveled off in Iowa in recent days and have stopped their steep descent, the same is true of all 11 other Midwestern states, with their variety of restrictions/openings.

Now in case you needed further evidence that so-called mainstream sources have exaggerated the Covid threat, note this survey from Gallup and Franklin Templeton asking people what they believe the likelihood of hospitalization is for a given Covid-19 "case."

The correct answer is between one and five percent. Note how few people get the answer right. A strong plurality have somehow managed to become so uninformed that they think the answer is over 50 percent:

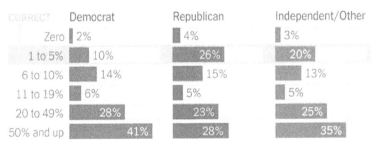

What are the chances somebody with Covid must be hospitalized?

	Democrat	Republican	Independent/Other
Zero	2%	4%	3%
1 to 5% (CORRECT)	10%	26%	20%
6 to 10%	14%	15%	13%
11 to 19%	6%	5%	5%
20 to 49%	28%	23%	25%
50% and up	41%	28%	35%

March 24, 2021 | Chart flattens Doomer governor

You'd think Phil Murphy, governor of New Jersey — which as of this moment has the worst Covid death rate of any American state — would have the decency to keep his mouth shut on the subject. Well, you'd be wrong.

When asked about Texas's decision to repeal its statewide mask mandate, Murphy replied that he was "stunned" and that he "couldn't conceive of lifting a mask mandate inside."

How about we see how both states are doing?

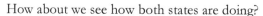
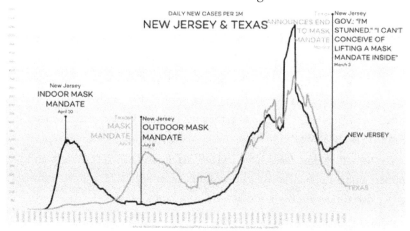

(Source: nytimes.com/interactive/2020/us/coronavirus-us-cases.html)

Well, how about that.

California, meanwhile, has seen its numbers come way down from their peak. They are of course pretending that their lockdown did the trick. The problem is this: Nevada didn't lock down as much and Arizona locked down even less, and yet:

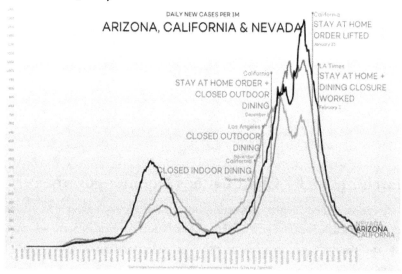

(Source: nytimes.com/interactive/2020/us/coronavirus-us-cases.html)

March 30, 2021 | The vaccine passport has resisters. Here's one

The Orwellian proposals keep piling up, and Ron DeSantis continues to be a hero.

When Joe Biden hinted weeks ago at the possibility of further lockdowns, DeSantis spoke to the press and said that that would absolutely not be happening in Florida.

When it sounded as if Biden might restrict travel to Florida, DeSantis pledged to resist.

Oh, and by the way: the anti-Florida ghouls are reduced to claiming that DeSantis must be suppressing Florida's true numbers.

Sure, that's plausible! So this theory is that the hospitals in Florida are actually bursting at the seams with Covid patients, but we can't know that because the official numbers aren't reliable?

I see. So every single hospital is in on it, too? Not even one bit of anecdotal evidence of hospital overflow has managed to escape a single hospital?

It's almost sad what the Doomers are reduced to. And they accuse *other people* of being "conspiracy theorists"!

In a way it's encouraging, though: these people cannot explain Florida's numbers without dreaming up wild conspiracies. That means they're implicitly admitting that Florida's numbers are great. Otherwise they wouldn't need to be explained away.

Well, now DeSantis is resisting vaccine passports — the Orwellian idea proposed by whoever is running Joe Biden — as well.

"It's completely unacceptable," he said. "You want to go to a movie theater, should you have to show that? No. You want to go to a game, [or] a theme park? No. So we're not supportive of that."

He is pledging to take executive action, as early as today.

As Jeff Deist put it, "No private business or industry would require vaccine passports without state sanction and a strong assist from lapdog media to overcome the terrible PR optics. It's a sick and crazy idea."

Meanwhile, check out media coverage of Florida. The *New York Times* just ran an article about rising "cases" in one of the four states in this chart. Which one do you suppose it was?

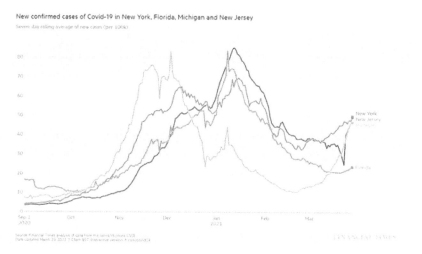

(Source: *Financial Times* analysis of data from the Johns Hopkins CSSE.)

Yes, they looked at those lines and decided to write an article about Florida's "rising cases."

Meanwhile, back on this planet, here's a comparison they won't make (but thanks to @yinonw on Twitter for making it):

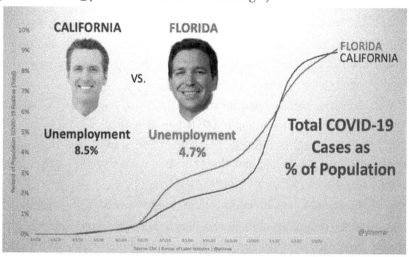

April 1, 2021 | Fauci and Birx defensive

Anthony Fauci and White House Coronavirus Response Coordinator Deborah Birx are trying to blame everyone but themselves for how things have turned out. They're trying to blame Scott Atlas, even though the lockdown policies Fauci and Birx advocated were in fact implemented almost everywhere.

Last night on *The Ingraham Angle*, Atlas responded:

> We are witnessing something incredible, really, which is people trying to overtly rewrite history....Of all the insanity I saw in the White House, this is the most despicable....These are people that advocated the curfews, the lockdowns, the school closures, the business restrictions, the lack of group visits for your own family — *and those were implemented!* Those were the policies on the ground of almost every single state....And now they're saying that the people who criticized the polices that were implemented are responsible for the failures of the policies that were implemented!

> This is insane. It is despicable. I am shocked, but...I shouldn't be, because I never fit in there. These people don't know truth if it hit them in the head. It's incredible what we're seeing here....

> What they advocated *was done.* I was the one brought in because I was the only one who cared what was happening by shutting down medical care, closing schools, closing businesses, destroying low-income families, sacrificing our children — they had no interest in even talking about it. I could go on and on about what they didn't know.

> I can guarantee you: the truth will come out.

April 6, 2021 | One photo from Texas shows it's all over

The divergence between the two Americas is growing wider. Remember Joe Biden's promise that if we just followed the voodoo for a few more months, we might be able to gather in small groups by July 4?

Here's a scene from Texas yesterday:

Texas and Mississippi opened fully a month ago. Here's how it's going:

New confirmed cases of Covid-19 in Texas, Michigan, New York, New Jersey and Mississippi
Seven-day rolling average of new cases (per 100k)

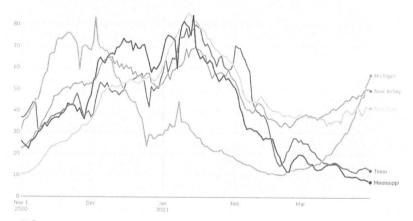

Of course, you can imagine the screeching if those lines were reversed, and Texas and Mississippi were the ones rising.

But because the numbers look like this, total silence.

Incidentally, even if this were all to go away tomorrow, it would still be crucial to talk about these numbers. We have to do whatever we can to make sure people don't conclude, "That sure was a tough year, but thanks to those of us who followed the mitigation measures, we got out of it."

As it is, despite our best efforts — and my 2009 book *Meltdown*, which spent 10 happy weeks on the *New York Times* bestseller list — people still think "deregulation" caused the financial crisis of 2008, even though when you ask them which repealed regulation would have prevented the crisis, they can't name one.

They still think laissez-faire capitalism caused the Great Depression. Those of us who have read Murray Rothbard's *America's Great Depression*, or understand Austrian business cycle theory, know the truth. But that's a tiny sliver of the public.

You'll note what all of this has in common:

Freedom causes crises, and the alleged experts fix them.

You need us, citizen. We keep you safe. We clean up the messes caused by allowing you too much freedom. We are smart. You are dumb. Trust us.

How about you go jump in a lake, and we'll live our lives?

As I posted in response to the Ohio governor's grandstanding during National Public Health Week:

> The "public health" establishment has disgraced itself with arbitrary decrees based on nothing. That anyone could still think any of these measures do the slightest bit of good after examining charts from other, less restrictive states is a testament to the power of belief over reason.

April 7, 2021 | Fauci stumped on national TV

Yesterday I showed you the numbers for Texas. They look good.

I had a whole bunch of people write to ask me for the source of the graph. I told them the answer: the *Financial Times*. They say that without the source, their friends wouldn't believe them.

In a way that's encouraging: it means that their friends are at a loss to account for reality. The best they can do is: I don't trust your source! Because if the source is correct, then their lockdown religion is in for a severe challenge.

What I also told some people who wrote to me was: nobody disputes that Texas's numbers are falling. Dr. Fauci himself addressed it on MSNBC just the other day! So your friends who refuse to believe you are completely out to lunch.

Now recall when Biden Covid adviser Andy Slavitt appeared on MSNBC two months ago. He was asked why Florida has a lower death rate than most states despite having no state-level restrictions, while California, with tons of restrictions, is only slightly better (and even that slight difference is entirely accounted for by California's much younger population).

I remember wondering to myself: maybe the so-called experts really do have a plausible-sounding explanation for this, even if it's nevertheless false.

Nope.

Slavitt was reduced to this: "Look, there's so much of this virus that we think we understand, that we think we can predict, that's just a little bit beyond our explanation." Translation: we've got nothing.

Well, Dr. Fauci just had his own Slavitt moment, also on MSNBC. At this point the ridiculous predictions have been so far off that MSNBC is asking Fauci about them. Wasn't Texas supposed to be a disaster?

Fauci's response: "It can be confusing, because…often you have to wait a few weeks before you see the effect."

It's been a month, Dr. Fauci.

And then this: "I'm not really quite sure. It could be they're doing things outdoors."

That's it. That's all he has. Things repeatedly happen the opposite of how he predicts, and he has nothing.

April 8, 2021 | *The Today Show* stumbles toward Covid truth

I know there is life beyond Covid. But it has planted the seeds for so much destruction and evil that I feel compelled to cover it consistently (if not exclusively).

Today we read this from *The Today Show*: "Some states with stricter rules are now seeing surges in Covid-19 cases, while many others that rushed to reopen are experiencing sizable drops. The numbers have experts scratching their heads."

Imagine that. And imagine it taking more than a full year for them to notice this. And further imagine consulting only the "experts" who are "scratching their heads." Any chance there might be worthier people to be talking to, *Today Show*?

Speaking of worthier people: YouTube keeps banning them.

Florida governor Ron DeSantis recently held a roundtable discussion with Sunetra Gupta of Oxford, Martin Kulldorff of Harvard, and Stanford's Scott Atlas and Jay Bhattacharya. YouTube evidently decided that it's best for roundtables featuring experts who are advising a major U.S. governor to be kept secret, because they took the video down.

According to the *Wall Street Journal*'s editorial page:

> In the hour-and-forty-five-minute video, Mr. DeSantis and the four panelists lambaste the U.S. coronavirus response as excessively draconian and ineffective. They emphasize unintended public-health harms from lockdowns and school closures, criticize mask mandates and generally celebrate Florida's response....
>
> YouTube told us Thursday in a statement that it removed the video "because it included content that contradicts the consensus of local and global health authorities regarding the efficacy of masks to prevent the spread of Covid-19."
>
> As an example, YouTube points to a video passage where Gov. DeSantis asks one panelist, Harvard biostatistician Martin Kulldorff, whether children need to wear masks, and Mr. Kulldorff says no. Dr. Jay Battacharya of Stanford adds that masking for children is "developmentally inappropriate." Gov. DeSantis notes, accurately, that "if we went back a year, a lot of the experts would say that wearing masks for the general public is not evidence-based."

And of course that's true. That is flat-out true. Remember, even now, after a year's worth of propaganda, the World Health Organization itself can muster only this: "At present there is only limited and inconsistent scientific evidence to support the effectiveness of masking of healthy people in the community to prevent infection with respiratory viruses, including SARS-CoV-2."

That's the World Health Organization! Did you realize its support for universal masking was so timid? I'll bet you didn't. That's because nobody is telling you.

According to YouTube, evidently, the progress of science occurs when certain ideas become unchallengeable orthodoxies, even when they have been directly contradicted in the very recent past, and even when one of their own authorities admits the evidence for one such orthodoxy is "limited and inconsistent."

Facebook hasn't been much better, as we all know.

These behemoths have gone out of their way to ensure that the Fauci line is consistently protected no matter how many times its predictions fail to come true.

April 20, 2021 | Former GOP rep: no liberties violated in 2020

If for some reason you've been trying to keep track of the craziest things said this year, well, I've got one that belongs at least in the top five.

MSNBC's Joe Scarborough was not happy with Congressman Jim Jordan (R-OH), who recently grilled Dr. Fauci and demanded specific answers as to when Americans could lead normal lives again.

Congressman Jordan described the various interventions as assaults on American liberties.

But according to Scarborough, this is all nonsense.

No liberties were taken away!

You think I must be joking. Woods, you say, surely you have misunderstood Joe Scarborough!

Here are his words:

"No personal liberties were taken away. The Supreme Court has reviewed the cases. The courts have reviewed cases. It's sheer idiocy playing for the lowest common denominator."

It almost takes your breath away, the sheer stupidity, does it not? *The Supreme Court has reviewed the cases?* So I can't tell if my liberties have been violated or not until the Supreme Court graciously informs me?

And what a surprise: a branch of government that tells us whether another branch of government has violated our rights has decided that it hasn't! Well, then, that's all I need to hear!

Scarborough went on: "Jim Jordan peddles the suggestion that Anthony Fauci somehow is the problem instead of a coronavirus that's spread across America and killed 550,000 people."

Of course, like his fellow lizard people, Scarborough acts as if it's simply obvious that the so-called mitigation measures did any good. Yes, Joe, Fauci "somehow" *is* the problem, since the states whose policies he recommended did no better than states he castigated, and he has spent virtually the entirety of the past 13 months acting as if lockdowns and restrictions cause no damage worth noticing.

Oh, and speaking of which, why don't we check in with Texas, over two weeks since that Texas Rangers game that had everyone up in arms? Surely a "superspreader" event, right? (And for fun, let's put the California/Florida rivalry in there as well.)

(Source: nytimes.com/interactive/2020/us/coronavirus-us-cases.html)

I'm sure everyone who predicted the apocalypse in Texas will promptly apologize.

April 30, 2021 | Let's check in on those Covid predictions

Today we're going to check in on how some predictions are going.

Let's start with California and Texas. Remember when Gavin Newsom, governor of California, described the decision to drop the Texas mask mandate as "absolutely reckless," and then continued with his own crazy policies of closing even outdoor dining and then had similar or worse results than Texas for seven weeks? I'm sure that was all over the news, right?

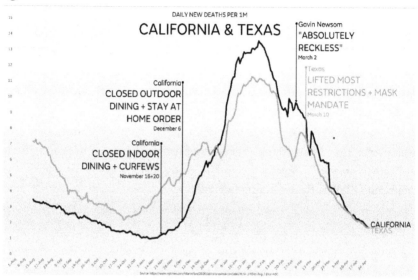

Let's shift to Iowa. Remember the *Washington Post*'s headline, "Welcome to Iowa, a State That Doesn't Care If You Live or Die"? Deaths are down 91.4 percent since then:

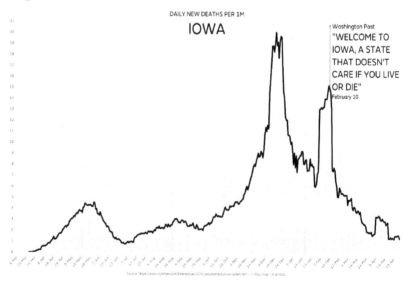

This one involves heavily masked Hungary against sparsely masked Sweden. Shouldn't these numbers be reversed?

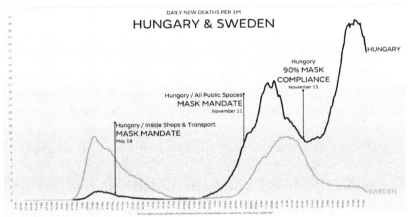

As usual, no clear pro-Fauci story emerges from the charts — as it darn well should if all the craziness and sacrifice had been genuinely necessary.

May 3, 2021 | The governor they hate just broke their hearts again

Well, Ron DeSantis is at it again.

Today he lifted the state of emergency in Florida and ordered all emergency mandates issued by local governments to be lifted immediately. In doing so, he pointed to what's still happening in some places across the country, even now. He mentioned Brookline, Massachusetts, extending its outdoor mask mandate at a time when virtually everyone now acknowledges the uselessness of outdoor masking. He mentioned Washington, D.C., which has outlawed dancing at weddings.

It's "insane," he said.

The mayor of St. Petersburg, meanwhile, is outraged:

> Cities like St. Pete, Tampa, Orlando, Miami and Miami Beach saved Florida and the governor's behind throughout this pandemic. Can you imagine if each city had been led by Ron DeSantis? How many lives would have been lost? What would our economy look like today?

The mayor hasn't looked at the charts.

You can't tell which place did what.

Meanwhile, the *New York Post*, in a story about the governor's action, added this: "Public health experts have said regions should aim for under a 5 percent positivity rate for Covid-19 tests before lifting restrictions....It recorded a daily positivity rate of 5.87 percent on Sunday, up from 5.7 percent the day before."

It astonishes me that "public health experts," with their arbitrary numbers and metrics, still have the nerve to speak at all. How many of their recommendations have been walked back at this point? How much damage do these people have to do, while relatively freer states continue to prosper, before they're embarrassed enough just to slink away for good?

May 5, 2021 | How I know the Covid tide has finally turned

Well, how about this.

The Atlantic, which hasn't exactly been on our side through all this, just published an article by Emma Green called "The Liberals Who Can't Quit Lockdown."

Subtitle: "Progressive communities have been home to some of the fiercest battles over Covid-19 policies, and some liberal policymakers have left scientific evidence behind."

Some excerpts:

> The spring of 2021 is different from the spring of 2020, though. Scientists know a lot more about how Covid-19 spreads — and how it doesn't. Public-health advice is shifting. But some progressives have not updated their behavior based on the new information....Some progressives have continued to embrace policies and behaviors that aren't supported by evidence, such as banning access to playgrounds, closing beaches, and refusing to reopen schools for in-person learning....

> Scientists, academics, and writers who have argued that some very low-risk activities are worth doing as vaccination rates rise — even if the risk of exposure is not zero — have faced intense backlash. After Emily Oster, an economist at Brown University, argued in *The Atlantic* in March that families should plan to take their kids on trips and see friends and relatives this summer, a reader sent an email to her supervisors at the

university suggesting that Oster be promoted to a leadership role in the field of "genocide encouragement."

Green spends some time discussing the treatment of dissidents in left-liberal Somerville, Massachusetts:

> In Somerville, a local leader appeared to describe parents who wanted a faster return to in-person instruction as "f***ing white parents" in a virtual public meeting; a community member accused the group of mothers advocating for schools to reopen of being motivated by white supremacy. "I spent four years fighting Trump because he was so anti-science," Daniele Lantagne, a Somerville mom and engineering professor who works to promote equitable access to clean water and sanitation during disease outbreaks, told me. "I spent the last year fighting people who I normally would agree with…desperately trying to inject science into school reopening, and completely failed."

As most Americans prepare to go back to normal, Green says in her conclusion, lockdown-addicted progressives "are left, Cassandra-like, to preach their peers' folly."

Nice to see progressives finally portrayed, accurately, as stubbornly refusing to listen to science, and addicted to restrictions as evidence of their good citizenship. But also nice to see a mainstream publication say: everyone else is going back to normal.

April 7, 2021 | An appeal from a "sad kid"

Today on Twitter someone shared a poem from a young person. I'm going to share it with you:

> *Let me be,*
> *let me go,*
> *let me be happy*
> *and not sorrow*
>
> *Let me play,*
> *let me dance,*
> *let me go*
> *be happy!*
>
> *Stop keeping me in*
> *let me out,*

I need my friends…
they need me!

I miss the wind
in my face, As I
run through
the fields

I miss dancing
I miss my friends,
I miss my old
life, Let me go!

Yours, a sad kid

Living in Florida as I do, it's easy to forget that in many places madness still reigns. They can't admit it does no good at all, even though a recent chart comparing hospitalization rates in the 25 strictest states and the 25 least strict states showed no difference. The disgraced public health establishment cannot admit that it ruined people's lives, decimated their savings, and caused all kinds of horrific collateral health damage, so they have to go on pretending. Same with the politicians.

Meanwhile, you have the ordinary people whose lives are so meaningless that they can find fulfillment only in false demonstrations of superiority over others — and the pointless so-called mitigation measures are perfect for that.

May 11, 2021 | The Covid follow-up question no reporter will ask

Back in January, Michael Osterholm, who's been an adviser to Joe Biden on the virus, warned that the next six to fourteen weeks would be the worst of the pandemic.

We're now beyond fourteen weeks from that moment. The case numbers are down 76 percent:

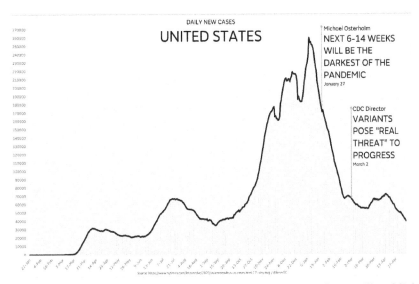

DAILY NEW CASES

UNITED STATES

Michael Osterholm
NEXT 6-14 WEEKS
WILL BE THE
DARKEST OF THE
PANDEMIC
January 27

CDC Director
VARIANTS
POSE "REAL
THREAT" TO
PROGRESS
March 2

"I want to be so wrong on this one," Osterholm said. "I will publicly celebrate me being wrong if this [surge] doesn't happen, because I just wish we didn't have to go through this."

Our inquisitive media will surely follow up with him and give him an opportunity to celebrate publicly.

They wouldn't fail to pursue a story like this just because it undermines the panickers. I mean, these are curious people, and professionals to boot!

Ahem.

This, by the way, is the same person who said on October 9 that Florida would be a "house on fire" within weeks because it wasn't listening to him. We know how that one turned out.

You'd think after a while he'd stop and wonder: "Maybe I don't fully understand this. Maybe I should keep the shaming and the unnecessary panic to a minimum. Because it sure seems as if the resumption of normal life doesn't affect anything."

But of course not.

I'm spending a few days in the Florida Panhandle. I cannot believe how (relatively) unmasked it is here compared to Central Florida, where I live. And everything is fine. No "overwhelmed hospitals," nothing.

This, I am convinced, is why many of them don't want the masks coming off. Not because they fear a spike, but precisely because *they fear nothing will happen.* At which point the handful of people still capable of independent thought will wonder how they got snookered into all this in the first place.

May 12, 2021 | They've broken young people

Professor Don Boudreaux of George Mason University, on his Cafe Hayek blog, shares this email from a reader who describes a weekend incident involving one of her daughters and her longtime friend (LTF):

> *We own a second house in Aiken, South Carolina. This daughter is an equestrian. SC is now fully open and Aiken lifted all mask mandates just this past week (thank God). With college classes over, my daughter and her longtime friend made a weekend trip there. Sounds like fun, right?*
>
> *My daughter made dinner reservations, and another friend invited them to see live music outside. It is important to note that my daughter has one shot of the vaccine, and that her LTF not only had Covid, but is fully vaccinated, and the friend they are meeting had Covid — and they are all under 25, so already not at great risk. They are about to enter the restaurant when LTF has a panic attack, starts crying, and declares that she cannot enter the restaurant because people are dining inside. LTF then declares that she also cannot go to the music event because there will be crowds there. LTF has become so terrified of other human beings that, despite being immunized, she cannot fathom living life normally. LTF is convinced that all the non-mask wearing people are going to infect her, and despite the fact that she, her parents, and her grandparents are all vaccinated, she is going to carry the illness to them and kill them. This is mental illness. This is what we've done to our young people. It is heartbreaking.*

After sharing a story of his own, Boudreaux concludes with this:

> *Despite nearly four months of steadily, and often dramatically, falling case counts in Virginia — despite steadily falling hospitalization numbers for Covid — despite falling Covid death rates — despite 50 percent of Virginians now having at least one vaccine shot and 38 percent being fully vaccinated, the government of this State which was home to Patrick Henry, George Washington, Thomas Jefferson, and James Madison officially advises citizens to double mask and to worry about "new variants of Covid-19."*
>
> *This attitude is deranged.*

May 18, 2021 | The last Covid-hysteric argument against us, exploded

Yesterday someone wrote to tell me that his friend was complaining that my various comparisons don't take population density into account (even though my comparisons often involve places that are right next to each other).

So let's take this opportunity to dispense with this objection once and for all. Here are population density and health outcomes graphed together. As you can see, the results are completely random:

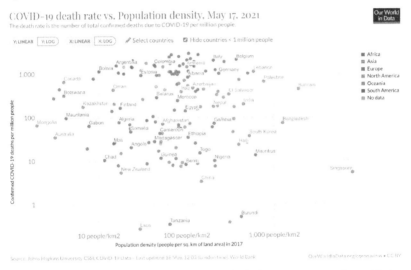

On another matter, yesterday the graph below was posted on Twitter, showing the results for the states allegedly following The Science, and the so-called neanderthal states. Well, how about that:

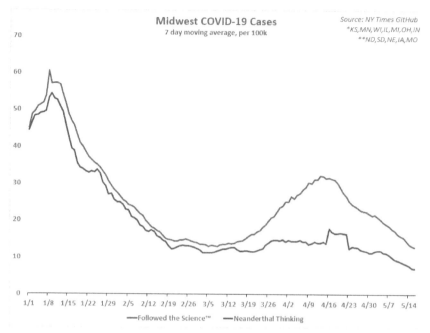

A self-described math teacher, evidently not knowing what "per 100K" means, claimed the graph didn't account for population:

Replying to @IAmTheActualET

Math teacher here...

Good try! Most Blue states have larger populations than Red states. % of population would be a better indicator!

2:09 PM · May 17, 2021 · Twitter for Android

So I replied: "Now that you know you're wrong, I guess you have to admit that the chart is a problem for your position. If it didn't pose a problem for you, you wouldn't have been so fast to try to correct it. Now that you know you're wrong, how are you changing your views?"

I hope you're sitting down: I have not received a response.

May 20, 2021 | The mask dead-enders

Masks have been taking a beating.

First it was the sudden Establishment consensus that outdoor mask mandates had no scientific merit and should be repealed. Then it was the CDC saying that the vaccinated don't need to wear masks. Then, from this foundation, big stores like Trader Joe's, Walmart, and Costco all announced that the vaccinated would not be required to wear masks in their stores — and added that they wouldn't be verifying anyone's vaccination status.

And yet in many places mask wearing is still overwhelmingly prevalent.

The wearers either don't believe their vaccines work, or they suddenly don't trust the CDC, or who knows what. Or they've simply been so terrorized and propagandized that they can't think clearly. Or the mask is a symbol of "science" and moral superiority, and they can't give that up.

The other day on Twitter someone asked people: why do you care if people are wearing masks outdoors? They've just been through a mass death event. Let them do what they want.

Well, of course I'll let people do stupid, pointless things if they want. But here's why I care:

(1) If people did a rain dance during a drought I wouldn't say, "Can you blame them? It's been a long drought."

(2) Many of the people still wearing masks, especially outdoors, are the very ones who spent the past year lecturing the rest of us about science. When they themselves act in defiance of science, it rightly makes us question what their true motivations were all along.

(3) Masks don't seem to do anything. The "studies" purporting to show that they do either involve arbitrary dates (and thus exclude huge spikes that would be embarrassing to have to explain away) or are just models, in which the model assumes from the start that masks work.

What we know in reality is that we have chart after chart after chart of countries around the world in which, just before a massive spike, some headline read, "How Country X Defeated the Coronavirus," and the story generally involves masks. After the spike, no journalist revisits the issue and says, "Maybe we were being too simplistic when we attributed Country X's success to masks, since its people are still wearing them but now the numbers are way up." The Florida Panhandle is mostly unmasked, and their health outcomes are no different from those in the rest of the state. Mandates have ended in numerous states with no ill effects.

(4) Human communication involves more than words (and even words can be hard to make out with masks on). Masks disrupt the full spectrum of human communication, thereby opening the door to misunderstanding.

(5) Are we seriously so debased that I actually have to argue in favor of seeing people's faces?

(6) Infants and toddlers need facial expressions for their proper development. We all know about the studies involving infants and a mother who is expressionless as opposed to a mother who is smiling. Infants and toddlers today are growing up in what must seem like a soulless dystopia.

(7) If you're wearing a mask outside in particular, you're either impervious to evidence or you're making some kind of statement, and neither possibility is particularly flattering. Nobody would do such a thing without at least a vague sense that it's scientifically justified. So that means they almost certainly look at my unmasked face and assume scientific ignorance. I don't particularly care for having that assumption made about me.

At first many of us wondered how the politicians would stand down from all these crazy restrictions and requirements. But now an equally compelling question is whether substantial segments of the American public itself will be willing to ditch these things.

I suspect the masks will come off in large numbers once a critical mass is reached. In other words, the remainder will fall quickly because I think many of those people complied in the first place out of a desire to do what was popular. As soon as masks cease to be popular, this group of people will rip them off without delay.

May 21, 2021 | I've stumped the Covid hysterics, and they're not happy

I've had a few people say: enough is enough, Woods. On to another topic. And I have indeed covered other topics. But just when I consider letting up, I get a news item like this, via Alex Berenson:

> The Canadians have lost their minds. Ontario has 14.7 million people. 1 in 11,000 is hospitalized for Covid. Cases are plunging, vaccinations soaring. Yet Ontario has a lockdown as

strict as any U.S. state had *last April*. No "nonessential" retail, playgrounds closed, etc.

And the premier, Doug Ford, just *extended* the lockdown — while promising if his subjects are good sheeple and hit vaccination targets, they may get 10-person outdoor gatherings in mid-June.

The U.K. has been saying they'll reopen on June 21 — an already absurd date — but that they can push that date back if not enough people are vaccinated.

Meanwhile, all of Europe has to pretend that Florida doesn't exist, ignore the American states that have dropped their mask mandates with no ill effect, and not mention the large events that have recently been held in the U.S. that led to no problems at all.

Earlier this week I released my Covid Charts Quiz (CovidChartsQuiz.com), which asks people to identify, on unlabeled charts, which state is the one with the heavier restrictions, and other questions of that kind. It's impossible to figure out the answer based on the charts because of course the results have been completely random.

I've received feedback from a handful of hysterics to the effect that I'm not taking into account this or that trivial thing differentiating the various states I'm comparing, even though a lot of the charts involve neighboring states that are demographically identical.

But think about it: had you asked hysterics in April 2020 whether in May 2021 they'd be able to distinguish the locked-down states from the open ones by looking at their results on a graph, they would have said absolutely yes. *They would have been sure that the differences between the two would be extremely obvious.*

The fact that today the graphs are in fact so similar that they're reduced to laughable (and invalid) nitpicking means *they were wrong*. You know and I know that in 2020 they were absolutely certain that the states that ignored them were going to be overwhelmed by deaths, no caveats about it, and that this devastation would be clear and unmistakable on any chart.

And now they see the charts, can't tell the difference, and have to make up phony explanations as to why.

May 24, 2021 | What a surprise: two superspreaders that didn't happen

Restrictions are falling left and right at this point. Las Vegas casinos are back to 100 percent, and with no mask requirements. Huge sporting events, and even concerts, are coming back (Foreigner performed in Orlando last week, for example).

And yet, even though the scolds' predictions of "superspreader" effects failed to materialize from the Super Bowl, the college football national championship, or that packed Texas Rangers game we were all warned about, they're still predicting it, and they're still wrong.

A couple of examples, courtesy of Ian Miller.

Back on May 8 the Atlanta Braves had their first full stadium since all this started. Nobody was asked about vaccination status. Sportswriter Peter King wrote on Twitter, above a picture of the event: "570,615 deaths. Nothing to see there."

Since King is a mainstream sports journalist, he still — still! — thinks the Fauci "mitigation measures" actually do something, and defying them leads to mass death.

Well, two weeks later, here's the massive carnage caused by that event:

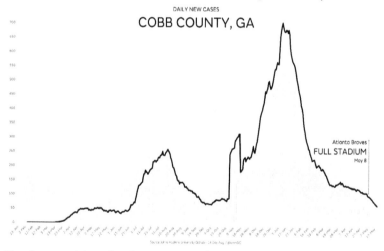

Here's something else from two weeks ago: the Canelo Alvarez fight in Texas, a fight attended by over 73,000 people. No indoor boxing event in history has been attended by more people. Nobody checked vaccination status, and not many masks.

Let's check in on the devastation this event surely caused:

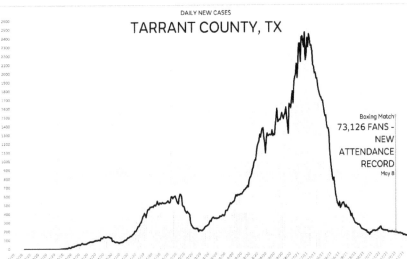

The ongoing wickedness in Canada and Europe is predicated on pretending that these things aren't happening. They have to pretend that mass events haven't been going on in the U.S. without any discernible effect.

You'd think the populations of those countries would be demanding an explanation as to why they're still locked down, but I guess they don't value living as much as you and I do.

May 31, 2021 | Warning: good news

This is a bit of a potpourri issue. Item #1 is crazy California, but the others are good.

(1) If you want to make sense of the various Covid restrictions, especially the insane ones that make no sense and will clearly do nothing to keep anyone "safe," this general principle seems to work every time: forget trying to find "science" in these restrictions. Imagine instead that the principle is "curtail or eliminate things that bring people joy, and demand things that cause them pain or grave inconvenience." That principle, rather than "science," appears to explain every restriction I've seen.

I just encountered another example of this.

I'm taking a quick trip to Southern California with my 11-year-old daughter next week so I've been trying to figure out, in light of the ongoing reopening, what is available for us to do while there.

She's never been to a drive-in movie, so I was considering that.

When I got to the website of one such theatre, I was met with this: "In accordance with L.A. County guidelines, double features are not permitted."

Evidently double features — performed while you're completely isolated in the car — are a driver of infection!

I give up trying to figure out how even the most superstitious person can believe this stuff.

(2) On the last day of May let's look back to the CDC's warning of a Covid surge because of the "variant" bogeyman. Since that prediction, cases are down by just about 50 percent:

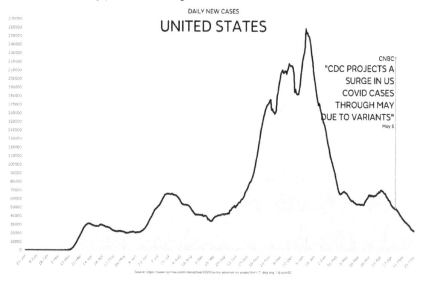

(3) And it wasn't that long ago that the CDC director was warning of "impending doom" if Americans started doing the very things Texas and Florida, with no ill effects, have been doing for a while:

THE CORONAVIRUS CRISIS

CDC Director Fears 'Impending Doom' If U.S. Opens Too Quickly

March 29, 2021 · 11:52 AM ET

Well, that sentiment sure faded fast and without explanation; here's a headline from May 28:

Dr. Rochelle Walensky to throw out first pitch at Fenway Park Saturday as capacity limits are lifted

There's still plenty of craziness, but there's also a lot that's moving in the right direction.

The resumption of large events is carrying on in more and more places. And the headline out of the *Telegraph* in the U.K. reads, "U.K. vaccine passport plans to be scrapped," with the subhead, "No legal requirement to show jab status at large events, as ministers go cool on proposals."

June 10, 2021 | Another "mitigation measure" they now admit is pointless

Now it's the plexiglass barriers.

Anyone with half a brain knew these things were stupid.

Joseph Allen of the Harvard School of Public Health had been saying from the beginning that plexiglass shields weren't going to do anything. "We spent a lot of time and money focused on hygiene theater," Allen said.

Not a single study has found that these barriers do a bit of good; if anything, by interfering with ventilation, too much plexiglass has even been found to be slightly detrimental.

Epidemiologist Shira Doron of Tufts Medical Center, while admitting that "there's no research" in support of the use of plexiglass barriers, insisted on the principle: "If it might help, and it makes sense, and it doesn't hurt, then do it."

It's been on that basis that all kinds of crazy and stupid measures have been forced on us that practically everyone has to know don't actually do anything.

It calls to mind the anecdotal evidence we read about people and masks. Even though they've gotten the shots and the CDC says they can take the masks off, people seem to keep them on for purely irrational reasons: because everyone is doing it, to signal that they're not Republican, to "show respect" (whatever that's supposed to mean), and so on.

If there's any "science" in any of this, it isn't exactly obvious.

Part VI: Summer 2021

July 5, 2021 | Masks on kids

Have a look at this headline:

Duke TODAY

Topics ∨

PUBLISHED JUNE 30, 2021 IN CAMPUS, MEDICINE

RESEARCH FINDS MASKS CAN PREVENT COVID-19 TRANSMISSION IN SCHOOLS

"With masking, the schools clearly can safely deliver face-to-face education for children and adults"

I'll bet you think they looked at schools with masks and schools without masks and drew a conclusion.

Nope.

Two Duke scholars examined a bunch of masked schools in North Carolina, found transmission to be low, and credited masks.

They said that all the quarantining and social distancing had been a waste — good so far, so I appreciate them to some extent — because masks alone had been so effective (an unsupported assertion).

And they even admit: "Because North Carolina had a mask mandate for all K-12 schools, we could not compare masked schools to unmasked schools."

Say what?

Without any unmasked schools, there's no control group, and without a control group there's no study! But this is the kind of study your friends trot out to prove to you how effective masks (or whatever other alleged mitigation measure they want to vindicate) are.

Lesson:

Don't take their word for anything.

Check everything.

I'm sure you've figured out that lesson already, but it can't hurt to be reminded.

When you're told to listen to the research, remember that *b.s. like this is "the research."*

August 2, 2021 | The science cult, smashed

The cult of "science" has got to be smashed.

Someone on Twitter just posted this, thinking himself profound:

> If you think you don't trust scientists, you're mistaken. You trust scientists in a million different ways every time you step on a plane, or for that matter turn on your tap or open a can of beans. The fact that you're unaware of this doesn't mean it's not so.

Saifedean Ammous, a great friend of the Tom Woods Show, wasn't about to let this stand.

Before going any further, let me add this: after the past 18 months, I think the dangers and absurdities of scientism have become clear enough. "Science" does not (and is not intended to) have the answers to all questions. It does not and cannot tell us what we should value, what our priorities should be, whether certain behaviors are morally acceptable or indeed required, and so on. Staring longingly at men in white coats, seeking the meaning of life, is contemptible superstition.

Not to mention: the standard story of how science progresses is completely wrong. We do not move forward because government-subsidized men in lab coats play around in laboratories doing "basic science" untainted by mundane concerns. It is generally men of action who actually do the work. (See episode #713 of the Tom Woods Show for elaboration — TomWoods.com/713).

Now for Saifedean:

> The Wright brothers and a century of airplane builders were engineers. Scientists first dismissed flight as impossible even after it happened, then made up a bunch of irrelevant equations to pretend to explain how it happened.

> Everything that matters to our modern life was built by engineers and workers who got their hands dirty. Scientists sat in cushy universities writing textbooks after the fact indoctrinating generations to think it was their post-hoc explanations that built things.

Lord Kelvin was one of the world's most important scientists when airplanes were invented. This is what he thought:

"I have not the smallest molecule of faith in aerial navigation other than ballooning, or of the expectation of good results from any of the trials we heard of."

Astronomer and polymath Simon Newcomb in 1903:

"Aerial flight is one of that class of problems with which man will never be able to cope."

This was the same year in which the Wright Brothers, two bicycle shop owner high school dropouts, built the first working airplane.

Three years after the Wright Brothers flew, *The London Times* dismissed their claims of flight as fake, and was instead writing:

"All attempts at artificial aviation are not only dangerous to human life, but foredoomed to failure from the engineering standpoint."

The first commercial steam engine was invented by Simon Newcomen, a barely literate ironmonger who had never come in contact with a scientist. James Watt was a technician, not a scientist, and explicitly denied that any scientific theories influenced his invention.

The scientific method is practiced by engineers building things, experimenting to see what works. Professional science consists mostly of nerds quibbling over each other's irrelevant papers and agreeing they all need more funding.

Nothing in science needs trust. I don't trust anyone to get in an airplane. I look at the track record of airplanes and decide the risks are acceptable given the benefits. "Trust science" is how you end up with billions of lives destroyed over virus hysteria.

I love Saifedean.

The real story of science is something like the opposite of what we've been told. Not to mention: countries that heavily subsidized science in the nineteenth century lagged behind the U.K., which spent no government money on it. The classic treatment of the subject is Terence Kealey's *The Economic Laws of Scientific Research*.

August 3, 2021 | Apartheid is coming September 13

New York has really gone off the deep end.

Andrew Cuomo had already been pressuring businesses not to serve the unvaccinated. Now Bill de Blasio, in the City itself, is closing indoor dining, gyms, and entertainment venues to the unvaccinated. It's officially beginning on September 13.

Big deal, you may say. You don't like New York anyway.

That's an inhumane response.

For one thing, there are plenty of New Yorkers who are not in a position to leave. They are people. They deserve normal human sympathy, not snooty superiority. Not to mention: leaving out the politics, New York is in my opinion a wonderful place. I spent five years in Manhattan getting my PhD at Columbia University, and I've visited dozens of times since then — I have so many friends there, so many places where I love to eat, so many cultural attractions that bring me joy. Many times in my life I've been rejuvenated by the energy of the city.

It's going to be hard to give that up. But give it up I will.

Stipulating for the sake of argument that the vaccines are everything their supporters say they are, there is precisely zero reason for someone like me, who's actually had Covid, to take it. It's all downside.

But even if I'd been vaccinated, I wouldn't let myself be part of a system that benefited me while oppressing other people.

August 13, 2021 | Vaccine passports and the two Americas

The list of cities I will take pleasure in not visiting is growing, what with "vaccine passports" being proposed and implemented in New York, San Francisco, Los Angeles, and New Orleans.

I could be wrong, but I honestly think this system will be a fiasco.

The crazies say it will be great for business, because it will make hypochondriacs feel better about dining out and visiting entertainment venues. Will it, though? A lot of these folks are the double-masked-even-after-vax types who don't strike me as dying to go hear local musicians until death itself is abolished.

And on the other hand, it drives away a solid 30 percent of these establishments' customer base, at the very time that a chunk of the other 70 percent is still too scared to go out and do anything.

How do businesses survive under these conditions?

They don't, which is why in Russia, Moscow just dropped its requirement that restaurant patrons show proof of vaccination. (Moscow's rule was actually more liberal than what's being proposed in certain American cities, since it also allowed a negative Covid test or proof of natural immunity.) According to the Associated Press, "The softening of restrictions reflects their devastating impact on restaurant owners, who pleaded with city officials to rescind them."

Also, this scenario is coming: vaccines get approved for kids. Any damn fool can see kids don't need them. But with availability for kids comes an end to the vaccine passport exemption that currently exists for kids. That means your kid won't be able to do anything. Will every city get away with that? I don't see that happening.

I'm not infallible. I could be wrong about this. But what I see happening instead is some places indeed making these ridiculous demands, and the result being major migrations to states without such a policy.

August 16, 2021 | Everything they say is a lie, and 2/3 of the country believes them

Well, just like that, masks have come back in quite a few places.

You and I know they don't do anything, because we've seen the charts. The charts are relentless and unforgiving. Try to figure out where on the chart widespread masking began and you'll always be wrong, because it's always at a random spot.

And one way you know that a country with 95–98 percent mask compliance is about to have a massive spike is that the Western media writes stories about how that country "taught us how to beat the coronavirus," with the main lesson being the alleged importance of masks.

I'm not much of a Bill Maher fan, but he wasn't wrong when he said, "Sometimes I think we have to cover our faces so other people can cover their asses."

Let's check in on Georgia, where several counties recently introduced mask mandates. Note that there is zero difference between masked and unmasked counties, with the exception that the masked counties appear to be doing slightly worse:

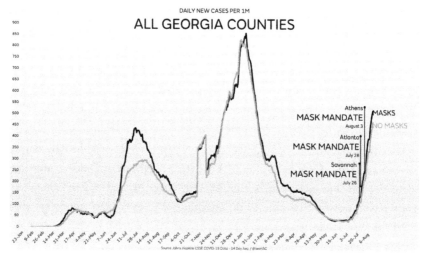

In Nevada, the governor recently reimposed mask mandates in 12 of Nevada's 17 counties. Let's check in to see how much worse the unmasked ones must surely be doing:

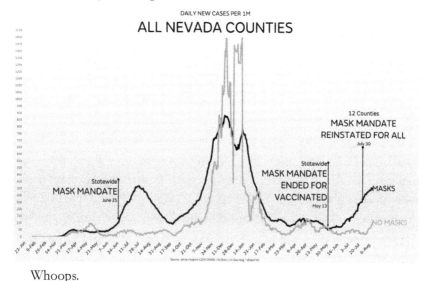

Whoops.

Let's check in with San Francisco, where hospitalizations just hit the same level as last summer's peak:

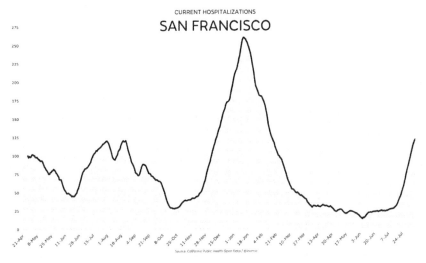

CURRENT HOSPITALIZATIONS

SAN FRANCISCO

Is this because they're not vaccinated in San Francisco, or not wearing masks? Of course not. They've been fanatics about Covid in San Francisco. Why is there zero curiosity about this?

Answer: the crazies enjoy demonizing people. Nothing brings them more pleasure than to blame health outcomes on people's failure to wear masks, or deprive themselves of joy, or whatever. So when bad outcomes occur in places where people are obsessively following whatever the latest "CDC guidelines" are, well, there's nobody to demonize. Not to mention: charts like these undermine the standard narrative that any of these "guidelines" accomplish anything.

So they just don't get mentioned.

If there's one point I've hammered away at more than any other over the past year and a half, it's this: the health outcomes of various places appear to bear no relation to the "mitigation measures" or "CDC guidelines" that place followed.

But virtually every talking head on CNN continues to speak as if it's just obvious that these "guidelines" really do "keep us safe," and they are never required to confront the mountain of evidence to the contrary.

It is truly like living in a Kafka novel. Nothing makes sense. People touted as experts on TV repeatedly tell you things you can disprove with three mouse clicks, and most people act as if this is normal.

August 17, 2021 | Next-stage insanity started today

Today New York City's vaccine passport went into effect. And although, strictly speaking, enforcement won't begin until September 13, lots of places are already demanding your papers. Virtually everything you can think of that you might want to do in the city will be closed to unvaccinated people.

Months ago I planned a trip to NYC in part to see a few old friends. I was supposed to head there tomorrow. But to hell with it. I'm not giving the vaccine fascists one cent.

I spoke to the head of catering today at a major New York institution (I'm sure he wants to remain anonymous). He seemed doubtful that this system would remain in place for even a year, though he conceded that it's impossible to know.

Regardless, it is unbelievable that this is happening at all — and when the FDA approves the vaccines, things will only get worse.

Some people are claiming that these kinds of policies will help business, but it seems clear to me that it will crush them.

Recently I spoke to the two brothers who comprise the musical group Right Said Fred (you'll surely remember "I'm Too Sexy," one of their numerous hits), who turn out to be extremely sound on Covid, the evil passport system, and all the rest. They are refusing to perform before what they call a "segregated audience," so that means they're not doing any shows or festivals at all for the time being.

This is what principled people sound like (not to mention they're a lot of fun): TomWoods.com/1945

August 19, 2021 | Tricks the maskers play: how to counter them

Remember my advice for when people try to tell you that masks brought the virus numbers down in some place: always check. In virtually every case the numbers were already coming down before masks were mandated.

In Florida, local officials, stymied by Governor DeSantis, are desperate for something that might make them look important. They're obviously hoping that mask-wearing, including in schools, can be implemented fast enough to take the credit for the obviously inevitable decline in Florida's numbers.

The problem for this scheme is that it looks like the death numbers are coming down already (and yes, that modest hump on the right-hand side of the graph is what had the lunatics screaming "DeathSantis" in recent weeks; they were basing their screeching on high but meaningless "case" numbers):

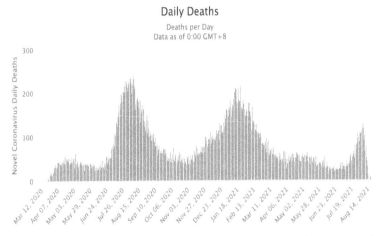

Now on the other hand, deaths in Germany appear to have come down after the introduction of a medical-grade mask mandate, so it's tempting to say, well, score one for the mask people.

But wait a minute: there's a nearby country, with virtually no masking of any kind, medical-grade or otherwise, showing exactly the same trend at the same time:

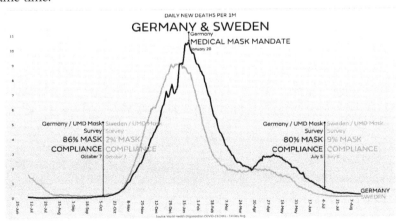

Meanwhile, the American Academy of Pediatrics, which has a case of childhood mask fanaticism, is now systematically removing references on its website to any previous suggestion that babies might need to see human faces.

Anything mentioning the importance of faces in child development, including "Face Time and Emotional Health," and a description of how adults can enrich infants four to five months old that involves repeated reference to facial cues and expressions, is now gone.

Who would ever trust people like this again?

August 20, 2021 | Can we cause them enough pain to make this stop?

I saw an interesting poll result today that I want to share with you. The Associated Press is reporting that 46 percent of vaccinated people polled say they have been "avoiding other people as much as possible."

Think about that for a minute. Nearly half of the vaccinated are still avoiding people. What does this mean for "vaccine passport" systems?

Imagine having a business, and the government now says: the only customers we'll allow you to have are people who, even after receiving the shots, are still avoiding people as much as possible.

Have fun catering to *that* clientele!

In case you're wondering, by the way, not a single word from the ACLU about governments closing off normal life to people who for whatever reason have declined a vaccine. Not one. (I know we shouldn't be surprised, but I just enjoy embarrassing them a little.)

[TW note: The ACLU eventually came out in favor of vaccine passports: "Far from compromising civil liberties, vaccine mandates actually further them," they said.]

Meanwhile, all eyes are on Florida, because the media establishment despises Ron DeSantis, but lunatic Washington state just set an all-time record for hospitalizations:

CURRENT HOSPITALIZATIONS
WASHINGTON

Source: Healthdata.gov / @anonSC

Oregon, according to news reports, just had someone die in the emergency room because no ICU beds were available, even though 70 percent of the public is vaccinated, kids are masked in school, and there's a statewide mask mandate.

But there's a different standard for red and blue states.

When the numbers go up in red states, this is a sign that people are misbehaving, not following science, being selfish, etc., and their political leaders are being stupid and irresponsible.

When the numbers go up in blue states, well, the experts are stumped and it's just one of those things.

Next week the FDA is likely to give final approval to the Pfizer vaccine, which will mean more mandates.

And more cities will — in effect — forbid entry by people with allergies and health problems that make vaccination dangerous, people with natural immunity who consider vaccination superfluous and carrying no net benefit, and those who simply prefer not to have the injections for whatever reason.

Those of us who believe in the free society have to resist this. Boycott these places. I just forfeited a large deposit at a venue in New York because I will not hold an event where people have to show their papers to get in. I'll have it in Florida instead. I did this because I have principles.

How are we going to deal with this new world? Do we have sufficient economic power to cause enough pain that the passport systems collapse?

August 23, 2021 | The good news, the bad news, and the really bad news

Some good news, some bad news, and some really bad news for today's issue.

Let's go out of order and start with the bad news: in Guam they've introduced a particularly hideous vaccine passport system. You pretty much cannot enter any indoor establishment, with few exceptions, unless you have proof of vaccination. Beyond that, you cannot take part in any social gathering with vaccinated people. Oh, and vaccinated people are themselves limited to gatherings of 100.

So what in heaven's name could be the good news?

It comes from Denmark, where they're phasing out all their restrictions. That includes their own passport system, the coronapas, which will be discontinued as of October 1. It requires proof of vaccination, a recent negative test, or recovery from a previous infection in order for people to enter most establishments.

So it is indeed possible for these kinds of interventions to be repealed. That's good news.

Now for the really bad news, courtesy of a reader in the Philippines:

> *My wife and I are teachers at an international school here in Manila, Philippines. We enjoyed our summer off back in the U.S. and Italy, where my wife is from: breathing fresh air, taking our young son to the playground, going out for ice cream — you know, all the normal things that humans do that we haven't been able to do over the past year because of the draconian restrictions imposed by the Philippine government. It certainly was a breath of fresh air. Despite all of the madness going on in both the U.S. and Italy right now, I am still green with envy at the freedoms enjoyed by the people living in those places. It jarred my brain to meet people this summer who have never had to submit to (multiple) PCR tests.*
>
> *You can imagine our morale as we returned to Manila a few weeks ago (we are contractually bound by our job). Here in the Philippines, it's as if time stopped in April of last year. Still, you must wear both a face mask and shield when you leave your house. Still, children under 18 and*

senior citizens are technically not allowed to leave their houses (although this summer that loosened up a bit, but after two weeks "delta" put an end to that). Still, schools are closed. Still, you must have a negative PCR/antigen test to travel to the next province, book a flight, or stay a night in a hotel. Still, gyms, theaters, cultural institutions, and outdoor sites (such as the American Memorial Cemetery — a cemetery!) are closed. Still, upon entering every shop or workplace one is subjected to a temperature check and a contact tracing form. Still, most restaurants are take-out, or reduced to 50% capacity (only on the lowest-level lockdown). Still, people think that if everyone "just gets the vaccine," Covid will just go away and all of this will be over. Still, what is considered the longest lockdown in the world continues.

Indeed, what is happening in places like France and Australia is very alarming, but it is frustrating to see that the Philippines is never acknowledged for its continued brutish restrictions that have been imposed as a result of the de facto martial law that has reigned over this country since all of this began. At least in other places people are beginning to question the narrative; there isn't even a shred of that here. People are too scared of the government.

Here in Manila, we finished our two-week hotel quarantine and went right into a hard lockdown, the third here since all this began in March 2020. Once again, due to the so-called "delta" variant, citizens are expected to remain at home for two weeks (a tired trope by now) and may only exit their residences for essential items with a quarantine pass (one per household). Outdoor exercise was allowed until yesterday, but the authorities probably got spooked into banning it when they saw people still outside enjoying themselves (or trying to be healthy) and not cowering in fear at home.

Naturally, only "essential" workers are allowed to leave their homes to go to work, and because teachers are somehow included in that category I consider myself lucky to be able to leave the house; our 4-year-old son, however, isn't so lucky. Our students are beginning the school year virtually, so you can imagine student (and teacher) morale. Most likely, the current round of hard lockdown will carry on until at least October: they always start out with two weeks, but then extend it by a month or more. It's always one step forward, five steps back here. I'm sure we'll get two weeks of loosened restrictions in November before the government panics about people wanting to be human for Christmas and then walks everything back.

I suppose what is particularly frustrating about this round of house arrest is that the government didn't even try to justify it with rising "cases." It was just, "We could have over 10,000 cases a day because we have 'delta' now, and we don't want the hospitals to be overrun." Reading the local news, the screeching about rising "cases" and the daily death toll that characterized previous stay-at-home lockdowns is conspicuously absent. Instead, the headlines praise the improved vaccine rollout, which until recently has been mostly farcical (and is one of the activities that has been allowed to continue during the lockdown)....

In a certain sense, there is some serenity to be found in the assurance that nothing will change here in the future, that lockdown will be on the horizon here indefinitely: at least you know where you are at. On the other hand, that can swing the other way, too, and with it come feelings of desperation and hopelessness. Additionally, the government makes decisions so quickly and capriciously that the small pleasures of life that can be squeezed out of the current situation can be snatched away at any moment, like outdoor exercise, or whether the policeman patrolling the local park will stop turning a blind eye to you taking your kid out to get some sunshine because of a new top-down order he received. All of this takes a heavy toll on the soul. Thank goodness that we have been spared the divide-and-conquer rhetoric regarding vaccines, so far.

When will this ever end? No one knows, and there is no answer, no stated goal.

I'll admit: I had no idea things were still so bad in the Philippines. Imagine a full lockdown and no dissident voices at all.

[Remember: I am giving away my book *Collateral Damage: Victims of the Lockdown Regime Tell Their Stories* for free at DiaryOfCovid.com. Please read it, because these people deserve to be heard.]

Still, although things could certainly be worse in the United States, where most of my readers and I live, we still have plenty of work ahead of us.

The CDC director herself, speaking about the vaccines being urged upon us, said that "what they can't do anymore is prevent transmission." So according to them, being vaccinated does not mean you cannot make someone else sick.

And with that, the logic of vaccine passports — or human movement passes — disintegrates.

Of course, if logic had been the driving force behind any of this, the world would look quite different right now.

August 24, 2021 | The forbidden country just scored another win against Covid

Today it's back to charts again. Let's start with California.

California has just matched its hospitalization peak from last summer, so I guess we can expect the media to pounce on Governor Gavin Newsom, right? (Ha, ha — sorry, you and I already know the answer to that.)

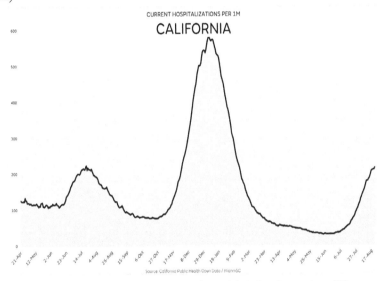

The chart below shows states in the mid-Atlantic region. These states have different policies when it comes to schools, masking, and vaccines, and yet you'll notice that their hospitalization trajectory is exactly the same:

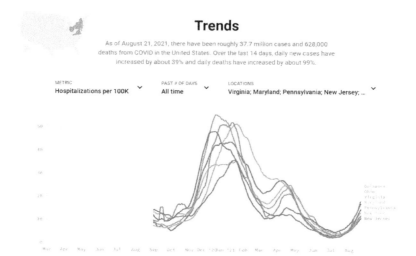

Trends

As of August 21, 2021, there have been roughly 37.7 million cases and 628,000 deaths from COVID in the United States. Over the last 14 days, daily new cases have increased by about 39% and daily deaths have increased by about 99%.

METRIC	PAST # OF DAYS	LOCATIONS
Hospitalizations per 100K	All time	Virginia; Maryland; Pennsylvania; New Jersey; ...

Now for probably the most important of my three graphs for today. This year Sweden, even during the Delta phase of all this, where mitigation measures have been light at best and schools have been open without masks or distancing, excess mortality has actually been lower than normal. I have included the United States in the graph for something to compare Sweden to:

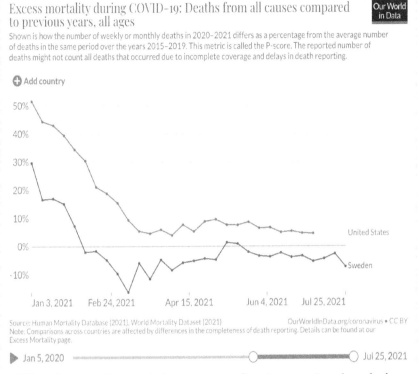

Excess mortality during COVID-19: Deaths from all causes compared to previous years, all ages

Shown is how the number of weekly or monthly deaths in 2020–2021 differs as a percentage from the average number of deaths in the same period over the years 2015–2019. This metric is called the P-score. The reported number of deaths might not count all deaths that occurred due to incomplete coverage and delays in death reporting.

Source: Human Mortality Database (2021), World Mortality Dataset (2021)   OurWorldInData.org/coronavirus • CC BY
Note: Comparisons across countries are affected by differences in the completeness of death reporting. Details can be found at our Excess Mortality page.

What does it all mean? It means we live in a society based almost entirely on lies. It's really extraordinary.

August 30, 2021 | A state that doesn't care if you live or die

Now is as good a time as any for some perspective.

Ask the average person in whatever country you choose what his chances of hospitalization with or death from Covid are and the answers will shock you. Nearly everyone you speak to is completely uninformed. It is impossible to make rational decisions amidst this degree of ignorance.

The survival rate for people in the 0–19 age group is 99.997 percent. For 20–29 it's 99.986 percent. You can find all the figures in the graphic below.

The data come from a recent paper by Stanford's Cathrine Axfors and John Ioannidis, "Infection fatality rate of Covid-19 in community-dwelling populations with emphasis on the elderly: An overview." Here's how it breaks down:

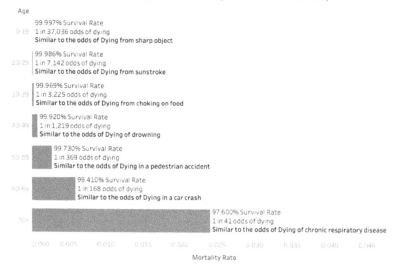

Mortality Risk COVID-19 - Chances of dying of C19 by Age Group with Comparable Overall Odds to the Population (Stanford Study - Ioannidis & Axfors)

Do you think the average person has any idea that the numbers for survival are this high?

A person under 50 is therefore at greater risk of death from drowning, choking on food, sunstroke, or from a sharp object.

In the U.K., the *Daily Mail* just published an article called, "Is it time to stop obsessing over Covid figures? Statistics reveal virus is NOT the biggest killer — with heart disease, dementia and cancer each claiming four times as many lives in an average week last month."

"Even before the rollout of the vaccine," the article notes, "fewer than one per cent of people who caught Covid died. Now, scientists say that figure is ten times smaller."

Much as I welcome this, it's pretty rich for the British press (or indeed any press) to publish an article and a chart like that, scratching their heads as to why people are obsessed about Covid, when they themselves are directly responsible for the misinformation that brought about that obsession.

Remember when the *Washington Post* called Iowa "a state that doesn't care if you live or die" when that state removed its Covid restrictions? That was seven months ago.

Here's the chart. Think we're going to hear any apologies, or any "gee, I guess I don't understand any of this as well as I thought," or…?

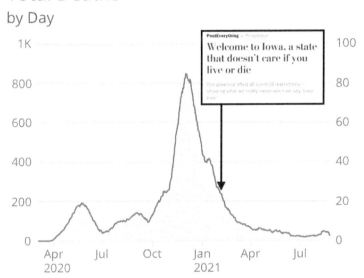

September 8, 2021 | So you think we can't get back to normal?

Last week I mentioned that the ban on entry into Sweden against people who live in seven countries (among them Israel and the United States) is interfering with a trip I had scheduled to take there.

I received replies from numerous people who live in either Denmark or Sweden, and I wanted to share this with you.

It's almost unbelievable, but this is what life is like in Sweden right now, as told by someone who's in the heart of it:

Hi, Tom; greetings from Stockholm, Sweden:

I have been a regular listener to your podcast since about episode 500, so I would consider myself a big supporter of your work.

The entry ban towards U.S. citizens is a huge surprise. The Swedish strategy against Covid-19 has so far been very successful, but is thanks not to wisdom but rather to the gigantic incompetence of the Swedish government — the social democratic leaders are so full of woke "value ground work" (Swedish: värdegrundsarbete*) that they can't implement any changes of any kind — and in the case of Covid that's just perfect! The fact that they managed to implement some random travel ban is most likely just due to some random event in the administration.*

Personally, I live close to the center of Stockholm (10 km from downtown), which has been the epicenter of epicenters in this pandemic (for a long period of time in 2020 Sweden had the highest numbers in Europe and Stockholm had the highest numbers in Sweden). Yet no one in my family or extended family has had the virus, and no one I know of has even been to the hospital due to the virus.

I can report from my daily trips to my office downtown, via metro or commuter train, that about 0–1% of Swedes are wearing masks today, the trains are full of people (almost close to pre-Corona levels), and the streets, shops, restaurants in Stockholm show no — ZERO — sign of some pandemic going on.

Life is 100% back to normal, as it has almost been the whole time....I leave my kids (ages 9 and 12) at school every day. The school is packed with happy, unmasked children, and the only difference from pre-Covid is that we leave them outside school rather than inside.

It is with great sadness that I see the development in some U.S. cities and states, and countries like Australia, NZ, Canada. I pray to God that your message can help prevent the same development in the U.S. — a country I used to love, have lived in for 18 months (Boston + San Francisco) and have visited about 25 times.

Imagine that. They're just living.

For the past two months there have been only a handful of Covid deaths in Sweden. In case you're wondering: Sweden is number 13 in Europe for percentage of the population fully vaccinated, so if your smart-aleck friend wants to claim their good results are due to vaccination, that'll be a tough mountain to climb.

Wouldn't it be nice to live in a world in which every time a politician acted as if it was simply obvious that his proposed restrictions were necessary for "public health," a reporter demanded that he account for the case of Sweden?

September 13, 2021 | They're coming for the kids next

Fauci keeps getting worse, just when you thought that wasn't possible.

He has been saying that the Biden vaccine mandates [that required the shots for health care workers and at companies employing at least one hundred people] are a "moderate" plan, because OSHA will allow for weekly testing as an option instead of vaccination. "Myself, I would make it just vaccinate or not," said Fauci.

Now Fauci wants vaccination as a requirement for air travel and — you knew this was coming — for children to be allowed to attend school.

"I would support that if you want to get on a plane and travel with other people, that you should be vaccinated," he said.

Kamala Harris, for her part, said the other day that we need to "protect the vaccinated."

So the message people are hearing, from Fauci and Harris and the rest, is: *The vaccines work so well that in order to protect people who get them, we need to do only one small additional thing: banish everyone else from society.*

Yeah, that message is sure to get people excited about the shots!

Naturally Fauci favors requiring children to be vaccinated, and we're now being told that authorization for children aged 5 to 11 to get the shot could be coming as early as next month.

This is no big deal, said Fauci: "I don't know what school you went to, but the school that I went to, you had to be vaccinated for measles, mumps, rubella, polio or otherwise you couldn't go to school. So it is not something new to mandate vaccines for school children."

Well, thanks for treating us like we're 7.

The point here is that Covid is of borderline zero danger to children. Even the CDC reports that "a total of eight in-hospital Covid-19–related deaths in persons aged 0–17 years occurred during August 2020–August 2021." And the shots appear to be more dangerous to them than Covid itself. (Incidentally, the shots he mentioned were *not* required when Fauci went to school.)

So brace yourself for fights over Covid vaccination in schools. And then, on a smaller scale, as part of the hysterics' ongoing destruction of society, unvaccinated kids being told by their parents that they can no longer play with some of their longtime friends, because those friends' parents are lunatics who won't allow their children to associate with the unvaccinated.

A total fiasco.

Homeschooling will get a shot in the arm, so to speak, from all this (so don't forget to check out the self-taught K-12 Ron Paul Curriculum at RonPaulHomeschool.com), and normal people's disdain for government at all levels will grow, but these silver linings are slim pickings when set against the damage the crazies will try to do.

Remember: evil bastards don't say, "We're extending our power over you because we're evil bastards." They say, "We're extending our power over you for your own good."

September 14, 2021 | They're scared: health-care workers are resigning

A few months ago normality was actually taking shape, at least in the United States.

In New York, Andrew Cuomo declared that since 70 percent of eligible state residents had been vaccinated, he was dropping Covid restrictions. New York!

By contrast, these days it's hard not to feel demoralized, what with all the hysteria and hatred toward the unvaccinated, and with the horrific Covid regimes around the world that show no sign of letting up.

Here in the United States we have a ruling class that doesn't hesitate to denounce other countries for their human rights abuses. Yet Australia has turned their country into a prison camp and imposed restrictions with exactly zero scientific basis, and children's lives are being flat-out destroyed — and not a word from the U.S. regime.

That should tell you something.

Meanwhile, I'm happy to report that my old friend, erstwhile co-author, attorney, and Tom Woods Show guest Chris Ferrara just threw a monkey wrench into the New York vaccine mandate for health care workers.

Today a federal judge issued a temporary restraining order that prevents New York from proceeding with that mandate because it failed to include an exemption for health workers who object to the vaccination on religious grounds.

Chris said, "Never in the history of New York State, never in the history of the world, has a government sought to forcibly impose mass vaccination on an entire class of people under threat of immediate personal and professional destruction. This is just another example of how Covid regimes are completely out of control. The federal judiciary has a duty under the Constitution to put a straitjacket on this institutional insanity."

Chris is great, as you can see.

And many health workers are sticking to their guns. At Olean General Hospital, for example, 11 employees have so far indicated that they will resign rather than get the vaccine. This, said a hospital spokesman, is "enough to push the hospital into a disaster status should these employees elect to leave the organization as a result of the mandate."

Keep fighting. There are more of us than they think.

September 15, 2021 | They're trying to shut one of our heroes up

Oxford's Carl Heneghan and Harvard's Martin Kulldorff are reporting that Jay Bhattacharya, a professor of medicine at Stanford who's been a voice of reason in a sea of monomaniacal Covid hysteria, has been the subject of an anonymous attack for his well-founded position against masking, and masking children in particular.

Posters featuring Bhattacharya's portrait have appeared around campus that link him to Covid deaths in Florida, even though Florida (contrary to the impression you'd get from the media) has one of the best rates of age-adjusted Covid mortality in the United States.

Further, Melissa Bondy, who chairs the university's epidemiology department (you know, the profession one third of whose members polled were afraid of opening their mail, out of fear of catching the virus from an envelope, as late as the summer of 2020), has circulated a petition criticizing certain faculty members for allegedly offering "recommendations [that] are disturbing and contrary to public health standards; they foster uncertainty and anxiety and put lives at risk."

The petition names no names but quotes Bhattacharya, who correctly observed that "there is no high-quality evidence to support the assertion that masks stop the disease from spreading."

"It is hard to understand," write Heneghan and Kulldorff, "how any scientist can claim there is high-quality evidence that masks on children are an effective public health measure." Again, hard to dispute this, since the evidence needed to do so does not exist.

This assertion should be uncontroversial even without reference to the relevant studies. The charts from all over the world show widespread masking to correlate with precisely nothing in the Covid numbers, and appear at entirely random points along the various countries' curves.

Countries with mask compliance rates of 95 percent and above have continued to see outbreaks that should not be occurring if masks had the effectiveness claimed for them. Masks have surely been the most outstanding and embarrassing public-health failures in living memory.

When it comes to masking children in order to "stop the spread" in schools, the fact remains that no randomized studies exist. What we know is that in Sweden, which kept schools in session and didn't mask children at all, teachers fared no worse than people in any other profession, and not one of that country's 1.8 million school-age children died.

The *New York Times* excitedly reported on a study out of North Carolina showing low Covid rates in that state's schools, but since it had no unmasked schools to compare them to, the study was worthless.

The recently touted Bangladesh study is alleged to show the effectiveness of masks, but most people reporting on it neglected the confidence intervals involved, which in fact lead us to the conclusion that masks have either no effect or a very limited one.

To act as if this question isn't even debatable, when all of the existing evidence is on Bhattacharya's side (spare me the mannequin studies that don't involve actual human beings, or studies that begin with the *assumption* that masks work), is inexcusable for anyone, but especially a scientist. And to try to create a chilling effect on campus for dissident voices, well, that's typical of the totalitarian instincts we've seen throughout this mess. One dissident voice, to these control freaks, is one too many.

Part VII: Fall 2021

September 21, 2021 | DeSantis just dropped a ten-megaton bomb

Florida's governor, Ron DeSantis, keeps lobbing bombs at his enemies.

Today he introduced to the press the new surgeon general of Florida, Dr. Joseph Ladapo.

An immigrant from Nigeria, Ladapo holds his medical degree from Harvard Medical School and his PhD from the Harvard School of Public Health. He will be joining the faculty at the University of Florida as well.

And as it happens, his name is affixed to the Great Barrington Declaration, which condemns lockdowns as a public-health measure.

Ladapo didn't waste time letting the press know that he is their enemy.

"Florida will completely reject fear as a way of making policies in public health....That's been...a centerpiece of health policy in the United States ever since the beginning of the pandemic. And it's over here. Expiration date, it's done."

"The risks and benefits of decisions haven't been considered wholly and thoughtfully," he added, because policymakers and the public have been operating from a position of fear.

He went on: "Public health is not one thing. Public health is not about a single item. It's not [only] about how many cases of Covid there are in a location....As all of you know, that's how public health has been treated for the past year and a half. So that's over. It's not going to happen here."

Vaccination, he said, "has been treated almost like a religion."

And he denounced lockdowns, which he described as both ineffectual and wrong.

The Covid hysterics are already trying to claim that this man, whose credentials are as long as my arm, isn't qualified to speak about Covid. These are the same people who hang on every word of "Eric Feigl-Ding," a nutritionist who took some classes in epidemiology.

Evidently the only people qualified to speak about Covid are nutsos who are monomaniacally obsessed with it. People urging reason and balance? Close your ears, citizen!

October 4, 2021 | Maybe no Christmas this year, says Fauci

It's "too soon" to say whether we'll be able to gather at Christmas, Dr. Fauci is now telling us. Well, we didn't listen to him last year and I have no intention of listening to him now.

But wouldn't it be nice to have a news media that challenged these clowns once in a while? For example, Fauci should have to explain this chart (the bold line represents the average):

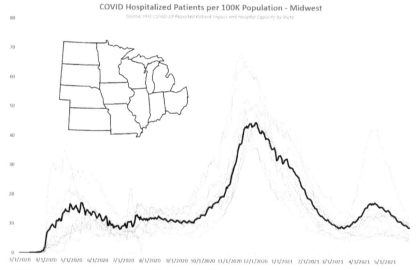

This graph traces Covid hospitalizations in the Midwest over time. Here's why it matters to the "maybe you can't have Christmas" insanity: the hospitalization peak occurs right around Thanksgiving, before the alleged effects of Thanksgiving gatherings would have had time to take effect. And then, instead of spiking in the wake of those gatherings, the numbers plummet — and continue to plummet consistently and without interruption all throughout Christmas, as if that holiday hadn't even occurred.

Would Dr. Fauci care to explain to us how, if his advice is sound, such a thing could have occurred? (Good thing for him no one is going to ask.)

Speaking of bad Fauci predictions, he said, "I don't think it's smart" for college football to be played in front of full stadiums. After he said that, Covid numbers in the South, where these games are being played regularly, began to plummet. As you can see below, they began to plummet almost immediately after Fauci warned them not to do it.

In a weird way you almost have to be impressed by someone who can be so precise in his wrongness:

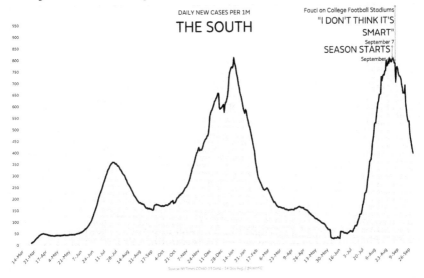

Meanwhile, courtesy of Worldometers, let's check back in with Florida. The drop in Covid deaths there has been extremely sudden and sharp, even though the general public has not modified its behavior at all. (I live here, so I know.) The chart says it all:

Daily New Deaths in Florida

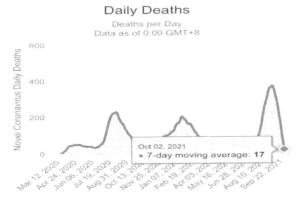

We can be sure the media will get right to the bottom of this!

October 5, 2021 | Another NBA player makes Fauci's head spin

Last week people cheered when I sent what Jonathan Isaac of the Golden State Warriors said about health, Covid, and vaccination.

Now it's Draymond Green of the Golden State Warriors who's got the thought controllers after him.

"To me," he told the press, the Covid issue

> has turned into a political war....For someone who's not extremely into politics...when you make something so political, and not everyone is into politics, you can also turn those people off. And I think there is something to be said about people's concern about something that's being pressed so hard. Like, why are you pressing so hard? Just pressing and pressing and pressing.
>
> I think you have to honor people's feelings and their own personal beliefs. And I think that's been lost when it comes to vaccinated and non-vaccinated. And it kind of sucks that that's been lost.
>
> You say we live in the land of the free. Well, you're not giving anyone freedom, because you're making people do something, essentially. Without necessarily making them, you're making them do something. That goes against everything America stands for, or supposedly stands for.

What I like about that statement in particular is his observation that not being a political person, he's being turned off by how political Covid and vaccination have become. And he wonders aloud about the fanaticism around it and the constant pressure on people.

It makes me wonder: how many other people, also not normally interested in politics, have also had enough of this, even if they might not say so in public, and who are also disturbed by the fanaticism driving it all?

They may say in public what the authorities want them to say, but how many people in their hearts can see something is very wrong?

It's easy to get discouraged that more people aren't actively opposing the craziness. At the same time, those filled college football stadiums tell us at least something: there are lots of people who aren't paying attention to the hysterics anymore.

But if we're going to push back on the coercion and the misinformation (isn't it rich that of all people the Fauci devotees have the chutzpah to accuse *us* of misinformation?), it's going to take more than just ignoring them. We have to fight back.

October 6, 2021 | *New York Times* finally admits: our behavior doesn't seem to matter

Well, it took only 19 months, but the *New York Times* is admitting that people getting sick with Covid does not appear to have a whole lot to do with our behavior.

In an article this week called "Covid, In Retreat," David Leonhardt of the *Times* observes that U.S. cases have fallen 35 percent in a month — a month that included Labor Day, whose celebrations were supposed to have made the numbers worse. (I am aware of the problems with "cases," but he later notes that this general trend extends to hospitalizations and deaths as well.)

The virus appears to move in two-month cycles, says Leonhardt, and epidemiologists "do not understand why" it works like that. It has occurred "even when human behavior was not changing in obvious ways."

"We've ascribed far too much human authority over the virus," says Michael Osterholm, the former Biden Covid adviser who has occasionally said sensible things.

Leonhardt is also cautiously optimistic that the worst may be behind us — a rare thing coming from a *New York Times* writer. He cites Scott Gottlieb, formerly of the FDA, as saying, "I'm of the opinion that this is the last major wave of infection."

Gottlieb could be wrong, of course. That's almost not the point. It's that they're talking in ways that are clearly different from the Fauci wing of all this, and that's better than nothing.

Now back to Leonhardt: his point about a two-month cycle, and Osterholm's point that we've been overemphasizing the role of human interventions, obviously extends to masks as well: nobody is wearing masks in two-month cycles, and yet the virus observes that pattern anyway. Nobody in the article extends the analysis to masks, but there's no other way to interpret what they're saying.

Still, despite this, we have kids masked in school all day and crazy deep-cleaning protocols as if we haven't learned a thing in 19 months. Someone joked that we should just pretend schools are restaurants so kids can just take their masks off when they sit down.

October 8, 2021 | Biden Covid adviser finally admits: we're clueless about viruses

Something is screwy: the *New York Times* has been sensible twice in a single week.

Now writer David Leonhardt is pointing out what a lot of us have been saying pretty much the whole time: (1) predictions of doom based on people's so-called "bad behavior" often turn out to be embarrassingly off the mark, and (2) the "moralistic fable" behind Covid (whereby good and virtuous behavior makes the numbers go down and "reckless" behavior does the opposite) is unhelpful.

Leonhardt writes:

> The fable we tell ourselves is that our day-to-day behavior dictates the course of the pandemic. When we are good — by staying socially distant and wearing our masks — cases are supposed to fall. When we are bad — by eating in restaurants, hanging out with friends and going to a theater or football game — cases are supposed to rise.

With school resuming and large crowds, often unmasked, assembling for all kinds of events, we heard plenty of stern warnings at the beginning of last month. Leonhardt cites Politico's headline "It May Only Get Worse." "The new school year is already a disaster," said *Business Insider*.

And then what happened?

Everything plummeted: cases, hospitalizations, deaths.

As I've said repeatedly over the past year and a half, I've just wanted to hear the so-called experts say, at least once in a while, "We don't know. We don't fully understand what's going on here."

But that's not as fun as lording it over the public with a false certainty.

Former Biden Covid adviser Michael Osterholm displayed the kind of humility I've been waiting for when he told Leonhardt: "We still are really in the cave ages in terms of understanding how viruses emerge, how they spread, how they start and stop, why they do what they do."

What a refreshing change from "Shut up and listen to the science." A little late, though. Some of us have been treated not too kindly for saying these very things. Now, as people begin to weary of it all, people like Leonhardt suddenly have the courage to say something.

But better late than never. I'm not a sore winner.

October 18, 2021 | Finally: Fauci gets fact-checked

Well, now the shoe is on the other foot.

NBC reporter Shaquille Brewster just fact-checked Dr. Anthony Fauci's claim that full football stadiums would lead to terrible Covid outcomes.

Today's Joy Reid said to Fauci, "As soon as I saw it, I thought Covid is about to have a feast. What did you think?" To which Fauci replied: "I thought the same thing. I think it's really unfortunate."

Brewster points out that Reid and Fauci had nothing to worry about. "It never happened. Cases are now in steep decline in every college football state across the South. Including Florida, where hospitalizations fell 64 percent last month, even as some 90,000 fans packed the [University of Florida] Gators' stadium."

(In fact, Florida now has the lowest Covid case rate in the entire continental U.S. — I'm sure the media will jump right on that!)

Do you suppose Joy Reid will ask Dr. Fauci how they could have been so wrong, and whether they're being too cartoonish in their analysis?

November 2, 2021 | Public opinion just took a major swing our way

An NBC poll finds Americans souring on vaccine mandates, perhaps as they begin to observe their consequences.

The question: "Do you strongly favor, somewhat favor, somewhat oppose, or strongly oppose requiring that everyone who is now eligible must get a Covid-19 vaccine?"

Results: Favor 47% (34% strongly), Oppose 50% (41% strongly).

Now expect those numbers to change if the Northeast has a bad winter, even though nothing about the vaccines themselves or the issues involved will have changed.

But still, that's a surprising result. We'd been told consistently that 70+ percent of Americans favored the mandates.

And incidentally, that's something the bad guys love: making you feel marginalized and alone.

As writer John Hayward puts it:

> One reason Dems are so comically furious over "Let's Go Brandon" is they understand it's the kind of thing that triggers preference cascades — a moment when people look around and realize that huge numbers of their neighbors share what the ruling party claims is a fringe opinion.
>
> The Left expends a huge amount of effort on making its adversaries feel marginalized. They mastered the dark art of making the majority *feel* like a fringe minority. The demoralization-destabilization-subversion strategy of the Left is designed to make normal people feel abnormal.

I think that's why people say the ol' Tom Woods Show (at TomsPodcast.com) and these emails help them feel normal — since every major outlet around them is trying to make them think the whole world opposes them.

November 3, 2021 | America to CNN: drop dead

Speaking in Palm Beach County this morning, Ron DeSantis said: "A recession is when your neighbor loses his job; a depression is when you lose yours. A recovery is when Fauci loses his."

He's speaking like someone who feels like things are going his way — and maybe they are.

You've heard about yesterday's election results, particularly in Virginia. Yes, Glenn Youngkin, the victor in the gubernatorial race, may not be the world's best Republican, but there is no doubt what he represents in the minds of voters: opposition to Covid stupidity and woke lunacy.

The GOP also took the lieutenant governor's office and the attorney general's office away from the Democrats, and flipped the Virginia House of Delegates as well.

In New Jersey the execrable Democrat Phil Murphy was very nearly driven from office in a state Joe Biden carried by just under 16 points. Ed

Durr, a truck driver who spent $153 on his campaign, is poised to defeat the current state senate president.

One commentator wrote, "I don't know why Democrats did so poorly last night, but one possibility is that their entire theory of governance is based on paternalism, hysteria, conspiracy theories, censorship, moral superiority, virtue signaling, and a complete indifference to people's material well-being."

Even with the tide evidently turning in blue states, the crazies are nevertheless undeterred: Boston elected a mayor who favors a vaccine passport system (even after these systems have, predictably, proven useless in "stopping the spread"), and San Francisco is looking forward to closing down virtually all of life to children 5 and over if they're not vaccinated.

That's all crazy and awful, though I personally think that anyone mandating vaccination for kids is going to find they've bitten off more than they can chew: the poll numbers find only about a quarter of parents ready to vaccinate their children at the first opportunity.

And as a member of my private group, the Tom Woods Show Elite, put it, "Things aren't all rosy for the narrative the media wants you to think is the truth. Even if they continue to mostly win, any indication that the people, in private, reject them, gladdens my heart."

We have a fight ahead of us, to be sure, but I'm tired of defeatists telling me that everything is hopeless and there's no way out. Normal Americans are beginning to reassert themselves.

November 4, 2021 | The crazies are fuming at the South's low Covid numbers

Within the past week someone who's more or less on our side of all this stuff took a bizarre swipe at your host here.

He thinks I'm saying that our political elites are innocently making mistakes and that showing them some mask charts will change their minds. I have never said or even thought such a thing, obviously. What, then, is the point of my charts?

Number one, to reassure you — yes, *you*, dear reader — that you're not crazy, and that you are correct to think the "public health" establishment is clueless, and possibly even sinister. And also to help raise doubts in the minds of your friends.

By the way, is this "preaching to the choir"? I suppose so. But I've never understood why that's supposed to be bad. The choir needs to be preached to! Have you ever been to a church where the pastor tells the choir they may as well just go outside and smoke while he delivers his sermon?

Number two, to show people who aren't strongly committed one way or the other that the morality play being pushed on us — "good behavior" makes the virus go away, while "bad behavior" makes it spread — does not in any way reflect reality.

But no, there's no changing the minds of the power elite, because for them this is all a golden opportunity to expand their power, portray themselves as indispensable saviors, and set the stage for future large-scale interventions.

So for example, the chart at the end of today's entry won't make Joe Biden change course, but it can make a normal person wonder.

Today on Twitter a *New York Times* reporter shared a map of the United States that depicted rates of active Covid in the various states. He was asking why the South would be doing so well despite its governors having ignored the CDC.

Since some people cannot give up the CDC religion no matter what the data tells them, one woman chimed in that the South probably isn't testing as much, because they don't really believe in Covid. So she's convinced that Covid *must* be bad in the South. It just has to be. Her religion *requires* her to believe this.

She doesn't know, apparently, that Florida's daily hospitalization numbers are lower than they've been in about a year and a half. How would she know that, even if she were a reasonable person with an open mind? Who's going to tell her?

And if it's a question of a lack of testing, that lack of testing must be incredibly well coordinated across the Southern states to produce such strikingly similar outcomes everywhere:

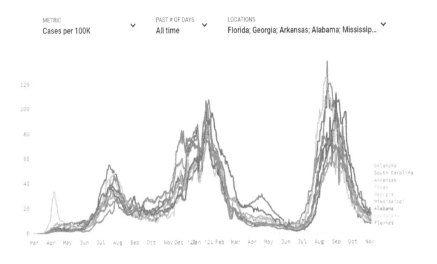

November 8, 2021 | How will they blame DeSantis now?

All of this is your fault, they say.

If you had just listened to the experts (I am trying to use that word with a straight face) and followed their mitigation measures, we could have conquered this thing long ago.

What you're seeing below are two maps of the United States, side by side, separated by roughly three months, depicting the Covid cases that our opinion molders profess to be so concerned about. These maps are generated on a regular basis by the *New York Times*.

Well, how about that.

August 12   November 7

283

Remember when the map on the left was the fault of Ron DeSantis? Not to mention the vaccination rates of those states, which were likewise blamed (although Florida's vaccination numbers for seniors have been quite high).

And yet with zero changes in behavior, the map on the left became the map on the right.

Are we supposed to believe that everyone in the Southeast suddenly started wearing masks at the same time, and everyone in the rest of the country stopped wearing them, also at the same time?

November 12, 2021 | The geniuses are locking down again

Today someone shared this chart, generated by the *Financial Times*. Try to pick out which one of these countries hasn't implemented a vaccine passport system:

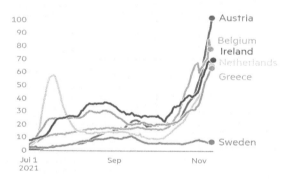

New confirmed cases of Covid-19 in Austria, Belgium, Netherlands, Greece, Ireland and Sweden
Seven-day rolling average of new cases (per 100k)

I'll bet you know which one it is.

Meanwhile, parts of Europe are going back into lockdown. Austria is locking down the one-third of the population that is unvaccinated. The Netherlands is 72 percent fully vaccinated and is going into lockdown for everyone, vaccinated and unvaccinated.

Wouldn't it be nice if, instead of inanely blaming "the unvaccinated" for this, the robots on social media would at least admit that this isn't how they expected it to go, and that there shouldn't be this level of cases and deaths after the introduction of vaccines?

It's like Sweden: we were supposed to believe that Sweden would have one of the worst death rates in the world because it ignored the so-called experts demanding lockdown. Well, Sweden is currently #53 in the world for Covid death rate. Number fifty-three. Not one. Not two. Not ten. Not twenty. Fifty-three.

The crazies are still criticizing Sweden, naturally. But my question is: when you were screaming hysterically at Sweden to lock down, did you think they'd end up all the way down at number 53 in the world in death rate? Aren't you the least bit curious about that? Is there a chance that if we hadn't wrecked societies it wouldn't have made any difference anyway?

Same with Florida: did the hysterics expect them to have one of the better rates of age-adjusted Covid mortality in the United States? Of course not. They were warning that Florida would be one of the worst.

And yet in none of these cases can they bring themselves to say: thank goodness things turned out better than we predicted! Instead, they just double down.

November 14, 2021 | They just admitted what the passport system is for

You've probably seen a handful of people on social media say that vaccine passport systems make them "feel safe." You know and I know that these systems have nothing to do with health or safety.

Well, some authorities in Canada just admitted what you and I knew: the aim is to punish the unvaccinated.

The British Columbia Recreation and Parks Association says:

> Remember, the purpose of the PoV card is to incentivize residents to be vaccinated, not to control the spread of the virus....This is an important shift to keep aware of for your decision-making; the province has shifted from actions that provide a Covid-safe environment to actions that provide discretionary services to the vaccinated.

Patricia Daly, Chief Medical Health Officer for Vancouver Coastal Health, added:

The vaccine passport requires people to be vaccinated to do certain discretionary activities such as go to restaurants, movies, gyms, not because these places are high risk. We are not actually seeing Covid transmission in these settings. It really is to create an incentive to improve our vaccination coverage....The vaccine passport is for non-essential opportunities, and it's really to create an incentive to get higher vaccination rates.

So even though cities and countries with these systems in place are doing no better than countries that don't, that isn't the point. The point, as I've said all along, is to punish.

November 15, 2021 | Pro-Fauci state senator is unhappy with ol' Woods

A state senator from Tennessee is very unhappy with your host here.

Heidi Campbell of the state's 20th senatorial district responded to the email I sent out some time ago letting you know that the video of my 2000th episode event was up. I must have made some side remark about Dr. Fauci.

As you will see in what follows, she evidently thinks that public health bureaucrats take some class in college that teaches them how to balance lockdowns against collateral damage and therefore gives them the exclusive right to make judgments in this area.

There is no such class, obviously. Not to mention: lockdown was universally rejected by the public health literature before 2020.

(So "trust the experts" both when they tell you definitely not to do X, and then also trust them when suddenly and without evidence they demand you do X.)

Here is what she wrote to me:

> *The puerility of a grown man who has been given so much opportunity in life actively attacking a doctor who has tried to disseminate good public health messaging is really just embarrassing. I realize that you are the kind of person who does not listen and just speaks, but I encourage you to take some time to think about your value system and what you're doing to make the world a better or worse place. If you're honest with yourself I suspect you'll find some areas where you might want to change some things.*

When I received this message I was out with my kids, so I wasn't in a position to draft the most eloquent of replies. But I did quickly dictate something into my phone:

> *If you're [sic; error caused by the dictation function on my phone] concern is science, health, or the norms of civilization, I cannot imagine how you could be criticizing me, of all people.*
>
> *What's embarrassing is somebody who continues to make excuses for this man despite being embarrassingly wrong on schools (or are you telling me Europe was wrong?), predicts superspreader events that never occur, and has literally, and I mean literally, no explanation for why states without lockdown have better age-adjusted Covid mortality.*
>
> *Tell me, what is your explanation for that? I'd love to hear it. Andy Slavitt doesn't know, either.*
>
> *Oh, and put masks on 2-year-olds, even though there are no randomized controlled trials on this. And Europe doesn't do it.*
>
> *The results of this fiasco include millions of deaths in the developing world (according to the* New York Times, *there will be 2 million excess deaths from HIV, malaria, and tuberculosis because of the irrational panic), tens of thousands of premature cancer deaths, the decimation of people's life savings and dreams, a huge loss in educational attainment, elderly people left completely isolated and begging for human contact, childhood poverty massively increased around the world, and on and on.*
>
> *And as we can see by using scatterplots, there is no connection between the alleged mitigation efforts and health outcomes.*
>
> *Infectious disease epidemiologists, as opposed to immunologists like Fauci, said from the beginning that the correct approach was to protect the vulnerable without shutting down society. That approach has been vindicated a million times over.*

Believe it or not, the following was her reply. Not a word about childhood poverty or the devastation of the developing world or anything. Just this:

> *Amazing that you have this long-running podcast and (I'm sure) a significant number of listeners and your response to an email encouraging you to take some time for introspection begins with a contraction that was obviously intended to be a possessive adjective. Lord help us!*

Now folks, I don't pull out the "I have a PhD" card pretty much ever, but I could not believe she was pretending that I must not know the difference between *your* and *you're*, so it was a quick proxy. I said: "It's dictation software. I hold a PhD from Columbia University; I assure you I can write. Anytime you care to share any answers to my questions, I'd love to hear them."

Her reply:

> *Informing people that you have a PhD is never a good look — it just makes you seem insecure. I don't need to answer those questions. 99.9% of the global public health community has already weighed in. I understand that you make money from spreading disinformation and it's apparent that you lack the depth of character to have any misgivings about doing so. Inevitably it's Veronica, Regina, and Amy who will suffer because of your actions. Your choice. Have a great weekend!*

I guess she looked up my children's names. She's not even good at that: she left out Elizabeth and Sarah. (None of them got sick, by the way, because they were at zero risk in the first place.) My reply:

> *I was not boasting about the degree, as is clear from the context, but pointing out that your frivolous comment about the misuse of a word was obviously misguided.*
>
> *What exactly have world authorities said about why there's no difference between lockdown and no-lockdown places? Can you at least repeat their explanation for me? Does their explanation satisfy you?*
>
> *Why is Sweden a distant #53 in death rate, without locking down? Sweden would be #43 out of 50 in terms of Covid deaths per capita were it a U.S. state. Were you expecting it to be #53 in the world? Seriously and honestly? If not, do you concede that perhaps the situation is a bit less comic-bookish than* Salon *has made it appear?*
>
> *Why aren't you the least bit curious about this?*
>
> *I have five daughters, all of whom are critical thinkers, and none of whom would look at the present situation and make an appeal to authority. If you think 99.9% of health experts believe in lockdowns, you are shockingly misinformed. You cannot possibly be serious.*
>
> *As soon as you can point out a single false statement I have made, I will retract it. But you'll need to explain to me why I'm wrong, and not just tell me that some public health bureaucrat disagrees.*

No response yet.

At every level we are governed by mediocrities like this.

She doesn't have to answer my questions because "the authorities" have answered them. Oh, have they? Andy Slavitt had no idea what the answer was when the subject came up on MSNBC. He just said that "there's so much of this virus that we think we understand, that we think we can predict, that's just a little bit beyond our explanation."

In other words, he has no answer.

Same with Dr. Fauci: when asked about the success of Texas, the best he could come up with was that maybe everyone was doing things outdoors now. In other words, an embarrassing non-answer.

We've ruined people's lives and dreams with nothing to show for it and what we laughingly call our expert class has no answers for us — and our state senator here has no answer, either. She points me in the direction of Fauci and Slavitt, both of whom admit they have no answer.

The complete lack of an answer does not make her curious at all. Needless to say, she never entertains the forbidden thought that maybe none of it did any good. Something tells me she has never had a thought that wasn't safely within the range of opinion permitted to us by the *New York Times*.

What I'm trying to do, and what enrages our state senator, is broaden the range of allowable conversation, to say the things we're all thinking. If at this point, after everything that's happened — and particularly after all the huge events even before the vaccine rollout (so they can't use that explanation) that resulted in no "superspreader" effect — people still think it all worked, they're probably unreachable.

But some people *are* reachable, as we can see from the packed football stadiums and other events.

November 19, 2021 | 90% vaxed country considers more restrictions

On my other email list today I shared this CNN headline: "The Definition of 'Fully Vaccinated' Is Changing to Three Covid-19 Doses." This comes two weeks after Ron DeSantis was "fact checked" for saying that this precise thing would happen.

Meanwhile, there are critics of the strategy of making vaccines the central weapon against the virus.

CNN recently summarized Robert F. Kennedy, Jr., as saying: "With so much yet to be learned about the virus, using vaccines as the main weapon against Covid-19 could lead to new variants. It has never been done before…and it would really be an inappropriate public health strategy to do so."

Wait, did I say that was Robert F. Kennedy, Jr.? My mistake. Those are the words, as reported by CNN, of Dr. David Nabarro, the World Health Organization's special envoy for Covid-19.

That's right — you're evidently now allowed to say that making vaccination the primary means of combating the virus is "an inappropriate public health strategy."

Meanwhile, it sure looks as if Austria is making vaccination its primary weapon, since it just announced that mandatory vaccination will be its policy beginning in February. The age requirement for the vaccine has not yet been determined, and exemptions will be given to those with medical reasons for declining, but they're planning to go ahead with this.

Not to mention: Austria has just gone into its third lockdown. I wonder how many times Europeans have to be locked down before they start wondering about how effective lockdowns are. That's just one of those questions it's apparently considered rude to ask.

Here's another such question:

Now that Michigan has a hospitalization rate five times that of Florida, can we expect the same media personalities who attack Ron DeSantis for every death in Florida to begin criticizing Gretchen Whitmer?

The question answers itself.

Here's yet another such question:

With Ireland's eligible population about 90 percent vaccinated, and with vaccine passports and indoor mask mandates in effect, they're still seeing an explosion in cases. They're bringing restrictions back and could be in full lockdown by Christmas. Who is still thinking any of these are good ideas?

December 15, 2021 | What you can no longer say on Twitter

The "You Can't Make This Stuff Up" Department is going to need to open a five-story annex at this point, but get this: Moderna just announced that it's withdrawing from the upcoming J.P. Morgan Healthcare Conference because of — get this — Covid concerns.

You heard that right. The same people whose vaccine was described as extraordinarily effective are afraid to attend a conference full of vaccinated people in a city that requires proof of vaccination to enter a huge array of indoor venues.

Meanwhile, New York University just mandated booster shots for the entire campus. So not just the initial two shots, but now the booster will also be necessary. All events and gatherings have been canceled. Oh, and you have 15 minutes to eat lunch, and you'll be taking your final exams over Zoom. By the way, know what the vaccination rate on the NYU campus is? Approximately 100 percent.

How do they maintain the narrative while doing all this crazy stuff?

Well, Twitter thinks it has the answer: not allowing us to tell people that the shots don't prevent the spread of Covid. Its Terms of Service now include this: "We may apply labels to tweets that contain, for example...false or misleading claims that people who have received the vaccine can spread or shed the virus (or symptoms, or immunity) to unvaccinated people."

Penalties can go as high as a permanent ban.

How even the dopiest of the dopes fail to realize, after everything we've seen, that Joe Biden was wrong to say you can't get Covid if you get your shots or that vaccinated people don't spread it or spread it significantly less, is beyond me.

The logic of the vaccine passport systems taking shape in various countries is based on the idea that the vaccinated don't spread the virus, or spread it much less. But after two or three months, any such difference has dissipated.

So maybe — how about this — there *isn't* any real logic behind them, and these systems are intended to punish political enemies and dissidents, and exert control for its own sake.

For its part, the U.K. has just instituted vaccine passports, and there is talk of lockdowns.

A U.K. resident posted this comment online, and as you read it, understand that this is what these people have done to the vulnerable of our society (capitalization and other usage as in the original):

> Would i be exempt for anxiety and panic disorder. Im really struggling immensely since all this has kicked off again and struggle to leave the house as it is. I have bipolar disorder. Ive had my 3 vaccines but this is killing me. My mental health is going down rapidly and im scared about whats to come, especially more lockdowns and schools closing as i have an autistic son under 10 who wanted to self harm last year he was that depressed.

This fills me with rage.

We have to keep fighting. We cannot let them demoralize us.

At the same time, we must positively rejoice in normality where we find it. Every "large gathering" — every concert, sporting event, convention, whatever — is cause for joy. Every one of these is, at least implicitly, a finger in the eye of what we laughingly call the experts.

Every human mind that even now, at this late date, is suddenly being opened — whether because of booster requirements, or the broken promises, or the refusal to let the thing go — is cause for thanks.

I am convinced that most people are just going through the motions at this point. The sliver of the public that is still sincerely hysterical has disproportionate influence on policymaking, but I don't think the number is as big as it once was.

Still, you probably know people whom you expected to have come to their senses by now, but haven't. It is a frustrating and bewildering phenomenon, unlike anything I have ever experienced.

Part VIII: Winter 2021–2022

December 21, 2021 | Discovered: Fauci part of campaign to demonize opponents

I'm sure you remember the statement last year by three experts — Jay Bhattacharya of Stanford, Martin Kulldorff of Harvard, and Sunetra Gupta of Oxford — decrying lockdowns as disastrous, and contrary to public health properly understood. It was called the Great Barrington Declaration.

Thanks to emails recently made public, we now know that Dr. Fauci and Francis Collins (of the National Institutes of Health) were part of an effort to smear these scientists and deliberately misrepresent their positions.

(Incidentally, when I was dealing with Covid myself, Jay — who has become a friend — wrote to me without being asked, to offer medical advice and answer my questions.)

For today's email, I want to share Jay's response, from a Twitter thread:

> On TV today Francis Collins doubled down on his lies and propaganda attack on the Great Barrington Declaration. If you read the GBD, you will not find the words "let it rip" because the central idea is focused protection of the vulnerable.
>
> We now know the origin of the term — it came from the mind of Collins and Fauci. When reporters started asking me why I wanted to "let the virus rip," I was puzzled. Now I know that Collins and Fauci primed the media attack with the lie.
>
> I was also puzzled by the mischaracterization of the GBD as a "herd immunity strategy." Biologically the epidemic ends when a sufficient number of people have immunity, either through Covid recovery or vax. Lockdown, let-it-rip, and the GBD all lead to that.
>
> As Martin Kulldorff has said, it makes as much sense to say "herd immunity strategy" as it does to say "gravity strategy" for landing an airplane. The only question is how to land safely, not whether gravity applies.
>
> So the question is how to get through this terrible pandemic with the least harm, where the harms considered include all

of public health, not just Covid. The GBD and focused protection of the vulnerable is a middle ground between lockdown and let-it-rip.

Lockdowners like Collins and Fauci presumably think that focused protection of the vulnerable is impossible. They could have engaged honestly in a discussion about it, but would have found that public health is fundamentally about focused protection. Some in public health did engage civilly in this discussion about strategies for focused protection with me and it was productive.

Instead, Fauci and Collins decided to smear Martin Kulldorff, Sunetra Gupta, me, and supporters of the GBD. They lied about the ideas it contains and orchestrated a propaganda campaign against us.

In this propaganda and smearing war, they joined Jeremy Farrar, the head of the Wellcome Trust, and Dominic Cummings, former consigliere to U.K. PM Boris Johnson.

They engaged in ad hominem smears, calling Sunetra Gupta, Martin Kulldorff, and me "fringe" epidemiologists. It is an odd argument given my decades of NIH-funded research. Do Collins and the NIH fund many other "fringe" scientists?

So, why do Fauci and Collins engage in ad hominem and lies instead of honest scientific discussion? I don't know fully, but part of the answer lies in another puzzle — their blindness to the devastating effects of lockdown on the poor and vulnerable.

For instance, the economic devastation of poor countries caused by rich countries shutting down has contributed to tens of millions facing starvation. I could list many more harms....We will need to work hard to reverse the damage.

Covid panic-mongering by Fauci and Collins led countless school districts to shut schoolhouse doors, especially for poor kids who could not afford private school, especially in blue states. The harm to our kids will last a generation.

Fauci and Collins are silent about lockdown harms because they are culpable. The sad fact is that they won the policy war, they got their lockdowns, and now with other lockdowners, own the harms. They cannot deny it. The GBD warned them.

They also cannot say that the lockdowns worked to suppress Covid. In the U.S., we followed the Fauci/Collins lockdown strategy and we have 800K Covid deaths. Sweden — more focused on protecting the vulnerable — did better and cannot be ignored.

Though lockdowns seem so sensible to some as a way to stop disease spread, in fact, they protect only a certain class of people — the laptop class — who are permitted to work from home. Lockdowns are a "let it drip" strategy.

Collins, in his interview with Bret Baier says that "history will judge," and he is right. It will judge those in charge of the Covid policy, and it will not judge kindly. He smears the GBD and its authors because he has no substantive argument left.

This would be damaging enough if Collins and Fauci were not also in charge of $41 billion that funds nearly every epidemiologist, immunologist, and virologist of note in the U.S. Their smear of the GBD is a signal to other scientists to stay quiet about lockdown folly.

The conflict of interest created here is at least as great as traditionally recognized conflicts that, for instance, pharma-funded scientists face. Collins and Fauci should have recused themselves from Covid policymaking.

Francis Collins' interview with Baier marks a sad end to an illustrious career, and I take no joy in saying so. Fauci should join him in retirement. They have done enough damage.

December 30, 2021 | Every word out of their mouths is a lie, including "and" and "the"

With so many positive test results for asymptomatic people, the CDC just declared that such people need to quarantine for five days rather than the previous ten.

What scientific insight led them to this policy? CDC director Rochelle Walensky said, "It really had a lot to do with what we thought people would be able to tolerate."

(This reminds me of when Alachua County, Florida, instituted a one-person-per-thousand-square-feet rule for retail establishments. When asked where they got that figure, the county commissioner said it was "because it's easy math for everybody to do.")

Then Dr. Fauci: "There is the danger that there will be so many people who are being isolated who are asymptomatic for the full ten days, that you could have a major negative impact on our ability to keep society running. So the decision was made of saying let's get that cut in half."

I'm glad that after nearly two years Dr. Fauci is giving some thought to keeping society functioning, but this is exactly the kind of thinking Fauci himself would have condemned as recently as two weeks ago, back when he was monomaniacally concerned with one issue and unable to entertain the possibility that there may be other things society needs to worry about.

It's strange, isn't it? To you and me, it's excruciatingly obvious that the people in charge are making it up as they go along, while the zombie population is just sure our overlords have some kind of master plan they learned in a textbook somewhere.

Oh, they laughed at people who thought Donald Trump was playing 4D chess and had his own master plan, but they are convinced that Dr. Fauci ruined their lives for a really good, 4D scientific reason.

Speaking of The Science, here's a New York City council member with some recommendations for schools:

(((Stephen Levin))) ● ✔
@StephenLevin33
···

If the incoming administration does not move to full remote, they should absolutely do a few easy things to reduce spread and mitigate risk: 1) keep a strict mask mandate in place 2) have lunches or any other eating time outdoors, even in the cold or inclement weather

His list of suggestions continues, but I think that gives you the idea.

We now have an avalanche of evidence that schools are safe, and that teachers are at no greater risk than anyone else and if anything have done even better than people in other professions. This evidence comes from all over the world. Yet it makes no difference to our council member, who wants us to think that the more unreasonable he is, the more seriously he's taking the virus.

Yes, yes, I know: the government's schools are terrible. I'm not encouraging people to attend them. I am saying it's psychotic to recommend that children eat lunch in 30-degree weather.

Regarding masks, Sweden's schoolchildren did not wear masks at all. There are 1.8 million of them. Zero of them died, and their teachers did fine.

It's just made-up craziness or outright lies. The Chicago mayor keeps screeching about overwhelmed hospitals, for example. But visits to the emergency room are lower than they were before Covid!

Chicago Hospitals' Weekly Emergency Department Visits: Week-Ending 10/10/15 - 12/25/21

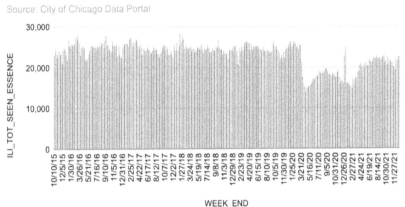

As Mary McCarthy said of Lillian Hellman, "Every word she writes is a lie, including 'and' and 'the.'"

January 6, 2022 | Time for the white flag: Covid outbreak in Antarctica

(I'll deliver on this chapter title. Just give me a minute.)

"This was never about a virus," people keep telling me. I hear you.

But I say back: "Billions of people to this day think it is."

Remember, I'm not trying to persuade Joe Biden or Dr. Fauci. I'm trying to reach people of good will who made the mistake — a mistake they were almost programmed to make, given their background in the regime's schools — of assuming that public officials had their well-being at heart. In other words, plenty of people went along with all this not because they were involved in anything sinister. They went along because they believed that the so-called experts were acting in good faith.

Others went along, long after doing so had clearly become unreasonable, because they had zero curiosity, they felt uncomfortable holding an opinion other than what the powerful told them to hold, or they're just dumb as rocks.

Thus Whoopi Goldberg, who recently tested positive. "I've done everything I was supposed to do," she protests.

"Since she's vaxxed and boosted, her symptoms have been very, very mild," said Joy Behar, her co-host on *The View*.

Hmm. You know who else has symptoms that are very, very mild, especially with the new variant? Practically everybody, vaxxed or not.

As for doing all the right things, etc., remember this: there was just an outbreak in Antarctica, among fully vaccinated scientists. Writes the BBC: "A Belgian scientific research station in Antarctica has been hit with an outbreak of Covid-19, despite workers being fully vaccinated and based in one of the world's remotest regions."

If this can happen as far away from civilization as it is possible to be, then forget about it. By depriving yourself of the joys of life all you're doing is stealing time from yourself that you can never get back.

And now, as I write to you, another of the things we're "supposed to do," namely mask wearing, is collapsing.

ABC News is running this headline on Twitter: "Studies are emerging that cloth masks are not effective in preventing the spread of Covid."

Did it really require "studies" for us to figure this out? When we have example after example of demographically similar populations right next to each other but with different levels of masking and yet the same Covid numbers, isn't that enough to make the effectiveness of masks extremely unlikely, or at least something a rational person would call into question?

January 13, 2022 | Supreme Court rules: here's the good news and the bad news

First, the bad news.

The Supreme Court has upheld the vaccination requirement for health-care workers as a condition for receiving Medicare and Medicaid funds.

Opinions like this one are maddening to read, because they confine themselves to questions such as whether the Secretary of Health and Human Services exceeded his congressionally granted authority when imposing this requirement. The Court then proceeds to explain that the Secretary has been understood to enjoy a very broad authority when it comes to imposing requirements regarding the administration of Medicare and Medicaid.

Not considered is where the federal government's authority to intervene in matters involving health, whether or not given statutory expression by Congress or delegated to a health bureaucrat, derives from in the first place or how it can be justified.

Perhaps this ruling will lead to further growth in direct primary care practices which accept neither Medicare nor Medicaid nor even traditional insurance. That is another question.

The good news is very good: the OSHA vaccine mandate for employees of businesses with 100 or more workers has been blocked.

Such a measure, the Court says, constitutes a vast overreach by OSHA into the more general field of public health, where it has not been granted authority.

It would have been nicer to hear an opinion based on the nature of what was being demanded as opposed to whether the institution doing the demanding was the correct one. But I'll take what I can get.

I pulled out some relevant passages from the opinion of the Court:

> Although Covid-19 is a risk that occurs in many workplaces, it is not an *occupational* hazard in most. Covid-19 can and does spread at home, in schools, during sporting events, and everywhere else that people gather. That kind of universal risk is no different from the day-to-day dangers that all face from crime, air pollution, or any number of communicable diseases. Permitting OSHA to regulate the hazards of daily life — simply because most Americans have jobs and face those same risks while on the clock — would significantly expand OSHA's regulatory authority without clear congressional authorization....
>
> OSHA's indiscriminate approach fails to account for this crucial distinction — between occupational risk and risk more generally — and accordingly the mandate takes on the

character of a general public health measure, rather than an "occupational safety or health standard."

Justice Gorsuch concurred with the Court, and was joined by Justices Thomas and Alito in a concurring opinion from which I draw the following passages (internal footnotes omitted):

> I start with this Court's precedents. There is no question that state and local authorities possess considerable power to regulate public health. They enjoy the "general power of governing," including all sovereign powers envisioned by the Constitution and not specifically vested in the federal government.
>
> The federal government's powers, however, are not general but limited and divided. Not only must the federal government properly invoke a constitutionally enumerated source of authority to regulate in this area or any other. It must also act consistently with the Constitution's separation of powers. And when it comes to that obligation, this Court has established at least one firm rule: "We expect Congress to speak clearly" if it wishes to assign to an executive agency decisions "of vast economic and political significance." We sometimes call this the major questions doctrine. OSHA's mandate fails that doctrine's test. The agency claims the power to force 84 million Americans to receive a vaccine or undergo regular testing. By any measure, that is a claim of power to resolve a question of vast national significance. Yet Congress has nowhere clearly assigned so much power to OSHA....
>
> The question before us is not how to respond to the pandemic, but who holds the power to do so. The answer is clear: Under the law as it stands today, that power rests with the States and Congress, not OSHA. In saying this much, we do not impugn the intentions behind the agency's mandate. Instead, we only discharge our duty to enforce the law's demands when it comes to the question who may govern the lives of 84 million Americans. Respecting those demands may be trying in times of stress. But if this Court were to abide them only in more tranquil conditions, declarations of emergencies would never end and the liberties our Constitution's separation of powers seeks to preserve would amount to little.

This does not solve all problems, obviously. Some private entities will persist in vaccine mandates despite their injustice, irrationality, and general uselessness. Other problems, like vaccine passports, are occurring at the local level and must be dealt with at the local level — though we can hope they will resolve themselves as they destroy business and tourism.

But it is a start.

January 17, 2022 | Revealed: what Democrats want to do to the unvaccinated

What's happening to the unvaccinated in some countries almost defies belief. We've endured some horrors here, to be sure, but not we're not Australia.

But that's exactly what many Democrats would prefer, and then some, if they could have their way. How do we know? Polling data. Rasmussen just reported the following:

- 59% of Democrats favor forcing the unvaccinated to stay home at all times except for emergencies.

- 55% of Democrats favor levying state or federal fines on people who decline the shot.

- 48% of Democrats favor fines or imprisonment for people who publicly question vaccine efficacy.

- 47% of Democrats favor a government tracking program to people who decline the shot.

- 45% of Democrats support temporary relocation to "designated facilities or locations" for those who decline the shot.

- 29% of Democrats favor temporarily removing your custody of your children if you decline the shot.

That's pretty twisted.

Not to mention that none of that has any connection to "public health," since the vaccinated are also spreading the virus. This is punishment of the noncompliant.

No wonder the idea of "national divorce" is trending. Who would want to share a country with people so hateful and irrational?

January 21, 2022 | How's that vax passport system going?

I've been wondering about what will happen with the various vaccine passport systems in certain American cities.

To me it's obvious that they will harm business and undermine tourism. Supporters say they will benefit business because (ignorant) people will feel "safe" going to restaurants now.

Even if that were true, any gains would still be less than the loss in business, but I'm not even sure it *is* true: anyone who, two full years later, is still fearful of restaurants is the kind of person who won't go even with a vaccine passport system in place. After all, patrons remove their holy masks while eating!

Inside the Tom Woods Show Elite, my private group, someone shared what's happening with the vaccine passport system in the Chicago area, and it sounds like good news to me:

> *I just listened to the latest episode with Lew Rockwell and based on what you mentioned about vax passports, wanted to shed some light on what's happening in Chicago. I live just outside of the city limits of Chicago so I'm mostly impacted by the rules of the Cook County Health Dept, which are mostly the same.*
>
> *Before the Cook County vax passport on everybody 5+ ever even took effect, they revised it to be 16+ for entertainment or fitness-related stuff. Only about a fourth of 5–11-year-olds even in Cook County are "fully" vaccinated, so this was going to be a death blow to all child activities. I was in the process of calling all extracurriculars for my kids before the revision to pull out my kids, and they said they had been getting flooded with similar calls and didn't know what they would do. I go to a small mom and pop gym, and when I called them to cancel my membership, they told me they would not be enforcing it — my first sign of hope.*
>
> *Many cities surrounding the Chicago core in Cook County have outright defied the order and said they will leave it up to the Cook County Health Department to enforce it, and in effect this means it's flagrantly violated. Cook County and Chicago are trying their hardest to get people in line with violations, but the disobedience to the order is so widespread. I went to lunch downtown last week and despite the signs of the vax and mask requirements, I walked right in unmasked and didn't hear a peep about any of it. Most people are just sick of this.*

I'm trying to find a place to schedule my kids' birthday party, and I'll ask them up front — plenty in the defiant suburbs have told me they are not enforcing.

The places that do seem to be enforcing the order are all major chain businesses and restaurants or places with a heavy concentration of Branch Covidians. Portillo's is a Chicago staple of a restaurant, and they are rigidly enforcing the order. When I went there with my family to test it, the restaurant was completely empty — unheard of on a Sunday afternoon. We went down the street to a small, family-owned restaurant and ate there just fine and it was packed.

Some places are also being upfront about their disobedience. I was also in another part of Chicago that is largely non-woke zealots to a Wendy's the other day and half the employees there weren't even wearing masks. I'm hearing through the grapevine from friends that in parts of the south and west neighborhoods of Chicago, businesses are laughing at people if they need to show vax cards. Those that are enforcing it are seeing massive drop-offs of about 50% of their revenue.

So there is hope. What I bet will happen is that when Omicron wave naturally dies down, they will get away from this order quickly, claim their fake victory, and then put it behind them.

I have the same hope.

I for one intend to vacation in places that actually want me there, and to avoid places governed and cheered on by deranged hypochondriacs.

January 24, 2022 | Fauci's poll numbers: bad for him, good for us

These days it seems as if everywhere I turn, a new person is saying the whole thing is stupid and I'm not doing it anymore.

This time it's an editorial writer for *USA Today*. Headline: "I am done with masks. We've been idiotic about them since the beginning."

He begins with this: "Who knew that little pieces of plastic or cloth worn over the nose and mouth could turn people into complete idiots?"

In response to Dr. Leana Wen's recent observation that cloth masks are nothing more than "facial decoration," he responds, "Well, I feel like an idiot for all the times I donned a facial decoration and forced my kids to do the same." He dismisses the drive for N95 masks as unreasonable, and concludes: "As for me, I've had it with masks. I feel like a fool, and I am not going to play anymore."

Then, too, Bari Weiss, formerly of the *New York Times* opinion section, made waves on Bill Maher's program recently when she declared herself "done with Covid," and swatted down the standard arguments with data.

The only thing missing was: I'm sorry for going along with it all this time and for having demonized people who said then what I'm saying now.

The whole "we now have new information" thing from Weiss and others is disingenuous. We knew very early on that the crazies were wrong and that nothing they recommended did any good. A simple "stay home when you're sick" would have been better than their entire mitigation program.

Having said that, I by no means decline Bari Weiss's membership in Team Reality, and I'm happy to see our ranks continue to grow.

Now before I reveal the happiest of the three items I have to report to you today, in terms of the evolution of opinion, I want to make sure you know a term.

Surely you know "red pill" and "blue pill," from *The Matrix*. You and I are red-pilled. We understand the nature of the regime that rules over us. We don't accept the establishment version of events.

The blue-pilled are those who even now still think the public health establishment just has the best interests of Americans at heart and should be trusted to do sensible things.

A white pill, meanwhile, is a source of optimism for us.

And now for a white pill: a recent NBC News poll — so not exactly biased in our favor — finds more Americans distrust Fauci than trust him. The question was, "In general, do you trust what Dr. Fauci has said about the coronavirus or not?" The results were 43% no, and 40% yes. Compare those results to 60% yes and 8% no in April 2020.

Meanwhile, Ireland just announced it's dropping most Covid restrictions, and England is dropping its mask mandate and vaccine passport system.

Austria keeps putting off its mandatory vaccination program, and there are murmurs in England about pushing the vaccine mandates for NHS workers back six months.

We're almost there.

With next to no high-profile support, and with every major opinion-molding institution against us, we've begun to turn the tide. What you and I say and do is not in vain.

January 25, 2022 | A reader from Italy

It's good news and bad news today.

First the bad news: a reader from Italy reminds us, as things are beginning to thaw in the U.K. and even the U.S., what the situation remains like there:

> *Dear Tom, thanks for your precious work. Fond listener here, and member of your LibertyClassroom.com.*
>
> *They all talk a lot about Nazi Australia but almost nobody talks of what's been going on here in Nazi Italy. I just want to give you an update and hope you may help sharing some info internationally.*
>
> *Our government, since February 2021, is made of a mega-coalition that includes all political parties with just one party feigning opposition, but actually doing no opposition at all.*
>
> *Emergency decrees are being enacted at a psychotic, compulsive rate and the "state of emergency" has now been extended to March 31st, 2022.*
>
> *As of December 2021, vaccination rate in Italy for people over 12 was about 91%, intensive care occupation was a meager 9.5%, all adults are currently running to get their 3rd jab but, still, they have made mask mandates more stringent: now you have to get masked even in open air, and if you have the guts to get on a bus, then you must wear an FFP2 mask.*
>
> *As a matter of fact, I can't even stand walking on a sidewalk now here in Milano because my stomach churns with every masked "covidiot" I see walking alone.*
>
> *Recently released official data admitted that 34% of Covid hospitalizations of the last two years were actually not Covid related and no wonder: they increased public contributions to hospitals for each Covid patient and so any patient admitted for a broken bone but testing positive for Covid became a Covid patient.*
>
> *Omicron is spreading fast these days, with its mild flu symptoms and no real emergency of course and, as other places are slowly getting to their*

senses — like England and Ireland, for example — our press is still in full propaganda mode. After all, a national law last year doubled public contributions to the media officially for them to "inform" about Covid. (A total of 386 million euros.)

We now need to have what they call a Super-GreenPass, that you can only get with vaccination or recovery, to do anything: going to work, using public transportation, entering bars and restaurants, playing sports, going to a bank or post office.

Starting from February 1st, we unvaccinated rats will not be admitted even into shops. Except to buy food or gasoline...thanks to their generosity.

And it must be the right thing because, even though we all know now that vaxxed souls are also widely spreading the virus, just last October our Führer Mr. Draghi (ex-ECB chairman, by the way) said on television that "the Green Pass is a measure with which Italians can be guaranteed to be among non-contagious people." Last July, Mr. Draghi also said: "You don't get vaccinated, you get sick, you die."

I am currently considering to run away from this hell of a country but, unfortunately, my triple-vaxxed wife is not sharing my view....

Please let people know, if you can, that Australia or Austria are not alone in their fascist delirium. As a matter of fact, we have a lot to teach about fascism!

No matter what good developments occur in the United States and elsewhere in the world we cannot abandon people like this. The story must continue to be told.

January 31, 2022 | Another mandate was just scrapped

Take a moment to appreciate the gravity of our situation.

For two solid years the world has been turned upside down by an elite bent on the suppression of alternative points of view. What we laughingly call the "mitigation measures" they imposed on us haven't done a bit of good, and instead have caused death and impoverishment everywhere they've been tried.

With only a handful of exceptions, every major institution has been an enemy of sanity.

You and I have been up against every channel of fashionable opinion.

That we've managed, under these impossible conditions, to win any victories at all is a miracle. But they keep on coming.

The most recent: in England, the National Health Service (NHS) mandate for health-care and home-care workers is being scrapped.

Remember, it was only a week ago that the *Daily Mail* was running this headline: "'No plans' to scrap Covid vaccine mandate for frontline medics in England, Downing Street says as it doubles down on plan despite warnings NHS could lose 80,000 workers overnight." So we went from "no plans" to "the mandate is scrapped" in a week.

Why did they do it? Some are trying to say it's because of the relative mildness of the Omicron variant, and that under these conditions a vaccine mandate is no longer a proportionate response. Maybe. But I doubt it.

Here's a more plausible answer. The *Daily Mail* reports that what prompted the revision were "fears it could force the NHS to sack around 80,000 staff who remain unvaccinated." According to Chris Hopson, chief executive of NHS Providers: "There were always two risks to manage here: the risk of Covid cross-infection in healthcare settings and the consequences of losing staff if significant numbers choose not to be vaccinated."

Stop and think about what this means: noncompliance forced them to abandon the mandate. And not even majority noncompliance. We're talking in the neighborhood of 10 to 20 percent.

I know there's plenty of hideousness still out there. I hear that. But when we get a win, let's be happy, and keep on pushing forward.

February 9, 2022 | Vaccine passport systems being withdrawn?

Some months ago on the Tom Woods Show I asked Stanford University's Jay Bhattacharya what he thought the future had in store for vaccine passport systems in certain cities, whereby "proof of vaccination" is necessary to enter many indoor businesses.

He said he thought they would be relatively short-lived. I hoped he was right.

Well, maybe he was.

Now it's true: not all problems are solved. But in Denver the requirement has been withdrawn. In St. Paul, Minnesota, the mayor says he hopes to lift the policy this week. In Minneapolis, the mayor is planning to lift the policy sooner than expected, possibly within the coming days. In Chicago the mayor is saying the policy could be lifted in a matter of weeks. In Boston the mayor has finally indicated that the policy is temporary and will be lifted when three metrics are reached. One of them has already been reached, and the others are well on their way to being reached.

Now before you think Woods has gone all wimpy on you:

I'm not saying that the people in charge of these places are good or reasonable. If they were, they wouldn't have enacted these policies in the first place. They are hopeless. And some of them support other terrible policies, still in place. Their crazy "metrics" are arbitrary and based on nothing. They insist that they have the power to reimpose these measures at any time.

We cannot pretend any of this is normal or acceptable, even as we celebrate the lifting of the stupidest and most destructive policies.

February 14, 2022 | DeSantis was just proven right two more times

Two related phenomena continue to develop: (1) more of the credentialed are finally speaking out about the Covid fiasco, and (2) more people are admitting — without directly saying so — that you and I have been right.

Let's start with Stefanos Kales, a professor at the Harvard T.H. Chan School of Public Health. "Public health is a balance," he recently said:

> How many businesses closed and did not make it through that first six to twelve months? A lot of these restaurants, their business is still way down. Large companies can survive, but a lot of small businesses have gone under. And that takes a toll on the health of people who work there or own those businesses.

In other words, "public health" is about more than the monomaniacal fixation on one thing.

In an appearance on CNBC, Kales said:

> This whole idea of we just ignore everything else in the economy and health and well-being to try to get to zero

308

Covid cases [was] never a realistic goal and it has failed miserably. We haven't balanced all these other things. The fentanyl overdoses in the U.S. are at a record high as well as other opioids. Suicidality in young people. It's a big mistake.

Good.

Even better has been to observe Ron DeSantis, governor of Florida, being vindicated again and again.

Exhibit A:

Opinions   Editorial Board   The Opinions Essay

Voices Across America

Opinion: Florida's new anti-masking law denies us key tools to protect our schools from future covid surges

And then:

Business • Analysis

Mask Mandates Didn't Make Much of a Difference Anyway

Here's another one. The first item is from August 2021, and the second from January 2022:

The Washington Post ✓
@washingtonpost

DeSantis blames Florida's surge on 'covid season.' That's misleading, experts say.

washingtonpost.com
DeSantis blames Florida's surge on 'covid season.'
That's misleading, experts say.

The Washington Post ✓
@washingtonpost

Covid-19 transmission may have seasonal spikes tied to temperature and humidity, increasing at different times of the year for different locations, a new study suggests

washingtonpost.com
Covid-19 may have seasons for different
temperature zones, study suggests

Incidentally, if after two years of fact-free insanity there's a more risible phrase than "experts say," I don't know what it is.

February 16, 2022 | Guess where "it's time to move on" is coming from now

Nobody expected it, but all eyes are on Canada now.

By now you probably know my feelings about politicians, and why I am so little inclined to cheer for any of them. What I report today is more for the purpose of demonstrating which way things seem to be trending.

And so:

Doug Ford, Premier of Ontario — who's been atrocious, by the way — just told the press the following:

> You can go to Costco, you can go to Walmart, you can go shopping, you don't know if the person has a shot beside you or not, but we also know that it doesn't matter if you have one shot or ten shots, you can catch Covid.
>
> See, the Prime Minister, he has triple shots, and I know hundreds of people with three shots that caught Covid.
>
> We just have to be careful, got to always make sure we wash our hands, and move forward. We can't stay in this position forever. We've got to learn to live with this and get on with our lives.
>
> I bet if I asked every single person in this room, do you want these damn masks or do you want them off, they want them off! They want to get back to normal. They want to be able to go for dinner with their families.
>
> And there's every single person, including myself, knows people who are unvaccinated. Sure, there are rabble rousers, and then there's just hardworking people who just don't believe in it. And that's their choice.
>
> This is about, again, a democracy and freedoms and liberties. And I hate as a government telling anyone what to do.
>
> We've just got to get moving forward and get out of this and protect the jobs.
>
> I think a lot of people, probably yourself, too, everyone's done with this. Like, we are done with it. Let's start moving

on, and cautiously. We've followed the rules, 90 percent of us,
for over two years. The world's done with it.

I know some of you are living in countries where this kind of hope
cannot be found. Even if we should get "back to normal" over here in
North America, there will still be a great deal left to do — not only in
helping the remaining places escape the Covid prison, but also in getting
our own societies in order. We have a massive number of people who have
been completely broken by this experience, and who are now incapable of
assessing risk or evaluating situations rationally.

But some places may indeed be reaching an endpoint.

February 17, 2022 | The psychosis is alive and well among private employers

With the momentum having shifted against the craziness, it's tempting to
overlook the remaining pockets of lunacy. But here's one.

Subscriber Allison Zatarain gave me permission both to use her name
and to share with you what she wrote to me this morning. At a time when
practically everyone is aware that the shots don't prevent transmission, the
monomania she writes about below is truly psychotic:

> *I was let go from my executive job at one of the "big 3" global major
> record labels yesterday because I am not vaccinated. I have 3 months left
> of (remote) employment should I stay. I was hired during the pandemic
> in August 2020.*
>
> *I quote from my official letter from HR: "Even if you were prepared to
> wear a mask, social distance and/or submit to regular Covid-19 testing,
> this would not adequately mitigate the direct threat of illness to you, your
> coworkers, or the third parties with whom you are expected to interact as
> part of your job without an undue burden on our business operations."*
>
> *I knew my days were numbered when the company sent out a very stern
> internal email top of November with a deadline for filing a religious
> exemption (which I did immediately) and a deadline for submitting a
> vaccination card. They even waved the carrot of an additional four days
> off during the holidays for compliance. In bold letters they said, "your
> employment will be at risk" and "all new hires are required to be
> vaccinated as a condition of employment."*

They have since announced that boosters are required after five months of initial vaccination. With a planned reopening in February, that's a lot of paper to chase.

I recently got married and we're trying for a baby. The experimental shot is not an option for me. Covid has been swirling around for almost two years and this is the most personal it's ever felt. And I had Covid in January! My ability to earn a living, especially in the music industry in NYC which was my dream and for which I have a Master's degree, is slipping away. But I know in my bones that now is the time to resist and stand up for liberty.

We're leaving NYC in the spring no matter what, currently targeting Charleston (but also looking at TN, TX, WI, and FL). Look out, SC — some music business mojo is coming your way.

Thank you for everything you do. You make us feel less alone.

February 21, 2022 | Vax passports: more useless than you thought

As I reported a week or two ago, the vaccine passport systems in various American cities seem to be on their way out. Since the last time I wrote, the system in Boston has also been removed. That holds special significance for me. I could not bear to see the city of my youth placed under those useless, cruel, and unscientific orders.

Here's a chart you can try to stump your friends with.

These are two neighboring counties in California: Los Angeles County, which has a widespread vaccine passport system, and Orange County, which has no passport system at all. These people live right next to each other. It's a perfect test.

We are told that the shots are supposed to reduce hospitalizations. So let's have a look. Hospitalizations in Los Angeles County vs. hospitalizations in Orange County. There had better be a huge difference in Los Angeles County's favor to justify all this.

And yet…

And yet.

Here is the chart, generated from CovidActNow.org:

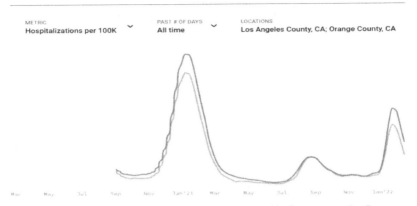

METRIC
Hospitalizations per 100K ⌄

PAST # OF DAYS
All time ⌄

LOCATIONS
Los Angeles County, CA; Orange County, CA

I haven't labeled the counties. Can you tell them apart? Can your friends? *Shouldn't they be able to?*

The answer almost doesn't matter, since the curves for the two places are essentially indistinguishable. But if you're really curious, I'll tell you that the line that's slightly worse is Los Angeles County, the place with county-mandated vaccine requirements to participate in normal life, and the slightly better line is Orange County, which has no such requirements.

They've destroyed businesses, torn families apart, turned people's lives upside down — all for nothing.

February 23, 2022 | Shutting down makes us richer, lizard people say

Three items you'll enjoy today:

(1) The chairman of the chemistry department of the University of Florida just released this statement to his professors, and I thought you might like to read it:

> In a department this size, conflicts occasionally burble up to the surface and the recent issues on masking have done so. Since they burbled on up to administrative levels above the department, said administrators have told me to remind you of the rules. They haven't changed and there they are (executive summary version):

> It's Florida here and this is the way it is. No, you cannot require masking (except to protect your personal space in your single-occupant office and then you offer a Zoom alternative). It is a personal choice. No, you cannot state or

even imply that there are consequences for not masking. No, you cannot cast aspersions on those who disagree with you on this topic.

Simple. Straightforward. Do it.

(2) Mark Levine, Manhattan Borough President, wants to make sure nobody puts two and two together about any of this and blames him for promoting society-destroying Covid hysteria, so he recently tweeted an article and told us that California's more favorable death rate than Florida's is the single most important thing to remember about this entire period.

Had he adjusted the two states for age? Of course not.

But here's the kicker: the very article he himself tweeted included this: "In the end, some states that adopted dramatically divergent policies had comparable outcomes (Florida and California, for example)."

(3) Remember all those "the economy will do even better in places where everything is shut down" people? Here's the data on the restaurant industry over the past few years. Note where there has been growth, and note where there has been decline:

Seated diners from online, phone, and walk-in reservations

14-day average of change from 2019 to 2022, February 8 to 21

https://www.opentable.com/state-of-industry

1 Las Vegas	+32.6%		24 Atlanta	-9.7%
2 Miami	+28.8%		25 Denver	-10.2%
3 Scottsdale	+25.0%		26 Kansas City	-12.7%
4 Austin	+23.4%		27 Beverly Hills	-12.9%
5 San Antonio	+22.8%		28 Cleveland	-13.0%
6 Houston	+17.9%		29 Los Angeles	-13.9%
7 Fort Lauderdale	+12.3%		30 Raleigh	-14.0%
8 Tampa	+11.3%		31 Boston	-15.4%
9 Nashville	+8.3%		32 Baltimore	-18.8%
10 Dallas	+6.0%		33 Boca Raton	-22.9%
11 Phoenix	+5.0%		34 New Orleans	-28.5%
12 Naples (US)	+3.4%		35 St. Louis	-29.6%
13 Louisville	+3.2%		36 Honolulu	-30.5%
14 Orlando	+3.1%		37 Washington	-30.8%
15 Charlotte	+2.9%		38 Philadelphia	-34.0%
16 San Diego	+1.8%		39 Chicago	-34.5%
17 Miami Beach	+1.3%		40 Cambridge (US)	-37.6%
18 Columbus	+1.1%		41 Brooklyn	-39.0%
19 Cincinnati	-0.1%		42 Seattle	-39.9%
20 Pittsburgh	-1.9%		43 Portland	-43.3%
21 Tucson	-4.4%		44 New York	-43.5%
22 Milwaukee	-5.9%		45 San Francisco	-48.4%
23 Indianapolis	-6.7%		46 Minneapolis	-52.4%

February 25, 2022 | Dem pollster: Biden must declare Covid victory

You've heard the expression: "The memo went out." In this case, a literal memo has indeed gone out.

And it's saying: Biden needs to declare victory over Covid and get remaining restrictions lifted.

Impact Research puts it this way:

> After two years that necessitated lockdowns, travel bans, school closures, mask mandates, and nearly a million deaths, nearly every American finally has the tools to protect themselves from this virus. It's time for Democrats to take credit for ending the Covid crisis phase of the Covid war, point to important victories like vaccine distribution and providing economic stability to Americans, and fully enter the rebuilding phase that comes after any war.

As you can see, they're sticking to the idea that the past two years "necessitated" lockdowns and restrictions, and of course they're trying to take credit for why we can drop it all now (because of all that work Democrats did!).

But what matters is their realization: if we keep on this restriction bandwagon, we're going to get slaughtered.

Another portion of the memo:

> **Recognize that people are "worn out" and feeling real harm from the years-long restrictions and take their side.** Most Americans have personally moved out of crisis mode. Twice as many voters are now more concerned about Covid's effect on the economy (49%) than about someone in their family or someone they know becoming infected with the coronavirus (24%). Two-third of parents and 80% of teachers say the pandemic caused learning loss, and voters are overwhelmingly more worried about learning loss than kids getting Covid. Six in ten Americans describe themselves as "worn out" by the pandemic. The more we talk about the threat of Covid and onerously restrict people's lives because of it, the more we turn them against us and show them we're out of touch with their daily realities.

Then this: "Don't set 'Covid zero' as the victory condition."

And this:

> **Stop talking about restrictions and the unknown future ahead.** If we focus on how bad things still are and how much worse they could get, we set Democrats up as failures unable to navigate us through this. When 99% of Americans can get vaccinated, we cause more harm than we prevent with voters by going into our third year talking about restrictions. And, if Democrats continue to hold a posture that prioritizes Covid precautions over learning how to live in a world where Covid exists, but does not dominate, they risk paying dearly for it in November.

It's all politics for these people. But the politics must be swinging in our favor if the Democrats are being advised like this.

March 1, 2022 | 8 things the Age of Fauci teaches us

When even New York City abandons its vaccine passport system (it's gone as of March 7), it's over.

At least in the non-California United States, anyway.

There is plenty still to talk about on the Covid front, of course, and we have to make sure not only that existing restrictions are lifted but also that they can never return again.

At the same time:

It's growing clearer that it's time for me to return to a more diverse array of topics, along the lines of what I covered in this newsletter before March 2020.

I have an extremely diverse subscriber base. Some people agree with everything I say. Some are here for Covid only. Some came for Covid but stayed for the whole libertarian package.

Regardless of whether any of those describe you, I think we can all say we learned (or had reinforced) certain key things from all this, among them:

(1) There is something seriously wrong with the American establishment.

(2) The American establishment does not have your best interests at heart.

(3) There is something seriously wrong with the American medical establishment in particular.

(4) A large percentage of the general public is prepared to go along with whatever the establishment demands of them, without the slightest hint of curiosity about whether it makes sense or not.

(5) Dissident voices may not always be right, but they're right a lot, and they are demonized by fashionable opinion.

(6) Central direction by an elite of alleged experts who cannot be questioned is a bad way to organize society.

(7) We should never believe these people again, if we ever did. Everything they say must be scrutinized. They do not deserve the benefit of the doubt.

(8) We may disagree among ourselves, but I respect every single one of you who stuck with me along this journey, and regardless of what

differences we may have from here on out I will listen to you with respect because you were right on the issue of our age — indeed of many ages.

March 7, 2022 | My morning with DeSantis

Saturday night I received a message: "The governor wants to invite you to a Monday event."

Soon enough after that, I had received the details: Ron DeSantis was planning a roundtable discussion with medical professionals (which I myself am not) for the purpose of assessing the merits of various Covid policies, particularly regarding children.

The roundtable was also intended to keep these issues alive at a time when their proponents seem happy to let the news shift to other topics. We cannot forget what was done to us and to children, and the quacks who recommended these things need to be held to account.

A small number of influencers (including your host here) were invited to attend in person in order to report on and live-Tweet the event to their followers. Those of you who follow me on Twitter — @ThomasEWoods — were treated to precisely that.

DeSantis himself, whom I got to chat with a bit after the event, struck me as informed, down to earth, and authentic. What you see on television is what you get in person, except in person he's funnier and edgier.

The event itself featured such notables as Dr. Robert Malone, Dr. Tracy Hoeg, Dr. Jill Ackerman, Dr. Christopher D'Adamo, Dr. Jay Bhattacharya, Dr. Martin Kulldorff, Dr. Harvey Risch, and Dr. Sunetra Gupta.

During the event an ER doctor named Joseph Fraiman offered a public apology to Professors Bhattacharya, Kulldorff, and Gupta, whose anti-lockdown Great Barrington Declaration he had once considered dangerous. He was sure that places without harsh Covid lockdowns would experience worse outcomes.

"You were right," he said to them. "I was wrong....The scientist in me...had to acknowledge that my hypothesis had been falsified."

Stanford's Jay Bhattacharya emphasized the various ways in which the people in that room had been correct from the start, and reminded people of his own work early on, in March and April 2020, showing how much more widespread the virus was than previously thought. That meant there was no way a lockdown strategy could possibly have worked, but it would severely harm the working class and ordinary people in general.

The event wrapped up with a striking announcement from Joseph Ladapo, the heroic Florida Surgeon General: Florida is now the first state to recommend against the vaccines for healthy children.

In short: we've got them on the run. (DeSantis even wondered recently whether Dr. Fauci, who seems to have disappeared, may have enrolled in the witness protection program.) But that's not good enough. We have to make them answer for what they did.

March 10, 2022 | The *New York Times* just made its biggest admission

At the *New York Times*, David Leonhardt is the writer whose job it's been to gently break it to his largely left-liberal audience that the various crazy things they did wound up not having much of an effect on anything.

No matter how calmly he utters these truths, he gets savaged in the comments. These people do not want to be told that nothing they did mattered.

I get his newsletter simply because I want to keep an eye on what influential voices are saying. In his most recent email he made some interesting observations.

One of them isn't hard to predict: in blue cities restaurants are getting killed. People still aren't going:

> The number of seated diners last month was at least 40 percent below prepandemic levels in New York, Philadelphia, Minneapolis, San Francisco, Portland, Ore., and Cambridge, Mass., according to OpenTable. By contrast, the number of diners has fully recovered in Las Vegas, Miami, Nashville, Phoenix, Charlotte, N.C., and Austin, Texas, as well as in Oklahoma, Nebraska and New Hampshire.

Further, mask wearing, school disruptions, and working from home have been much more common in blue than red areas.

So, Leonhardt says, we have an almost perfect experiment: did any of these things help? He shares charts that show no obvious difference.

On the other hand, Leonhardt then shows some charts pitting counties where a majority voted for Trump against counties where a majority voted for Biden, and sure enough, there are more deaths in the Trump counties. He is taking "Trump counties" as a proxy for unvaccinated, and "Biden counties" as a proxy for vaccinated. He is concluding that the higher death numbers in Trump counties prove the vaccines work.

But hold on a minute. He isn't adjusting for age. Young people went strongly for Biden. Of course they're not going to be dying in significant numbers, whether vaccinated or not. Older people were more likely to vote for Trump. And those people, vaccinated or not, were more likely to be among the disease's casualties, simply because of the thousandfold difference in Covid mortality between the oldest and youngest.

If we adjust the numbers for age, therefore, it seems likely that any differences would disappear — as indeed they do between California and Florida.

Back to Leonhardt now, who urges his readers to recognize the costs of masking and social distancing: "Masks hamper people's ability to communicate, verbally and otherwise. Social distancing leads to the isolation and disruption that have fed so many problems over the past two years — mental health troubles, elevated blood pressure, drug overdoses, violent crime, vehicle crashes and more."

But then the other shoe drops: "If a new variant emerges, and hospitals are again at risk of being overwhelmed, then reinstating Covid restrictions may make sense again, despite their modest effects. But that's not where the country is today."

He's just finished telling you that those "modest effects" are more or less zero, but he then says we'll resort to them again if we have to. That's why we have to keep fighting. We cannot let this nonsense come back.

Part IX: Spring 2022

March 25, 2022 | Broadcaster reveals: government told us to toe the line

Yesterday our friend Jay Bhattacharya brought to the public's attention what he called an "explosive interview" with former Sky News and ITV executive Mark Sharman about the way the U.K. government pressured the media to portray Covid and the government's response a particular way.

Sharman spoke of a "warning" issued to media outlets by the U.K.'s Office of Communications, or Ofcom, that said in effect, "Do not question the government line." "I've never seen a warning from Ofcom like that," Sharman noted.

You could feature opposing voices, the warning said, but your host must intervene if there's any danger of "misinformation," which of course means dissent from the government line.

"I think that warning affected all broadcasters," said Sharman, who agreed that news hosts had been turned into representatives of the regime:

> Rather than question the government, they became cheerleaders for the government....They really were spreaders of panic and fear."
>
> We've all been trained to give both sides and let the viewer decide. But clearly, all the way through the pandemic, only one side of the story was given. It's created an environment that will lead to the biggest assault on freedom of speech and democracy I've known in my lifetime.

Sharman has a bit of the naivete of someone who's genuinely old school and is thus surprised by the media's recent behavior, but if we can look past that, it is a profoundly revealing interview.

The regime told broadcasters: don't question us. Just like that.

At the same time, I find most broadcasters are all too happy to be toadies of their ruling regime, so Ofcom's warning may have been superfluous.

April 19, 2022 | Guess where Covid stupidity may be returning

The rubber is about to meet the road in New York City, where I spent several days last week.

And let me pause to say: the place was better than I expected. More masking than there should be, but less than I thought I'd see. Nobody asked me for proof of vaccination. I even went to the Harvard Club, which I was sure would have continued demanding vax proof in order to demonstrate its superiority over the rest of us, but nope. In fact, someone I spoke to there got defensive about it and said the policy had been the city's, not theirs.

I still won't go to a Broadway show (they're demanding vax proof plus compliance with an almost comically strict mask mandate). But there was life in the place, and I wasn't sure if I should expect that or not.

Anyway:

We're about to find out whether New York City is determined to remain on the Covid hamster wheel, or whether it will quietly move on. New York City's Department of Health lists a series of risk levels (low, medium, high, very high). The city has been at the low level for some time now, but as the city's health commissioner recently noted, it appears to be trending toward medium.

Now if New York City is going to take those levels seriously, it has to bring back its pointless and disastrous "Key to NYC" vaccine passport program — requiring boosters this time — once the risk level hits medium. That's what it says on the website under "medium."

Virtually everywhere else has dropped all this, seemingly for good. Is New York really prepared to bring it all back, or will they instead simply continue on as if this "guidance" doesn't exist?

The answer to that question will speak volumes.

[TW note: New York ended up pretending those numbers didn't exist, and did not bring the program back as promised.]

April 22, 2022 | Fauci is hopping mad about the courts

Not everyone is happy that we're not wearing masks on airplanes anymore.

Some people are saying it's too risky to take the masks off. But that means they're assuming the masks do anything in the first place, and they clearly don't. We've observed the uselessness of masks for a very long time now. That anyone at all is still clinging to them is astonishing.

In case you'd like to buttress your own case against them, here is the definitive masks-don't-work episode of the Tom Woods Show: TomWoods.com/2051

The Fauci response to the decision is worth hearing, because it says so much:

> [I'm] both surprised and disappointed, because those types of things really are the purview of the CDC. This is a public-health issue. And for a court to come in — and if you look at the rationale for that it really is not particularly firm. And we are concerned about that, about courts getting involved in things that are unequivocally public-health decisions. This is a CDC issue. It should not have been a court issue.

We already knew that's how Fauci felt about restraints on him or on "public health" at large, but it's refreshing to hear him state it so clearly: you can't have legal recourse against us because we're looking out for what's best for you.

This is how every dictator speaks. Dictators rarely say: "I'm ruling over you because I'm evil."

Not to mention: so-called public-health experts have been embarrassingly wrong about masks again and again. Their so-called studies amount to isolating a narrow period of time in which a masked area had better results than an unmasked area. But when you zoom out and look at the entire Covid period we've lived through, that pattern no longer holds. They are trying to snow the public. There is no other explanation for behavior like that.

Even someone like CNN medical commentator Leana Wen, who went so far as to favor mandatory vaccination for interstate travel, has said that cloth masks — which Dr. Fauci still defends — are nothing more than "facial decoration." But we're supposed to believe that enough unanimity exists on masks that challenging them is unthinkable?

Fauci's star keeps fading, as fewer and fewer people care about his recommendations.

It's about blankety-blank time.

May 12, 2022 | The final numbers are coming in: Fauci a disaster

There are some numbers going around that the Faucis are going to want to ignore or explain away.

The excess death numbers among age groups less vulnerable to bad Covid outcomes are quite striking. It wasn't Covid that killed these people. It was the alleged mitigation measures that did it.

These two charts tell the story (the source for the top one is page 23 of the Society of Actuaries Research Institute report):

Table 5.6

EXCESS MORTALITY BY DETAILED AGE BAND

Age	Q2 2020	Q3 2020	Q4 2020	Q1 2021	Q2 2021	Q3 2021	4/20-9/21	% COVID	% Non-COVID	% Count
0-24	119%	127%	108%	102%	121%	129%	118%	2.7%	15.2%	2%
25-34	129%	135%	124%	120%	131%	181%	136%	11.4%	25.1%	2%
35-44	124%	136%	129%	129%	132%	217%	144%	19.8%	24.7%	4%
45-54	123%	127%	130%	133%	121%	208%	140%	23.8%	16.5%	10%
55-64	117%	123%	130%	129%	116%	170%	131%	21.0%	10.0%	18%
65-74	116%	115%	133%	130%	108%	133%	122%	16.8%	5.6%	17%
75-84	113%	113%	132%	122%	105%	116%	117%	13.3%	3.7%	20%
85+	111%	102%	123%	110%	90%	98%	106%	10.4%	-4.6%	27%
All[10]	116%	115%	128%	122%	107%	139%	121%	15.6%	5.7%	100%

United States Deaths Analysis, By Age Group, Jan-Mar 2019 vs Jan-Mar 2022
(2022 data as of 11 May 2022; 2022 will change as CDC receives updated data from the states)

Age Group	2019 All-Cause Deaths Jan-Mar	2022 All-Cause Deaths Jan-Mar	Change in All-Cause Deaths 2019 v 2022	2022 Covid Deaths Jan-Mar	2022 Non-Covid Deaths Jan-Mar	Change in Non-Covid Deaths 2019 v 2022	Percentage Change 2019 v 2022	Percentage Increase Due To Covid
Under 1	5,179	4,321	(858)	60	4,261	(918)	-16.6%	1.2%
1 to 4	897	850	(47)	44	806	(91)	-5.2%	4.9%
5 to 14	1,366	1,340	(26)	84	1,256	(110)	-1.9%	6.1%
15 to 24	6,819	8,231	1,412	370	7,861	1,042	20.7%	5.4%
25 to 34	13,915	18,459	4,544	1,471	16,988	3,073	32.7%	10.6%
35 to 44	20,214	28,600	8,386	3,409	25,191	4,977	41.5%	16.9%
45 to 54	41,264	50,171	8,907	8,643	41,528	264	21.6%	20.9%
55 to 64	97,487	118,035	20,548	21,486	96,549	(938)	21.1%	22.0%
65 to 74	144,650	189,189	44,539	34,920	154,269	9,619	30.8%	24.1%
75 to 84	180,484	229,992	49,508	39,333	190,659	10,175	27.4%	21.8%
Over 84	233,096	260,094	26,998	36,177	223,917	(9,179)	11.6%	15.5%
Total	745,371	909,282	163,911	145,997	763,285	17,914	22.0%	19.6%

Note: 2022 All-Cause Deaths includes deaths assigned to Covid plus those assigned to Non-Covid causes. Non-covid includes all deaths minus Covid Deaths

Sources:

2019 data: https://wonder.cdc.gov/

2022 data: https://data.cdc.gov/NCHS/Provisional-COVID-19-Death-Counts-by-Sex-Age-and-S/9bhg-hcku (11 May 2022)

Is Fauci going to concede anything at all? Of course not: "I'm not sure the lockdowns itself did it, and I'm wondering why you're asking me about lockdowns because there were not complete lockdowns in this country," Fauci said. "There were restrictions, obviously, but there were not lockdowns."

That's the latest one from the crazies: we didn't really have lockdowns. Real lockdowns were done by the Chinese, says Fauci. "China is now going into a real lockdown. So I would disagree characterizing whatever went on during this country as a full lockdown."

Stanford's Jay Bhattacharya shot back:

> It is shocking that Dr. Fauci remains blind to the strong scientific evidence that the lockdown approach that he championed has caused devastating harm to the poor, vulnerable, and working class. His only regret seems to be that we did not lock down hard enough like China did, where healthy residents have been force-quarantined, children separated from parents, pet dogs and cats killed, with no discernible effect on the spread of the disease.

Do these sound like people deeply invested in your well-being?

May 18, 2022 | Guess where the disinfo has been coming from

This is one of my favorite things of the past two years.

Apparently the Office of the Surgeon General has asked each of the 50 states to submit examples of Covid misinformation and the impact that such misinformation has had.

The response by Indiana is priceless.

Indiana Attorney General Todd Rokita acknowledged the harms done by misinformation, and then proceeded to list "the following examples of disinformation from the CDC and other health organizations that have shattered the public's trust in science and public health and will take decades to repair."

Beautiful.

The document then lays out the problems with lockdowns and masks, refutes the claim that the jabs could prevent transmission (the basis for the various vaccine passports and mandates), and criticizes the authorities for overcounting Covid deaths and denying natural immunity.

Then, too, it criticizes the practice of mass asymptomatic testing:

> Mass testing of asymptomatic individuals with contact tracing and quarantining of people who test positive has failed to substantively slow the progress of the epidemic and has imposed great costs on people who were quarantined even though they posed no risk of infecting others.

> Three facts are crucial to understanding why this policy has failed. First, even close contacts of someone who tests positive for the SARS-CoV-2 virus are unlikely to pass the disease on. In a large meta-analysis of household contacts of asymptomatic positive cases, only 3% of people living in the same home got sick.

> Second, the PCR test that has been used to identify asymptomatic infections often returns a positive result for people who have dead viral fragments, are not infectious, and pose no risk of infecting others.

> And third, the contact tracing system becomes overwhelmed whenever cases start to rise, leading to long delays in

contacting new cases. At precisely the moment when contact tracing might be needed, it cannot do its job.

At the same time, quarantining people is costly — for workers without adequate sick leave, absenteeism due to contact tracing means pay cuts, lost opportunities, and perhaps even an inability to feed families. For children, it means more skipped lessons and missed opportunities for academic and social growth at school, with long-run negative consequences for their future prospects. In the U.K., an official government review determined that its 37 billion pound investment in contact tracing was a waste of resources. The same is undoubtedly true in the United States.

Then Rokita takes on the implicit and sometimes explicit claim and goal of total eradication of Covid, even though it bore none of the characteristics of a disease that could be eradicated. The process of trying to do so, meanwhile, would cause incalculable damage:

First, we have no technology to reduce the spread of the disease or meaningfully alter disease dynamics. Lockdowns and social restrictions fail because only people who can afford to work from home without losing their job can comply over long periods....

Second, there are many animal hosts for SARS-CoV-2 and evidence of transmission between mammals and humans. One USDA study in late 2021 found that nearly 80% of white-tailed deer in the U.S. had evidence of Covid-19 antibodies. Dogs, cats, bats, mink, and many other mammals can get Covid-19. So even if the disease were eradicated among humans, zoonotic transmission would guarantee that it would come back.

Finally, eradication takes a global commitment from every country — an impossible goal since Covid-19 eradication is far from the most pressing public health problem for many developing countries.

So as usual, the real misinformation comes from the official sources, and the statement by the Indiana Attorney General is a rare case in which this problem is publicly acknowledged and countered.

June 5, 2022 | What happened after masks disappeared from planes?

We all remember Anthony Fauci's response to the striking down of the transportation (and especially airplane) mask mandate: only "public health" authorities may make these decisions.

So what do we do if the geniuses who run our public health establishment do something stupid, or overstep their (imagined) authority?

No answer.

You will be ruled by public health bureaucrats, and you will like it.

Last week Fauci even went so far as to say that the battle over the airplane mask mandate has less to do with masks on planes than it does with who gets to say whether we're forced to wear masks on planes:

> One of the issues that I have articulated in the past, and I will in the future, [is] it's less about mandates on the plane than it is about who has the right and the authority and the capability of making public health decisions.

> And I believe that the Department of Justice is operating on the principle that decisions that are public health decisions belong with the public health agency, in this case, the CDC.

As long as we're on the subject, let's take a look at the death trends since the mandate was lifted. Remember what a catastrophic health decision this was supposed to have been? The numbers must be through the roof, right? Let's take a look:

You must be shocked at this graph. Take all the time you need before continuing. Have a glass of water.

The great Ian Miller, author of *Unmasked*, just said that one of his favorite 2022 headlines has been "California extends mask mandate amid record Covid cases," because it showed not a hint of awareness of what this said about the effectiveness of mask mandates.

The main reason they've fought against the lifting of mandates is that we'll see that *no catastrophe occurs when the mandates are lifted*.

June 6, 2022 | Public health's DeSantis problem

The lockdowners and mandators have tried two strategies to explain away Florida's health outcomes over the past couple of years.

(1) They've tried to claim that Florida has actually done very badly. It's been hard to make this stick, though. People can see with their own eyes that there aren't piles of corpses on the side of the road in Miami or Orlando.

Also, even if Florida were doing slightly worse than some other places, it should still be doing *much, much* worse after ignoring the entire public health establishment's dire warnings.

And then people point out that you can't compare Florida to California on raw numbers, because that's apples and oranges. Covid is worse on people who are older, obese, or diabetic.

Correct for those population characteristics and there's no difference between Florida's outcomes and those of California.

(2) So some of them decided to abandon this approach and instead to claim that Florida must be fudging its numbers.

Stop and think about what an admission that is. Anyone arguing like this is essentially saying: if what we believe about "mitigation" strategies is true, Florida cannot possibly be doing this well. Therefore, the only explanation has to be that the numbers are fake. It isn't that our Covid religion is wrong. It's that Florida is deceiving us.

That's a dangerous road to take. If Florida's numbers can be shown to be accurate, where does that leave these people?

Well, the Inspector General just completed a full investigation of the claim and found nothing to support it.

Such a claim had been advanced by an employee named Rebekah Jones, and indeed I examined her allegations in an episode of the Tom Woods Show some time ago.

The lockdowners wanted and needed her story to be true.

But after interviewing a dozen people involved in Covid tracking in Florida, including Jones's own superiors, no basis for the story could be found.

According to the *Wall Street Journal*:

> Some said she had told them she was pressured to alter Covid case and death counts, but her allegations didn't make sense to them, not least because she didn't have access to the raw data to do so. Ms. Jones, a geographer by training who previously worked on hurricane tracking systems, merely assisted with the Covid data's online dashboard.

With this story buried, what is left for those who can't bring themselves to believe that Florida did well without Fauci?

My best guess is that they'll be talking a lot less about Florida now.

And yet isn't it funny: those people have absolutely no problem spreading their discredited ideas. They never have to wonder whether they should make that YouTube video or post that podcast episode. They get a free pass.

But those of us who can point to actual data and the real experiences of real places in the world? We have to sit in anticipation of the "disinformation" hammer.

June 9, 2022 | Crazies in White House still panicking parents about Covid

The downright nasty Dr. Ashish Jha, tapped by the Biden White House to be its Coronavirus Response Coordinator, is continuing with the crazy hysteria about Covid and children.

Everybody knows Covid is of essentially zero danger to children. The White House, on the other hand, *wants* it to be a problem for children. So Jha is now spreading the claim that Covid is "a far greater threat to kids than the flu," following the lead of Harvard Medical School Instructor Jeremy Faust. (He says Covid claimed the lives of 600 children in 2021, while the flu causes an average of only 120 pediatric deaths per year.)

You know that's false, but do you know the specifics?

The great Jay Bhattacharya just provided three reasons in the *Wall Street Journal* that the Jha claim is false.

First, flu tests are relatively rare compared to Covid tests. From October 2018 to September 2019, for example, 1.4 million flu tests were given. But as of last month, some 897 million Covid tests had been given.

You think that might skew the results a teensy-weensy bit?

Second, even the CDC admits, based on audits of death certificates, that 35 percent of reported pediatric Covid deaths couldn't actually have been caused by Covid.

Third, Dr. Faust's figure comes from a source known to underestimate flu deaths. The National Center for Immunization and Respiratory Diseases, realizing the challenge posed by the lack of flu testing, corrects for it with its estimate of 1,161 pediatric flu deaths in 2012–13, as opposed to Dr. Faust's claim of 142.

So as usual, ignore these people.

June 13, 2022 | Disinformation board: now 37% creepier

You may recall the "Disinformation Governance Board" (DGB) that was contemplated by the Department of Homeland Security (DHS), and to be headed by Nina Jankowicz, herself a serial spreader of misinformation.

(It has since been "paused.")

We were all told that it was actually no big deal, that concerns about it amounted to right-wing conspiracy theories — in other words, the kinds of things they say when something is absolutely true.

NPR ran a headline about our supposedly exaggerated fears of this new board: "How DHS's disinformation board fell victim to misinformation."

But thanks to new whistleblower documents, we know that a much broader scope for the Disinformation Governance Board was in fact contemplated than our rulers let on.

They were seeking with this board to regulate "disinformation related to the origins and effects of Covid-19 vaccines or the efficacy of masks," for example. Further, the Department had been "working on plans to 'operationalize' its relationships with private social media companies to implement its public policy goals."

Senators Chuck Grassley and Josh Hawley, in a letter to the Secretary of the Department of Homeland Security, laid out their concerns:

> Collectively, whistleblower allegations and the documents we've reviewed raise concerns that DHS could be seeking an active role in coordinating the censorship of viewpoints that it determines, according to an unknown standard, to be "MDM" [mis-, dis-, or mal-information] by enlisting the help of social media companies and big tech. The DGB's charter also specifically states that the DGB should "serv[e] as the Department's internal and external point of contact for coordination with state, local, tribal, and territorial partners, the private sector, and nongovernmental actors regarding MDM." The First Amendment of the Constitution was designed precisely so that the government could not censor opposing viewpoints — even if those viewpoints were false. DHS should not in any way seek to enlist the private sector to curb or silence opposing viewpoints. It is therefore imperative for DHS to provide additional clarity regarding its policies

and procedures for identifying and addressing "MDM," as well as its efforts to "operationalize" public-private partnerships and the steps it is taking to ensure that it does not infringe on the constitutional rights of American citizens.

The two senators have requested the following clarifications (the ten points that follow are their exact words):

1. Has DHS at any point in time asked or suggested to Twitter, Facebook, TikTok, or any other social media executives that they should censor, flag, add context to, or remove any social media posts that it believes to be disinformation?

2. Has DHS at any point in time asked or suggested to Twitter, Facebook, TikTok, or any other social media executives that they suspend or ban the account(s) of individuals believed to be promoting information it believes to be disinformation?

3. Please provide all documents, including all written and electronic communications, memoranda, and organizational documents, related to the DGB from the point that DHS first considered establishing a DGB until the present.

4. Please provide all documents, including all written and electronic communications and memoranda, related to Nina Jankowicz's selection as Executive Director of the DGB.

5. Please explain why, in your public statements and testimony before Congress, you have not fully explained the key role that the DGB was designed to play in coordinating among DHS components and engaging the assistance of the private sector.

6. Please explain how DHS defines "MDM" and how DHS decides whether a given news story or other piece of information fits its definition of "MDM." Please identify who exactly is ultimately responsible for making this determination.

7. Please explain the criteria DHS uses when deciding whether to spend taxpayer resources addressing a particular news item or narrative that it has classified as "MDM."

8. Please describe all safeguards that DHS has put in place to ensure that its efforts to counter the spread of disinformation

do not infringe on Americans' constitutional right to free speech.

9. Did DHS Under Secretary for the Office of Strategy, Policy, and Plans Robert Silvers meet with Twitter executives on April 28, 2022? If so, please provide a summary of topics discussed during the meeting.

10. Please define what DHS means by the phrase, "operationalizing public-private partnerships."

All excellent questions and points.

Now even though the prospect of a Disinformation Governance Board horrifies you and me, we should be aware of how many people favor such a thing.

A 2021 Pew Research Poll found that 65 percent of Democrats thought the U.S. government should take steps to restrict false information online, even if it limits freedom of information. Some 76 percent of Democrats thought Big Tech platforms should do so.

Also, not considered amidst all this is who gets to decide whether something is "false" in the first place. The U.S. government doesn't exactly have a stellar track record here.

Of course, the best approach is no censorship at all, and it's bizarre that in the United States, of all places, this has suddenly become controversial.

June 16, 2022 | One chart smashes critics of "DeathSantis"

I think I can say this without fear of contradiction: most of my readers do not watch *The View*.

Neither do I, dear reader. Neither do I.

But as a daily chronicler of mass imbecility, I come across clips from time to time.

The panelists were recently discussing who might be the Republican presidential nominee in 2024. Sunny Hostin spoke briefly about "DeathSantis." "I think he handled Covid miserably," she said. "I think he's a fascist and a bigot.…Those are his good points."

She added, "I like Gavin Newsom because he's really pretty to look at."

So it's all right to be imprisoned in your home or cut off from normal social life if the person doing it is "pretty to look at" and insists that doing so is "scientific."

As for "DeathSantis" and handling Covid "miserably," I'll say this: opinions regarding how DeSantis governed these past two years have become an IQ test, and people like "Sunny Hostin" haven't scored too well.

DeSantis minimized all the death and suffering caused by lockdowns — death and suffering never acknowledged by Sunny Hostin — while at the same time his state had an age-adjusted Covid mortality well below the national average (the lighter line in the graph below is Florida):

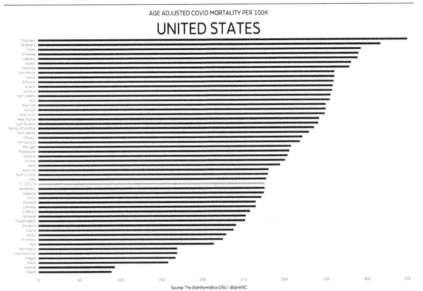

See all those states above Florida? Do you suppose Sunny Hostin is going to say all those places handled Covid "miserably"? I won't hold my breath.

(There's no need to bother addressing the claim of "fascism," because something tells me Sunny Hostin doesn't have the faintest idea what that word means.)

June 17, 2022 | Next up: shots for infants

Now that the FDA has approved the Covid shots for infants and toddlers, it's just a matter of waiting for the CDC to sign off on them.

Florida is the only state that has not ordered the shots for these children.

So CNN's Bill Weir went to Twitter to say, "49 states preordered Covid vaccines for kids under 5 so they'll be ready as soon as there is FDA approval. Take a guess which state did not."

Christina Pushaw, press secretary for Ron DeSantis, replied: "The state everyone is moving to?"

In New York, a major cultural center known as 92NY has already announced, even before the CDC has said anything, that they will be enforcing a vaccine requirement on everyone above six months old.

They wrote in an email:

> We are also anticipating the release of the Covid-19 vaccine for children under the age of 5 and have made the decision to extend 92NY's vaccine mandate to that age group once they are eligible. Currently, we plan to require proof of vaccination for children under 5 beginning in September. We will share more details once the vaccine is released.

At this point there's no sense in bothering to point out that the shots don't stop the spread. The people making the decisions at 92NY surely know that. They are almost certainly now using the vaccine as a proxy, a way of keeping out the riff-raff. It's a very particular kind of elite that will go to the extreme of doing this to an infant, and that elite is evidently their target clientele.

Given that the shots for young children already failed to get much traction, it is inconceivable that many normal people will want it for toddlers or infants. Even the Democrats aren't going to run on mandating this.

Vinay Prasad, a left-leaning commentator who has been pretty good on the lockdown regime, put it this way:

> If someone says vaccines for kids under 5 lower the risk of severe disease or death, it's important to remember that no data on earth proves that conclusion. The data we will soon get will be hopelessly confounded. And seroprevalence is already so high.

In related news, Senator Rand Paul confronted Anthony Fauci again. A couple of key moments:

Paul: "Can you tell me if anyone on the vaccine approval committees ever received money from the people who make vaccines?"

Fauci: "People who receive royalties are not required to divulge them."

Jay Bhattacharya observes:

Undisclosed royalty payments are a conflict of interest, no matter what Tony Fauci says. Having him as de facto head of Covid policy and also in charge of billions of dollars for government grants to scientists is also a conflict of interest. Why are government ethics watchdogs silent?

Another exchange:

Paul: "Are you aware of any studies that show reduction in hospitalization or death for children who take a booster?"

Fauci: "Right now there is not enough data…to indicate that."

That's our world, ladies and gentlemen.

But thank goodness for the courageous few who have risked so much to tell us the truth.

June 20, 2022 | Is this the Covid crazies' worst crime?

Earlier this week I wrote about the drive to give the shots to children as young as six months, and not long before that I wrote about how the hysterics manipulated the numbers to make Covid seem like a worse threat to children than it really is.

So what we have, then, is a disease that is of essentially zero danger to children, but in response to it the lizard people — and this is the understatement of the century — implemented a series of policies that did serious harm to children.

I just read (I had somehow missed it) from several months ago the first paper that attempted to estimate the mortality effects on children caused by economic damage done by lockdowns and restrictions.

Remember when people tried claiming that you and I cared only about the economy, but they, being morally superior to us, cared about saving lives?

And remember how we understood that implementing a strategy that wasn't going to save lives anyway but that would do massive and gratuitous damage to the economy would itself wind up taking people's lives? Remember how we understood that this dichotomy between "the economy" and "saving lives" was juvenile and inane?

We were right yet again.

And by the way, I'm not looking for kudos here. Anyone without brain damage had to know what the consequences of these things would be.

The paper, by the way, which has five authors and was published in the peer-reviewed *PLOS ONE*, is called "Estimated impact of the 2020 economic downturn on under-5 mortality for 129 countries." From the paper:

> Between 1990 and 2019, there has been a sustained trend of decline in global poverty and infant mortality in LMICs [Low and Middle Income Countries]. However, as hypothesized above, Covid-19 related economic downturns of 2020 are likely to reverse these positive trends....
>
> We estimate that the economic downturns of 2020 significantly increased loss of life among children younger than five years old in LMICs. Many of the countries in this analysis have relatively young populations with tenuous access to stable housing, clean water, food, and primary care. The health of these children is highly susceptible to reductions in the economic well-being of their families. Children in these lower income countries are also subject to a high rate of exposure to other infectious diseases, besides Covid-19, which makes them more susceptible when the economy reduces their access to nutrition, housing, water, sanitation, and parental care. Disruptions to primary health care service supply and demand will compound these threats, and thus may be a likely driver of increased mortality in these settings.

According to the study, assuming a conservative scenario of a five percent reduction in GDP per capita, the additional number of under-5 deaths (in other words, over and above the number of deaths that would have occurred under normal conditions) is 282,996. In the scenarios of 10 or 15 percent reductions in GDP per capita, the excess loss of life among children under age five is 585,802 and 911,026, respectively.

You have surely heard some people in our camp call for hearings, trials, imprisonments, and maybe some of you have thought those demands are over the top.

Look at those numbers again, and then consider what the perpetrators of this catastrophe deserve.

Part X: Summer 2022

June 21, 2022 | We want more power, say public health crazies

You would think, if we were dealing with normal people, that what we laughingly call our "public health" establishment would have offered a few apologies here and there, or at least indicated they had a little humility, after the disaster of the past two years.

Instead, the public health establishment is now clamoring for more power.

The *New York Times* reports that a panel of so-called "health experts" is calling for "an overhaul of the U.S. public health system that would expand the role of the federal government, giving Washington the authority to set minimum health standards and coordinate a patchwork of nearly 3,000 agencies."

They don't like the decentralized approach that exists in the United States with its federal system and states that can make their own decisions.

Former CDC Director Julie L. Gerberding, who served under George W. Bush, said the past two years had "taught us that we have to have a coordinated, integrated public health network that functions — and the only way that we can bring that together is by having a national approach."

The panel likewise calls for the creation of an Under Secretary of Public Health within the existing Department of Health and Human Services. It would coordinate the efforts of federal agencies that deal with public health, and could set minimum health standards for the states.

So the people who sat back and did nothing while Michelle Obama forced "low fat" lunches — as if no progress had been made in our understanding of human nourishment since 1977 — on hapless schoolchildren are going to set minimum health standards for the states.

I vote no on that.

June 30, 2022 | Surgeon General publicly responds to Woods

Well, I wasn't expecting this.

Today Donald Trump's Surgeon General, Jerome Adams, responded to me.

Here's the background:

In episode #2149 of the Tom Woods Show — TomWoods.com/2149 — Kelley Krohnert explained how she figured out that the commonly repeated claim in recent weeks that Covid was among the top five killers of children was bogus. All across the public health establishment this obviously false claim was uncritically repeated. Anyone following Covid had to know it was false, but they all repeated it.

Kelley Krohnert is a smart woman with corporate experience but she's not a statistician or in public health. Yet she exposed this particular case of fakery, while no journalist or public health specialist did.

Then, on Twitter, Kelley pointed this out to Jerome Adams.

The following exchange ensued:

Tom Woods @ThomasEWoods · 4h
Check out @JeromeAdamsMD telling a citizen -- who is 100% correct -- that she's not as smart as the "experts," so she's therefore not allowed to make a true statement

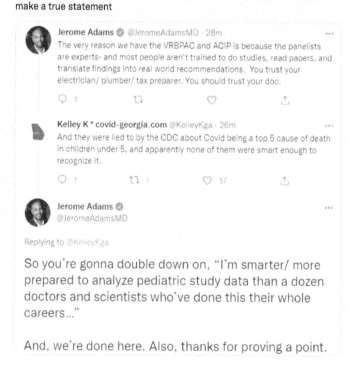

Jerome Adams ✔ @JeromeAdamsMD · 28m
The very reason we have the VRBPAC and ACIP is because the panelists are experts- and most people aren't trained to do studies, read papers, and translate findings into real world recommendations. You trust your electrician/ plumber/ tax preparer. You should trust your doc.

Kelley K * covid-georgia.com @KelleyKga · 26m
And they were lied to by the CDC about Covid being a top 5 cause of death in children under 5, and apparently none of them were smart enough to recognize it.

Jerome Adams ✔
@JeromeAdamsMD

Replying to @KelleyKga

So you're gonna double down on, "I'm smarter/ more prepared to analyze pediatric study data than a dozen doctors and scientists who've done this their whole careers..."

And, we're done here. Also, thanks for proving a point.

Jerome Adams ✅
@JeromeAdamsMD

Replying to @ThomasEWoods

Tom:
1) I apologized for being snarky because I got sucked into the back and forth
2) I never said she 0wasn't allowed to" make a statement. I said that the fact that she was correct in this instance doesn't mean the collective group of doctors/ scientists is wrong on all else.

Tom Woods
@ThomasEWoods

But anyone following this would have known that that stat had to be bogus. I'm just some schmuck and I knew it. How do people who do this for a living not immediately know that's false? And then they wonder why we don't trust them? The public health establishment is a joke

I don't think there's any real reply to that. How could someone who's been seriously engaged on this topic actually think Covid was among the top threats to children? What does this tell us about our "public health" establishment?

July 22, 2022 | The wrong lessons are being drawn from Covid

In some places they're trying to bring the hysteria back, but in general we seem to have moved on to the "lessons learned" stage.

It's hard to imagine that the kind of people who thought putting arrows on supermarket floors, distinguishing "clean" from "dirty" pens in doctors' offices, and putting small plexiglass barriers (that everyone simply evaded) in front of cashiers would "save lives" are capable of learning any lessons, but let's be sports about it and give them a chance.

The great Sunetra Gupta of Oxford, one of the three drafters of the Great Barrington Declaration, tells us that in the U.K., at least, the regime is drawing the wrong lessons.

A public inquiry has been opened into the government's handling of the situation there. And unfortunately, some people are trying to popularize the idea that the problem was that the government didn't lock society down at precisely the right moment or in just the right way.

But as Gupta says:

> The most important question to consider is not whether the Government locked down the country at precisely the right moment, but rather whether lockdowns and other restrictive measures were justified at all, given the uncertainties that existed at the time concerning their efficacy in containing the spread of SARS-CoV-2 and the negative knock-on effects on the health and well-being of the population.
>
> We now know that many of the measures imposed during the pandemic did not have a significant effect on reducing the spread of the virus and led to an entirely predictable set of concerning outcomes of extraordinary proportions among the most vulnerable sectors — children, the elderly, and the economically deprived.
>
> This is because, as any standard epidemiology text will tell you, measures restricting activity are unlikely to stop the spread of a novel virus in the long term. Such interventions, however, will alter the dynamics of endemic diseases (such as RSV, influenza, adenovirus) causing them to transiently disappear and subsequently re-emerge at unusual times with some attendant perverse consequences....
>
> Locking down "earlier" or locking down "properly" would not have avoided any of the unconscionable harms inflicted upon those whom society has always agreed to protect — children, the elderly, the economically disadvantaged.
>
> It is also unlikely that it would have had much impact on the spread of the virus.

Indeed it is.

For me, the Covid nuttiness had two primary effects:

(1) It made me realize I had been far too naive about the world's ruling classes — and I say this as someone who had had nothing but cynicism and contempt for them before 2020. These people, and whatever their sinister agenda is, are far worse than I thought.

(2) It drastically lowered my estimation of mankind. I am still flabbergasted at the nonsense so many people went along with, when the

truth was not hard to find — and when these people's very lives hung in the balance! They couldn't even take a few minutes to figure out whether their lives were being ruined for a good reason or not?

Because of (2), I began to shift my emphasis toward all those good people who did see through it all, who weren't afraid to be unpopular by speaking forbidden truths, and who themselves may have suffered professionally, financially, socially, or in any number of other ways because of the stands they took.

I want to use my resources to help *those* people.

I still promote my ideas on my podcast, because I do believe in freedom.

But a lack of knowledge of how to argue about antitrust law is not keeping people up at night.

What is?

A looming sense of dread about the future. If they pulled this Covid b.s., what else will they try? And do we have any choice other than to sit back and take it?

Or:

How do I carry on in a soul-crushing job that makes irrational and unjust demands of me, and could be yanked away at any time?

Or:

What do I do with my money, when the geniuses in charge seem hell-bent on destroying it?

Or:

How do I keep these people from colonizing my children's minds?

How about those for starters?

Everybody already knows what the problems are. What the world needs now isn't more articles telling them about the problems.

What the world needs is someone to hoist a flag and say: I'm determined to do something about this, and if you are, too, then come join me.

I've hoisted that flag: TomSchoolOfLife.com

August 8, 2022 | Guess what this mask mandate accomplished

One of the most maddening parts of the nuthouse we've been living in for close to 30 solid months now is that real-life events constantly contradict the official version of things, yet that version still persists as if nothing ever happened.

I expect politicians to refuse to understand things. But even your own neighbors pretend these things don't exist.

Florida's age-adjusted Covid mortality is better than that of most states. That should not be possible. Not a single, solitary Covid hysteric would have predicted that outcome, and they would have called you crazy and irresponsible for predicting it. Yet it occurred, and it didn't change their minds one iota, even though it explodes their entire worldview.

When it lifted its state-level restrictions in February 2021, Iowa was called by the media "a state that doesn't care if you live or die," but then when you track its health outcomes against other Midwestern states over the ensuing months, you cannot tell the difference between Iowa and any other state. If the hysterics were right, this could not be possible. Yet it occurred, and it didn't change their minds one iota.

Having said all that, let me now share with you another chart from the heroic Ian Miller. This chart, like the other pieces of evidence I've mentioned, will likewise do nothing to change anyone's mind, even though it obviously should.

Athens, Georgia, recently brought back its mask mandate. Athens, Georgia, must therefore be doing so much better than other places in Georgia that it just jumps right off the chart, right?

See for yourself:

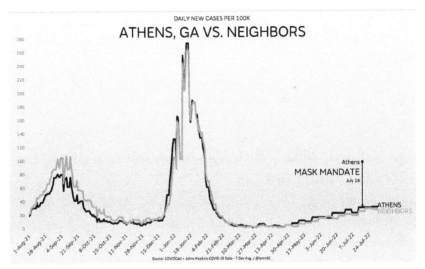

Wait, what's that? It's indistinguishable from its neighbors — like all other such charts? How about that. Not to mention: Athens and its neighbors imposed and lifted mask mandates at all different times, and yet their numbers are identical.

August 17, 2022 | The fate of blue-city businesses

Blue cities that saw violent protests in 2020 are finding that their effects, combined with the damage caused by lockdowns and Covid hysteria, continue to take their toll.

We can see this in the restaurant industry, thanks to a recent report using data kept by the restaurant reservation service OpenTable, but we can presumably extrapolate to other industries as well.

When we compare numbers from July 2019 with those of July 2022, the results are in some cases downright catastrophic.

In Minneapolis, with its draconian lockdowns, vaccine passports, and violence, the number of daily diners is down by more than half.

Not to mention, two-thirds of Minnesota restaurants took on debt during the madness. The average amount of that debt? $500,000.

In Seattle, those restaurants fortunate enough to still be open find themselves in an average of $160,000 in debt.

In New York City, 50,000 fewer people work in the restaurant industry today than on the eve of the lockdowns, and some 4,500 restaurants have closed.

Meanwhile, the numbers are excellent in Florida and up over 30 percent in Miami, Fort Lauderdale, Naples, and Tampa.

(You probably guessed that part.)

September 1, 2022 | Biden's suppression of dissident voices is coming out

Attorney Jenin Younes, whom I interviewed on episode #1947 of the Tom Woods Show, discussed a lawsuit today in which her firm is representing prominent lockdown critics Jay Bhattacharya (Stanford), Martin Kulldorff (Harvard), and others who were victims of censorship campaigns at the direction of the federal government.

"Thousands of pages of documents have exposed a censorship campaign both unprecedented and formerly unimagined in scale and in scope," said Younes.

We also heard today from the attorney general of Missouri; an excerpt follows:

> In May, we filed a landmark lawsuit against top ranking Biden Administration officials for colluding with social media companies to censor free speech. We have already received documents that show their cozy relationship, and now we're demanding more.

> In July of 2022, MO and LA served discovery requests and third-party subpoenas, demanding documents from top-ranking Biden Administration officials and social media companies over their alleged collusion to suppress freedom of speech.

> The Department of Justice is refusing to produce communications between the most senior officials and social media companies — yesterday we filed a joint petition asking the Court to compel them to produce those documents.

> Here's what we know so far. DOJ identified 45 federal officials who have interacted with social media companies on misinformation.

Beyond DOJ, Meta identified 32 additional federal officials including White House Officials who communicated with them, and YouTube identified 11 federal officials including White House Officials who communicated with them, many of whom were not disclosed by DOJ.

This is a vast censorship enterprise, and the American people deserve to see the truth. Here are examples that already prove that federal officials and social media companies are coordinating on censorship, and we're not close to being done yet:

A senior FB official sent an email to the Surgeon General stating, "I know our teams met today to better understand the scope of what the White House expects from us on misinformation going forward." This email chain follows the SG's "misinformation health advisory" in July 2021.

The same senior official sent a later email to HHS and noted, "Thanks again for taking the time to meet earlier today." Then, the official continued to discuss how Facebook is taking even more steps to censor freedom of speech.

Further communications show that Facebook is "increasing the strength of our demotions for Covid and vaccine-related content that third party fact checkers rate as 'Partly False' or 'Missing Context.' That content will now be demoted at the same strength that we demote any content on our platform rated 'False.'"

Twitter scheduled a meeting to debrief top White House Officials on "vaccine misinformation."

There are several instances where Facebook wouldn't proceed with censoring freedom of speech on their platform until they had input, or a "debunking," from the CDC. Twitter followed the same course in at least one email.

The CDC also proposed a monthly debunking meeting with Facebook to help them censor free speech as well as regular "Be on the Lookout" calls with major social media outlets.

A White House official was even concerned about parody Fauci accounts and coordinated with Facebook to take them down.

September 5, 2022 | The booster fanatics aren't giving up

Two and a half years later, most people are truly over the nonsense.

There are far too many Americans still pointlessly wearing masks, but some of that has to be a way of telegraphing to the world that they're anti-Trumpers. Mask usage has not correlated in any way to improved health outcomes, as many hundreds of charts can amply demonstrate. A continued devotion to them on the part of the general public has to be either politically motivated or the result of an extreme lack of curiosity.

As I mentioned last week from Scotland, we saw next to no masks there — far fewer than in the United States. A friend who lives there told me, "It's really something: it's as if a switch suddenly turned off, and nobody cared anymore." And during our visit to Sweden in May, if even one in 700 people was wearing a mask I would be surprised.

But the fanatics ye have always with you, and so even now we have items like this:

Jay Bhattacharya responded to that headline this way:

> In 2021, the Biden administration, Fauci, and the CDC made a bet on the basis of incomplete randomized trial data that the vax would stop Covid transmission. Vax mandates and discrimination followed. For the new booster, some are making the same bet, based on data from 8 mice.

He's not kidding about the eight mice part. I'd share more with you about that, but the results from the eight mice are part of a paper *in preparation*, and not even available as a preprint yet.

September 14, 2022 | New York did better than Florida, say the liars

They just can't let Florida go.

They *need* Florida to have been a disaster, because if it isn't/wasn't, then all their destruction was pointless.

So we've just had to endure Vincent Rajkumar, editor of *Blood Cancer Journal*, showing us this graph depicting Florida surpassing New York in Covid deaths:

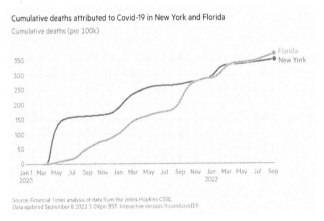

Cumulative deaths attributed to Covid-19 in New York and Florida
Cumulative deaths (per 100k)

Source: Financial Times analysis of data from the Johns Hopkins CSSE.
Data updated September 8 2022 3:09pm BST. Interactive version: ft.com/covid19

Jay Bhattacharya responded:

> How is it that an editor of a medical journal still does not understand the concept of "age adjustment" when comparing states on Covid mortality? It's been 2.5 years. More than enough time for people like him to understand the thousand-fold difference in mortality risk by age.

A reporter from the *Palm Beach Post* made a similar claim, to which Kyle Lamb responded with this data, showing Florida fared better than key lockdown states of California, Illinois, Pennsylvania, and New York:

Provisional Mortality Statistics, 2018 through Last Month Results
Deaths occurring through August 20, 2022 as of September 04, 2022

Residence State	# Deaths	Population	Crude Rate Per 100,000	Age Adjusted Rate Per 100,000
Florida (12)	63,824	65,199,936	97.9	65.3
California (06)	90,109	118,154,234	76.1	65.9
Illinois (17)	33,195	37,762,530	87.9	70.2
Total	295,166	317,426,850	93.0	71.1
Pennsylvania (42)	41,878	38,346,762	109.2	76.0
New York (36)	66,160	58,010,326	114.0	85.7

But look again at that first chart. Adjusting for age is obviously necessary for an apples-to-apples comparison. But suppose age weren't a factor, and that the graph above was a reliable indicator of how Florida and New York did when compared to each other.

The difference is completely trivial.

Suppose in March 2020 we had asked the crazies, "If Florida more or less defies all the recommendations you're making, what do you think the results will be?" They would have answered: *absolute carnage*. They would have predicted that Florida would wind up at least *an order of magnitude* worse than states with lockdowns and vax passports.

No matter what charts they try to mislead you with or what nit-picking they do, there is no escaping this fact: nothing like what they would have predicted actually occurred.

So now they're reduced to: look at this tiny difference between Florida and New York — a difference that more than goes away when correcting for age.

That's pretty sad.

September 15, 2022 | Progressivism, brought to you by Pfizer

It's hard to believe now, but not even one human lifetime ago the slogan "question authority" was associated with the left-liberal project.

That's long gone, having been replaced by "shut up and obey."

This more recent, more authoritarian approach is much more in line with historic progressivism, which began in the Progressive Era as an elitist movement that favored the management of society by a self-identified expert class, albeit concealed beneath a veneer of "democracy."

So it should not surprise us that *Mother Jones*, a progressive publication, isn't really so skeptical of authority or of big corporations after all. It's now more or less an unpaid division of Pfizer.

We've learned that senior editor Kiera Butler is preparing a hit piece on Dr. Vinay Prasad, himself a political liberal, for questioning the safety of the "boosters"; Prasad has correctly noted that the so-called safety data consists of results on eight mice.

Butler sought comment from Jay Bhattacharya, whom I mention quite a bit in this newsletter. Jay has since reproduced her email, along with his answers.

So here's Kiera Butler:

> I'm writing about the bivalent vaccines, and I saw that you had retweeted Dr. Prasad's video questioning their safety. I'm wondering if your past activism around opposing Covid protections — with the Brownstone Institute, Hillsdale College, and the Great Barrington Declaration — influenced your opinion on this at all? And I'm wondering if you think it's fair to characterize your takes on Covid as contrarian?

Jay's response:

> (1) The FDA did not require any human clinical study before approving the bivalent ba4/5 booster, so I don't have any opinion at all about their safety profile. I simply don't know.

> (2) The GBD was signed and supported by tens of thousands of scientists and doctors around the world. It is not a contrarian position, but represents the standard way of dealing with respiratory virus pandemics that the world has followed for a century until 2020.

> (3) I am not paid by any of the organizations you mentioned and received $0 from them. My thoughts reflect my professional training in medicine, epidemiology, and health policy.

Let's see how much of that winds up in Kiera's Pfizer press release. (Sorry, *article*.)

Part XI: Fall 2022

September 22, 2022 | Top scientist writes book: *The Year the World Went Mad*

Joe Biden declared the pandemic over a few days ago, and that made some people very unhappy.

I look at it this way: without a doubt we are at the stage now where what matters most is making sure we get the story of what happened right, so future generations are not misled.

Mark Woolhouse, one of Scotland's top infectious disease epidemiologists, just released *The Year the World Went Mad: A Scientific Memoir*. It's certainly a step in the right direction.

I thought I'd share bits and pieces with you (I've preserved the U.K. spelling):

- "My main aim in writing this book is that lockdown scepticism will become the mainstream view."

- "There is comfort in following the crowd even while it is stampeding in the wrong direction. We wouldn't let go of lockdown even after the evidence of the harm it was causing became so compelling that the WHO itself came to reject it."

- "The advisory system was dominated by clinicians and public health specialists who weren't looking at the bigger picture, such as economists, ethicists…which is why they kept recommending lockdown….The response was being driven too much by epidemiology, and I'm an epidemiologist."

- "Lockdown was never going to solve the problem; it just deferred it to another day, and it did so at great cost….Everyone needs to understand what such a harmful intervention can and cannot achieve before we introduce it. They didn't."

- "During the pandemic, several politicians adopted the position that 'no death from Covid is acceptable.'…This made it impossible to tackle the virus in a rational manner….We do not treat any other public health issue this way."

- "Will the cure turn out to be worse than the disease?…As early as April 2020, ONS used quality adjusted life years (QALY) lost to weigh harms and benefits....The best estimate was three times more harm....We got the balance wrong."

• "I was not prepared for the hate mail either, as vicious as any I received throughout the pandemic....People who spent the past year indoors did not want to be told that it had been safe to go out all along....Decision-makers had lost all sense of proportion."

An interesting book, as you can see.

And it reminds us of all the looniness from "public health" officials and even from your local doctor, who more often than not endorsed these measures. Your local doctor to this day thinks he's saving lives by separating the "clean" pens from the used pens.

Who can blame all those people who watched this spectacle and reached the obvious conclusion that if the medical establishment could take such consistently irrational and destructive decisions, maybe there's something rotten at the heart of it?

September 23, 2022 | Huh, I wonder what's causing this children's health issue

For the life of me I cannot understand people who don't respect Tucker Carlson.

Sure, like any of us he's wrong from time to time. But he says things nobody else will say, and he'll resist the entire establishment, including Conservatism, Inc., without batting an eye.

One of many ways you know progressives are phonies is that they should be saying of Carlson: he's awful on so much, but excellent on the military-industrial complex. But since progressives have evidently made their peace with the military-industrial complex, or don't consider it all that important, they never in fact say this.

Carlson just did a segment on the Covid shots and myocarditis in children. He said that in some people who received the shots, there "appears to be serious heart damage far more than the experts thought would occur."

He went on:

> *The Lancet* just surveyed young people ages 12 to 29 who suffered from myocarditis heart damage after taking the

Covid shot. According to *The Lancet*, 90 days after myocarditis symptoms emerged, roughly 26% of young people surveyed still needed daily medication because their hearts were so damaged, 20% said they had problems with their daily activities, 30% said they experienced pain. How will they be at age 60? You wonder. And of course, you know the answer.

Carlson then showed an ad by New York Presbyterian Hospital making it seem as if myocarditis in children is just a normal thing that happens. The voiceover in the ad is that of a young girl, and says:

I've been into fashion since I can remember. But one day I had a stomachache so bad I didn't want to do anything. The team at New York Presbyterian said it was actually my heart. It was severely swollen, something called myocarditis. But doctors gave me medicines and used machines to control my heartbeat. They saved me. So now I can become the next great fashion designer.

Tucker's response to this bizarre ad:

Severe heart damage in otherwise healthy children. Oh, yeah, we've always had that! No, we haven't, actually.

And Dr. Marty Makary [of Johns Hopkins University] was virtually alone in the medical community when he warned about the risks of this. He warned for months. In March, he wrote to the CDC and said, "You've got a duty to rigorously study the long-term effects of vaccine-induced myocarditis." He was not celebrated for this, of course. He was attacked, as always.

Makary, Carlson's guest, noted the CDC's downplaying of myocarditis concerns:

The CDC director last year said if we vaccinate a million children, there might be 30 or 40 cases of mild myocarditis. And they said, if you get myocarditis from Covid, that's worse or it happens at a higher rate. But that's not true. The studies have come out. Europe reacted by banning the Moderna vaccine altogether in young people, in many parts of Europe. And [in some places] everybody under 30, and in other places everybody under 40.

The tragedy is that we're now learning that there's significant heart damage: 31% of people having physical activity restrictions. The Seattle study that 63% of children after myocarditis had evidence of heart swelling months down the road on MRI. So we were playing with fire. We didn't know what we were dealing with. They undercounted the complication rate, making the vaccine look safer than it really was, overcounting cases in young people and hospitalizations, making the Covid infection look more dangerous than it really was.

Carlson concluded: "It's shocking. If your child has heart damage at the age of 14, how is she going to do at 50? And no one seems to be thinking about the future."

October 6, 2022 | Guess who just got canned for being "unvaccinated"

One headline put it this way: "Biden Congratulates Coast Guard Hero He's Trying to Fire."

Zach Loesch is "unvaccinated," so he's going to have to leave the Coast Guard.

This is the same man Joe Biden, not even a week ago, described as a hero for his work in Florida.

In fact, he called Loesch on the telephone to "personally thank" him for his "heroic work," and then praised him again in a public speech.

And Loesch did indeed deserve praise: he kicked through a wall to rescue a 94-year-old disabled woman and her husband, getting them and her wheelchair hoisted onto a helicopter even with heavy winds.

Loesch applied for a religious exemption and was denied, and his appeal of the denial was also denied, so now he has no choice but to leave.

When Karine Jean-Pierre, White House press secretary, was asked about Loesch and whether the President would ever consider lifting any of these mandates or issuing more exemptions, here is the answer we received:

> As you can imagine, the President has the deepest respect for the U.S. Coast Guard. That is something that you would hear from him directly. And the President and the country are grateful for all the U.S. Coast Guard heroes that have led the effort to save lives in Florida. We have seen that with our very own eyes these past couple of days. I would refer you specifically to the U.S. Coast Guard on this issue, on this

individual question. It's not something that I would comment from here. But there of course have been multiple vaccination requirements, as you know, in place for quite some time, but again I'm not going to comment from here on an individual case.

What on God's green earth is the point of that non-answer?

As Viva Frei put it, Jean-Pierre's response when asked an even remotely challenging question goes something like this:

"Uh uh"

turns page for no reason

"Uhhh…uhhh"

turns page she just turned back for no reason

"uhhhhhh uhhhhh"

Proceeds to lie / avoid answering

As Loesch himself put it, "If I had asked any of the people I saved yesterday if they wanted to come with me even though I am unvaccinated, every single one of them would have said 'yes.'"

October 10, 2022 | State surgeon general issues warning on Covid shots

Everybody knows about Ron DeSantis, but surprisingly few people I encounter are familiar with Dr. Joseph Ladapo, Florida's surgeon general.

An immigrant from Nigeria, Ladapo holds both an MD and PhD in health policy from Harvard University.

Here is how the second paragraph of his Wikipedia entry describes him:

> During the Covid-19 pandemic, Ladapo has promoted unproven treatments, opposed vaccine mandates, questioned vaccine safety, and associated with America's Frontline Doctors, a right-wing group known to promote falsehoods about the pandemic. In March 2022, as the Surgeon General of Florida, he misrepresented work by fellow scholars to recommend that healthy children not be vaccinated against Covid-19, a decision that also went contrary to the Centers for Disease Control and Prevention and American Academy of Pediatrics. Since then, Ladapo has banned gender-affirming counselling, hormonal therapies, and related medications for transgender and nonbinary children,

contravening relevant guidelines by a host of professional organizations.

All that propaganda is supposed to scare me, but since I don't have a television for a brain, it instead makes me think: he sounds like a great guy!

Well, the other day he released a report regarding safety concerns with the Covid shots. I thought you would be interested to see the press release, which reads as follows:

> Today, State Surgeon General Dr. Joseph A. Ladapo has announced new guidance regarding mRNA vaccines. The Florida Department of Health conducted an analysis through a self-controlled case series, which is a technique originally developed to evaluate vaccine safety.
>
> This analysis found that there is an 84% increase in the relative incidence of cardiac-related death among males 18–39 years old within 28 days following mRNA vaccination. With a high level of global immunity to Covid-19, the benefit of vaccination is likely outweighed by this abnormally high risk of cardiac-related death among men in this age group. Non-mRNA vaccines were not found to have these increased risks.
>
> As such, the State Surgeon General recommends against males aged 18 to 39 from receiving mRNA Covid-19 vaccines. Those with preexisting cardiac conditions, such as myocarditis and pericarditis, should take particular caution when making this decision.
>
> "Studying the safety and efficacy of any medications, including vaccines, is an important component of public health," said Surgeon General Dr. Joseph Ladapo. "Far less attention has been paid to safety and the concerns of many individuals have been dismissed — these are important findings that should be communicated to Floridians."

When I had a chance to meet DeSantis earlier this year, he said he doesn't even have to check on whether his surgeon general is hard at work or not. All he needs to see are all the outraged headlines, and he knows Ladapo is doing his job.

October 12, 2022 | A Pfizer admission

There was a time when you could have been banned from a social media platform for denying that Pfizer's shots prevented the spread of Covid.

Anthony Fauci, you may recall, said that once you've had the shots you become a "dead end" for Covid.

Well, now we have the truth from the horse's mouth. In an exchange days ago before the European Parliament, Pfizer executive Janine Small made clear that the company never even tested to see if its product prevented transmission.

Strange, isn't it? All your friends *knew* it prevented transmission! They made sure to let you know how crazy you were for disagreeing. All the respectable people on TV knew!

But how could they, if the company that developed the shots itself did not know?

Meanwhile, we just got this statement from the new premier of Alberta, Canada, Danielle Smith:

> The community that faced the most restrictions on their freedoms in the last year were those who made a choice not to be vaccinated. I don't think I've ever experienced a situation in my lifetime where a person was fired from their job or not allowed to watch their kids play hockey or not allowed to go visit a loved one in long-term care or hospital, or not allowed to go get on a plane to either go across the country to see family or even travel across the border.
>
> So they have been the most discriminated against group that I've ever witnessed in my lifetime. That's a pretty extreme level of discrimination that we have seen. I don't take away any of the discrimination that I've seen in those other groups that you mentioned, but this has been an extraordinary time in the last year in particular. And I want people to know that I find that unacceptable. We are not going to create a segregated society on the basis of a medical choice.

I know how easy it can be to get discouraged, especially when the other side seems so powerful and well organized. But we cannot forget: we defeated these "vaccine passport" systems. You know the so-called public health establishment and its hapless followers wanted those systems to be permanent. But enough of us refused to comply that they had to dismantle them.

October 17, 2022 | Pfizer CEO caught saying what they say he didn't say

I guess you've probably followed the recent uproar surrounding a Pfizer executive's admission that they hadn't tested to see if their shots stopped transmission at the time they released them.

The gatekeepers are trying to assure everyone that there's nothing to see here, that we already knew this, that they didn't test for this until later, etc.

Nice try, bootlickers.

Here's the Pfizer CEO in September 2020, speaking on the subject in an interview:

> And I want to tell them that their decision, they need to understand, will not affect only their lives, which at the end of the day is their judgment, but will affect the lives of others. Because if they don't vaccinate, they will become the weak link that will allow this virus to replicate. So I want to send the second message for those that are reluctant maybe to do a vaccine, and they need to understand that this decision, unfortunately, in this case does not affect only their health. Unfortunately, by making this decision, they will become the weak links in the way that the virus is transmitted and they will enable the virus to live there and they will risk society's health rather than [their] own health....
>
> Secondly, in the beginning, when fewer of the population is vaccinated, we should not, I think, relax — and I'm sure the authorities will not relax — all the other measures that are needed, like social distancing, masks, etc. But the more we vaccinate and the more we create herd immunity and the more we create the majority of the population being protected, then the less, I think, the other measures will have to be implemented. And as a result, the economy will open.

How much clearer can the guy be?

You need to take the shots to protect others and to work toward herd immunity, he said.

So once again, not a word these people say can be taken at face value, and when the media swarm to "correct" what you and I say, you can be sure you and I were right the first time.

October 24, 2022 | What we just learned about the you-know-whats

Today I discovered something in Steve Kirsch's Substack that I thought you might want to know about.

Evidently a new study out of Switzerland discussing the effects of the Covid shots on the heart generated some disturbing results. This is a genuine study, in a respected medical journal, by Professor Christian Mueller, whose expertise and record of publication make him difficult to dismiss. It's called "Myocardial Injury After Covid-19 mRNA Booster Vaccination."

Dr. Vinay Prasad, in turn, just made a video about the paper, though who knows how long YouTube — which opposes adults having conversations — will let it remain up. It's especially compelling since Dr. Prasad has been an advocate of the shots.

Here's what Prasad says:

> Troponin is a type of protein found in the muscles of your heart. Troponin isn't normally found in the blood. When heart muscles become damaged, troponin is sent into the bloodstream. As heart damage increases, greater amounts of troponin are released in the blood.

Then, discussing troponin levels in people post-shot, compared to people without the shots:

> It's not just the tip of the distribution that has elevated high-sensitivity troponin; it's that the entire distribution is right shifted. Everybody's having a little bit of elevation in high-sensitivity troponin. That's what this graph would have you infer.

This elevation, incidentally, would presumably have been higher had people been tested before days three and four, as they were in the data used in the study.

What is the cumulative effect of this if people continue to get boosters again and again? Do we even know?

Isn't that something we would want to know?

October 27, 2022 | Dissident doctors are being punished

Whatever craziness is going on in the United States, these days it always seems to be worse in Canada.

Dr. Kulvinder Kaur Gill is being persecuted by Canadian authorities for her entirely sensible dissident opinions on Covid. Jay Bhattacharya writes:

> Two weeks ago, I attended Dr. Gill's long-awaited appeal of a decision by the College of Physicians and Surgeons of Ontario (CPSO) to censor her for her advocacy against many of Canada's draconian Covid policies.

> Dr. Gill is a physician-leader with an excellent track record of patient care. She has never had a single patient complaint. She devotes her life to her patients. In 2020, she tweeted against the Canadian lockdowns. For this crime, CPSO is threatening her license.

> Dr. Gill's tweets in early 2020 focused on a few themes, supported by scientific literature: (1) the harms of lockdown; (2) the importance of T-cell immunity; (3) the folly of ignoring age-stratification of Covid mortality risk; etc. She was prescient and right about it all.

> In August 2020, a coordinated campaign to smear Dr. Gill resulted in the CPSO opening seven separate complaints about identical tweets. Five were dismissed, including a tweet about HCQ for Covid. The CPSO accepted two complaints on a very shaky basis.

> Here's the first tweet. Dr. Gill was spot-on here. The damage done by lockdowns to children, the poor, and the working class is incalculable. In any case, at the very least this is a legitimate opinion, not misinformation:

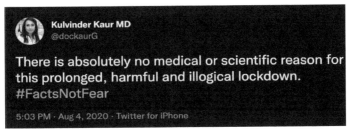

Kulvinder Kaur MD
@dockaurG

There is absolutely no medical or scientific reason for this prolonged, harmful and illogical lockdown. #FactsNotFear

5:03 PM · Aug 4, 2020 · Twitter for iPhone

In its decision against Dr. Gill, the CPSO cited the "success" of the lockdown in China as a reason to doubt the accuracy of Dr. Gill's tweet. Even at the time, this was ridiculous. Subsequent events have proven CPSO's position even more laughable.

Here's the second tweet. Note the date — August 2020, before the vaccines were introduced. In context, Dr. Gill was arguing that we did not need a vaccine to lift lockdown, which was a legitimate opinion (witness Sweden), not misinformation.

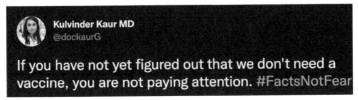

Kulvinder Kaur MD
@dockaurG

If you have not yet figured out that we don't need a vaccine, you are not paying attention. #FactsNotFear

Dr. Gill's experience with the dystopian actions by CPSO is a harbinger of what doctors in California can expect under the new AB 2098, which imposes a similar regime. Patients will wonder whether their doctor has their interest or the government's at heart.

These CPSO actions against Dr. Gill have already done considerable damage to Canadian science and medicine. They are deeply unjust, and I hope the appeals board reverses them. Dr. Gill is a Canadian hero.

I have followed Dr. Gill's commentary for over two years, and I second Dr. Bhattacharya's sentiment: let's hope she's completely vindicated.

Of course, her persecution is what our deeply corrupt establishment wants: one acceptable version of events, and penalties for people who dissent from it.

November 1, 2022 | Reporter just revealed the feds' censorship efforts

Remember the "Disinformation Governance Board" they tried to roll out?

Everyone ridiculed it, and of course the perpetrators tried to claim it had all been a big misunderstanding, that it wasn't at all what we feared it would be.

Well, that board may be gone, but thanks to reporting by *The Intercept*, we know that government censorship efforts are far from dead.

It may not come as a surprise to many people reading this, but it is still a major story: the Biden Administration is using Big Tech to advance its interests. We now know that government officials can pinpoint Facebook and Instagram posts they want throttled or suppressed.

Early this year, Microsoft executive Matt Masterson, formerly with the Department of Homeland Security (DHS), texted a DHS director to say, "Platforms have got to get comfortable with gov't. It's really interesting how hesitant they remain."

The DHS has indicated its intention to focus on the alleged problem of "inaccurate information" on such topics as "the origins of the Covid-19 pandemic and the efficacy of Covid-19 vaccines, racial justice, U.S. withdrawal from Afghanistan, and the nature of U.S. support to Ukraine" — in other words, everything you might want to talk about.

The DHS justifies this move into monitoring online disinformation (so-called) on the grounds that disinformation can radicalize people and lead to violence.

It looks as if federal authorities are trying to dance around the First Amendment by doing their dirty work through Big Tech platforms. As I reported some weeks ago, the attorneys general of Missouri and Louisiana have filed suit over the federal government's targeting of individuals for suppression by the platforms, and a lot of information is already coming out thanks to that suit. Not to mention: the judge has authorized them to depose Anthony Fauci himself, along with a variety of White House officials.

We'll see what else we find out.

I remember when Fauci would tell people that maybe we could have our lives back next Mother's Day, or two Christmases after this one, etc., but only if everyone got jabbed.

Meanwhile, half the country just proceeded to take their lives back, and did no worse health-wise than the hypochondriacs.

The "Fauci saved us" narrative cannot be pushed back on hard enough.

November 11, 2022 | We just won the Covid argument

What you're about to see says it all.

We all remember — how could we forget? — the hysteria around Sweden in 2020. Why, if they didn't have a proper lockdown, Neil Ferguson and his Imperial College model said, they'd have 96,000 deaths by June!

The actual number turned out to be 4,000.

So then the crazies fell back on: it did worse than the other Scandinavian countries, and that's the proper comparison. (These are the same people who thought the United States and the island nation of New Zealand was a legitimate comparison, however.)

The Organization for Economic Cooperation and Development looked at excess mortality in 31 countries, including Sweden (and New Zealand, for that matter), during the Covid era.

Want to take a guess as to which country wound up doing the best out of them all?

Yes, it was Sweden:

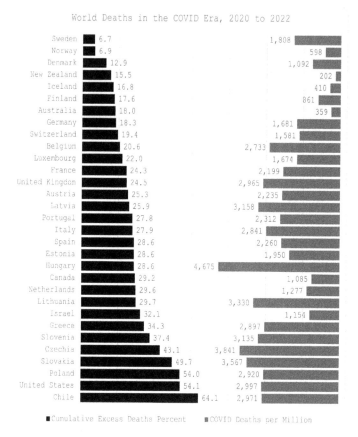

World Deaths in the COVID Era, 2020 to 2022

Country	Cumulative Excess Deaths Percent	COVID Deaths per Million
Sweden	6.7	1,808
Norway	6.9	598
Denmark	12.9	1,092
New Zealand	15.5	202
Iceland	16.8	410
Finland	17.6	861
Australia	18.0	359
Germany	18.3	1,681
Switzerland	19.4	1,581
Belgium	20.6	2,733
Luxembourg	22.0	1,674
France	24.3	2,199
United Kingdom	24.5	2,965
Austria	25.3	2,235
Latvia	25.9	3,158
Portugal	27.8	2,312
Italy	27.9	2,841
Spain	28.6	2,260
Estonia	28.6	1,950
Hungary	28.6	4,675
Canada	29.2	1,085
Netherlands	29.6	1,277
Lithuania	29.7	3,330
Israel	32.1	1,154
Greece	34.3	2,897
Slovenia	37.4	3,135
Czechia	43.1	3,841
Slovakia	49.7	3,567
Poland	54.0	2,920
United States	54.1	2,997
Chile	64.1	2,971

■Cumulative Excess Deaths Percent   ■COVID Deaths per Million

Why focus on "excess deaths" rather than Covid deaths? (1) because there's no universally agreed-upon standard for what constitutes a Covid death, and (2) what good does it do to lower Covid deaths while increasing non-Covid deaths by even more?

I'm sure lots of apologies will be forthcoming!

December 1, 2022 | Does looking like a duck protect you from Covid?

The dead-enders have been calling for a return of masking, though they don't seem to be making much headway among normal people.

The uselessness of masks is nevertheless important to emphasize, so that (1) perhaps fewer people will be taken in should the public health establishment ever seriously try to impose them again, and (2) people will begin to perceive how unreliable (to put it kindly) our public health officials are.

By now you've probably heard people say: of course the masking didn't work, because we should have been wearing N95 masks.

(That isn't what Dr. Fauci said, by the way. He said all masks were protective to some degree.)

Well, we now have a randomized trial, just published in the *Annals of Internal Medicine*, studying what difference in results, if any, can be perceived from the use of one over the other: "Medical Masks Versus N95 Respirators for Preventing Covid-19 Among Health Care Workers: A Randomized Trial."

What did they find?

Fifty-two out of 497 (10.46%) people wearing medical masks wound up getting Covid, and 47 out of 507 (9.27%) wearing N95s got it — a difference too trivial to amount to anything.

Germany, for that matter, broke all its records for the spread of Covid at a time when it had among the highest N95 usage in the world.

I might add that Todd Zywicki, a professor from the law school at George Mason University whom I've interviewed on the Tom Woods Show, says a doctor told him: "If you can wear an N95 for more than about 30 minutes you are wearing it wrong."

I remind you, dear reader, that I had one of my Tom Woods Show interviews with Congressman Thomas Massie removed from YouTube presumably because we questioned the utility of masks. (I can't be certain that that was the reason, because our betters at YouTube do not deign to disclose the reasoning behind their various bans and deletions, but it's the only thing I can think of.)

December 9, 2022 | Liars just caught red-handed

Well, the liars have been caught red-handed.

As you may know, Elon Musk has been releasing batches of documents revealing what's been going on at Twitter in terms of "content moderation," which really means suppression.

He has been releasing them to journalists Matt Taibbi and Bari Weiss.

The way you can know it's a significant story is that the mainstream press is downplaying or ignoring it.

Twitter's Vijaya Gadde and Kayvon Beykpour, both of whom have since been fired, once stated flatly: "We do not shadow ban....And we certainly don't shadow ban based on political viewpoints or ideology."

Oh, really? In Weiss's installment yesterday she revealed that Jay Bhattacharya, a vocal critic of lockdowns, was placed on a "trends blacklist" to prevent his Tweets from trending. Talk show host Dan Bongino was hit with a "search blacklist." Charlie Kirk's account was set to "Do Not Amplify."

A Twitter engineer said, "We control visibility quite a bit. And we control the amplification of your content quite a bit. And normal people do not know how much we do."

There's plenty of material, too, on the "Libs of TikTok" Twitter account, which has been punished multiple times for allegedly violating the platform's rules on hate and harassment, but all the account does is post TikTok videos showing leftists, particularly in school settings, behaving in extremely bizarre fashion.

When someone doxxed the anonymous operator of that account, Twitter didn't mind at all. This doesn't violate our policies, they said.

Deranged.

We're told there's more to come. I already reported on the FBI spook on the Twitter payroll (thanks to previous Twitter leadership) who'd been vetting the documents until Musk fired him.

Lots of people discussing lots of topics had their reach restricted, but one specific conclusion we can draw from all this is: even those scientists who weren't banned outright from the platform were nevertheless muted, which means Twitter contributed, perhaps significantly, to the ridiculous and science-free Covid response in the United States.

Since the censors consider themselves morally superior and entitled to rule, they probably never expected any of this activity to be exposed. But it's happening, and even though it's telling us what we long suspected anyway, there's no substitute for having the proof in black and white.

Part XII: Winter 2022–2023

December 23, 2022 | Disappeared: the vaccine injured

As of yesterday I have released 2,257 episodes of the Tom Woods Show — you can subscribe for free at TomsPodcast.com — and I think yesterday's ranks in the top ten.

The subject matter: the vaccine injured in the age of Covid.

These people have had their stories scrubbed from social media (they're contributing to "vaccine hesitancy," so they can't discuss what happened to them). Their friends, for political reasons, often don't know what to do with them. (We discuss one young woman who reports that her Democrat friends don't know how to interact with her, because she and her injuries undermine their religious convictions in the sacred shots.)

They have no health care, because few people seem interested in researching what's happening to them and what possible treatments there might be.

They've lost careers (you can't have some of these side effects and still be an orthopedic surgeon, for example), they've lost their life savings, and they've lost their voice.

But these are real people with real stories who deserve to be treated with humanity, rather than the way the Pfizer/CDC medical complex wishes to treat them.

I know this is a busy time of year, but while you're getting your last-minute arrangements done give this episode a listen and remember those people who have been without a voice. These people — and certainly not the universally lauded Black Lives Matter or transgender movements, whose sympathizers are all over the media — are the truly marginalized people in our society.

The link: TomWoods.com/2257

December 27, 2022 | Another thing we were right about

The latest episode of the "Twitter Files" involves Twitter and Covid, and the suppression of alternative voices (no matter how well supported by actual data).

We learn that the Trump Administration asked the Big Tech platforms, including Twitter, to suppress stories about runs on grocery stores — even though there actually were runs on grocery stores.

By far the worst offenses came under the Biden Administration, which specifically targeted "anti-vax" accounts.

We already knew, because it came out in Alex Berenson's lawsuit, that Berenson had been targeted by name by the White House. People like him were "killing people," according to Joe Biden, because he warned people to be cautious about a novel technology.

An internal memo at Twitter reveals that the Biden White House was "very unhappy" with Twitter for not being aggressive enough in silencing dissident voices.

Martin Kulldorff of Harvard Medical School, who is more favorable to the shots, nevertheless said on Twitter that there was no reason to inject the entire population, and certainly not children or the recovered.

Even though this was the exact policy that some other countries followed, it was deemed "misinformation" by the geniuses at Twitter.

David Zweig, who broke this chapter of the Twitter Files, adds that "after Twitter took action, Kulldorff's tweet was slapped with a 'Misleading' label and all replies and likes were shut off, throttling the tweet's ability to be seen and shared by many people, the ostensible core function of the platform."

Now how about this.

On episode #2149 of the Tom Woods Show I talked to Kelley Krohnert, who had exposed bogus claims being made by numerous official sources that Covid was currently the leading cause of death in children. That has never even been close to the truth, as anyone even casually acquainted with the data knows. This false claim was obviously intended to panic the population into giving children the shots. An examination of the CDC's own numbers showed it to be wildly off the mark.

Everyone now concedes that Krohnert was correct in ridiculing this claim about Covid and children. But even though she used the CDC's own numbers to make her point, and even though she herself was responding to misinformation, it was *her* writing that Twitter branded as misinformation!

The examples go on and on.

Honestly, imagine claiming you're fighting misinformation while simultaneously claiming that Covid is the number-one killer of children.

December 29, 2022 | The land where everyone complied

I haven't shared anything from the ol' mailbag in a while, and someone wrote to me in response to my recent appearance on Michael Malice's podcast:

> *I was just listening to your conversation with Michael Malice on his podcast where you talked about how the restrictions and mandates disappeared in the U.S.*
>
> *People do not appreciate enough how much power they have in situations like this. I come from Czechia but I have been living in Taiwan for a decade. And the contrast between the two could not be more striking. While pretty much the whole of Europe got rid of most of the ridiculous restrictions (Czechia completely), it's the opposite in Taiwan. They only removed outdoor mask mandate at the beginning of December 2022, although pretty much everybody still wears them. They still put them on toddlers and schoolchildren, as they have for the past two years.*
>
> *In Taiwan, there has never been any pushback from the people or businesses; they all gladly followed everything. You can't imagine the number of masked cyclists and scooter drivers (in rural areas most of the scooter drivers wear no helmet but cover their nose and mouth with a mask). It's the opposite in Europe and the U.S., where people might have given it a chance but after a few months, at most a year, they just stopped.*
>
> *As for Taiwan, what is most surprising and disappointing to me is that it is the same generation, the very same people, who in 2014 gathered in huge numbers around the presidential palace and parliament in Taipei to protest a trade agreement with China because they saw it as a threat to their freedom. And they managed to get it canceled (see "Sunflower Student Movement").*
>
> *Disobedience works.*
>
> *Thank you for being such an inspiration.*

This reminds me of what a listener told me about the Philippines: there was no resistance to the Covid insanity there at all. Everyone simply complied.

This testimony about Taiwan is simply stupefying. All they need to do is take a brief glance around the world and see entire unmasked countries having no worse outcomes than they themselves do. And they can't even be bothered to do that.

Regardless of the extent to which the various restrictions have receded, we cannot forget what a load of b.s. it all was.

January 9, 2023 | Creepy Pfizer board member

There's a certain fellow who sits on the board of a certain company who — we now know — has been trying to silence critics of a certain product.

I'm talking about Scott Gottlieb, who served as commissioner of the FDA from 2017 to 2019, and who also happens to sit on the board of Pfizer.

And he's not just any board member: he sits on the board's executive committee and directs its regulatory and compliance committee.

Thanks to Alex Berenson's work with the "Twitter Files," we know that Gottlieb, too, has been pushing to get dissident voices silenced.

One such voice he went after was that of Brett Giroir — who in fact served as FDA commissioner after Gottlieb.

Here's what Giroir said that was so dangerous:

"It's now clear Covid-19 natural immunity is superior to vaccine immunity, by *a lot*. There's no science justification for #vax proof if a person had prior infection. @CDCDirector @POTUS must follow the science. If no previous infection? Get vaccinated!"

So note: Giroir is actually encouraging the shots for people not yet infected and recovered, and yet this still isn't enough for Gottlieb, who objects to the claim about natural immunity being superior to vaccine immunity.

An outraged Gottlieb contacted Todd O'Boyle, Twitter's point of contact with the White House, and got the Tweet labeled "Misleading." From that point on it was essentially invisible.

That wouldn't be the only time Gottlieb would use his clout to go after dissidents, according to Berenson, but it's sufficient for us today. A Pfizer board member is going to tell us what we can and can't say about his product?

There will no doubt be plenty more revelations like these, although at this point they're probably just confirming what we already suspected or assumed. But we need these revelations, at the very least because historians will need more to go on than our hunches. An actual paper trail will help them tell this sordid story.

January 23, 2023 | Booster propagandists confronted

Last week I pointed out that a robust study in the *Journal of Medical Ethics* showing net harm for college populations from booster shots was sent to student newspapers at dozens of institutions that require them for attendance, and I noted that not one bothered to respond to an invitation to interview the authors.

Well, now we do have a response at the institutional level, and it's stupid.

Health directors at Boston University, Tufts University, Harvard, and MIT sent a response to the journal. They made no effort to contest its data. They said instead that there's more to health than number of hospitalizations averted, so they're not really going to focus too much on that:

> We read with interest this risk-benefit and ethical analysis of the utility of SARS-CoV-2 vaccine boosters in university students. We have some major concerns about the choice of hospitalization as the primary measure of benefit....
>
> Hospitalizations averted is not the only marker of morbidity that is relevant to the college student population and given the rarity of severe disease requiring hospitalization in young, generally very healthy adults, hospitalization is not a good choice for a marker of Covid-19 related morbidity.

Stop right there. They admit that the risk of hospitalization, much less death, in student populations is very low. So we're halfway there. But they say nothing — as in not one single word — about the myocarditis risk, which is the whole point of the paper.

Then this:

> We are also cautious about changing policy in reaction to a single study, although we are actively reviewing new information. As the authors allude to in their discussion of limitations, it was not possible to comprehensively address the

impacts of Covid-19 on mental health, time lost from academics, and other activities that are uniquely relevant to a college population.

We're supposed to be impressed with how scientific they are — why, they're not going to change their policy in response to a single study!

So where is their study showing net benefit of boosters for college students? Crickets.

I might add that Harvard alone received nearly $2 billion in research grants from the National Institutes of Health in 2021, so one wonders if there's a chance — just a chance, I say — that university administrators and health officials might be inclined to toe the party line.

There's a graphic going around social media that says, "I keep trying to follow the science, but it keeps leading me back to the money." Cynical? Sure. But it's hard not to be these days.

February 7, 2023 | The maskers just took a beating

I'll bet you're like me: you see someone wearing a mask in 2023, and you wonder what on Earth the person could be thinking. Either the person hasn't paid attention to anything at all, or is trying to make some kind of warped statement.

Well, the Cochrane Library just released a study on masking that really puts the nail in the coffin.

The Cochrane Library describes itself as "a collection of databases in medicine and other healthcare specialties provided by Cochrane and other organizations. At its core is the collection of Cochrane Reviews, a database of systematic reviews and meta-analyses which summarize and interpret the results of medical research."

The crazies are hysterical about it. But they can't refute it.

Vinay Prasad puts it like this: "It is irrational to mask."

Prasad sums it up:

> Here is the big summary finding. With 276,000 participants in RCTs or cluster RCTs, masking does nothing. No reduction in influenza-like or Covid-like illness and no reduction in confirmed flu or Covid. That's stone-cold negative. See those effect sizes and confidence intervals.

(To read the study yourself, do a search for "Physical interventions to interrupt or reduce the spread of respiratory viruses," from 2023.)

This includes the ballyhooed N95 mask as well.

Everybody in the medical establishment knew masking didn't do anything, Prasad says:

> There was a reason why Tony Fauci went out initially and said it didn't work. There was a reason why the CDC said not to do it and the WHO said not to do it. And between March 1st and April 15th of 2020, there ain't no new evidence that was generated of any plausibility. But two things happened.
>
> There was a concerted movement by activists who don't know evidence-based medicine to hashtag #wearaclothmask and hashtag #savelives and…you know, making stupid TikTok videos.
>
> Why? Because they're scared. They're in their house, they're scared. They don't know what to do. They just grasp for anything, just like our primitive ancestors would have maybe slaughtered a chicken or done a rain dance. They're doing the same thing.…
>
> They saw that Donald Trump didn't do it. And the moment he didn't do it, they knew they were right, because if he didn't do it, I got to be right on it. It's got to be right if he doesn't do it, because he always does the wrong thing.

That was truly how juvenile the universal masking movement was.

Actually, that's the wrong word. It was frankly sinister.

As with "social distancing," you were accused of essentially being a murderer if you didn't go along. It didn't matter that a scatterplot of places in the U.S. showed no connection between Covid restrictions and health outcomes.

This was never about science or evidence. It was a sinister confluence of some people's irrational fear with other people's desire to control, shame, and isolate.

February 7, 2023 | Covid Commission? Here's what to ask it

Yesterday I received an email from our old friend Martin Kulldorff, who's currently on leave from Harvard Medical School, and who was one of the three drafters of the anti-lockdown Great Barrington Declaration.

He and seven colleagues have drafted an 80-page document outlining the questions they would pose to any Covid commission that gets established, along with the science that informs those questions.

I'm planning to discuss these questions with Professor Kulldorff this week on the Tom Woods Show, and at that time I'll upload the document to my website.

The document is far more thorough and covers far more subject areas than the questions I've chosen might indicate, but what follows should give you an idea of what's in it. I have omitted ellipses, so simply be aware that the questions below do not necessarily appear in this order in the document:

• Why was so much influence on public health policy accorded to Drs. Collins and Fauci? They control the largest source of infectious disease research funding in the world. How many infectious disease scientists, who should have been strong voices during the pandemic, kept quiet for fear of losing the research funding on which their livelihood depends?

• Diabetes care was interrupted during the pandemic. How many Americans did this affect? What will be the long-term consequences and who will be responsible for defining and collating them?

• Physical exercise is important for preventing diabetes. How did closing exercise venues such as parks and gyms, affect diabetes incidence?

• What were the effects of Covid-19 restrictions on people with lupus, rheumatoid arthritis, Sjögren's syndrome, and other auto-immune diseases?

• People with dementia have suffered extraordinarily during the pandemic. Why were there not more efforts to ensure the well-being of dementia patients? To what extent did isolation protocols, cessation of physical therapy, cessation of group activities and restriction of mobility contribute to increases in dementia and to dementia deaths?

• Why were activities and sports for low-risk young people suspended without considering the harms of isolation and lack of physical activity?

• Anxiety and depression increased during the 2020 lockdowns. CDC data show that, in 2021, 37 percent of American high school students reported experiencing poor mental health during the Covid-19 pandemic, and 44 percent reported they persistently felt sad or hopeless during the past year compared to 36.7 percent in 2019. Why did public health authorities not consider such adverse effects? What is now being done to address and treat this problem?

• Why were people discouraged from going outside to exercise?

• Why were beaches, basketball courts, playgrounds, and similar venues closed, preventing people from exercising and socializing in low-risk environments?

• Why were many gyms closed by local and state governments?

• Why were sports programs for children terminated?

• In children ages 2–19, the rate of BMI increase approximately doubled during the pandemic compared to the pre-pandemic period. What are the long-term consequences on childhood obesity and diabetes? Was this taken into account when local governments restricted physical activity?

• As of March of 2021, 42 percent of adults reported gaining weight during the pandemic, with an average weight gain of 29 pounds. What are the long-term consequences on adult obesity, diabetes, cardiovascular disease, etc.? Was this taken into account when local governments restricted physical activity?

• Lockdowns forced many small businesses to close permanently. How did this affect the health and well-being of small business owners and their employees?

• When small businesses were forced to close, much of their business was taken over by large corporations that were allowed to operate when small businesses couldn't. Why were larger businesses provided this competitive advantage? Can this be reversed? If not, what are the long-term health consequences of having fewer small businesses?

• In 2020, one pro-lockdown argument was that it was more important to save lives than to save the economy. However, a healthy economy is important for public health, especially among lower-income populations. Did this view prevail because the people making it were mostly work-from-home professionals, who themselves did not suffer economically?

• Why is long-Covid-19 of greater concern than, e.g., "long influenza" or "long norovirus disease"? Is it a distinct clinical entity?

• In February 2021, NIH allocated $1.15 billion in funding for long Covid-19 research over a four-year period. Is this a reasonable amount? Historically, how much has NIH spent on research concerning long-term effects after other infectious diseases?

• Why didn't more modelers speak up about the difficulty of accurately predicting Covid-19 cases, hospitalizations, and deaths? Did epidemiological disease modelers sufficiently explain inherent model limitations to politicians and other consumers?

• In March 2020, the federal government invoked the Defense Production Act to force General Motors to produce more ventilators. At the same time, the New York State and City governments demanded more ventilators, even though current supply was not exhausted, claiming that "without a ventilator, doctors cannot save lives."

• Did government officials ask for clinical evidence to support this intervention? If not, why not?

• Physicians in New York stated that they intubated patients early to "control the spread." How many patients were intubated in New York City in March/April 2020 and what were their outcomes stratified by age and comorbidities? Could rapid gathering of such data have ended the practice earlier?

• In September of 2022, a study used data from the Pfizer and Moderna randomized trials to show an excess serious adverse event rate post-Pfizer of 1/990 and post-Moderna of 1/662 compared with controls who received placebo. Why was a study such as this performed by independent scientists and not requested by the FDA or from the manufacturers in 2020 or 2021?

• Given the clear relationship in this demographic [young men] between myocarditis and the second dose of Pfizer, why was Pfizer not questioned further when they stated they had not seen a higher-than-expected rate?

• In 2021, without supporting evidence, the CDC claimed that the Covid-19 vaccines "can keep you from getting and spreading the virus that causes Covid-19." Was this messaging deliberate or an honest mistake by the CDC?

• Why did it take so long to correct this information? Were CDC officials with knowledge of the shortcomings of the vaccine afraid to speak against official CDC views?

February 27, 2023 | Actor tells truth, media goes berserk

By now you may have heard about the opening monologue that actor Woody Harrelson delivered on *Saturday Night Live* this past weekend.

Given the hysteria surrounding it, I assumed it had to be a full-throated attack on Big Pharma.

So I watched it, and 95 percent of it was just normal comedy.

I'm about to share with you the entirety of the portion that sent the Establishment, and those poor and pathetic souls who for some reason feel compelled to defend the Establishment, into a fit.

Harrelson tells a fanciful story about reading a movie script:

> Okay, so the movie goes like this. The biggest drug cartels in the world get together and buy up all the media and all the politicians and force all the people in the world to stay locked in their homes. And people can only come out if they take the cartel's drugs and keep taking them over and over. I threw the script away. I mean, who is going to believe that crazy idea being forced to do drugs? I do that voluntarily all day long.

That's it.

It's obvious enough that the story is a reference to our Covid experience, with the lockdowns and the mandates. But note that he even softens the blow by ending it with a joke about his drug habit.

Well, this little passage — which, for heaven's sake, *obviously has the ring of truth to it* — sent the media into hysterics.

Remember, Harrelson is insinuating that the media are all bought and paid for. And here's how they reacted, as if trying to prove his point:

Note the verb choices, too — "spews," "rambles" — intended to denigrate the speaker. And of course "conspiracy," the ultimate dumb-guy putdown.

To my mind Harrelson is wrong about 90 percent of the time, but when he's right, it tends to be — as in this case — about something fairly important.

But good for him, making the kind of observation that hundreds of people in public life would be making if we lived in a normal society.

February 28, 2023 | The 18 questions everyone should have asked

Remember how reliably the music industry complied with lockdown demands, such that we can count dissidents on one hand?

Eric Clapton and Van Morrison were two of the best-known such dissidents.

Van Morrison was just interviewed for *Mojo* magazine by Billy Bragg. After the interview, which didn't mention the Covid lockdowns and Van

Morrison's position on them at all, Morrison posed these questions to Bragg, and I thought you'd enjoy seeing them:

1. How did you feel about the Covid-19 lockdowns and restrictions and enforcement of [the] same?

2. Did you just comply and go with the government narrative? Did you question any of it?

3. How did you feel about Rishi Sunak saying musicians should retrain and get another job?

4. Were you aware of Neil Ferguson's track record in relation to mad cow disease and other things he got very wrong?

5. Did you know about the vast sums of money politicians were making off the face mask contracts?

6. Were you aware of the Sage Report and the terms used to get the public to comply, i.e., there must be a threat to get the public to comply?

7. Did you know of the books *The State of Fear* by Laura Dodsworth and *Covid-19: The Great Reset* by Klaus Schwab?

8. Are you aware of the agendas of the World Economic Forum?

9. Were you aware of the number of millions of people having protest marches all over the U.K. and the world? Anti-lockdown protests that weren't being reported by the BBC or any of the mainstream media. When they were forced to report, they lied about the number of people that were in the protests, i.e., millions not hundreds.

10. Did you know that at least one of the Partygate parties was reported at the time and someone had to resign?

11. Were you against people like myself that spoke out in opposition to the lockdowns?

12. Do you think everyone should just have complied?

13. Do you think wanting freedom is some sort of political stance and, if so, are you pro-freedom of the people or pro-government overreach and enforcement?

14. Did you not approve of me protesting?

15. Did you do any research or look up Event 201 that was in October 2019 in New York and sponsored by the Bill and Melinda Gates Foundation and the World Economic Forum, to name but two?

16. Were you aware of other medical experts on the pandemic like Dr. Robert Malone, Dr. Mike Yeadon, Dr. Peter McCullough, and many more, and would you see this as political also?

17. Are you aware that Neil Ferguson, Chris Whitty, and Patrick Vallance received millions from the Bill Gates Foundation? I wonder why.

18. Matt Hancock…?

Incidentally, is it not ridiculous that Van Morrison is practically the only well-known musician even asking questions like these?

March 17, 2023 | They knew it was true

If we have any honest historians out there, a true chronicling of 2020 to 2023 is going to make the hairs on your neck stand on end.

Matt Taibbi has just released another installment of the so-called "Twitter Files," and this one looks closely at something called the Virality Project (VP), based at Stanford University.

On the eve of Taibbi's congressional testimony we had started hearing about what it had been up to, but we now know a lot more.

VP worked with the major Big Tech platforms to suppress dissident voices even when by VP's own admission, what those voices were saying was true. It worked with the Office of the Surgeon General and the Centers for Disease Control as well.

Writes Taibbi:

> This story is important for two reasons. One, as Orwellian proof-of-concept, the Virality Project was a smash success. Government, academia, and an oligopoly of would-be corporate competitors organized quickly behind a secret, unified effort to control political messaging.
>
> Two, it accelerated the evolution of digital censorship, moving it from judging truth/untruth to a new, scarier model, openly focused on political narrative at the expense of fact.

Through July of 2020, Twitter's internal guidance on Covid-19 required a story be "demonstrably false" or contain an "assertion of fact" to be actioned. But the Virality Project, in partnership with the CDC, pushed different standards.

VP told Twitter that "true stories that could fuel hesitancy," including things like "celebrity deaths after vaccine" or the closure of a central NY school due to reports of post-vaccine illness, should be considered "Standard Vaccine Misinformation on Your Platform."

Raising objections to vaccine passport programs also attracted the attention of VP, which advised, "We expect the vaccine passport debate to continue as a key talking point especially bridging the anti-vax community with the right-wing media sphere."

Therefore, "concerns" over such programs could be considered a "misinformation" event.

When the AstraZeneca vaccine began to be banned in Europe because people experienced blood clots, VP grew concerned that "increased doubts in one manufacturer's vaccine may lead to hesitancy about vaccination overall." Therefore, VP would "continue to monitor discussions about these suspensions."

By March of 2021, writes Taibbi, Twitter personnel "were aping VP language, describing 'campaigns against vaccine passports,' 'fear of mandatory immunizations,' and 'misuse of official reporting tools' as 'potential violations.'"

VP urged platforms to "hone in" on an "increasingly popular narrative about natural immunity."

VP falsely described "breakthrough infections" as "extremely rare events" and should of course never be cited to claim that "vaccines are ineffective." VP also claimed it was misinformation to say that the shots did not prevent transmission, even though it is a commonplace that they do not.

Even as research continued to vindicate natural immunity, this didn't matter because according to VP, "Whether or not…scientific consensus is changing, 'natural immunity' is a key narrative…among anti-vaccine activists."

In April of last year, VP sought a "rumor-control mechanism to address nationally trending narratives," and — see if this sounds familiar — a

"Misinformation and Disinformation Center of Excellence" at the Department of Homeland Security (DHS).

It certainly should sound familiar, because the very next day the director of DHS announced the creation of a Disinformation Governance Board.

The truth is coming out, dear friends.

We need someone to write *The Secret History of the 21st Century*. (I am too burned out to do it, but some young whippersnapper should make a name for himself by doing it.)

Part XIII: Spring 2023

March 22, 2023 | Suppressed voices have struck back

The case of *Missouri v. Biden*, in which the attorneys general of Missouri and Louisiana are accusing the federal government of assaults on free speech during the Covid madness, will go forward, despite the Biden White House's efforts to get it dismissed, thanks to a memorandum ruling by Judge Terry A. Doughty.

I am very happy about this. We cannot pretend none of this happened and simply resume normal life. The insanity has to be confronted in as many aspects as possible.

The memorandum is over 70 pages long, though most of it involves laying out various precedents in order to respond to the Biden team's legal technicalities.

It's clear that the judge has sympathy for the plaintiffs, who include our friends Jay Bhattacharya and Martin Kulldorff, both of whom were censored for opposing the ridiculous government Covid response.

I thought you'd like to see it, so I'm going to share bits and pieces of it with you here. Even when the judge is simply paraphrasing the plaintiffs' arguments, it's still a good opportunity to see how strong those arguments are. (Again, the "States" referred to are Missouri and Louisiana.)

Some excerpts:

> Because of the alleged coercion and collusion by the Defendants to suppress speech, the States assert "at least eight forms of imminent, continuing, irreparable injury." The States list these eight alleged injuries as follows:
>
> (1) "The federal censorship program directly undermines Missouri's and Louisiana's fundamental policies favoring the freedom of speech, and thus it inflicts a clear and direct injury on the States' sovereignty";
>
> (2) "The States and their agencies and political subdivisions have suffered government-induced online censorship directly";
>
> (3) "State agencies — such as the Offices of the States' Attorneys General — closely track and rely on free speech on social media to understand their citizens' true thoughts and

concerns," and "censorship of social-media speech directly interferes with this critical state interest, because it 'directly interferes with [our] ability to follow, measure, and understand the nature and degree of [constituents'] concerns'";

(4) "Social-media censorship thwarts the States' ability to provide free, fair, and open political processes that allow citizens to petition their government and advocate for policy changes";

(5) "Federally induced social-media censorship directly affects Missouri, because it has resulted in the extensive censorship of Plaintiff Dr. Bhattacharya";

(6) "Missouri and Louisiana have a quasi-sovereign interest in protecting the free-speech rights of a sufficiently substantial segment of its population," and "preventing ultra vires actions against those rights";

(7) "Missouri and Louisiana 'ha[ve] an interest in securing observance of the terms under which [they] participate in the federal system'"; and

(8) "Missouri and Louisiana have a unique interest in advancing, protecting, and vindicating the rights of their citizens who are listeners, readers, and audiences of social-media speech."

The Private Plaintiffs, primarily through the use of individual Declarations, allege their own ongoing injuries as a result of the alleged government action described above. The Private Plaintiffs state that the alleged censorship "is achieved through a wide variety of methods, ranging from complete bans, temporary bans, insidious 'shadow bans' (where neither the user nor his audience is notified of the suppression), deboosting, de-platforming, de-monetizing, restricting access to content, imposing warning labels that require click-through to access content, and many other ways..."

For example, Jay Bhattacharya, one of the Private Plaintiffs, stated in his declaration, "Because of my views on Covid-19 restrictions, I have been specifically targeted for censorship by federal government officials." Bhattacharya, the Professor of Health Policy at Stanford University School of Medicine, specifically alleges that a publication entitled the "Great Barrington Declaration," which Bhattacharya co-authored, was subject to "immediate backlash from senior government officials who were the architects of the lockdown policies" for Covid-19.

The Great Barrington Declaration "called for an end to economic lockdowns, school shutdowns, and similar restrictive policies on the ground that they disproportionately harm the young and economically disadvantaged while conferring limited benefits." Bhattacharya stated that, because the Great Barrington Declaration "contradicted the government's preferred response to Covid-19," its content was suppressed in various ways.

Specifically, Bhattacharya alleges that "Google deboosted search results for the Declaration, pointing users to media hit pieces critical of it, and placing the link to the actual Declaration lower on this list of results." Further, a "roundtable" discussion between Bhattacharya and others, posted via video to YouTube, was removed from the social-media platform, with YouTube claiming that the video "contradicts the consensus of local and global health authorities regarding the efficacy of masks to prevent the spread of Covid-19."

Additionally, Bhattacharya alleges that he and his co-authors of the Great Barrington Declaration were personally censored on social media, primarily on Twitter and LinkedIn.

Martin Kulldorff, another of the Private Plaintiffs, made similar allegations in his declaration. Along with Bhattacharya, Kulldorff co-authored the Great Barrington Declaration and allegedly "experienced censorship on social media platforms due to [his] views on the appropriate strategy for handling the Covid-19 pandemic."

In addition to the alleged suppression of the Great Barrington Declaration itself on platforms such as Google and Facebook, Kulldorff asserts that his individual opinions were censored on his private social media accounts....Kulldorff echoed Bhattacharya's belief that the censorship of Covid-19-related opinions on social media was driven by government officials....

The Court finds that Plaintiffs have stated plausible claims on the merits in all counts of the Complaint....

Traditionally, the First Amendment imposes limitations only on "state action, not action by private parties." However, plaintiffs "may establish a First Amendment claim based on private conduct if that conduct 'can fairly be seen as state action...'"

The Complaint contains over 100 paragraphs of allegations detailing "significant encouragement" in private (i.e., "covert") communications between Defendants and social-media platforms....

The Complaint even alleges...that President Biden threatened civil liability and criminal prosecution against Mark Zuckerburg if Facebook did not increase censorship of political speech. The Court finds that the Complaint alleges significant encouragement and coercion that converts the otherwise private conduct of censorship on social media platforms into state action, and is unpersuaded by Defendants' arguments to the contrary....

Plaintiffs have plausibly alleged joint action, entwinement, and/or that specific features of Defendants' actions combined to create state action. For example, the Complaint alleges that "once in control of the Executive Branch, Defendants promptly capitalized on these threats by pressuring, cajoling, and openly colluding with social-media companies to actively suppress particular disfavored speakers and viewpoints on social media." Specifically, Plaintiffs allege that Dr. Fauci, other CDC officials, officials of the Census Bureau, CISA, officials at HHS, the state department, and members of the FBI actively and directly coordinated with social media....

The Complaint alleges that federal officials set up a long series of formal meetings to discuss censorship, setting up privileged reporting channels to demand censorship, and funding and establishing federal-private partnership to procure censorship of disfavored viewpoints. The Complaint clearly alleges that Defendants specifically authorized and approved the actions of the social-media companies and gives dozens of examples where Defendants dictated specific censorship decisions to social-media platforms....

Plaintiffs have clearly and plausibly alleged that Defendants engaged in viewpoint discrimination and prior restraints. As discussed in great detail above, Plaintiffs allege a regime of censorship that targets specific viewpoints deemed mis-, dis-, or malinformation by federal officials.

Because Plaintiffs allege that Defendants are targeting particular views taken by speakers on a specific subject, they have alleged a clear violation of the First Amendment, i.e., viewpoint discrimination. Moreover, Plaintiffs allege that Defendants, by placing bans, shadow-bans, and other forms of restrictions on Plaintiffs' social-media accounts, are engaged in de facto prior restraints, another clear violation of the First Amendment. Thus, the Court finds that Plaintiffs have plausibly alleged their First Amendment claims.

And so the case proceeds, thank goodness.

I've had the pleasure of getting to know Jay and Martin over these past few years, and as you've seen, these are mild-mannered academics who never imagined themselves ever becoming the public faces of an international resistance movement. But their convictions compelled them to do so all the same.

March 30, 2023 | Looks like it's over — for now

A Republican bill declaring the Covid-19 emergency over is about to hit Joe Biden's desk, and word is that he'll sign it.

The bill consists of a single sentence, declaring that the national emergency declared in the name of Covid-19 "is hereby terminated."

Over three years after the "fifteen days" thing.

We can hope that this means international travelers to the United States will soon no longer be required to subject themselves to the ridiculous vaccine requirement that the vast majority of countries have long since abandoned.

Given everything that even official sources now concede about the shots, there is no rationale for keeping that restriction in place.

As I look back over the past few years, I'm left flabbergasted at the wreckage.

I won't catalogue it all, because you know it well enough. But just for starters, people had their life's work destroyed, their savings decimated, their health compromised, their businesses ruined — and that's not to mention the far more devastating consequences for the developing world.

Just the other day I had a mother write to me: her daughter can't proceed with her chosen profession, because the only school for it she can afford is still for some reason demanding the shots.

Beyond that, families and friends were torn apart, and dissidents demonized and isolated.

Then, too, you and I observed with our own eyes how readily our neighbors and countrymen instantly adopted the official line, displaying no curiosity at all, and not even bothering to see if any of the social destruction was actually doing any good.

And of course a central point I think we all grasped but rarely saw illustrated was what governments can get away with under cover of emergency.

Call something an emergency or a crisis, and all thought goes out the window on the part of the public — a situation officials are all too happy to exploit.

May 26, 2023 | Scorecard

The CDC has released its numbers for age-adjusted Covid mortality. These are the CDC's own numbers, I repeat, so you and I can't be accused of using obscure sources, or whatever other excuse the crazies normally use. In these rankings, number one is the worst.

Date generated: Thu May 25 2023 22:36:52 GMT-0400 (Eastern Daylight Time)

	State/Territory	Total Death rate per 100000			State/Territory	Total Death rate per 100000
1	Mississippi	422.9		25	North Dakota	281.2
2	Oklahoma	422.3		26	District of Columbia	279.5
3	Kentucky	366.9		27	Iowa	267.7
4	New Mexico	356.5		28	Montana	267.3
5	Alabama	355.9		29	North Carolina	266.7
6	Texas	353.1		30	Rhode Island	266.1
7	West Virginia	345.2		31	Illinois	260.9
8	Tennessee	342.1		32	Idaho	259.1
9	Arkansas	335.0		33	Delaware	255.8
10	Ohio	331.6		34	Connecticut	250.4
11	Nevada	329.5		35	Maryland	245.5
12	Louisiana	327.5		36	Florida	245.0
13	South Carolina	325.1		37	Nebraska	244.6
14	Indiana	324.1		38	Colorado	244.4
15	Arizona	321.7		39	California	242.7
16	Georgia	313.3		40	Massachusetts	232.9
17	New York	311.5		41	Virginia	232.5
18	Wyoming	301.8		42	Wisconsin	229.8
19	New Jersey	300.0		43	Minnesota	222.7
20	Kansas	298.0		44	Alaska	222.0
21	South Dakota	296.5		45	Utah	195.5
22	Michigan	293.9		46	New Hampshire	176.5
23	Pennsylvania	293.0		47	Oregon	173.4
24	Missouri	287.8		48	Washington	170.3
	United States of America	282.7		49	Maine	161.3
				50	Vermont	112.4
				51	Hawaii	93.8

New Mexico is the fourth highest. You may not remember, because you're not the fanatic I am, but the media once trumpeted New Mexico as a success story. It was one of their drearily predictable "Here's how [insert name of state] beat the coronavirus" stories. And of course it was the usual thing: they followed the useless "public health" protocols, etc.

And yet there it is at number four.

(I would also adjust this chart for obesity levels, because I think we'd get a clearer picture still. Some of the red states are home to demographics with unusually high obesity levels. If we corrected for this issue the result would be more random still.)

Iowa, a "state that doesn't care if you live or die," in the words of *The Atlantic*, is all the way down at 27.

And of course the major story is Florida, at 36!

California, the land of bizarre, irrational, and endless restrictions, is at 39 — a trivial difference from Florida, and in any case Florida's all-cause mortality figures turned out better than California's.

Remember when people were screaming at Florida for defying all the recommendations? If you had asked them where they expected Florida to wind up when all was said and done, precisely zero of them would have said #36. It would have been at least top five, if not number one.

In other words, the crazies were wrong, period, and we win. All the destruction and disruption was for nothing.

June 1, 2023 | More on the Censorship Regime

We've been learning in recent months about a vast censorship and suppression regime running through academia, the corporate world, and government in the United States.

In the case of *Missouri v. Biden*, victims of this regime are fighting back, both for themselves and for the sake of all of us.

Dr. Aaron Kheriaty, who's among the plaintiffs in the case, reports that their lawyers were in court last week "seeking a temporary injunction to halt the government's censorship-industrial complex." In their petition, they described this regime's activities with the following analogy:

> Suppose that the Trump White House, backed by Republicans controlling both Houses of Congress, publicly demanded that all libraries in the United States burn books criticizing the President. The President, in turn, made statements implying that the libraries would face ruinous legal consequences if they did not comply, while senior White House officials privately badgered the libraries for detailed lists and reports of such books that they had burned. The libraries, after months of such pressure, complied with those demands and burned the books.
>
> Suppose that, after four years of pressure from senior congressional staffers in secret meetings threatening the libraries with adverse legislation if they did not cooperate, the FBI started sending all libraries in the United States detailed lists of the books the FBI wanted to burn, requesting that the libraries report back to the FBI by identifying the books that they burned and the libraries complied by burning about half of those books.
>
> Suppose that a federal national security agency teamed up with private research institutions, backed by enormous resources and federal funding, to establish a mass-surveillance and mass-censorship program that uses sophisticated techniques to review hundreds of millions of American citizens' electronic communications in real time, and works

closely with tech platforms to covertly censor millions of them.

The first two hypotheticals are directly analogous to the facts of this case. And the third is not hypothetical at all — it is a description of the Election Integrity Partnership and Virality Project.

(In case the analogy isn't clear, the libraries represent social media companies, and the books being burned represent posts or accounts being suppressed.)

I'm sure you won't be surprised to learn that the same thing went on in Australia, as recently uncovered documents reveal. Meanwhile, last year Australia suffered its highest level of excess mortality since World War II. Is anyone in Australia other than the embattled minority of dissidents even bothering to try to figure out what could have caused that?

It's more important that they censor you than that they figure out the excess deaths problem (which was definitely not caused by That Thing You're Secretly Suspecting).

Afterword – Beyond Covid:
The madness is everywhere

In the blink of an eye, crazy and sinister people gained control of every major institution in the Western world.

Today you have to worry that despite your best efforts, your children will have their minds colonized by people with weird and destructive ideologies.

The federal government pressures businesses to make unreasonable health demands of you, or you're fired.

The Federal Reserve makes prices go up and strips away what savings you've managed to accumulate.

And that's just for starters.

The question is: what do we do about it? Write some more articles? Argue more on social media? Wallow in *woe is me*?

As the Covid fiasco wore on, I observed to my horror how many people went along without question with pointless restrictions that were ruining their lives — and never even bothered to find out if any of it accomplished anything.

At that point I made a decision: there's only so much I can do for people who have televisions for brains.

But there's plenty I can do for people who are capable of independent thought and who are doing their best to navigate their families through a world that hates them.

Stop and think for a minute. They came for your job and (let's not sugarcoat it) they're coming for your kids' minds. Who wants to navigate a world like that alone?

But put us all together, and we're a force.

When the great Harry Browne wrote *How I Found Freedom in an Unfree World*, he was hardly talking about politics at all.

He was talking about how to make your life better right now, regardless of what happens in politics. Because despite how the state demoralizes us, far more is within our control than we think.

And not all of our problems are connected to the regime. I personally know so many people in their 30s who are absolutely miserable in their corporate jobs, for example, and they can't see a way out.

I understand why people look to the future with dread. If the ruling class got away with the Covid madness, they're not liable to stop there. But do we have to sit back helplessly as we await the next thing?

I want to try to make us unbreakable.

In the midst of the Covid chaos, I arranged a two-hour private meeting with Jay Abraham, one of the most sought-after executive coaches in America. You want a day-long consult with him? That'll be $150,000.

Until now my contributions to the movement I believe in have been entirely academic: books, courses, speeches, and the like. Nothing wrong with that, but I felt like the times called for something different, something more practical and here-and-now. But I didn't know what. Did he?

Of course he did. He's Jay blankety-blank Abraham. He told me flat out: "You should start the Tom Woods School of Life."

And that's precisely what I did, with the goal of helping people create prosperous and fulfilling lives even under regimes that despise them.

Let me tell you a story:

One of our members, Kevin Stokes, just opened the second successful business he's started since being a School of Life member. It's a food and meat co-op.

Before they launched their first sale they began building their email list: "We have reached 739 email subscribers....Not bad for 1 week of marketing....All I did was follow some of the training in the Tom Woods Email Domination program." (The Tom Woods Email Domination Program is one of the many goodies that await members of my community.)

The day they opened their doors, Kevin wrote to say that in less than an hour they were completely overwhelmed with sales. Because of a contractual arrangement he has, he can't publicly disclose the numbers. (Not knowing this, I mistakenly gave out the numbers in an internal email to members, but I can't here.) I can tell you this: he exceeded the expectations of friends in a similar business by 10 times.

Then I heard from Kevin again later that day. They were doing so well that they were running up against the limits of what their existing trucking capacity could handle. What would he do?

The School of Life solved his problem, thanks to the community of extremely impressive people we have. Kevin told me:

> *One of your members...runs a logistics company. He schedules trucks for a living, makes $3 million a year doing so....He offered to help with the trucks.*
>
> *Our lives just changed in ways I was wondering if we would ever get to.*
>
> *In summary:*
>
> *This would never have happened without the School of Life and the encouragement from members of my accountability group.*
>
> *TWSOL is a life-changing platform.*
>
> *It would take me the rest of my life to give back one-tenth the value you have given me....I have spent the majority of my adult life thinking I was borderline anti-social. I was wrong. I've just been hanging out with the wrong crowd.*
>
> *You've created something special.*

Now what "accountability group" is Kevin talking about?

Every week small groups of between 8 to 12 members of the School of Life meet together with a facilitator. Many of them are starting or growing businesses, while others are still trying to nail down their business idea. Others are trying to lose weight, eat better, finish writing that book — whatever their goals might be.

And whatever your goal, you'll get there a lot faster in a group of like-minded people keeping you focused, giving you suggestions, making connections for you, and cheering you on. When you work alone and hit a snag, that can take the wind out of your sails. You're tempted to quit. And maybe, in the past, you have. But here, your fellow group members are there to help you out of it and carry you along on the next step of your mission.

We keep each other accountable: we all pledge to accomplish some finite task before the next meeting in order to get closer to our goals.

"I had no idea what to expect with the accountability groups," one of our members said. "Three weeks in and I kid you not: they are the best thing Tom's ever done."

In other words, we do something. We take action. We network with people who can help us.

Now it's true: you can find other sites that offer groups like this. But try saying in one of those groups, "I'd like to make more money so my wife can stay home with the kids," and see what happens to you. There's no substitute for working with people who see the world the way you do, and who won't become hysterical if you utter an unapproved opinion.

Another member, Darren, led a rebellion at his firm against the vaccine mandate. Although he ultimately got an exemption, he decided: I don't want to work here anymore. *Because if it's not this, it'll be something else.* And he didn't want to be a second-class citizen, having to eat lunch apart from everyone else and all the rest of the nonsense.

With the help of his accountability group, he's replaced his (high) income working on his own, and now nobody can tell him what to do.

Still another member, Liam, lost his job one day — and later that very day, thanks to our job board, had another job all lined up, with no reduction in pay. Just like that.

Here is my message to you: If you know what you want, we can help you get it.

And not just in business. We've built accountability groups on health and fitness, freelance copywriting, Bitcoin, content creation, tech, a women's group, and more. We have the technology for you to start your own group on any other topic you choose.

Our community director, Kevin Dolan, recalls a person in his fitness group who kept showing up, but every time he was reporting a failure. "I had a piece of cake because I attended a wedding" — that kind of thing. But after eight months, guess who by far had lost the most weight? That guy.

Consistency pays. And consistently checking in with smart, like-minded people who are rooting for your success pays even more.

But my School of Life is more than just the groups.

Twice a month I bring on someone who can teach us something essential to living a prosperous and fulfilled life in a hostile world.

My members have learned about investing, real estate, homeschooling, peaceful parenting, fitness, homesteading, preparedness, creating a secure home, how to build online and offline businesses — dozens of topics so far, with many more to come.

All action, no theory.

So in addition to the accountability groups, here's some of what I have in store for you inside the Tom Woods School of Life:

• A man in his mid-30s whose words have sold $400 million in goods and services, on an occupation perfect for liberty lovers that requires no formal training, that you can't be fired from, and that you can learn in a month (Henry Bingaman video).

• Fitness facts and fallacies: exercises that waste your time or risk injury, and exercises that actually help you make progress (Henri Pellerin video).

• An accomplished physician who showed us how to get cheap telemedical care and stay out of the broken and corrupt medical system. He also revealed his own step-by-step plan for maximizing health (session 13).

• An expert on getting other people to pay for your kids' schooling (if you know where to look, you can start getting scholarships in first grade!). (Session 11.)

• How to keep your homeschooled kids engaged and motivated (forget the threats and bribes — this is a much easier and more practical solution) (AMA session).

• A former U.S. congressman, in fact the last Republican opponent of the Iraq war to retire, taught us about relocation in an age of psychotic state governments (session 5).

• Business expert Marlon Sanders, who showed us how to earn an income online and work from anywhere (session 7).

• How to master the rare skill that will get you ahead in business (and in life), and make you look like a boss to your friends (session 15).

• A libertarian professor from Columbia Business School (I promise he's a good guy) who revealed the best investments for today's upside-down world (session 3).

• The owner of a 7-figure cooking website, who taught us how she built it (and she happens to be one of our members; as I said, this community is full of impressive people). (Session 9.)

• A hostage negotiator on how Harvard's myths about negotiating, believed by everyone, are making you not get what you want — and how to turn that around (session 21).

• The most canceled filmmaker in America, and how he's more successful and fulfilled than ever (session 26).

• Libertarian hero Eric July on how he went from idea to execution in building a new comic-book company and generating seven figures on the first day (session 29).

• A famous libertarian's secret for becoming debt-free in just seven months (session 2).

• Why the secret to earning more money can be working fewer hours (session 7).

• How two working parents can homeschool their kids without stress (AMA session).

• How not to write like a dork, and instead stand out from the pack with your writing (session 27, with *New York Times* bestselling author Tom Woods — that's me).

• How to de-program the heavily propagandized (CJ Killmer video).

• How to raise money to start a business and declare your independence (John Foster video).

• The best-performing asset class of the past four generations — and it isn't even close (session 3).

• How to quiet that inner critic that undermines your every move (session 16).

• The most freedom-friendly places to live — they're not always the ones you think (sessions 5 & 6).

• How to come up with a business idea you can implement and scale in record time (session 7).

• The supposedly "dying industries" that are generating massive returns (session 3).

• How about this one: how far you should live from a nuclear power plant (and did you know it depends on whether you're east or west of the plant?) (Session 6.)

• Specific strategies to win in a blue state when you're hopelessly outnumbered (Ali Rak video).

Recordings of all of this training, and a whole lot more — and I mean a whole lot; we've covered tons of essential topics — is waiting for you inside the members' area, with more to come every month.

And even that's not all. Every year I host an optional in-person event that will be free for you to attend, because I'm paying for it as a gift to you. It's a blast. As one attendee put it, "It was awesome to see a well-attended event with normal people, normal conversations, and normal things to laugh about and discuss. In a room of people who are clearly more intelligent than average, I was all ears and my learning muscle was on."

Said another: "It was a fantastic event and a great time. I have pages of notes and many more To Do's from all the great points the speakers shared with us."

I provide entertainment, too — in 2022 it was a free comedy show with the great Dave Smith, whom I flew down just for our event, and in 2023 it was world-class magician Doc Dixon, who fooled Penn & Teller on their TV show and sawed me in half at my 2000th Tom Woods Show episode.

Why am I doing this?

Because I'd like my tombstone to say something a little more memorable than "He recorded 7,000 podcast episodes."

There isn't a lot more I can tell people about the nonaggression principle that I haven't said already, but with my knowledge and connections I can certainly help them create the lives they want for themselves, even in a world that hates us.

It's been made abundantly clear that nobody is coming to save us. We have to do it ourselves.

This is how to find freedom in an unfree world — for you, your children, and your grandchildren.

Join us: TomSchoolOfLife.com

Sneak Preview of Volume II –
Collateral Damage: Victims of the Lockdown Regime Tell Their Stories

Some of us write email newsletters, and do our best to spread the word. Others make serious sacrifices.

One of those is Broadway actor Clifton Duncan. You need to know what happened to him.

He had an extraordinary background, and everything was going his way on the eve of 2020.

He held an MFA from New York University's prestigious graduate acting program. As Duncan explains it, the program is "a subsidiary of the Tisch School of the Arts, one of the world's most elite conservatory programs for young actors. It's considered on par with or often superior to America's other elite institutions, those being Juilliard and the Yale School of Drama."

Duncan is not the boasting sort, but he needs to tell you about himself in order for you to appreciate the full scope of what happened. So:

> Just to give you an idea of how competitive this institution is, at that time they would audition a thousand young hopefuls from around the country, sometimes around the world. And out of that thousand, they would call back 50. Out of that 50 they ultimately offered spots to 18. Now, many of my classmates had to audition multiple times to get into the program. I got in my very first try....
>
> I graduated from supporting to lead roles at many of America's top theaters. And eventually, after a bunch of near misses, I finally landed on Broadway in the hit comedy *The Play That Goes Wrong*, which Tom Woods is very, very, very obsessed with, and probably knows far more about than I do. And I was in it.
>
> Soon thereafter, I found myself working with renowned directors and starring opposite Tony-winning actors and actresses and doing television with guys like Jimmy Smits and a personal favorite of mine, Scott Bakula, who was awesome in *Quantum Leap*. And I was earning praise and effusion from

legends such as Joel Grey and the late Stephen Sondheim, and even garnering award recognition for my work.

But, Duncan says, "the contrast between what my life was and what it is now, to be completely candid, often drives me to despair." Because just like that, he lost it all. Everything he had worked for, everything that brought him joy and fulfillment, gone.

What happened? I think you know. But I'll let him tell it:

> So now I'm staring down the barrel of 40 years of age. I no longer reside in the city formerly known as New York, a place I called home for a decade and a half. I wait tables for a living, something I hadn't had to do since I was 22 years old. I no longer have a powerful manager sending me auditions for lucrative, high-profile, life-changing projects, and I no longer have the prospect of earning a five-figure weekly salary working in TV or on Broadway. And so now the prospects of paying off all those NYU loans, maybe even starting a family, have become even more distant dreams.

> I'm now shut out of the entertainment industry. I have few marketable skills because I never needed them. The few skills I did work on centered around acting and singing, skills which are highly valued in New York and Los Angeles, but which, as you might imagine, have very little value outside of the arts and entertainment sector. I feel as though I'm starting over from scratch....

> And so you may be asking yourself, well, what the hell happened? Why have I gone from having a billboard with my likeness on it in the middle of Times Square, winning standout notices in the *New York Times*, and guest starring on network television, to where I am now?

> Well, it's quite simple. I refuse to allow any employer — or, by extension, the government — to act as my health care provider and to dictate what I inject into my body. I refuse to be bullied or coerced or shamed into taking a medical product that I neither want nor need. I've been extraordinarily vocal in my opposition to what I view as grotesque and egregious state overreach into private affairs and personal freedoms.

> Indeed, even if things were to magically return to normal tomorrow, I'm greatly disturbed by the precedent which has been set, wherein government officials and bureaucrats can

take it upon themselves to determine who is essential and who is not, to decide who gets to operate their business and who does not, and in some cases decide who is allowed to travel and who is not.

I couldn't have improved on any of this.

Duncan has a profound understanding of every aspect of the issue, and rather than yield on a principle he held dear, he made an extraordinary sacrifice.

The world I want to live in is one in which a man like Clifton Duncan can stick by his principles and yet continue to do what he's trained to do, and what brings him joy.

Get *Collateral Damage: Victims of the Lockdown Regime Tell Their Stories* for free at DiaryOfCovid.com.

Acknowledgments

I learned so much from so many people during these terrible years, but I wish to single out a few for particular thanks.

First and foremost I wish to thank Jay Bhattacharya for his generous foreword and for being such a good example to us all: scholarly, even-tempered (even when he had every right not to be), and courageous. I can say much the same for Martin Kulldorff, who was likewise thrust into the national spotlight during these years. Both men were kind enough to send unsolicited good wishes, and medical advice, when I myself was hospitalized in July 2021.

Tim Scott did tremendous work on the tech side of my CovidChartsQuiz.com site, which I mention in this book, and I remain truly grateful.

I repeat my thanks to Ian Miller, which I extended in the introduction, for his tireless work in creating the charts that allowed curious people — of whom there should have been many more — to evaluate for themselves whether what was being demanded of us was having the effects claimed for them.

A special word of thanks goes to the editorial and layout team at the Libertarian Institute, on whose board I am privileged to serve. First and foremost Ben Parker, for his skill and superhuman speed, but also Scott Horton, Mike Dworski, and Grant F. Smith.

Finally, my wife, Jenna, patiently read everything I wrote on this subject, and we had many hours of discussions together that in turn clarified my thoughts. We got to meet many fine people we would not have known otherwise — from the time we had lunch with Martin Kulldorff near Harvard, to our house party for supporters in October 2020, to our illicit event in Orange County in early 2021 (with restrictions still in effect in California and in many other places), when hundreds of good folks thanked us for being normal and getting them out of the house.

I dedicate this book to her, because while nothing can excuse or undo what was done to us, the time we spent together during those awful days — corny as it may sound — showed that love truly can overcome anything.

About the Author

Tom Woods is the winner of the 2019 Hayek Lifetime Achievement Award, given in Vienna by the Hayek Institute and the Austrian Economics Center. He holds a bachelor's degree in history from Harvard, and his M.A., M.Phil., and Ph.D. from Columbia University.

Tom is the *New York Times* bestselling author of 13 books, including *The Politically Incorrect Guide to American History*, *Meltdown* (on the 2008 financial crisis, and featuring a foreword by Ron Paul), and *Real Dissent: A Libertarian Sets Fire to the Index Card of Allowable Opinion*. His books have been translated into Italian, Spanish, Polish, Lithuanian, German, Dutch, Czech, Portuguese, Croatian, Slovak, Russian, Korean, Japanese, and Chinese. Tom is also co-editor of *Exploring American History: From Colonial Times to 1877*, an 11-volume encyclopedia. He created 400 videos on history for the self-taught K-12 Ron Paul Curriculum (RonPaulHomeschool.com).

A senior fellow of the Mises Institute, Tom has appeared on MSNBC, CNBC, FOX News, FOX Business, and C-SPAN, as well as hundreds of radio programs. His writing has been published in dozens of popular and scholarly periodicals, including the *American Historical Review*, the *Christian Science Monitor*, *Investor's Business Daily*, *Catholic Historical Review*, *Modern Age*, *American Studies*, *Intercollegiate Review*, *Catholic Social Science Review*, *Economic Affairs* (U.K.), *Quarterly Journal of Austrian Economics*, *Inside the Vatican*, *Human Events*, *University Bookman*, *Journal of Markets & Morality*, *New Oxford Review*, *Catholic World Report*, *Independent Review*, *Journal of Libertarian Studies*, and *Human Rights Review*.

Tom won the $50,000 first prize in the Templeton Enterprise Awards for his book *The Church and the Market*, as well as the Gary G. Schlarbaum Prize for excellence in research and teaching, the George F. Koether Free Market Writing Award, the O.P. Alford III Prize for Libertarian Scholarship, and the Independent Institute's Olive W. Garvey Fellowship.

Tom hosts the popular podcast The Tom Woods Show (TomsPodcast.com), which as of this writing has released nearly 2,500 episodes.

The Libertarian Institute

Check out the Libertarian Institute at LibertarianInstitute.org. It's Scott Horton, Sheldon Richman, Laurie Calhoun, James Bovard, Kyle Anzalone, Keith Knight and the best libertarian writers and podcast hosts on the Internet. We are a 501(c)(3) tax-exempt charitable organization. EIN 83-2869616.

Help support our efforts — including our project to purchase wholesale copies of this book to send to important congressmen and women, antiwar groups and influential people in the media. We don't have a big marketing department to push this effort. We need your help to do it. And thank you.

LibertarianInstitute.org/donate or

The Libertarian Institute

612 W. 34th St.

Austin, TX 78705

Check out all of our other great Libertarian Institute books at LibertarianInstitute.org/books:

Hotter Than the Sun: Time to Abolish Nuclear Weapons by Scott Horton

Enough Already: Time to End the War on Terrorism by Scott Horton

Fool's Errand: Time to End the War in Afghanistan by Scott Horton

Questioning the COVID Company Line: Critical Thinking in Hysterical Times by Laurie Calhoun

The Fake China Threat and Its Very Real Danger by Joseph Solis-Mullen

Voluntaryist Handbook by Keith Knight

The Great Ron Paul: The Scott Horton Show Interviews 2004–2019

No Quarter: The Ravings of William Norman Grigg, edited by Tom Eddlem

Coming to Palestine by Sheldon Richman

What Social Animals Owe to Each Other by Sheldon Richman

Keep a look out for more great titles to be published in 2023 and 2024.

Printed in the USA
CPSIA information can be obtained
at www.ICGtesting.com
LVHW010405180624
783019LV00010BA/79/J

9 798988 403166